Hobbes's Political Philosophy

Hobbes's Political Philosophy

Interpretation and Interpretations

A. P. MARTINICH

Roy Allison Vaughan Centennial Professor Emeritus in Philosophy
University of Texas at Austin

OXFORD
UNIVERSITY PRESS

OXFORD
UNIVERSITY PRESS

Oxford University Press is a department of the University of Oxford. It furthers the University's objective of excellence in research, scholarship, and education by publishing worldwide. Oxford is a registered trade mark of Oxford University Press in the UK and certain other countries.

Published in the United States of America by Oxford University Press
198 Madison Avenue, New York, NY 10016, United States of America.

Library of Congress Control Number: 2021933670

ISBN 978–0–19–753171–6

DOI: 10.1093/oso/9780197531716.001.0001

1 3 5 7 9 8 6 4 2

Printed by Integrated Books International, United States of America

To some of my favorite editors and co-authors, whom I esteem and thank:
Jeff Dean, Marissa Koors, S. A. Lloyd, Roger Louis, Peter Ohlin,
Tom Palaima

Contents

Contents

Preface

Almost all of the chapters of this book were published in various books and journals over twenty-five years. The philosophical content of the chapters is the same as in their first publication. Typographical errors have been corrected; some mystifying phrases have been demystified; and some mental slips, such as writing "John Knox" for John Foxe, have been silently corrected. Because the editorial formats of the chapters in their original publication varied greatly from chapter to chapter, some uniformity has been imposed on the chapters—for example, changing all endnotes to footnotes. Two chapters appear here for the first time: "The Author of Sin and Demoniacs: Two *Ch. 11* Calvinist Issues in Thomas Hobbes and Some Contemporaries" was originally published in French; and "Hobbes on Sovereignty by Acquisition in *Ch. 9* *Leviathan*" was written expressly for this volume. The chapters are ordered according to overlapping themes, not chronologically. The chronological order is given in the List of Permissions.

Some points are made in more than one chapter because they were part of the immediate background of my position and could not be reasonably assumed to be part of the readers' beliefs, or because they were the best way to advance or defend my position. Almost fifty years ago, a mathematician told me that a new theorem is not proved until it is published at least three times.

Acknowledgments

I want to thank my editor Peter Ohlin of Oxford University Press and his colleagues, Emily Bang and Madeleine Freeman, for their extraordinary work. I am also grateful to the project manager, Preetham Raj, and his colleagues, Peter Jaskowiak and Munusamy V., at Newgen Knowledge Works for their labor on the production process. And Leslie Martinich, as always.

Introduction

The central concepts of Thomas Hobbes's political philosophy, especially as they appear in *Leviathan*, are explained in this book: the state of nature, the laws of nature; covenants; authorization and representation; sovereignty by institution, by acquisition, and by nature. The chapters are self-contained and should be intelligible to readers with only rudimentary knowledge of Hobbes's political philosophy. Hence the title, *Hobbes's Political Philosophy*. Many of the chapters took form as I responded to criticisms of my book, *The Two Gods of Leviathan* (1992), by theorists with competing interpretations. Reflecting on their competing interpretations moved me to think about the nature of interpretation itself. Hence the subtitle, *Interpretations and Interpretation*.

My interpretation of Hobbes's "science" of political philosophy is that he tried to show that absolute sovereignty was the only genuine kind of government by using Euclidean geometry as his mode (cf. Stauffer 2018: 66–72). He would deduce theorems about politics from carefully formulated definitions. Political philosophy was to result from reason alone, not empirical experience. When he mentioned empirical facts in his exposition, it was for the sake of illustrating a point, not proving it.

The idea that Hobbes was either an early liberal theorist or a proto-liberal is a mistake. His premises that all persons are equal and are absolutely free in the natural condition of human beings, the state of nature, are imposters of liberal premises, because for him, equality is equal ability to kill any other person and freedom is the right to do whatever one wants, no matter the harm that comes to others. With these premises, plus the proposition that the dominant or strongest desire of human beings is self-preservation, he argued that human beings ought to create their sovereign and commit to obeying it, no matter what it does.[1] This is the heart of his "timeless" political philosophy.

---

[1] I will typically refer to sovereigns with neuter pronouns to emphasize that the sovereign is an artificial person, which has no gender.

Hobbes's Political Philosophy. A. P. Martinich, Oxford University Press. © Oxford University Press 2021.
DOI: 10.1093/oso/9780197531716.003.0001

In addition to his formidable, timelessly true political philosophy, I argue that he had two time-bound projects. The first was to prove that authentic Christianity is not politically destabilizing, contrary to what the opponents of King Charles I maintained during the years prior to and during the English Civil War. This project should have been crystal clear, given the number of sermons preached and published against the king's policies by the English and Scots. In his history of the Civil War, he wrote that "the interpretation of a verse in the Hebrew, Greek, or Latin Bible, is oftentimes the cause of a civil war and the deposing and assassinating of God's anointed." He was alluding to the execution of Charles (Hobbes 1679: 202). The second project was to show that Christian doctrine, properly conceived, is compatible with the new science of Copernicus and Galileo. Several of Hobbes's friends had the same project, but they carried it out in different ways. Pierre Gassendi Christianized Epicurean atomism; Kenelm Digby and Thomas White Christianized atomism and Aristotelianism; and Marin Mersenne, the leader of a circle of intellectuals that included those just mentioned, "was indubitably an heir to the Thomistic view of a necessary synthesis between Christian faith and philosophy, . . . the tacit assumption being that 'true philosophy never contradicts the teachings of the Church'" (Hamou 2018).[2] That is, Hobbes's time-bound projects were not unique to him. To distinguish Hobbes from his philosophical friends, we can appeal to three facts: he was an English Calvinist; he was better informed about the Bible than they were; and he was a better philosopher. In short, Hobbes was both a powerful political philosopher and a person of his age.

That Hobbes's historical projects were closely connected to his philosophy is a fact that even atheist interpreters—that is, those who think that Hobbes was an atheist—admit. For example, Leo Strauss wrote that Hobbes made "use of the authority of the Scriptures for his own theory," but he also wanted to "shake the authority of the Scriptures themselves" (Strauss 1952: 71). Recently, Devin Stauffer gave a more sophisticated defense of the same basic position. As one reviewer described it: "Hobbes's reinterpretation of Scripture is designed to bring the Bible into alignment with his political philosophy" and to "dispel the reigning darkness, chasten religion, and bring a new dawn of enlightenment" (Franco 2020: 127). One problem with the Straussian interpretation is that it attributes to Hobbes the incoherent intentions of

---

[2] Rene Descartes also wanted his philosophy to be consistent with Christianity, but it was less central to his aspirations than it was for Hobbes and others, and Descartes was not a friend (Martinich 1999: 163–79).

wanting to use Christianity and to subvert it at the same time.[3] Hobbes may have been a blockhead, but Strauss or Stauffer have not discovered how (cf. Hobbes 1682a: 7). The more palpable interpretation is that Hobbes's project was the one that made perfect sense in the middle of the seventeenth century. If it is impossible to reconcile science and Christian doctrine and impossible to show that Christianity is a religion of peace, most intellectuals only came to know that a century or more later, and many intellectuals today still do not know it.

Hobbes's characterization of the different realms of faith and reason is straightforward and neat. Reason generates science from definitions by proving universal and necessary propositions about the natural world. Faith generates religion by revealing individual, contingent events that show the road to salvation. Because they reign in different areas of cognitive life, they cannot contradict each other. Of course, if the tenets of a religion are non-sensical or superstitious, then the distinction would be futile. So Hobbes's description of biblical Christianity needs to be sensible and not superstitious; and it is. But equally important is that Hobbes's account is one that most mainstream, biblical scholars today accept. His penchant for absolute sovereignty worked well with familiar Christian adages such as "No man can serve two masters"; "Servants, obey your earthly masters with fear and trembling"; and "Let every person be subject to the governing authorities, for there is not authority except from God" (Matthew 6:24, Ephesians 6:5, and Romans 13:1, respectively).

I hope that what I have already said explains why I think understanding Hobbes's time-bound projects is important. However, to be explicit, at least three values motivate me: respect for the philosopher, truth, and the belief that studying the philosopher's actual beliefs repays the effort. These values are consistent with judging the adequacy of the philosophy and improving it when viable.

Chapter 1 discusses the place of Hobbes's political philosophy within his general scheme of philosophy. In logical order, his philosophy has three parts: *De corpore* (1655) (*On Body*) or physics; *De homine* (1658) (*On Man*) or human beings; and *De cive* (1642, 1647) (*On the Citizen*). Hobbes's titles have to be taken with a grain of salt. The first of his three parts is about

---

[3] Another criticism is that what Stauffer wants to prove does not entail that no version of Christianity is true: "thoroughgoing critic of traditional Christianity, . . . [and the desire] of over-throwing a 'Kingdom of Darkness' . . . [and] offering . . . a rational and secular 'Kingdom of Light'" (Stauffer 2018: 7).

bodies; but it begins with chapters about the nature of language and concepts of logic. His second part, about human beings, is as much about optics as it is about any other aspect of human beings. (My guess is that he had worked so long and hard on optics that he wanted his final version published.) Oddly, his treatment of human beings does not discuss families. The reason is that for him, human beings are no more familial animals than they are political ones. When Hobbes begins the third and last part of his philosophy, *De cive* (*On the Citizen*), human beings are mature individuals with no history and no emotional attachments. They are, as Hobbes suggests, like mushrooms, fully developed creatures when they first appear. Parental authority appears in the middle of *De cive*. It is treated as a special case of sovereignty as dominion; and dominion has the connotation of things such as household property belonging to an owner (*dominus*). The default condition of authority over children, in the original condition, belongs to the mother who is the first to have power over a child. In *Leviathan*, his comments about families or social relations are limited and ill fitting (cf. Hirschmann 2016).

Another oddity of *De cive* is that it says little about citizens and a great deal about sovereignty and government. The problem with Hobbes's political philosophy (mentioned at least once by Quentin Skinner) is that he has no theory of society. Hobbes's political philosophy provides no space for social relations among one's fellows. His occasional comments about "social" behavior are unflattering.

A second theme of chapter 1 is the importance of historical context. No interpretation of the actions performed by using sentences can be reliable or complete without information about the context of its utterance and at least the intentions of the speaker. Donald Davidson's T-sentences illustrate one feature of language, namely, that a satisfactory semantics has to appeal to no more than finite intellectual resources. But his semantic theory is not supposed to be a theory of interpretation, as he himself says (Davidson 2005: 89–107). Take the method of disquotation, for example:

"This board is strong enough" is true if and only if this board is strong enough

gives the lexical meaning of a sentence but not an interpretation in the sense relevant to theories of textual interpretation. For Davidson interpretation is not a rule-governed activity. The interpreter has to use various contextual resources to arrive at an interpretation. Suppose the context indicates that the speaker is talking about a wooden board. More is required. Does the author mean that the board is strong enough for battering down a door, prying up a tree trunk, or supporting the weight of a human being, or something else? Is the speaker asserting, recommending, hypothesizing, or something else? (See chapters 2 and 3.)

The third theme of chapter 1 concerns Hobbes's subversive motives. He was quite open about wanting to subvert long and deeply held false political and religious beliefs (e.g., Hobbes 1651: A2ᵛ). And it should not be surprising that his criticisms would apply to all but a narrow conception of religion— Erastian, episcopal, high liturgy, orthodox, and Calvinism as the English understood it. This is was the religion of King James I, Hobbes's sovereign from the formative years of seventeen to thirty-seven. He was generally not religiously tolerant because the English were not tolerant; and almost every denomination in England denounced every other in harsh terms. Until recently, each Christian denomination professed itself to be the one true religion. For Christians, the great variety of false religions is a consequence of human perversity. Hobbes wrote that it was "almost impossible for men without the special assistance of God to avoid both Rocks of *Atheism* and of *Superstition*" (Hobbes 1647: 16.1, spelling modernized).

Scholarly disagreement about the proper interpretation of Hobbes's philosophy is almost as deep and fierce as religious disputes in the seventeenth century. Not long after the publication of *Two Gods*, I began to think about the nature of interpretation and the reason that interpreters are intransigent. Chapter 2 explains that a deep source of disagreement is the fact that each person comes to a text with a complex network of beliefs acquired over decades of experience, partially shaped by the person's dispositions. And this has the consequence that different people will understand complex texts differently. Although relatively few beliefs in a network are held tenaciously, often they are the ones that are crucial to interpretation. These beliefs are largely impervious to contrary evidence, even in learned, brilliant scholars. These differences do not make discussions impossible, but they do reduce the likelihood of rational persuasion.

The extent of differences in networks should not be exaggerated. The networks of beliefs of people in the same culture at the same time greatly overlap. Although networks of beliefs of people living at different times and places have less overlap, education enables them to embed subnetworks roughly of the form, "People in place p and time t, believed . . . ," by which people of the present can understand people of the past.

Chapter 2 also describes the main properties of beliefs and the network, such as unity, generality, and tenacity and how they relate to interpretation. Good interpretations have defeasible virtues such as simplicity, generality, consistency, and coherence (see also chapter 4). Usually a simpler interpretation that uses general principles to explain the text and is also coherent and consistent in doctrine is better than a more complex one. However, sometimes a simpler interpretation is incorrect. The serpent of Genesis is not identical with the Satan of the book of Job, because they had different origins and the author of Job did not intend it to be the serpent. Sometimes texts do not hang together as neatly as they should. And some texts, especially philosophical ones, are not consistent. For example, Hobbes contradicts himself because he asserts both that the sovereign is never a party to a sovereign-making covenant and sometimes, it seems, that he is a party to the covenant (see chapter 9, "Hobbes on Sovereignty by Acquisition in *Leviathan*"). So sometimes an interpretation that reports incoherencies and inconsistencies in a text is the better and the correct one. Some of the ideas in chapter 2 are continued in chapter 4, which relates the role of networks of belief to Hobbes's understanding of covenants.

Chapter 3, "On the Proper Interpretation of Hobbes's Philosophy," is a response to criticisms of *Two Gods* by Edwin Curley (1996a). Much of his disagreement with my interpretation turns on the applicability of a conversational device that Curley calls "assertion by denial," a type of irony or sarcasm ("I would never think that your approval of Pol Pot's domestic behavior was morally insensitive"). Assuming that interpretations require networks of beliefs and acknowledging that differences in those networks account for much scholarly disagreement, I discuss the conditions under which a conversational context is ripe for sarcasm and when it is not. The standard or default way to understand an author's words is in their literal meaning. If doing so would result in a falsehood that the speaker would expect the hearer to recognize, then an interpreter thinks about alternative ways of taking the words, for example, as a figure of speech or as sarcasm when appropriate.

Where Curley can find no plausible, literal interpretation of many of Hobbes's sentences, I identify aspects of the seventeenth century that make the sentences literally reasonable. The major context is Jacobean, the complex of beliefs promoted by King James VI and I, namely, support for absolute sovereignty, Erastianism episcopacy, a high liturgy, orthodoxy in doctrine, and English Calvinism in theology. Unfortunately for Hobbes, this culture began to wane in the 1620s and was largely nonexistent by 1651.

Sometimes Hobbes's failure to develop a satisfactory theory for some religious doctrine is mistakenly interpreted as a sign of irreligion. While his attempt to explain the doctrine of the Trinity as one god and three persons who represent that one god fails, as he later admitted, no other scholar produced a logically and religiously sound theory. The doctrine is arguably inconsistent; and no scholar to my knowledge has identified a logically satisfactory doctrine of the seventeenth century or earlier. The distinguished Roman Catholic theologian Bernard Lonergan quipped, "The doctrine of the Trinity has four relations, three persons, two generations, one substance, and no explanations." Scholars who are hard on Hobbes for his Trinitarian theory should compare it to John Wallis's view. Wallis wrote that each person of the Trinity is

wont to be called *Personality*. By which word, we mean, that Distinction (what ever it be) whereby they are distinguished each from other, and thence called *Three Persons*.

If the word *Person* do not please, we need not be fond of Words, so the Thing be agreed: . . . And we have no reason to wave the Word, since we know no better to put in the Place of it.

If it be asked, what these *Personalities* or *Characteristicks* are, whereby each *Person* is distinguished from other; I think we have little more thereof in Scripture, than that the *Father* is said to *Beget*; the *Son*, to be *Begotten*; and the *Holy-Ghost*, to *Proceed*.

If it be further asked, what is the full import of these Words (which are but Metaphorical), and what is the adequate Meaning of them, I think we need not trouble our selves about it: . . . we may be content to be ignorant.

In brief, "person" does not mean *person*; and Christians do not know what it means as regards the Trinity. Any other word would work as well, as long as it makes sense to say that one begets, one is begotten, and one proceeds. Then Wallis says,

And we who know so little of the Essence of any thing . . . need not think it strange that we are not able to comprehend all the Particularities of what concerns that of God, and the *Blessed Trinity*. (Wallis 1690: 3–4; cf. Hobbes 1651: 31.33/191)

Hobbes's views about Christian doctrines look less objectionable when they are considered against the background of numerous theological efforts. Almost all of them eventually break down. But Christian intellectuals continue to deal with the same problems. Recent efforts to escape the conundrum of reconciling God's universal causality with the causality of free will continue to come up short, I think (see Tracy 1994: 96n20, and Vicens 2018). Curley and others claim that Hobbes advanced so many implausible or impossible religious views that he must have been doing so deliberately. But many of Hobbes's views about political philosophy, geometry, and natural science are similarly implausible or impossible.[4]

In "The Interpretation of Covenants in *Leviathan*," Curley again criticized my interpretation (Curley 2004). He argued that Hobbes's discussion of covenants is suspiciously ambiguous and that his appeal to mediators in covenants with God is intended to show that it is impossible for human beings to enter into a covenant with God. Chapter 4, "The Interpretation of Covenants in *Leviathan*," is my reply. Putting our debate into a larger context of interpretation in order to explain why it is difficult for scholars to resolve their disagreements, I say more about the role of networks of belief in interpretation and more about the properties of networks. However, the networks of contemporaries are similar, and a community of scholars can evaluate competing interpretations against principles or marks of good interpretations, some of which have been mentioned above. Scholarly arguments about interpretations do not need to end in disagreement to be fruitful. They may help the scholars to clarify their positions or to shore up their evidence.

Curley argues that the best explanation for the contradictory opinions that Lord Clarendon and Robert Filmer had concerning Hobbes's treatment of biblical covenants is that Hobbes was willfully ambiguous (Curley 2004: 199). But that is implausible, since Hobbes's treatment of non-religious

---

[4] Also, Hobbes is sometimes criticized for espousing standard Christian views. One of the most egregious examples is his assertion that God is incomprehensible and no creature knows his nature (Stauffer 2018: 92). But probably hundreds of examples of this doctrine could be assembled. I give just one from the document currently at hand: "We firmly believe and confess that there is only one true God . . . incomprehensible and ineffable" ("Fourth Lateran Council: Constitutions," https://www.ewtn.com/catholicism/library/history-and-text-1465, accessed June 19, 2020). When Hobbes says that human beings "cannot have any idea of him in their mind answerable to his nature," he means that God, subtle body, does not affect the senses. Thomas Aquinas also denies that human beings know God's nature. Stauffer then seems to commit a non sequitur via a rhetorical question. Hobbes's definition of a true religion as one in which "the power imagined is truly such as we imagine" moves him to ask whether any religion could fit this description. Obviously, it could. And one could have faith in and believe that religion. But one may not *know* that it is the true religion: "Blessed are those who have not seen and yet have come to believe" (John 20:29).

concepts was equally ambiguous and has generated contradictory interpret-ations. I discuss nine absurdities in parts of Hobbes's philosophy that do not concern religion and allude to others. No scholar holds that Hobbes was intentionally ambiguous about these topics.

Curley thinks Hobbes's position that "there is no covenant with God but by mediation of somebody that representeth God's person" (Hobbes 1651: 18.3/ 89) is a good example of Hobbes's surreptitious project. Curley thinks that because he can prove that there could not be such a covenant, Hobbes must have thought the same. But Curley is projecting his own belief onto Hobbes. All Christians believe that Jesus is the mediator of the new covenant between God and human beings, just as Moses was the mediator between God and the Israelites. To assume that Hobbes did not believe that Jesus could be the mediator is to beg the question. It also renders absurd Hobbes's long discussions of divine covenants in chapter 35 and elsewhere in Parts III and IV. Curley's interpretation is an exercise of reading between the lines, when understanding the lines themselves is satisfactory.

In chapter 5, "Four Senses of 'Meaning' in the History of Ideas," I discuss four different senses of that key term for interpretation. These four senses can be identified by their syntactic and semantic features. Briefly, "mean" in the sense of *intend* takes an infinitive complement and intentions are often not fulfilled; "mean" in the sense of *try to communicate* takes a "that"-clause as its complement and the sentence asserting meaning does not entail its complement; "mean" in the way that logical and causal relations *mean* also takes a "that-clause as its complement and is entailed by the sentence that expresses the meaning. Finally, "mean" in the sense of significance or importance has to be relativized to a person or group, "for x" or "to x," and entails its that-clause. Historians are most concerned with meaning as significance and search for meaning in the other senses as clues to the relevant significance. Using a classic article by Quentin Skinner, I show how a confusion of these various senses produced a confused theory of interpretation.

A central principle of Skinner's theory of interpretation is considered in chapter 6, "Law and Self-Preservation: On Misinterpreting Hobbes's Philosophy, 1650–1700." Skinner espoused the principle that a philosopher's contemporaries have a privileged position for understanding what the phi-losopher meant. I think the principle is falsified by the facts. Ironically, Skinner expresses his perplexity after reading articles about his theory by distinguished scholars: "Reading my critics, I . . . learn that I am at once an idealist, a materialist, a positivist, a relativist, an antiquarian, an historicist, and a mere methodologist with nothing to say" (Skinner 1988: 231). The explanation for these facts, in my opinion, is that the contemporaries of a first-rate philosopher are generally not reliable interpreters because the originality of such philosophers usually consists of creating new concepts or reconfiguring familiar concepts in unfamiliar ways that second- and third-rate readers cannot appropriately fit into their networks of belief. Taking Hobbes's views about law and self-preservation as my central example, I explain the misinterpretations of his views by his contemporaries. They thought that self-preservation was one of Hobbes's laws. But that could not be true. Self-preservation is a desire, the dominant or strongest one that humans have; and because desires are physiological conditions, they cannot be laws. Rather, the concept of self-preservation is part of the definition of "law of nature." But the definition of a law of nature is no more a law of nature than the definition of an elephant is an elephant.

What then are laws of nature? Chapter 7, "The Laws of Nature Are the Laws of God in *Leviathan*," answers this question. Against the standard interpretation that the laws of nature in *Leviathan* are not laws because Hobbes calls them "theorems," I argue that the theorems or "dictates of reason" constitute the content of the laws of nature, but not the laws themselves. To be laws, the dictates of reason need to have the force of a command, as Hobbes says. He uses reason to prove theorems; and reason is the "undoubted word of God" and one of the three ways that God communicates with human beings, according to Hobbes. So the laws of nature are "properly called Lawes." John Deigh's ingenious defense of the standard view is that terms that have a certain sense outside of a technical term such as "law" may not retain that sense inside the technical term such as "law of nature." The technical term "law of nature" should be taken as if it were a fused expression such as "law-of-nature" or "lawofnature" (Deigh 2016a). If that is true, then "civil laws" and "natural liberty" may not be laws or liberty, respectively. Also, if the laws of nature are not laws, then Hobbes's division of two kinds of law, civil and natural, would be analogous to the division of two kinds of horses into equine animals and hobbyhorses.

I criticize the interpretation of another distinguished philosopher in chapter 8, "Leo Strauss's Olympian Interpretation." I argue that Strauss is mistaken about three foundational concepts in Hobbes's *De cive*: (a) Concerning rights, I argue that in the state of nature they are not normative, contrary to Strauss's view. For Hobbes, rights exist simply where no law excludes them. They contribute to conflict; but no one violates another person's right in that state. (b) As for self-preservation, it is a desire and is not necessarily guided by reason. (c) Finally, Strauss is mistaken in thinking that Hobbes was an innovator in understanding law in terms of will. God's laws in the Bible are laws because God wills them. Also, Hobbes's laws of nature depend on reason.

Chapter 9, "Hobbes on Sovereignty by Acquisition in *Leviathan*," shows that Hobbes's philosophy had better resources to explain the nature of sovereignty when it arises from conquest than Hobbes actually used. When he first explains sovereignty, he says that the two kinds of sovereignty differ only in the incidental way in which they come to exist. But he says that sovereignty by institution consists of a covenant among all and only the future subjects of a sovereign; and he seems to say that sovereignty by acquisition does not. The conquering sovereign seems to be a party to a covenant and the newly acquired subjects seem not to covenant at all. They consent. These differences are not incidental, because if they exist, then several unfortunate consequences follow: (1) Commonwealths could contain two kinds of sovereigns governing the same territory, with two corresponding kinds of subjects, with different obligations to their sovereign. (2) The kind of commonwealth that occurs most frequently in history would have a less prominent place in Hobbes's philosophy and it would be less clearly and more briefly described. And (3) sovereignty by acquisition would lack the two most innovative aspects of sovereign-making in *Leviathan*, authorization and representation. The alternative interpretation of sovereignty by acquisition offered here contains the essential features as sovereignty by institution; and the unfortunate consequences are eliminated or mitigated. The application of Hobbes's theory to several historical or nearly historical examples of new sovereigns arising for a population shows that the phenomena to be explained is much more varied than Hobbes seems to appreciate.

Chapter 10, "Natural Sovereignty and Omnipotence in Hobbes's *Leviathan*," completes the treatment of Hobbes's views about sovereignty. Because his discussion of natural sovereignty—that is, the sovereignty that God has in virtue of his omnipotence—occurs in the last chapter of Part II, "Of the Commonwealth," it is properly part of his political philosophy. Two significant differences between human and divine sovereignty are that the power and authority of God depends neither on a transfer of rights from subjects to the sovereign nor on a covenant. These two differences are grounded in the same fact, namely, God's "irresistible power." He does not need his subjects for his power and his authority does not depend on a covenant they make among themselves. Hobbes's views allow for a special covenant to be made between God and his subjects. This special covenant does not fit his other models of sovereignty; but he has to accept it since it is biblical.

Seventeenth-century divines and philosophers used their conception of divine sovereignty to explain the sovereignty of absolute monarchs. In Psalm 82, God calls kings "gods." So human monarchs are analogs of the divine sovereign. They have a monopoly on power; their judgments resolve contested facts and statements; they administer justice, and they save people (usually) from enemies and criminals. Sometimes the model of the human sovereign is used to explain properties of God. The question "Should human beings obey God or their sovereign if there is a conflict?" has an easy answer in Hobbes's philosophy. There can be no conflict because God commands people to obey their human sovereign. Locating the source of God's sovereignty in his power contrasts with standard seventeenth-century views, which located the source in his goodness or creation.

In chapter 11, my interpretation of Hobbes extends to one of the principal controversies between English Calvinists and Arminians, whether God is the author of sin or evil, and to another issue, the nature of demoniacs in the New Testament. Concerning God and sin, Arminians claimed that Calvinists were committed to the following inconsistent set of propositions:

1. God is the cause of everything.
2. God is the cause of Adam and Eve's sin of disobedience.
3. Whoever is the cause of sin is culpable of the sin.
4. Whoever is caused to perform a sinful action is not guilty of the sin.
5. God is culpable for Adam and Eve's sin; and Adam and Eve are not guilty of the sin. (From 1–4)

The creation story in Genesis is the evidence for (1) and accepted by both Arminians and Calvinists. Calvinists claim that (1) entails (2); Arminians say either that God is the cause only of good things or that he only permits evil actions like disobedience. Propositions (3) and (4) are supposedly obviously true; and (1)–(4) entail (5). Thus, God is the author of sin or evil. Calvinists less insightful than Hobbes often simply denied (3) and (4) without giving a good explanation, and occasionally denied (2). Hobbes's resolution is ingenious. He accepted (2) and denied (3) on the ground that not everyone who causes a sin is culpable for the sin. Concerning (4), he pointed out that in order to commit a sin, one has to be subject to a law and God is subject to none; and Adam and Eve were subject to God's law or command not to eat the fruit of the tree of the knowledge of good and evil and broke it.

Hobbes's debate with John Bramhall on these issues was only one of at least two other extensive debates at roughly the same time. The debates between the English Calvinists William Twisse and William Barlee and the Arminians Thomas Jackson and Thomas Pierce are similar in structure and argumentation to the Hobbes-Bramhall debate. The same lines of reasoning were pursued by other Calvinists too. I will mention only one more here, that of Thomas Whitfield, whose view is expressed in the title of one of his books, *A Treatise Tending to Shew that the Just and Holy God, may have a Hand in the Unjust Actions of Sinfull Men: and that in such a Way as shall be without any Impeachment of his Justnesse and Holinesse, or Diminution of his Power and Providence* (1653).

The second topic of chapter 11 concerns Hobbes's position that the people possessed by demons (daemons) in the Gospels were madmen. Although John Bramhall attacked him for this view, it was accepted by Twisse and originated with the respected and renowned Joseph Mede (aka Meade), one of the great New Testament scholars of the seventeenth century. Bramhall criticizes the view either because it was new or because Hobbes accepted it. Hobbes ably defends his position (Hobbes 1682a: 58).

The Act of Supremacy (1534 and 1559) was of great consequence. When Hobbes scholars mention this act, they usually say that the Church was subordinate to the monarch. That is at best misleading. State and religion are united; neither is subordinate to the other (cf. Evrigenis 2020: 131). In chapter 12, "Hobbes's Erastianism and Interpretation," I explain how the illustrated title page of *Leviathan* illustrates the unity of church and state (see also Martinich 1992: 362–7). The sovereign is pictured with a sword in one hand and a bishop's crozier in the other. Down the left side of the page are images proper to secular government, such as a castle; and down the right side of the page are images proper to the Church, such as a cathedral. If Erastianism is defined as the view that the Church is governed by the monarch, then England was Erastian and Hobbes was a good Englishman. If it is defined as the view that the Church is subordinate to the monarch, it is less clear whether England or Hobbes was Erastian.

The focus of my criticisms is the scholarship of Jeffrey Collins, who argued that Hobbes was Erastian, a proponent of Independency, and irreligious. While I agree that Hobbes was Erastian, Hobbes's support for Independency was hedged at best; and he was not irreligious. Collins sometimes omits evidence that is crucial for correctly understanding Hobbes's positions and sometimes draws an inference not justified by the evidence. These criticisms bear directly on my view that interpretation is inference to the best explanation.

The concept of a covenant is central to Hobbes's political theory. He very likely was exploiting the biblical concept of covenants in his political theory. While the concept of a covenant in *Leviathan* is the focus of chapter 4, other problems are dealt with in chapter 13, "Sovereign-Making and Biblical Covenants in *On the Citizen*." For Hobbes, it is important that human sovereigns not be a party to the covenants that create them. Indeed, they could not be, since they are the creatures of sovereign-making covenants. In contrast, God is not created by covenants, and he is a party to them. I argue that Hobbes did not try to give a unified account of both types, possibly because such an account would have been controversial. In fact, his philosophy had the resources to give a unified account. He could have pointed out that divine covenants in the Bible are not sovereign-making. For the covenants involving Moses and Jesus, he could have said that they were mediators of a covenant among the Israelites and Jews, in which God was a third-party beneficiary. A significant element common to human and divine covenants is faith (see also Baumgold 2013).

This book extends the interpretation I presented in *The Two Gods of Leviathan*. My interpretation improved as a result of criticisms by such scholars as Jeffrey Collins, Edwin Curley, John Deigh, and Quentin Skinner. Scholarship at its best is dialectical, thesis being criticized by antithesis, followed by a more refined thesis. Hobbes's philosophy is so rich and paradoxical that it invites theorizing about the nature of interpretation itself. While agreeing with Skinner's emphasis on context, my views on interpretation developed in a different direction. Scholars need to study the writings of both the target philosopher's first readers and the authors that the philosopher probably read or knew about in order to understand what problems the philosopher considered, his background beliefs, what he meant, and what he intended to do. I hope that my articles will help others to increase our understanding of Hobbes and the nature of interpretation.

1

Hobbes's Political-Philosophical Project

Science and Subversion

Thomas Hobbes conceived of his political philosophy as a science.[1] Due to the circumstances in England, he intended it to be subversive. The scientific dimension is accepted by virtually all Hobbesian scholars, including Leo Strauss, who famously held that the scientific trappings obscured his political philosophy (Strauss 1952).[2] The character of that science and the place of politics within it is the topic of section 3. Whether Hobbes's subversion was supposed to be subterranean, and if so, how, is complicated and will be the topic of section 4. Both sections need background information to be understood, and that is provided in sections 1 and 2.

1. Textual and Contextual Interpretation

Many interpreters adopt formalism in theory. They believe that the meaning of a text is discovered by careful attention to the meaning of the words and to the syntax of the sentences. Those who read between the lines by a careful reading of the text are, somewhat ironically, the best-known textualists.[3]

A problem with textualism appears when considering a brief but important text: "Congress shall make no law . . . abridging the freedom of speech." The text does not exclude a law that prohibits people from listening to speech. So by textualism freedom of speech does not include freedom of listening. The text of the Second Amendment provides an equally good example. It allows laws against the loading and shooting of arms. The source of the problem with textualism is that the meanings of words underdetermine

---

[1] I want to thank S. A. Lloyd and Leslie Martinich for their help with this chapter.

[2] On Hobbes's humanism, see Skinner 1996, Paganini 2003, and Nauta 2009.

[3] Only textualism and contextualism will be discussed in this chapter. Intentionalism and a form of reader-response interpretation both have a role to play in contextualism, described below. Deconstructionism is not treated at all.

Hobbes's Political Philosophy. A. P. Martinich, Oxford University Press. © Oxford University Press 2021.
DOI: 10.1093/oso/9780197531716.003.0002

the communicative meaning that audiences care about. For a textualist to object that the context of the text is implicit is to concede that the theory is inadequate.

Contextualism, which asserts that context supplements text, obviously does not deny the importance of the text. Text and context have to be balanced against each other with an eye toward identifying the most likely meaning. Applied to a historical text like *Leviathan*, a judgment as to what Hobbes meant to communicate is or should include evidence from his life and activities, his culture and circumstances, the judgments of his contemporaries about what he meant, propositions about human psychology generally, and seventeenth-century intellectuals in particular. The reason for considering these multiple factors is that successful communication depends upon mutual understanding of the author and audience, plus the author's reasonable expectation that his audience can recognize his communicative intention. Mutual knowledge conditions what an author is likely to mean and able to communicate (Davidson 1984, Grice, 1989, Quine and Ullian 1978; cf. Skinner 2002: 1: 1–7).

While contextualism puts the right elements of interpretation into play, it does not prevent disagreements about the interpretation of a text. Contextualists do not agree about what Hobbes thought the proper relationship between religion and politics is because they cannot agree about his beliefs about religion. One opinion that rests heavily on Hobbes's reading and the dominant religious practice of the early seventeenth century is that Hobbes was a particular kind of theist, that is, episcopal, orthodox, Erastian, an English Calvinist, and preferring a rich liturgy.[4] Such interpretations are "the theistic interpretations" because of what they attribute to Hobbes, not to the interpreter. Non-theist interpreters claim that Hobbes was a deist, agnostic, or atheist.[5] Logic would suggest that those who think that Hobbes was a heretic are theistic interpreters, since "heretic" presupposes being a believer. However, they usually have more in common with the atheist interpreters.

---

[4] Johnson (1974) and Glover were perhaps the first to present this kind of interpretation. Glover wrote, "Some of the ideas which Hobbes derived from the Reformation were, as a matter of fact, as disturbing to his contemporaries as anything resulting from his rationalism or materialism . . . [Other Protestants] who held very similar views [used] terminology that obscured implications Hobbes laid bare . . . Against the God of the Platonists Hobbes defended the Biblical tradition of a God who acts directly in nature and history, a God who is the source of righteousness" (Glover 1965: 142–3).

[5] A view on the border between the theist and non-theist interpretations, and possibly the best one, is that Hobbes was a deist who thought the best institutional structure of religion was episcopal monarchism and who found a high liturgy spiritually or emotionally most satisfying.

The claim that Hobbes was an English Calvinist is often mistaken as the claim that Hobbes accepted all of the salient beliefs of John Calvin. However, several Western European countries developed their own versions of Calvinism, England being one (McNeill 1954; see also Martinich 1992, 1996, and 2012a). Alan Cromartie gives the impression that Hobbes was not Calvinist enough to be any kind of Calvinist. He indicates that Hobbes differed from John Calvin on some important points, and that "the more Hobbes's view is scrutinized, the less Calvinistic it seems" (Cromartie 2018: 96; cf. Muller 1986: 180). Hobbes's belief about salvation is relevant here. One mark of any kind of Calvinism is belief that salvation is completely a matter of faith, not works. While Cromartie does not think that Hobbes believes it, consider Hobbes's assertion in the first sentence of this passage:

> For by the Law of *Moses*, which is applyed to mens Actions, and requireth the Absence of Guilt, all men living are liable to Damnation, and therefore no man is iustified by Works, but by Faith only. But if Workes be taken for the endeavour to doe them, that is, **if the Will be taken for the Deed, or Internal, for External Righteousness, then doe works contribute to Salvation.** And then taketh place that of S. *James*, Chap. 2.24. *Ye see then how that of works a man is iustisted [sic], and not of faith only.* And both of these are ioyned to salvation, as in S. *Mark.* 1.5. *Repent and believe the Gospel. . . .* But though both **Faith and Justice (meaning still by Justice, not absence of Guilt, but the Good Intentions of the Mind, which is called Righteousness by God, that taketh the Will for the Deed)** be both of them said to iustifie, yet are their Parts in the Act of Justification to be distinguished. (*De corpore politico*, II.6.10, 138–9)

Cromartie denies that Hobbes is a Calvinist because of the words in bold-face, the only words of the passage that he quotes. But Hobbes had just asserted the *sola fide* tenet with the words, "no man is iustified by Works, but by Faith only." The rest of the passage has to be understood in light of that assertion. Maybe Cromartie does not see this because he discounts the first sentence and does not give enough weight to the "ifs" in the second sentence. Acts of will are usually not regarded as deeds; but *if* they are so regarded, then God takes them for deeds. St. Paul is the source for the view (2 Corinthians 8:12). Such Calvinists as John Bradford and William Perkins wrote that God accepts "the will for the deed" (in Foxe 1583: 1923; Perkins

1592: 7).[6] Other expressions of the doctrine may found in Attersol 1618: 258; Abbot 1617: 8; Bennefield 1615: 21; Bernard 1626: 269; Bolton 1626: 316; and Byfield 1615: 8, to consider only divines with last names beginning with A or B.[7] Taking the will for the deed was an aspect of respectable English Calvinism. This example also shows how historical contextualism enjoins "To the texts themselves!"

To discuss the proper interpretation of Hobbes's views more generally, we need to judge the likelihood of his having a particular communicative intention. The issue is not so much about whether we have a "right to suppose that Hobbes could see what we see" (Curley 1996a: 270), but whether he could have expected his audience to understand what he meant. Roughly, theistic interpreters think that Hobbes could have expected his audience to believe that he believed (a) that sovereignty is absolute; (b) that religion is subject to the authority of the sovereign in order to preserve civil stability; (c) that God exists; (d) that reason belongs to science and faith to religion; and (e) that faith is compatible with reason, among other things. Non-theist interpreters generally think that Hobbes expected his audience to attribute to him (a) and (b), possibly (c) and (d), but not (e). Those who accept (c) think that Hobbes is a deist; and those who accept (d) usually think that Hobbes believed that superstitions are religions that result from putting faith in a person like Moses. Non-theist interpreters think that the clerics John Bramhall, George Lawson, and William Lucy were perceptive readers, and presumably that Hobbes's philosophical friends, such as Mersenne, Gassendi, Digby, White, and the Cavendishes, who left no evidence of Hobbes's non-theism, were not. John Aubrey, a friend but not a philosopher, judged that Hobbes's "writings and virtuous life testify" that he clearly was "a Christian" (Aubrey 1898: I. 353; cf. Martinich 2007). But Edwin Curley thinks that Aubrey's report that Edmund Waller refused to write a memorial poem for Hobbes because Waller apparently said that Hobbes had "pulled down all the churches . . . and laid open their priestcraft" is strong evidence of Hobbes's non-theism (quoted in Aubrey 1898: I: 358; and Curley 1996a: 271). I'm not convinced because the first part of Waller's quotation seems hyperbolic. The second almost certainly applies only to the priests and bishops of the restored Anglican Church. In any case, I am comfortable in the company of Mersenne and the others.

---

[6] Spelling is modernized for most seventeenth-century texts except for those by Hobbes.
[7] Space does not allow me to give Cromartie's work the discussion it deserves.

Undoubtedly, Hobbes failed to communicate with many people; but most original thinkers do (cf. Skinner 1988: 231–2). In addition to their bigotry and mental rigidity, interpreters could misunderstand Hobbes's sometimes obscure and apparently contradictory texts (*Leviathan* 17.13/18.1, and 21.14; see also Martinich 1996: 275–6 and Martinich 2001). If Hobbes's obscurities and contradictions existed only in his theological discussions, these failings might be telling. But they occur in his political philosophy, his natural philosophy, and mathematics.[8] It is not acceptable to say that our judgments about the significance of Hobbes's religious contradictions are not subject to the same criteria as those in other fields because religion is . . . religion. Isolating religion from the other parts of his philosophy is special pleading and requires a needlessly complex explanation for what he was doing. Also relevant is Hobbes's distinction between explicit atheism and "atheism by consequence" (*An Answer to a Book Published by Dr. Bramhall*, 130–1). Atheists are conscious of their disbelief in God. But atheists by consequence are all those who hold beliefs that entail that God does not exist, whether the person is conscious of this consequence or not. If Christian theism includes inconsistent propositions, then every Christian theologian is an atheist by consequence.[9]

Also contributing to misunderstanding Hobbes was his unique attempt to yoke the old with the new. The old was his adherence to *sola Scriptura*, English Calvinism, and absolutism. *Sola Scriptura* was a standard Protestant tool for purging the Bible of pagan and Roman Catholic elements, as it was in the work of many who decried the use of philosophy in religion (*Considerations upon the Reputation, Loyalty, and Religion of Thomas Hobbes*, 32, 37; see also Byfield 1626: 50, and Martinich 2013). Hobbes's arguments against belief in immaterial spirits and free will are consonant with a commitment to the literal interpretation of the Bible, which he shared with the prominent theologian William Perkins: "*There is one only sense, and the same is the literal*" (Perkins 1609: 31). Hobbes thought that the theology imbued with Aristotelian concepts distorted biblical teaching and introduced false doctrines into Christianity. He was at one with Tertullian on this issue: "What has Athens to do with Jerusalem?" As for absolutism, his promotion of it in *Leviathan* was incompatible with the spirit of limited government in the

---

[8] On political philosophy, see *Leviathan* 17.13/87, versus 18.1/22 and 21.14/112; on natural philosophy, see *De corpore* 7.1–2 and 25.1–2; on mathematics, see Jesseph 1999.
[9] Section 4 contains more about Hobbes's contradictions.

early Commonwealth. The new view was his scientism and sophisticated knowledge of biblical interpretation, which far outstripped the common run of English divines. It led him to adopt interpretations that some of his readers thought undermined the Bible through mockery or refutation by his espousal of the new science (see Malcolm 2002). In fact, these interpretations were consonant with the English Calvinist theology of double predestination and a literal interpretation of the Bible.

Some of his views, which his adversaries thought to be novel, were not. Calvinists had distinguished between faith and reason long before Hobbes (see Pearson 1659: 1–5; cf. Frith in Tyndale 1573: 334, second pagination; Hemmingsen 1579: 60; Whitaker 1585: 188). What he provided was an elaboration of the consequences of that distinction. The elaboration did not denigrate faith. He could hardly have done that since he required subjects to keep faith in creating a sovereign (*Leviathan* 7.5/31, 14.18–20/68, and 15.3/71; see also John 20:29). If two people covenant "to performe hereafter . . . , he that is to performe in time to come, being trusted, his performance is called Keeping of Promise, or Faith; and the fayling of performance (if it be voluntary) *Violation of Faith*" (*Leviathan* 14.11/66; see also 14.20/68; 30.4/ 175–6).[10]

His temperament often worked to his disadvantage. As Seth Ward reported, Hobbes "had a good conceit of himself, and was impatient of Contradiction: . . . he also thought himself Wiser; if any one objected against his Dictates, he would leave the Company in a passion, saying, his business was to Teach, not Dispute" (see Pope 1697: 118). His mien reflected his personality: "Those who remember Mr. *Hobbs,* as I perfectly do (and whose Pictures are perfectly like him) might discover in his very Looks, a supercilious, Saturnine *Opiniatrety* [*sic*], pleased with himself (Evelyn, 1697: 340– 1). Some resented that the low-born Hobbes had risen so high (Clarendon 1676: 181; Skinner 2002: 2: 324–5; see also Jackson 2007: 51). Hobbes aptly

---

[10] It is tempting to think that religious faith and political faith are different things. But they are not. Hobbes's explanation of faith or belief in chapter 7 of *Leviathan* covers the faith that people have in religion and the civil state. It would be difficult for him to hold that there are two kinds of faith, since he wants a union of the civil state and religion. In sovereign-making covenants, "*faith in* the man" is faith in the other parties to perform the terms of the covenant and then faith in the sovereign to protect them. And in religion, "*faith in* the man" is faith that the founder of the religion is revealing the true god and then, properly, protecting them as the sovereign (*Leviathan* 7.5/31). A distinction that should be drawn is between rational and non-rational faith, and within non-rational faith, between irrational and non-irrational faith. Faith in Naziism is irrational political faith, and not different, as faith, from an irrational religious faith. I think that the Christian or Jewish faith of some prominent philosophers has the same character as their faith in their political party. Neither religious nor political faith needs to be uncritical or unreflective.

described himself as a man who loved his own opinions (*Leviathan*, "To My Most Honor'd Friend").

Quentin Skinner, one of the great theorists of contextualism, urged making the guiding question for interpreters "What is the author doing with words in such-and-such a book?" Inspired by Austin's theory of speech acts, Skinner said that authors' intentions are revealed through linguistic conventions. In answering the question about what an author is doing, it is essential to distinguish between illocutionary and perlocutionary acts, that is, between what an author does "in saying" something and what the author does "by saying" something (Austin 1975; and Skinner 2002: 1: 104–5).

Skinner departs from Austin's view of illocutionary acts in that while such acts for Austin apply only at the level of individual sentences (Austin 1975; cf. Fotion 1971), Skinner is primarily concerned with the author's intentions for an entire text, whether article or book. About *The Shortest-Way with the Dissenters*, he says that Defoe's "illocutionary intention is that of ridiculing the intolerance that would be embodied in" recommending certain cruel practices (Skinner 1988: 270).[11] Skinner seems to be more interested in a fine-grained theory or classifications of genre than in individual speech acts. About the passage, "it is necessary for a prince to learn how not to be good," in Machiavelli's *The Prince*, Skinner says, "it cannot I think be doubted that the crucial question to raise is what Machiavelli was *doing in* counselling rulers in this way." He answers that Machiavelli's intention was

> to challenge and repudiate an accepted moral commonplace. We can know he was doing this because there was not only a highly conventionalized genre of writing against which to measure Machiavelli's utterance of it. There is also a clear presumption that Machiavelli was aware of the genre and the conventions governing it. (Skinner 2002: 1: 136, 142)

Even if Machiavelli was giving counsel, trying to persuade the prince that politics is exempt from morality is a perlocutionary act.

Illocutionary and perlocutionary acts are asymmetric. Illocutionary acts are either governed by conventions or rely on open, communicative intentions, in contrast with perlocutionary acts, which cause some natural state or reaction in the audience, such as a change of beliefs, attitudes, or values (Austin 1975, Grice 1989, and Strawson 1971). Discovering the

---

[11] However, the intention to ridicule is a perlocutionary intention.

perlocutionary act is often important for understanding the history of a text. So identifying the reactions of an author's contemporaries is important. But unlike illocutionary acts, perlocutionary acts may be unintended. An author who intends to get his audience to see that covenants ground a sovereign's authority may succeed in convincing or reinforcing their belief in patriarchy, as it was with Robert Filmer. Hobbes's insistence that his state of nature was part of a thought experiment was sometimes misunderstood or ignored (cf. Filmer 1652). Similarly, an author who wants to rid Christianity of superstition and unjustified clerical claims to authority and reconcile it with science may instead succeed in convincing his audience that he is non-Christian. Hobbes was often misunderstood. John Bramhall was convinced that Hobbes had, perhaps inadvertently, written a "Rebells Catechism" (Bramhall 1656: 515). In short, while the understandings of a philosopher's audience are relevant to understanding what the philosopher has done, they should not serve as a criterion for what the philosopher meant. Our particular interest is in showing that dissembling would have been at odds with what Hobbes was trying to do in his book *Leviathan*.

Recognition that an author's audience misunderstood him does not always lead a contextualist to draw the right conclusion. In his investigation of "how Hobbes's contemporaries reacted to his claims" in order to find evidence about Hobbes's views, Jurgen Overhoff discovers that Hobbes correctly described the views of Luther and Calvin, that "Bramhall did not, and that the Calvinist William Barlee held the same view as Hobbes about free will." He might have added that William Twisse, prolocutor of the Westminster Assembly, also held Hobbes's view. But Overhoff discounts this evidence and says there is "room for doubts about" Hobbes's sincerity—why?—because Hobbes did not exhibit the "spiritualism" of Luther and Calvin. (Overhoff 2000: 157, 158, cf. 155; cf. Martinich 2013). The issue should not be about devotion but doctrine. Truly, Hobbes did not cry, "Lord, Lord" (Matt. 5:20, 7:21). However, he worshipped according the rubric of the Church of England even when it was illegal; when he was near death, he made his confession and took the sacrament on the condition it be performed according to the rite of the Church of England (Aubrey 1898); and some of his discussions are theologically insightful:

> By this Ransome, is not intended a satisfaction for Sin, equivalent to the Offence; which no sinner for himselfe, nor righteous man can ever be able

to make for another: The dammage a man does to another, he may make amends for by restitution, or recompence, but sin cannot be taken away by recompence; for that were to make to make the liberty to sin, a thing vendible. (*Leviathan* 38.25, misnumbered as 248; see also *An Answer to a Book Published by Dr. Bramhall*, 77)

Another problem with Overhoff's conclusion that there is "room for doubts" is that there is room for doubting most things. The pertinent issue is whether the doubts lead to the right judgment, all things considered. Overhoff's earlier judgment that "most of the theological doctrines developed by Hobbes in his letter *Of Liberty and Necessity* clearly corresponded with Luther's and Calvin's own doctrines on these themes" is better explained by Hobbes's being a theist (cf. Overhoff 2000: 155).

A recalcitrant problem for interpretation is that different interpreters will assign different weights to the available evidence. Hyperbole is for one interpreter evidence of ignorance, whereas for another it is evidence of bad judgment. When John Donne wrote in "Anatomy of the Word," "[N]ew philosophy calls all in doubt / The sun is lost, and th' earth, and no man's wit / Can well direct him where to look for it," was he expressing cognitive dissonance hyperbolically or skepticism unreasonably? While many intellectuals evaded dissonance by ignoring science, Hobbes thought he knew the location of sun and earth and how to live on the latter too. His approach to religion was in the spirit of Cardinal Baronius and Galileo: "the intention of the Holy Ghost is to teach us how one goes to heaven, not how heaven goes" (Galileo 1615: 186).

2. Circumstances and Audiences

Hobbes's first book on politics was finished in spring, 1640, though not published until the 1650s, when the king's authority was breaking down. Handwritten copies of it circulated among lingering members of the Short Parliament, "those whom the matter it containeth most nearly concerneth" (*Humane Nature*, "Epistle Dedicatory"). He thought that adoption of his "opinions concerning law and policy" contained in it would be "an incomparable benefit to commonwealth," since doing so would end "mutual fear" and create "government and peace," an expression of his belief that philosophy should have salutary practical consequences ("Epistle

Dedicatory"). He wanted to end England's strife, not exacerbate it. His book was quasi-scientific in that it contained more logic than rhetoric ("Epistle Dedicatory"), and his exposition of his views is similar to that in *De cive*, which is explicitly scientific. Since it was published in the Dutch Republic, his primary audience was continental intellectuals (cf. *Vita Carmine*, 223, line 155).

Hobbes's primary audience for *Leviathan* was the ruling class of England during the Commonwealth (*Considerations*, 19–20). Edward Hyde's report that Hobbes told him that he wrote it because "I had a mind to go home" rings true and illustrates how infuriating his candor could be. A more irenic answer would have gone something like this: "England now has a stable government, albeit not the most desirable one. I am old and English. I want to go home. But because of my royalism, it's prudent for me to smooth the way by showing how my principles are consistent with a non-monarchical, non-episcopal commonwealth."[12] His secondary audience was the educated class of England. He wanted them to understand the foundations of authority and the obligation of obedience. It would have been reckless for him to be communicating prosecutable doctrines either openly or surreptitiously. He made this point himself in 1656:

> But do not many other men as well as you read my *Leviathan*, and my other Books? And yet they all find not such enmity in them against Religion. Take heed of calling them all Atheists that have read and approved my *Leviathan*. Do you think I can be an Atheist and not know it? Or knowing it durst have offered my Atheism to the Press? Or do you think him an Atheist, or a contemner of the Holy Scripture, that sayeth nothing of the Deity, but what he proved by the Scripture? You that take so heinously that I would have the Rules of Gods worship a Christian Common-wealth taken from the Laws, tell me, from whom you would have them taken? From yourselves? Why so, more than from me? From the Bishops? Right, if the Supreme Power of the Common-wealth will have it so; If not, why from them rather then from me? From a Consistory of Presbyters by themselves, or joyned with Lay-Elders, whom they may sway as they please? Good, If the Supreme Governour of the Common-wealth will

---

[12] Outrage at the execution of Charles I probably also moved him to write *Leviathan*. (See *Vita Carmine*," 234, lines 189–9; on regicides, *Leviathan* 18.3/89; 18.7/90; and 29.14/170–1.)

have it so. (*Six Lessons*, 62; see also *Seven Philosophical Problems*, "Epistle Dedicatory")

At the Restoration, he explained how he had also been writing for royalists (*Considerations*, 25–6). His political philosophy could serve the interests of both "commonwealth men" and royalists because it is a form of loyalism, allegiance to an established government, whether it came to rule by legal or illegal means (*Six Lessons*, 56–7). Royalists for the Commonwealth in 1650, and republicans for the monarch in 1660.

If it is paradoxical that he could honestly justify both sides of a dispute, it is Hobbesian (although not only Hobbesian) (Wilson 1615; Parkin 2016). He gloried in paradox and enjoyed showing people who claimed he had contradicted himself that he had not. So he wrote that Bramhall had

> not yet found the place where I contradict either the Existence, or Infiniteness, or Incomprehensibility, or Unity, or Ubiquity of God. I am therefore yet absolved of Atheism. But I am, he says, inconsistent and irreconcileable with myself, that is, I am, (. . . he thinks) a forgetful blockhead. I cannot help that: but my forgetfulness appears not here. (*An Answer to a Book Published by Dr. Bramhall*, 5–6; see also *Questions Concerning Liberty*, 283; cf. Holden 2015)

The mistake was in Bramhall's inattention or ratiocination, not in Hobbes's argument.

Non-theistic interpreters typically argue that Hobbes's assertion that God's nature is incomprehensible is a sign that he believes there is nothing to comprehend by the word "God." In evaluating this interpretation, it is necessary to consider his view that people cannot know the nature of the smallest creature (*Leviathan* 31.33/191); that negative theology was an ancient and honorable Christian tradition; and that both Arminians and Calvinists asserted the fact of divine incomprehensibility (Jackson, T. 1628: 3, 7–8, Wilson 1600: 15, and Wilson 1615: 6–7). As I was writing this paragraph, a group email about Herbert McCabe, a distinguished twentieth-century theistic philosopher arrived, which included this sentence: "A second message of McCabe is . . . [that] we do not know what/who God is, neither by reason nor by faith" ("Philosophy in Europe," on behalf of Franco 8/4/2020).

3. Political Theory as Scientific Philosophy

In *Leviathan*,[13] Hobbes defined philosophy or science as

> *[1a] the Knowledge acquired by Reasoning, from the Manner of the Generation of any thing, to the Properties; or [1b] from the Properties, to some possible Way of Generation of the same; [2] to the end to bee able to produce, as far as matter, and humane force permit, such Effects, as humane life requireth.* (*Leviathan* 46.1/367)

Philosophy has two major aspects, [1] methods and [2] goal. The methods of philosophy are also two, indicated by "a" and "b." Each method connects the way things are generated or come to be with the properties of those objects. The first method, the "synthetic" one, consists of connecting the manner of generation (the cause) with the properties or effects, [1a]. The second method, the "analytic" one, connects effects to possible causes of those effects, [1b] (see *De corpore*, 6.1).

Clause [1a] comes from Hobbes's conception of Euclidean geometry. Definitions, in general, should give instructions for constructing figures such as this: a circle results from fixing one leg of a compass and drawing a line with the other until a plane forms. This definition depends on a definition of line, and the definition of a line on a definition of a point. [1a] is the preferred method of the first chapters of *De corpore* and of *De cive*.

The method of doing science indicated in [1b] is to begin with an effect and then to conjecture that some particular thing or event is its cause. So suppose that a roughly circular figure appears. One way to find out whether it actually is a circle is to propose a generation like the one described above. If the result of the generation is a line that is equidistant from a given point within the figure, then it is a circle. While Hobbes considers the propositions of both methods to be formally hypothetical, the propositions used in reasoning according to [1b] are also hypothetical in the sense of a hypothesis that may be confirmed or disconfirmed by an experiment. Applied to politics, [1b] characterizes the reasoning of someone who thought that the destruction of a commonwealth could be the effect of people, acting on the belief that the authority of a sovereign is not absolute, or the belief that they did not transfer their rights to the sovereign, and so on (*De corpore* 6.7). The scientist

---

[13] Hobbes's first published definition of "philosophy" or "science" is in *Humane Nature* 6.4.

of politics formed a hypothesis consisting of a possible cause and the actual effect, which this proposition expresses: "If people believed that the authority of their sovereign was not absolute, the commonwealth was destroyed" (*Leviathan* 29.3/167–8, and 46.1/367; see also *De corpore* 6.4). The methods described in [1a] and [1b] are asymmetrical. The conclusions of [1a] are the effects of the actual causes. The premise or some of the premises of [1b] are only possible causes of the effects (cf. Talaska, 1988).

The second feature of philosophy, indicated by [2], has to do with the goal of philosophy (see Hoekstra 2006). The "*end* or *scope* of philosophy" is some benefit to human beings. The importance of practical consequences in Hobbes's conception of philosophy is consonant with his assertion, "*Scientia potentia est*" ["*Science is power*"][14] (Latin *Leviathan* 2012: 10.15/135; cf. Bacon 1597: 13ᵛ: "*ipsa scientia potestas est*"). The word "end" in [2] suggests that Hobbes violated his stricture against final causes, as he also seems to have done at the beginning of chapter 17 of *Leviathan*:

> The final Cause, End, or Designe of men . . . in the introduction of that re-straint upon themselves . . . is the foresight of their own preservation, and of a more contented life thereby; that is to say of getting themselves out of that miserable condition of Warre. (*Leviathan* 17.1–2/85)[15]

However, the phrase, "final Cause," is a *façon-de-parler* expression, re-placeable with a literally true mechanistic paraphrase: The desires for self-preservation and a contented life cause human reason to calculate the means of maintaining that preservation and even producing a more contented life. The apparent reference to the final cause of entering a commonwealth dissolves into human desires (cf. Hyde 1676: 27).

In *De corpore*, Hobbes restricts the definition of philosophy to its methods, described above:

> PHILOSOPHY *is such knowledge of Effects or Appearances, as we acquire by true Ratiocination from the knowledge we have first of their Causes or*

---

[14] Hobbes then adds "*sed parva.*" The parallel passage in *Leviathan* is "The sciences are small power" (10.14/42).

[15] This definition appears at the beginning of chapter 46, "Of Darkness from Vain Philosophy, and Fabulous Traditions." It seems to be out of place unless chapter 46 was written as a stand-alone essay, say, in response to discussions with members of the largely Roman Catholic Mersenne circle. Then it occurs right where it should, at the beginning of the essay.

> *Generation: And again, of such Causes or Generations as may be from knowing first their Effects. (De corpore* 1.2)

However, Hobbes's discussion of the end or goal of philosophy shortly after indicates that it is essential to his conception of philosophy:

> The *End* or *Scope* of Philosophy, is, that we may make use to our benefit of effects formerly seen; or that by application of Bodies to one another; we may produce the like effects of those we conceive in our minde, as far forth as matter, strength & industry will permit, for the commodity of humane life. (*De corpore* 1.6)[16]

While Hobbes's entire philosophy was supposed to consist of three parts—of body, of the human being, and of the citizen—the last was published first. It begins with adult human beings who shoot up like mushrooms (*Philosophical Rudiments*, 127; cf. Lloyd 2009: 75–6). The humans are adults because the results of the second part of the triad, *De homine*, which ends with human beings as individuals, is presupposed. Not understanding this, critics objected to his beginning with mushroom men (*Philosophical Rudiments concerning Government and Society* 8.1; see Eachard 1672: 117–8). In fact, publishing the third part first was not objectionable in principle. It was analogous to publishing a book on solid geometry before one on plane geometry. The geometer may assume the definitions of point, line, and plane, and begin with definitions of face, edge, base, vertex, and so on (cf. Sorell 1988).

Both the methods and the aim of philosophy presuppose the tools of philosophy, namely, clear and unambiguous words, used literally. Insinuation and suggestion are not the ways of science or philosophy. Reason is attained

> first in apt imposing of Names; and secondly by getting a good and orderly Method in proceeding from the Elements, which are Names. . . . To conclude, The Light of humane minds is Perspicuous Words . . . And on the contrary, Metaphors, and senseless and ambiguous words, are like *ignes fatui;* and reasoning upon them, is wandering[17] amongst innumerable absurdities; and their end, contention, and sedition, or contempt. (*Leviathan* 5.1/18 and 5.20/22)

---

[16] Sharon Lloyd has noted that "self-preservation" does not appear in this description of the end of philosophy.

[17] Hobbes is continuing the analogy introduced by "like."

He had a strong motive for using perspicuous words and speaking clearly about religion in the second half of *Leviathan*. False and nonsensical language in religion caused contention and sedition. His chief complaint against Aristotelian philosophy was its unintelligibility; and its intrusion into religion was a source of superstition (*Leviathan* 1.5, 4.1, 12.31, 44.3, and 46.11). Hobbes found the philosophical terminology in the Nicene Creed offensive (Springborg 2008: 230–5). However, he was willing to profess it because the sovereign commanded it. To object that Hobbes's allegiance to clarity is a good cover for his surreptitious subversion is to beg the question of his need or desire to dissemble. It is also to oppose the weight of evidence. Hobbes's goal of establishing political stability through the development of politics as a science, his commitment to clarity and precision in philosophy, his aversion to accusations of error, and his self-satisfaction in holding paradoxical views, suggest that he would not try to communicate surreptitiously.

At the beginning of chapter 32, Hobbes says that he had

> derived the Rights of Soveraigne Power, and the duty of Subjects, from the Principles of Nature onely; such as Experience has found true ... and from Definitions. . . . But in that I am next to handle . . . the Nature and Rights of a CHRISTIAN COMMONWEALTH . . . the ground of my Discourse must be, not only the Naturall Word of God, but also the Propheticall. (*Leviathan* 32.1/195)

In short, the method and the content of the second half of *Leviathan* is substantially different from that of the first. The first half aspires to science; the second does not. This difference between the first and second half does not mean that there is any change in Hobbes's communicative style. He seems to discuss this particular issue:

> we are not to renounce our Senses, and Experience; nor (that which is the undoubted Word of God), our naturall Reason. For they are the talents which he hath put into our hands to negotiate ... and therefore not to be folded up in the Napkin of an Implicite Faith, but employed in the purchase of Justice, Peace, and true Religion. (*Leviathan* 32.2/195)

In other words, Hobbes is recommitting himself to the ideals of clarity and precision. His allusion to "the Napkin of an Implicite Faith" is an insult to

Roman Catholic theology.[18] Some think that Hobbes's succeeding comment that "the mysteries of our Religion," should be "swallowed whole" because chewing them would likely cause them to be "cast up again" (*Leviathan* 32.3/195) may imply revulsion for Christianity. But I think that twenty-first-century sensibilities are being projected onto the seventeenth century (cf. A. D. 1624: 18; Abbot 1594: 181–2; and Abbot 1623: 267). Religion has mysteries that cannot be broken down and understood. Breaking down is a method of science that produces understanding of those phenomena that are proper objects of scientific study.

4. Subversion and Surreptitious Subversion

Hobbes was open about his subversive projects. He wanted to subvert the mistaken religio-political views that led to the English Civil War, the belief in limited sovereignty, the practice of superstitious religion in Roman Catholicism, and the pretension that religion should be independent of the sovereign's authority. He wanted to initiate a "cultural transformation" that had "roots in the humanist and polemical traditions of the Renaissance" (Johnston 1986: ix and xx; on Hobbes's humanism, see especially Nauta 2009, Paganini 2003, and Skinner 2008: 1–17). But he did not expect people to give up religion, *pace* David Johnston (1986; cf. *Leviathan* 12.2/52). As for the numerous false religions, his account of them fits the standard understanding of the time, that they were deviations from the original, true religion (Calvin 1559: I.4.1; Raleigh 1614: 84–97; Martinich 1992: 62–7 and 372n4). He thought that self-interested people could be made obedient through a proper education in the universities and from the pulpit, as S. A. Lloyd (1997) has rightly emphasized. (During her reign, Elizabeth I prescribed politically correct sermons to be read at Sunday worship services; see Jewel 1571; cf. Anonymous 1623). Hobbes did not believe "the human psyche [could be transformed] into the mold of rational egoism" (Johnston 1986: 216; cf. Lloyd 1992: 374–5). Human nature was fixed. Education could instill the fundamentals of government, and training could inculcate a desire

---

[18] According to Roman Catholics, Christians did not need to know doctrine in detail. As long as they believed whatever the Church believed, they had implicit faith, and that was sufficient faith for salvation (see Thomas Aquinas, *Summa Theologiae* 2a2ae, Q. 2, art. 5. For Protestant criticism of implicit faith, see, e.g., Anonymous 1611: 80–1; Attersoll 1612: 77; and Beard 1616: 143, 349, and 528; cf. Ball 1617: 9).

to obey. He wanted not a brave new world, but a safe old world, reinforced by an accurate understanding of the Bible and compatible with the new science.

Hobbes looks more modern in politics than he was because he exploits the concepts of liberty and equality (cf. Skinner 1998 and 2008). However, his conceptions of them are not the liberal conceptions. Not even a radical libertarian could love Hobbes's liberty because it provides no protection for property; and equality is equal ability to kill or vulnerability to being killed. Absolutism saves. It is the lesson of the Bible in the stories about the leadership of Moses, David, and Solomon. England's rule came close to that ideal in the quasi-absolutist reigns of Henry VIII, Elizabeth I, and James I (*Leviathan*, chapter 40).

Was there also an important strain of surreptitious subversion as non-theist interpretations claim? I do not think so. Adrian Blau has, in my opinion, definitively refuted the Straussian interpretation that Hobbes communicated his genuine beliefs between the lines and that "the careful reader" could identify them (Blau 2012). As for other non-theistic interpretations, they depend less on surreptitious messages than on supposed conversational implicatures. They hold that Hobbes's materialism, anti-Catholic, anti-Presbyterian, anti-jure-divino clericalism was on the surface. I agree. But those positions do not imply that Hobbes was a non-theist. Tertullian was a materialist, as are Mormons; and Hobbes is right in holding that the Bible is not committed to immaterial substances. As for anti-clericalism, Luther and the thousands of signers of the root and branch petitions were anti-clerical. Religious reformers and zealots were "anti" one traditional Christian thing or another, and often many things. Many of Hobbes's "offensive" religious views were held by undeniably religious authors or are understandable as his attempt to show that faith is compatible with reason, as Mersenne and others did.

To read the polemical religious treatises of the Elizabethan and Jacobean reigns is to be shocked by the uncharitable recriminations among Christians. So it should not be surprising that any rigorous, original thinker is castigated by his contemporaries.

A more subtle form of argumentation for Hobbes's non-theism has been offered by Curley. He says that Hobbes engages in "suggestion by disavowal" (Curley 1996a: 261–2); that is, a speaker asserts a proposition by supposedly denying it: "In this rhetorical device a writer presents a series of considerations which might reasonably lead his reader to draw a certain conclusion, but then denies that that conclusion follows" (Curley 1996a: 262).[19] Curley

---

[19] By "his reader," Curley must mean a generic reader. But it is doubtful that Hobbes had a generic reader when it comes to his religious views. Different particular readers drew different conclusions

illustrates his point by claiming that Hobbes reports his skepticism about miracles, prophets, and scripture (hereafter, "the triad"). Hobbes supposedly leads his readers to the conclusion that none of the members of the triad exist, and then unconvincingly disavows his own lack of belief. I do not agree with Curley's position, partially because I think he misdescribes the texts. Hobbes explains why members of the triad are not objects of knowledge, but of faith or belief. It was not a novel position (see Barnes 1573: 344, third pagination). His discussion was supposed to protect the triad that is grounded in faith from criticism supposedly arising from reason. Science uses reason; religion uses faith (*Leviathan* 32.5/196, 37.5/234, 43.8/324; Luke 7:50, 18:42). Since all covenants depend on faith, as mentioned in section 1, Hobbes would have been fighting against himself if his point was to convince his readers to abandon faith. Also, before Hobbes explains why instances of the triad cannot be known, with some exceptions, he either asserts or presupposes that there have been revelations, miracles, and true prophets (revelation: *Leviathan* 32.3–7/195–7; miracles: 37/233–8; cf. 26.39/148–9; prophets: 36.8–13/225–8). This order of assertion or presupposition is important in that he settles the issue of *fact* before raising the issue of *knowledge*. *Pace* Curley, Hobbes does not lead the reader to the conclusion that members of the triad do not exist, only to disavow that conclusion.

Curley's interpretive device of "suggestion by disavowal" is faux cancellation of what would be otherwise conversationally implicated. In genuine cancellation, the speaker forestalls the conclusion that the listener might otherwise have drawn (Grice 1989). If a speaker says to Lee's manager, "This is the third time this month that Lee has submitted his report late," she might add, "but that is not a reflection on Lee's competence; Lee's been given too many duties." If suggestion by disavowal is in play, a person is caught in a Catch-22. The person would be incriminated whether asserting atheism or denying it. Attributing suggestion by disavowal to a speaker is easily uncharitable and difficult to determine. The comedy *Seinfeld* created a meme by having characters end an apparently negative description of some behavior with "Not that there's anything wrong with that."

Non-theist interpreters make much of the effort by some Restoration clerics to have Hobbes investigated for atheism. Usually omitted is the fact that the accusers wanted Thomas White, a Roman Catholic priest,

---

from his texts. The readers most inclined to conclude that Hobbes was anti-religious were the most inquisitorial ones.

investigated at the same time. Both could be exasperating; and that largely accounts for the clerical threat. Much is also made of the condemnation of Hobbes's works by Oxford University in July 1683. What is usually omitted is that the Presbyterians Richard Baxter and John Knox, the Independents John Milton and John Owen, and the "philo-Catholic" Godfrey Goodman were condemned in the same document (see *Judgment and Decree* 1683; and Martinich 1992: 38). And why was the condemnation issued against dead authors? It was a ripple of the reaction to the Rye House Plot.

The reliability of suggestion-by-disavowal can be put to the test outside the realm of religion. Consider Hobbes's position that people are equal. He purports to prove it using the premises that people are generally satisfied with the amount of intelligence they have and that "there is not ordinarily a greater sign of the equal distribution of anything than that every man is contented with his share" (*Leviathan* 13.2/61). Actually, variations in strength and intelligence seem to be evidence of inequality; and many stupid people do not know that they are and are content with the talents they have. So, suggestion-by-disavowal yields the result that Hobbes's assertion of equality should be taken as suggesting that he thought people were unequal. But that is the wrong result, for if he actually held that people were naturally unequal, he undermined his political philosophy in three ways. One is that he needs equality in order to generate war in the state of nature. Another is that the few of superior strength and intelligence would have a claim to natural sovereignty. The third is that Hobbes believes scientific progress depends on the method he discovered. (See *De cive*, "Preface," 2–3; *De corpore*, chapter 6; and *Leviathan* 5.17/21 and 5.21/22; cf. *Leviathan* 8.11/34.)[20] (See also section 3 above.)

Some non-theist scholars claim that Hobbes's words constitute plausible deniability, and they imply that almost any offensive position can be protected with a denial. No. Powerful scoundrels sometimes pretend to give a plausible denial of their bad behavior; and they often get away with the pretense because their opponents lack the power to press the point. But Hobbes was in no such position.

Since space does not allow as full a discussion of other non-theistic interpretations as they deserve, I will need to paint in broad strokes. Any argument that depends on showing that Hobbes's professed Christian views entail a contradiction is weakened by the fact that Christian doctrine seems

[20] Descartes placed the same high value on the method of rightly conducting the mind.

to concern numerous contradictions, as mentioned in section 1 above (see Martinich 1978; and Martinich 2019 for another example). A favorite non-theist argument for Hobbes's subreption concerns the Trinity. He allegedly uses his novel theory of persons to show that the doctrine of the Trinity is inconsistent. But it is implausible that Hobbes had this intention. (Although the doctrine is demonstrably inconsistent in predicate logic, seventeenth-century philosophers did not know this.) He was trying to show the power of his theory of persons to explain that well-entrenched doctrine. It is hard to believe that he would not have known that faced with a choice between (i) and (ii),

> (i) accept Hobbes's novel theory of persons and reject the doctrine of the Trinity, or
> (ii) reject Hobbes's novel theory of persons and retain the doctrine of the Trinity,

virtually everyone would chose (ii). Attributing "a clearly ironical strategy aimed at attacking the very substance of the doctrine" to Hobbes does not seem plausible (Paganini 2003: 192n103, referring to Curley's view; see also Trinkhaus 1996). If no cogent treatment of the Trinity had been given in 1,000 years and more—non-theist interpreters do not cite one that is— then Hobbes's failure is not revealing. Scotus's theory is no better that that of Thomas Aquinas (Bach 1982, 1998). Appealing to an irreligious motive is *de trop*.

Non-theist interpreters think that Hobbes's treatment of the Bible is clear evidence that he was anti-Christian. However, it was merely one of the most advanced understandings of the Bible in the mid-seventeenth century (Malcolm on biblical scholarship). Also, almost everything that Hobbes said about the Bible is accepted by biblical scholars today, theists and non-theists alike, except when their views are more radical than Hobbes's

Let us now consider a special problem that Hobbes has. Curley argues that Hobbes's theory of covenants is incompatible with the biblical conception of them and that this is evidence that Hobbes was a non-theist (Curley 2004). Curley does not mention that the Bible contains at least two incompatible conceptions of covenants, each of which is problematic with respect to the standard model of a transcendent God. Hobbes was in an impossible situation. I think Hobbes made a good effort in trying to make biblical covenants consistent with his theory (Martinich 2004a).

The contextual elements of English law and the Bible support the theist interpretation of Hobbes. According to law, the monarch was the supreme head of the church. Henry VIII had asserted it; key bishops had supported it; and Parliament had enacted it in the Law of Supremacy. Elizabeth I's parliament re-installed it. Most Elizabethan[21] and Jacobean bishops were comfortable with it. It is not surprising that the Act of Supremacy was part of the law, since it was also part of the law that all English subjects were Christians. The ideal of the Old Testament was that the leader was the head of state and religion. The three greatest leaders of the Israelites, Moses, David, and Solomon, headed both religious and secular affairs, as Hobbes explained in chapter 40, "Of the Rights of the Kingdom of God, in Abraham, Moses, the High Priests, and the Kings of Judah." The two dimensions of Christian sovereignty are represented on the title page of *Leviathan*, in which Leviathan holds the sword of secular authority in one hand and the crozier of episcopal authority in the other. Running down the left- and right-hand sides of the page are five boxes. On the left, aspects of secular power are pictured; and on the right, religious power. Religious elements are coordinate with secular ones (Martinich 1992: 362–7; see also Lloyd 1992: 224–6). Both Protestants and Catholics thought that every commonwealth needed a religion: "Without Religion, Societies are but like soapy bubbles, quickly dissolved" (Bramhall 1657: 465; see also, for example, Hakewill 1616: 111; and Fitzherbert 1610: Preface, n.p.). And in sixteenth- and seventeenth-century Europe, the sovereign often had regular control over the religion.

That many of Hobbes's contemporaries would think he was irreligious is attributable to many factors: his innovative and nonstandard theories, his desire to resurrect an old-time religio-political system (rejected by both royalists and non-royalists), and arrogance and a flinty personality (cf. Malcolm 2002: 317–5; Pope 1697: 117–8; cf. Aubrey 1898: 348).

5. Conclusion

Hobbes's political philosophical project was to make politics scientific, according to his geometrical conception of science, which begins with

---

[21] Elizabethan clerics had to pledge, "I, A. B., now elect bishop of C., do utterly testify and declare that the Queen's Highness is the only supreme governor of this realm . . . as well in all *spiritual and ecclesiastical things or causes as temporal*" (Elton 1982: 375).

"perspicuous words but by exact definitions first snuffed and purged from ambiguity," for such words are "the light of human minds" (*Leviathan* 5.20/21–2). Ambiguity and verbal legerdemain are the stock in trade of dissemblers. Hobbes's audiences were educated men in England and on the continent, many of whom had power and influence; few of whom were non-theists. Also, he hoped his theory would come to be taught to the elite in universities and to the masses from the pulpit (*Leviathan*, "Review and Conclusion," 16/395). Like others, he believed that religion was important to civil stability. So conveying an anti-religious view would have been counter-productive.

The argumentation of *Leviathan* is at least as cogent as that in *De cive*; and the second half of the book has at least the same clarity as the first, and arguably more. Finally, since he wrote *Leviathan* because he had a mind to go home, he had to have known that insinuating anti-religious views would have been against his self-interest.

2

Interpretation and Hobbes's
Political Philosophy

Hobbes's beliefs about God are important to his political philosophy because of his use of the laws of nature. On the one hand, if he thinks that God exists, then he can use God to command the laws of nature; this would ensure that they are genuine laws and hence have force, and thus the transition to the civil state would be eased. On the other hand, if he thinks that God does not exist, the laws of nature would not be genuine laws and hence not obviously have force; thus it would be difficult to establish the civil state on firm ground. Although these are not the only two lines of thought that can be developed from Hobbes's theism or atheism, they are obvious ones. Also, although theism and atheism are not the only possibilities—he might have been a deist, pantheist, or agnostic—for the sake of simplicity, I will consider only the theist- and atheist-interpretations of Hobbes's philosophy.[1]

This article has two parts. In Part Two, I defend my version of the theist-interpretation of Hobbes's philosophy. The defense is consonant with what I take to be principles of good interpretation. The main principles involved here are consistency, completeness, connectedness, and defensibility. They naturally come to the fore when a debate is mature, that is, when over a long period scholars have elaborated their own views, have replied to objections, and have raised objections to opposed views. The debate over Hobbes's religious views is mature, and not, I think, senescent.

For many years now I have wondered why debates such as this one persist among intelligent, knowledgeable, and well-meaning scholars. I have come to believe that it can be explained in large part by the conditions under which interpretation occurs. One might think that these conditions could be overcome by the principles of good interpretation; but in fact, some of these

---

[1] "Theist-interpretation" means an interpretation that holds that Hobbes was a theist, and "atheist-interpretation" means an interpretation that holds that Hobbes was an atheist. Neither interpretation says anything about the beliefs of the interpreter.

Hobbes's Political Philosophy. A. P. Martinich, Oxford University Press. © Oxford University Press 2021.
DOI: 10.1093/oso/9780197531716.003.0003

principles may exacerbate it, particularly conservatism, frugality, palpability, and generality. I discuss this issue, with application to Hobbes, in Part One.

Part One

The Difficulty of Rational Persuasion

Every interpreter comes to a text with her or his own complex Network of Beliefs,[2] by which one understands the world. Linguistic interpretation is just a special case of understanding the world, and not even separable from it, partially because language is itself part of the world, and because knowing a language requires interaction with the nonlinguistic part of the world. Textual interpretation is impossible without a complex Network of Beliefs. To judge that Hobbes is a theist/atheist presupposes an enormous set of beliefs about people in general, people in the seventeenth-century more particularly, and about philosophy and religion. Although the beliefs may be literally pre-judgments in the sense that one has them before the interpretation of a target text occurs, they are not necessarily biased. The Network of Beliefs is a largely true representation of the world. Survival could hardly have it any other way. It is misleading at best to call the beliefs in the Network "prejudices," as some hermeneutic philosophers do.

The goal of interpretation[3] is to update the Network in the most satisfactory way. (What counts as the most satisfactory way will be discussed below.) But some properties of the Network reduce the possibility of agreement between scholars. Consider just one of these, tenacity: beliefs are held more or less strongly. Tenacity is essentially the degree to which a person is unwilling to give up a belief, even in the face of what otherwise would be disconfirming evidence. For some people, belief in God is something that they will not give up, no matter what the evidence against it. In the extreme, they take the position, "I believe because it is absurd." Analogous remarks could be made about some atheists, Marxists, utilitarians, Kantians, (American) Democrats, Republicans, and Libertarians. Such tenaciously held beliefs are

---

[2] My idea of the Network is very close to the idea of the "web of belief" (Quine and Ullian 1978) and the idea of the Network (Searle 1983). A belief in my general sense is a proposition that a person thinks is true. So, I may use the word "proposition" rather than "belief" when English style invites it.

[3] The word "interpretation" has a process/product ambiguity. I trust that the context will indicate the intended sense.

usually irrational, but they do not need to be. When the Copernican theory was first presented, there was more evidence for the Ptolomaic scheme, but the Copernican theory had other virtues that made it preferable.

The tenacity of a belief is not perfectly correlated with the amount of evidence in favor of the belief, although there is a high correlation between the two. In contrast with tenacity, certainty concerns a person's degree of confidence in the truth of a proposition, usually inversely related to the likelihood that evidence could disconfirm it. Most people, when asked, are certain that "$1 = \overline{.99}$" is false. However, once shown a simple proof that the equation is true, most of them immediately change their mind. Their belief that "$1 = \overline{.99}$" is false was certain but not tenacious, partially because it has little to do with their practical lives.

The distinction between tenacity and certainty is important because it partially explains why one scholar will not give up belief in a certain interpretation even when the evidence is or appears to be against it. An opponent may point out that the tenacity of this belief is not justified by the evidence, but the scholar (typically) will not see it.

Let's now turn from properties of the Network to properties of a good interpretation.

Virtues of a Good Interpretation

A good interpretation is such because it has certain properties.[4] It might seem then that a judgment could be made between incompatible interpretations by comparing their virtues. However, these virtues do not provide a simple criterion for judging between two interpretations, because each interpretation is relative to a Network, and the source of disagreement is often in the Networks themselves. That is, one interpreter can judge between Interpretation I_1 and Interpretation I_2, precisely because her Network is the same for each. But two interpreters, A and B, each of whom has her own Network, determined by her own native dispositions and experiences, may not make the same judgment between I_1 and I_2, precisely because the interpretations are related to two things. Interpretation I_1 may be better with respect to A's Network than to B's, and Interpretation I_2 may be better with

---

[4] Although good interpretations tend to be correct interpretations, the two concepts are not identical. For simplicity's sake, I will discuss only good interpretations.

respect to B's Network than to A's.[5] The virtue of conservatism provides an example.

Conservatism

A good interpretation will update one's Network by changing as few beliefs as possible. Given two interpretations, I_1 and I_2, I_1 is better than I_2 if I_1 changes fewer of the beliefs in the Network than I_2 *ceteris paribus*. (Since all the principles I will describe apply *ceteris paribus*, I will usually not make this explicit for the others.) The reason behind conservatism should be obvious. The Network has served at least to help keep its owner alive and possibly to flourish. Since its beliefs have succeeded in the past, there is a presumption in their favor. However, since interpreters come to a text with different Networks, the degree of conservatism of each I_i will vary. Again, the general problem is that while two theories can be compared with respect to some virtue with respect to the same Network, they cannot easily be compared if the Networks differ with respect to those parts relevant to the interpretation itself. This point is also made clear by the virtue of frugality.

Frugality

While conservatism concerns the number of beliefs that need to be subtracted by an interpretation, frugality concerns tenacity. Given two interpretations, I_1 and I_2, I_1 is more frugal than I_2 just in case the beliefs that I_1 requires to be subtracted are overall less tenaciously held than the ones that I_2 requires to be subtracted. Since two interpreters may hold the same beliefs with different tenacities, I_1 may be more frugal than I_2 for one person and less frugal for the other. Even for one person it may be impossible to determine which of two interpretations is more frugal, because for most beliefs there is no way to assign numerical values to tenacities.

---

[5] I say "cannot always judge between two interpretations" because in all cases most of the beliefs in a Network are not relevant to the interpretation of a text. Only a relatively small part of the Network comes into play, usually a part that is largely common to all interpreters. Consequently, in most cases, the differences in Networks do not interfere with interpretation. Since scholars focus on differences, intense debates may obscure extensive areas of agreement.

Even though the virtues of a theory, at least taken singly, may not determine which of two interpretations are better, it does not follow that anything goes. People have roughly the same sensory and cognitive equipment, and those living in the same culture will to a large extent share values and experiences. So the virtues of an interpretation can often be recognized even if a settled judgment about the ultimate preference of one to another cannot be given.

Palpability

A palpable interpretation may be thought of as the one most obvious, most available, or closest at hand.[6] According to one version of the story, when Freud took out a cigar, cut off its tip, and turned it inside his mouth to moisten it, he said to his aghast audience, "Remember, sometimes a cigar is just a cigar." On my view, the interpretation that it is just a cigar is more palpable than a "deeper" interpretation, and hence better unless other facts suggest that it is more than just a cigar. A palpable interpretation is better than an extravagant or implausible one. Given two interpretations, I_1 is better than I_2 if I_1 depends on explanations or hypotheses that are more likely to occur than the ones on which I_2 depends. Suppose a teacher has to decide which of the following is the likeliest (true) explanation for why a student did not hand in his homework: (a) he did not do it; (b) his dog ate it; (c) space aliens stole it. The explanation or interpretation that uses (a) is more palpable, and hence preferable to those that use (b) or (c), even if the teacher believes that space aliens have stolen some things. This is an easy case.

Interpreters of Hobbes's philosophy often disagree about the palpability of explanations. Although my critics and I probably agree that relative to an arbitrary sentence by Hobbes the proposition that he is not being ironic is more palpable than that he is being ironic, we disagree about its palpability relative to certain sentences of *Leviathan*.[7] Moreover, it is difficult for people to change their belief in the palpability of an explanation because it depends upon their own native psychological dispositions and experiences, which are relatively few. Hobbes recognized this: "let one man

---

[6] Although I am unhappy with the term "palpability," I am even more unhappy with other possible names: "banality," "mundaneness," "obviousness," and "straightforwardness."

[7] I do not deny that Hobbes was sometimes ironic; I deny that he intended any of his irony to undermine what he thought was the correct understanding of Christianity.

read another by his actions never so perfectly, it serves him only with his acquaintance, which are but few" (Hobbes 1994b, Introduction). But there are ways to overcome the narrowness of our own first-hand experience. Hobbes thinks it comes with reasoning by analogy: "whoever looketh into himself, and considereth what he doth, when he does *think, opine, reason, hope, fear, &c,* and upon what grounds; he shall thereby read and know, what are the thoughts, and passions of all other men." Although I do not think that reasoning by analogy is the method (Malcolm 1988), it certainly is the case that we usually learn how other people think and feel by paying attention to their behavior. Hobbes agrees with this to at least some extent when he writes:

And though by men's actions we do discover their design sometimes; yet to do it without comparing them with our own, and distinguishing all circumstances, by which the case may come to be altered, is to decipher without a key, and be for the most part deceived, by too much trust, or by too much diffidence; as he that reads, is himself a good or evil man. (Hobbes 1994b, Introduction.)

Hobbes's words seem to imply that if the theist-interpreters are mistaken, they are too trusting; and if the atheist-interpreters are mistaken, they are too diffident. I can live with either result.

To be more serious, I believe that for the disputed sentences, the interpretation "Hobbes means what he says" is more palpable than "Hobbes is communicating that atheism is true," given that Hobbes was a physical coward, knew that professing atheism was a serious crime and knew that he had powerful enemies, knew that he was already suspected of atheism, and knew that publicly trying to spread atheism and mocking religion would be dealt with more harshly than keeping it within a small circle of friends. I believe that Hobbes's behavior[8] is plausibly explained as the work of a philosophical, Christian reformer, not an enthusiast, like John Knox, but someone more like Richard Hooker with on chip on his shoulder, the kind of person who, when his views were challenged at a social gathering, would say in effect, "I come to teach, not to dispute" (Pope 1697: 117–8). A somewhat arrogant or prideful reformer would be inclined to write sarcastically. The sarcasm would overlap

---

[8] It is important that my judgment would apply not just to Hobbes but to anyone like him in the relevant respects. The judgment has to be based on one or more general propositions, otherwise it is indefensibly ad hoc.

with irony. And that combination of sarcasm and irony would complicate the problem of determining exactly what he meant.

Edwin Curley would partially reject my judgment because he thinks that Hobbes was not a coward (1996a: 262). But then he needs to explain why Hobbes left England in late 1640, returned to England in 1651, and wrote in his verse autobiography that he did so because he was afraid of civil war and the French clergy. Curley says that Hobbes "likes to boast of his fearful nature." But that is not a palpable explanation. As Hobbes well knew, people like to be honored or respected, and cowards are not (Hobbes 1994b: 13.5).

Generality

A proposition is general, in my sense, when it explains a large number of things, especially, seemingly diverse things. The proposition does not need to be syntactically general. For example, the interpretation expressed by the singular proposition *that Hobbes is an English Jacobean Calvinist* has the power to explain his opposition to many English Arminians, his belief that God is the cause of everything, his belief in determinism, his support for episcopacy, and for sovereign supremacy even in matters of religion.

It is natural to call highly general interpretations "highly theoretical," in the sense that they rely upon many interconnected propositions, the truth of which is not immediately obvious. A good example of such an interpretation is *Reason and Rhetoric in the Philosophy of Hobbes* by Quentin Skinner. His view at one level is that Hobbes's understanding of the best method of conveying his philosophy to his readers underwent a sea change between the completion of *De cive* and the composition of *Leviathan*; the change consisted of his reappraisal of the value and role of rhetoric. If this were all Skinner was trying to establish, his achievement would be much more modest than it in fact is. What makes Skinner's view important and even magnificent is the extent to which his interpretation of Hobbes fits within highly general claims about the humanistic culture of Renaissance England and its historical relation to rhetoric and political philosophy in ancient Greece and Rome. He displays a virtual omniscience about these matters. Hobbes's intellectual development is in fact only a moment in a much greater story about early modern political philosophy.

Interpretations as general as Skinner's are often hard to accept because their consequences may be so far ranging that they clash with the Networks of their readers. That is, being highly general may contribute to the theory's being perceived by readers as having a low degree of conservatism, frugality, and possibly palpability.

Not nearly as general as Skinner's theory—and it need not be—is the theistic-interpretation, according to which, whenever Hobbes talks about religion, what he says presupposes or entails that God exists. For example, when he says, "miracles now cease," that presupposes or entails that God exists because miracles are by definition events caused by God.

Because theist-interpreters claim the vast majority of Hobbes's statements about religion as evidence for their view, David Berman, an atheist-interpreter, says their position rests on what he tendentiously calls "the quantity argument." He wants to transmute this virtue into a vice. To himself he attributes the "quality" argument, a supposedly insightful analysis of a few key sentences that reveal Hobbes's "crypto-atheistic" position (Berman 1988: 64–5). Here is a representative passage:

> In eight (folio) pages, Hobbes soberly describes nearly 50 emotions. In the middle of this psychological chapter, however is the following paragraph:

> Feare of power invisible, feigned by the mind, or imagined from tales, publiquely allowed, RELIGION, not allowed SUPERSTITION. And when the power imagined, is truly such as we imagine, TRUE RELIGION.

> *Prima facie*, this paragraph does not particularly stand out from its surrounding text. . . . Yet the first sentence can be and was read as a superbly condensed statement of unbelief. Hobbes's epigrammatic gem can be seen alone, even though it is embedded in a different duller story. It is also hidden in the sense that the last sentence (about true religion) covers up and effectively denies the first provocative statement. Yet Hobbes's real or latent meaning was in the daring first sentence, rather than in the forest of psychological description or cover-up sentences. . . . He would probably have known of Cicero's injunction that the good orator will choose "the strongest points for the opening and closing, and insert the weaker points in between." By implication, the middle of a work (like the middle of a thicket) would be an ideal place to hide something. (Berman 1988: 64–5)

There are at least three objectionable aspects to Berman's attempt to over-throw the quantity argument. First, he seems to reason from how Hobbes's sentence "can be read" to how it is to be read. This is the fallacy of *a posse ad esse*, reasoning from what can be to what is. And he reasons from how Hobbes's sentence "was read" to how it should be read, an analogous fal-lacy. Second, Berman's argument relies on special pleading. On the one hand, he admits that the beginning and end of a text are the most important positions, and he uses this fact as evidence that the first clause ("sentence") defining religion is "a superbly condensed statement of unbelief" and the last clause ("sentence") defining true religion "covers up and effectively denies the first provocative statement." On the other hand, the paragraph's location in the middle of the chapter is an important fact, according to him, because it allows Hobbes both to hide there (because it is least conspic-uous) and (for the very same reason) to reveal his most important thoughts. The degree of importance that Berman attaches to a text's location seems to depend upon how well it supports his interpretation. The third defec-tive aspect is that Berman's argument requires reading Hobbes's definition of religion out of context: the definition is to be "seen alone, even though it is embedded in a different, duller story." The conclusion Berman aims at is driving his premises.

The last sentence of Berman's chapter indicates that he is begging the ques-tion: "If we suppose that Hobbes wished to express and disguise his atheism in *Leviathan*, I cannot see how he could have done it more effectively than by the esoteric technique I have tried to exhibit here" (Berman 1988: 67). Hobbes's atheism is to be proved, not to be supposed.

Let's now return to generality. Another reason it alone is unlikely to settle a dispute is that many of the propositions used by rival interpreters are logi-cally independent of each other. For example, Skinner's thesis that Hobbes's political philosophy was greatly affected by Renaissance humanism is in-dependent of the theistic-interpretation. Generality has special force when coupled with palpability. A literal interpretation of a text is better than a nonliteral interpretation (*ceteris paribus*). A literal interpretation does not need initially to justify itself because it is the default mode. The apparent triviality of T-sentences like " 'Snow is white' is true if and only if snow is white" depends on the primacy of literal meaning. A nonliteral inter-pretation bears the burden of showing that the default modes need to be overridden.

Part Two

Let's now consider four properties of good interpretation that are not so easily stymied by differences in Networks: consistency, completeness, connectedness, and defensibility.

Consistency

A good interpretation is both internally consistent and consistent with the Network of which it becomes a part. It is a truism that inconsistent propositions (and hence interpretations) are untenable because they are logically too strong: everything follows from an inconsistency. This is obvious—and two things almost as obvious need to be added.

First, it should go without saying that the beliefs attributed to the author of the text need not be consistent with the beliefs of the interpreter.[9] Let's suppose that Hobbes believes that the laws of nature are genuine laws, and the interpreter *in propria persona* does not. Her belief that the laws of nature are not genuine laws is consistent with her interpretation that Hobbes did believe that the laws of nature are genuine laws. As obvious as this is, some people believe that interpreters who believe that Hobbes was a theist must themselves be theists. When this latter belief is conjoined with the Straussian belief that atheists are more intelligent than theists, they think they have additional evidence against the theist-interpretation, though they are usually not so crass as to say it. While I have no opinion about how intelligence is distributed, the Straussians should provide good evidence that scholars who are theists are in fact intellectually disadvantaged. It is ironic that so many seventeenth-century theists were able to read between Hobbes's lines with the acuity of a Grand Inquisitor.

Second, it is not necessary for the beliefs attributed to the author of the text to be self-consistent (cf. Skinner 1969: 41–2). Many philosophers have contradicted themselves. Although interpreters often try to resolve what they take to be purely verbal contradictions, I think it is often better to recognize that since philosophers try to clarify poorly understood concepts or determine the limits of them, they will sometimes fall into contradiction.

---

[9] I had thought this was too obvious to mention, until I discovered that a colleague who has written several books on interpretation was mistaken about this very point.

It happened famously to Gottlob Frege, one of the greatest logicians of all time. It happened to Hobbes perhaps more often than usual among first-class philosophers.[10] He believed the false mathematical proposition that a construction could be given that would square the circle. Since all true mathematical propositions are necessarily true, all false mathematical propositions are necessarily false. So Hobbes's mathematical beliefs were (at least virtually) contradictory, unless he was being ironic about the existence of mathematical entities. Also, Hobbes wrote, "Who is so stupid, as both to mistake in Geometry, and also to persist in it, when another detects his errors to him?" (Hobbes 1994b: 5.16). Yet during the 1650s and 1660s, Hobbes both made mistakes in geometry and persisted in them when mathematicians whose views he trusted, some of whom were friends, pointed out his errors, unless, again, he expected the attentive reader to combine his "so-stupid" statement with his seeming mathematical obtuseness and conclude that he was being ironic about the existence of mathematical entities. Numerous additional contradictions or absurdities in Hobbes's views could be pointed out. For example, Hobbes thought that because "Necessarily, it will rain tomorrow or it will not," either "Necessarily, it will rain tomorrow" is true or "Necessarily, it will not rain tomorrow" is true (Hobbes 1839a: 4: 277).

How should apparent contradictions in an author's work be handled? There is no one way. Sometimes the contradiction is genuine and ineliminable. Sometimes it is only apparent, and the appearance can be removed by showing that one or both sentences are inexplicit and that explicit renderings make their consistency evident. Sometimes it is a mark that the author changed her mind about the issue. And sometimes it is a mark of irony. There is no algorithmic way to know what tactic should be employed in any particular case. Interpretations are guided in each case by the desire to find an inference to the best explanation, and each inference begins from an interpreter's unique Network, which includes maxims and principles of interpretation. This is a generality. How should the alleged contradictions in Hobbes's religious views be handled?

In the space available here, I will say that I do not know of any legitimate way of both acknowledging that Hobbes sincerely but stubbornly defended novel and obviously contradictory mathematical beliefs and also maintaining that he insincerely but stubbornly defended novel and obviously contradictory

---

[10] See Martinich 1996: 275–6. While not agreeing with all of my examples, Curley concedes the general point in Curley 1996b: 285.

religious/political beliefs, as some atheist-interpreters do, *ceteris paribus*. It is simpler to explain Hobbes's stubborn defense of both his nonstandard mathematical and religious views by the general principle that, because he was proud, he would stubbornly defend a theory that he proclaimed was original with him, even if it provided evidence to his opponents that he was obtuse or insincere.

Atheist-interpreters might respond that it is legitimate to distinguish between Hobbes's stubborn defense of his mathematical absurdities and his religious absurdities because the former do not affect the interests of people and the latter do. Although the distinction between "mathematical and dogmatical" learning is Hobbes's own, it does not help the atheist-interpretation. Since Hobbes claims that mathematical learning "is free from controversies and dispute, because it consisteth in comparing figures and motion only" (Hobbes 1994a: 19), there is all the more reason to think that he is being ironic when he persists in advancing absurd mathematical views than when he does so in religion or politics. Everyone knows that we can expect sincere and stubborn absurdity from a theologian and that we should not expect that from a sincere mathematician. If we do happen upon a mathematician stubbornly supporting surds, we may judge that he is being ironic. I will return to this point below.

Completeness

A good interpretation is one that needs to account for all of the evidence relevant to understanding the text. What counts as relevant varies from theory to theory. Formalism (the old New Criticism), for example, claimed that nothing outside the text should count for anything and only the meanings of the words of the text itself are important. Certainly, it is a necessary condition for a good interpretation that it explains almost all of the evidence that the text itself provides. I say "almost all" because some texts, including some of the most interesting ones, resist any compelling complete interpretation. However, most interpreters of Hobbes recognize that understanding the text requires understanding what the author's intentions were, and those can best be discovered by taking the context, linguistic and nonlinguistic, into account. Consequently, most interpreters of Hobbes in effect subscribe to a kind of Nonformalism, because they think that the correct interpretation depends on understanding either Hobbes's intentions or some contextual matters. Among the evidence that I have appealed to is Hobbes's letter of July 1645 to Edmund Waller:

> My odd opinions are baited. But I am contented with it, as believing I have still the better, when a new man is set upon me that knows not my paradoxes but is full of his own doctrine, there is something in the disputation not unpleasant. He thinks he has driven me upon an absurdity when 'tis upon some other of my tenets and so from one to another till he wonder and exclaim and at least finds I am of the antipodes of the schools. (Malcolm 1994: 124, spelling modernized)

Hobbes is reveling in the fact that some of his views are paradoxes, in the first sense of "paradox" in the *Oxford English Dictionary*: "A statement or tenet contrary to received opinion or belief; often with the implication that it is marvelous or incredible; sometimes with unfavorable connotation, as being discordant with what is held to be established truth, and hence absurd or fantastic; sometimes with favorable connotation, as a correction of vulgar error."[11] I trust that all interpreters agree that Hobbes in this letter is speaking straightforwardly and not ironically, and that he thinks his views belong to the category of the "marvelous" and uses the word "paradox" "with favorable connotation." If he generally, or even occasionally, spoke ironically in expressing his own views, it would have been appropriate for him to say so in this letter. Yet he says nothing about it.

Hobbes again discusses his views as paradoxes in his debate with Bishop John Bramhall, who was championing free will. Bramhall claims that Hobbes's espousal of determinism combined with his belief that he can resolve to do things and deliberate about doing things generates paradoxes (Hobbes 1839a: 5: 30–2). Hobbes is sanguine.

> The Bishop speaks often of paradoxes with such scorn or detestation, that a simple reader would take a paradox either for felony or some other heinous crime, or else for some ridiculous turpitude; whereas perhaps a judicious reader knows what the word signifies; and that a paradox, is an opinion not

---

[11] Consider some of Hobbes's paradoxical metaphysical and political beliefs: nature is artificial; machines are alive; human beings are machines; the judgment of the sovereign is the criterion of all truth; democratic premises lead to the conclusion that the sovereign is absolute; the person to whom one alienates her rights is the one who acts for you; mothers, not fathers, have natural dominion over infants; and so on.

yet generally received. Christian religion was once a paradox . . . Insomuch
as when a man calleth an opinion [not his own] a paradox, he doth not say it
is untrue, but signifieth his own ignorance; for if he understood it, he would
call it either a truth or an error. He observes not, that but for paradoxes
we should be now in that savage ignorance, which those men are in that
have not, or have not long had laws and commonwealth, from whence
proceedeth science and civility. (Hobbes 1839a: 5: 304)

Again, he says nothing about his speaking ironically. Hobbes could be hu-
morous in various ways, especially when reporting or attacking the views of
others. But when he explains his own positions, he is mostly humorless. We
may think his views are funny, but he does not.

To my knowledge, no atheist-interpreter has commented on the significance of this letter or the passage attacking Bishop Bramhall. So, in this
matter at least, the theist-interpreter has a more complete theory than her
opponent.

Connectedness

Completeness is often joined to another virtue. It is implausible in my
opinion to rest one's interpretation on a few passages if that interpretation does not also explain how other parts of the text are connected or
fit together. For example, Curley defends his atheist-interpretation by
focusing on Hobbes's allegedly blatant misrepresentation of the Nicene
Creed in Appendix 1 of the Latin *Leviathan*.[12] But he does not explain how
this supposed misrepresentation connects with the rest of the Appendix.
Consider, for example, these passages that set the tone for most of the
Appendix:

For my part I do not find fault with those who think this [that the soul is
naturally immortal]. For one who thinks very well of his own soul will
generally take care not to dishonor it with a shameful life. But I do not
grant that a person will take less care to avoid that result if he believes
firmly that his soul has been redeemed by the blood of Christ, and made

---

[12] For a further defense of the theist-interpretation of Hobbes's treatment of the Trinity, see
Martinich 1996: 279–81; chapter 3 of this volume.

eternal . . . Let others expect what immortality they wish. I expect that
which Christ, having conquered death, acquired for us by his blood . . .
(Hobbes 1994b: 510, 511)

Passages like this forestall an ironic interpretation of Hobbes's views about
the Nicene Creed in my opinion. If the atheist-interpreter replies that it is just
the part about the Trinity that gets satirized, he still owes us an explanation of
why only that doctrine. Why, for example, does Hobbes not mock the virgin
birth, which is just as incredible?

Only the blood of the woman is the matter of the fetus, growing by daily
nourishment until the proper time for birth. The semen in the uterus is
the efficient cause of fertility, not the matter of the fetus. So if you believe
that a woman can become pregnant by the virtue of human seed, why do
you doubt that she can become pregnant by virtue of God's omnipotence?
(Hobbes 1994b: 511–2)

Because he does not require the human seed to supply the "form" of the fetus,
Hobbes's variation on the standard reproductive biology of the time actually
makes the virgin birth less incredible.

My point about taking into account the general structure and tenor of a
work is in line with Hobbes's own view: "For it is not the bare words, but
the scope of the writer that gives the true light, by which any writing is to be
interpreted; and they that insist upon single texts, without considering the
main design, can derive no thing from them clearly" (1994b: 43.24). Another
way to put my point is that Curley, like some other atheist-interpreters,
appears to give great weight to a few passages that they privilege and little
weight to the rest of the text.

Defensibility

When an interpretation is able to rebut criticisms made against it, it is defensible in that respect. Consequently, the defensibility of an interpretation can
be judged only after the interpreter has had a chance to reply. Because I treat
interpretations as fundamentally products of a particular person or persons,
not abstract sets of propositions independent of being produced at a particular place and time, defensibility is not reducible to some of the other virtues.

Also, since it is most important when debates are mature, as this one is, my discussion of objections is extensive.

There have been several recent occasions on which atheist-interpreters of Hobbes should have defended their theory and have not done so adequately. For example, Paul Cooke, in *Hobbes and Christianity*, maintains that Hobbes's philosophy is inimical to Christianity. He purports to refute the theistic view but directs almost all of his fire against Howard Warrender's position, from which I had already dissociated myself in some respects (Cooke 1996: 76–86; Martinich 1992: 134–5). So he is attacking a straw man as far as I'm concerned. While he expresses large agreement with my interpretation, he maintains that Hobbes's "entire treatment of Christianity constitutes an exceedingly clever illusion" without refuting my arguments (Cooke 1996: 32–3). Although he thinks that Hobbes wrote ironically, he does not consider that Judith Sklar's comment to him may have been ironic: "Bishop Bramhall would have been proud of you" (Cooke 1996: xiv). I think any philosopher should prefer to have Hobbes proud of him or her. While a point by point response to my interpretation may not have been feasible, the absence of a detailed reply to my most important arguments makes Cooke's interpretation score low with respect to defensibility.

Curley too can be criticized for not showing his interpretation to be defensible in our debate. For example, he says nothing to rebut my claim that the same form of reasoning that leads to the conclusion that Hobbes is an atheist should lead to the conclusion that Hobbes is an "amathematician" (Martinich 1996: 276). If Hobbes's contradictions about religion indicate that he believes that God does not exist, then his contradictions about mathematics should indicate that he believes that numbers and figures do not exist.

Curley's interpretation is also not defensible insofar as he misrepresents my position that Hobbes was a Calvinist in the sense it had in early seventeenth-century England and slightly later. In this sense, the primary mark of Calvinism was subscription to the doctrine of double predestination. Curley writes: "I welcome Martinich's clarification of his use of the term 'Calvinist.' It was silly of me to think that he intended to imply substantial agreement with the theology of John Calvin. I see now that he intended it to imply only acceptance of the doctrine of double predestination" (Curley 1996b: 285).[13]

---

[13] Here are some of the issues mentioned by Curley on which Hobbes's views differ from Calvin's: "the nature of God and of the soul, the immortality of the soul, the eternal punishment of the damned, and the status of Jesus's commands," and others (Curley 1996a: 261n15). I was quite aware of these divergences.

Curley is probably being sarcastic, but, "silly" or not, he should have realized the sense in which Hobbes was a Calvinist, because more than once I said so explicitly. On the first page of *Two Gods of Leviathan* I said Hobbes was committed to "the Calvinist Christianity of Jacobean England" (Martinich 1992: 1), and I made the same point in "On the Proper Interpretation of Hobbes's Philosophy" (Martinich 1996: 278, chapter 3 of this volume). Moreover, it is simply not true, *pace* Curley, that Hobbes was Calvinist only on the issue of double predestination. To quote myself: "I said [on page 15 of *The Two Gods of Leviathan*] that Hobbes was an orthodox Calvinist in theology, 'insofar as it emphasizes that the Atonement is achieved through the mercy, in contrast with the justice, of God'" (Martinich 1996: 278, chapter 3 of this volume). Other features of Hobbes's brand of Calvinism that I mentioned are (complete) causal determinism, "the belief that Jesus died only for the elect, the belief that salvation (after the fall of human beings) comes from faith and that good works do not merit it" (Martinich 1996: 279, chapter 3 of this volume). (I realize that some of these doctrines are also marks of Lutheranism.)

Curley rests a large part of his case that what Hobbes says about the Trinity is ironic on the premise that he made the "manifestly false claim . . . that the Nicene Creed is untainted by Greek philosophy" (Curley 1996a: 269; cf. 268). Because the assertion is supposedly "manifestly false,"[14] he concludes that Hobbes knew it was false, and hence must have meant his assertion to be taken ironically. According to Curley, Hobbes wants his audience to reason something as follows: Since Hobbes is making the manifestly false assertion that the Nicene Creed is untainted by Greek philosophy, he ironically means that the Nicene Creed is tainted by Greek philosophy; and consequently not even the Nicene Creed satisfies the fundamental test of reformation theology, namely, that only what is scriptural is to be accepted. Presumably the reasoning would not stop here but should continue as follows: Any church that accepts the Nicene Creed, which includes virtually every Protestant denomination, is false.

If this were Hobbes's communicative strategy, then, given the repressive atmosphere created by the Restoration Church of England, it would have been

---

[14] Curley gave the impression that he would produce a clear example of "suggestion by denial." This is irony introduced by a phrase similar in form to, "I will not suggest that *p*," where the speaker implies that *p*. In fact, his example turns on the principle, "When someone says something manifestly false, we often take that as a sign of an ironic utterance." According to Curley, Hobbes ironically asserts that *p*, when it is (allegedly) obvious that *not-p*.

an incredibly imprudent one. I mean "incredibly" literally. Overall, Hobbes toned down his controversial religious views in the Latin *Leviathan* (Skinner 1996: 3n15). The supposed strategy would also be vain because it conflicts with the apparent intent of the paragraph in which it occurs:

> But that synod [Nicaea] condemned, not only Arius, but also all heresies which had arisen since the birth of Christ, summing up briefly the orthodox faith in the creed called Nicene, taken from Scripture itself, with no admixture of Greek philosophy at all: *that Christ is true God, and born of the son of God, and is of the same substance as God*, which faith the following three general councils also confirmed with an article added concerning faith in the Holy Ghost. They also condemned the heresy of the Africans which had arisen under Cyprian, concerning the rebaptism of those who had returned to paganism, and added to the creed the article: I believe in one baptism for the remission of sins. These doctrines, acknowledged by the synod of Nicaea from Sacred Scripture, and not yet supported by pagan philosophy, found favor and were confirmed. For at that time philosophers were not a majority of the Fathers. (Hobbes 1994b: 470–1)

The entire paragraph suggests that Hobbes was showing off his command of the history of Nicaea and confirming his credentials as an interpreter of Church history.

Curley in effect requires the reader to ignore 90 percent of the paragraph, fixate on the 10 percent that says that the orthodox faith in the Creed was "taken from Scripture itself, with no admixture of Greek philosophy at all" (the proposition that Curley claims is manifestly false) and interpret it out of context. I won't judge whether that proposition is "manifestly false" in itself, but it was not manifestly false to Restoration Englishmen because the eighth of the Thirty-Nine Articles declares it to be true: "The Nicene Creed, and that which is commonly called the Apostles' Creed, ought thoroughly to be received and believed; for they may be proved by most certain warrants of Holy Scripture." Curley might object that anyone can see that the eighth article is false. However, as I have said before, for thousands of years religious people could not see that the Bible contained inconsistent stories about creation and Noah's flood; it is plausible then that they would not see any falsehood in the proposition that the Nicene Creed was philosophy free (Martinich 1996: 276–7). Moreover, as I shall now explain, Hobbes has an explanation for why the Creed has no admixture of philosophy even though the

Greek version contains the word "*homoousion*," which occurs in late Greek philosophy.

First note that the Greek word does not occur in Hobbes's Latin text, quoted above. For "of the same substance with God," Hobbes writes "ejusdem cum Deo substanitiae," so the controversy about "*homoousion*" is not on the face of the text.

Second, I think that Curley will agree that whatever else Hobbes wanted to do, he did not want philosophy to dictate religious doctrine. That is one reason why he ends the paragraph saying, "at that time philosophers were not a majority of the Fathers." The Christian Church had not yet been taken over and corrupted by the philosophers. Although pagan philosophy was at the gates of the Council of Nicaea and had some presence in the Council, it did not get into the Creed. After the Council, the influence of pagan philosophy increased. This is a theme that Hobbes pursues in the very next paragraph of chapter 46:

> But in explanations of the Nicene creed—and of those whose writings are still extant, there is hardly any doctor of the church in the five hundred years after this council who did not publish some explanation of that creed—not so much concern is shown for the opinion of Scripture. For where in Sacred Scripture (or in the Nicene Creed itself) do we find what is said in the Athanasian creed: that God and man are one Christ, in the same way that the rational soul and the flesh are one man? The constitution of a man from flesh and soul was never considered a mystery. But *Christ in the flesh* is the greatest mystery. (Hobbes 1994b: 471)

In short, although pagan philosophy had infected theology before the Council and made it gravely ill afterwards, the Creed itself was unaffected.

In addition to the proposition I have been discussing in the last several paragraphs, Curley thinks there is another, in which Hobbes states something "manifestly false" about the Trinity, namely, this one: "almost all those theologians who published explanations of the Nicene creed use definitions taken from the logic and metaphysics of Aristotle, when they ought to have proven the holy Trinity from Sacred Scripture alone . . ." (Hobbes 1994b: 518, Curley 1996a: 267–8). Here Hobbes's point, which Curley missed, is that although "*homoousion*" is a philosophical term and was explained in philosophical terms by philosophizing theologians before and after the Nicene Council, the term was not used in any philosophical sense in the Creed. The proposition appears in appendix I of the Latin *Leviathan*, a dialogue between A and B. Hobbes has A, the less perceptive of the two interlocutors, say, "I am amazed also that the Nicene Fathers, so many of whom were philosophers, did not bring into the creed itself those terms of art which they used in their explanations" (Hobbes 1994b: Appendix i.90). A is not including "*homoousion*" in "those terms of art," because it is not a philosophical term "from the logic and metaphysics of Aristotle." He is amazed that the Aristotelian terms that the philosophizing theologians had used to explain the fact expressed by "*homoousion*" did not get into the Creed. At this point, B, the astute interlocutor, says, "To me that's not surprising." It is not surprising because the majority of the Council "approved only those arguments which had been brought from Sacred Scripture." Further, the majority of biblically oriented theologians outvoted the philosophizing theologians, "so that nothing would be admitted into the creed except what was inferred plainly from Scriptures" (Hobbes 1994b: 518–9). (Inferring what is "plainly from Scriptures" does not violate the rule of *sola Scriptura*.) Hobbes is contrasting the minority of philosophizing theologians, "who can plead a case and debate boldly," with the majority of biblically oriented theologians, who carried the day and preserved the integrity of the creed.

In my criticism of Curley's interpretation, I have been emphasizing the importance understanding texts contextually, in contrast with looking for so-called proof texts. There is one additional contextual fact that needs to be mentioned. In the part of appendix i, devoted to the Trinity, Hobbes's primary target is Robert Bellarmine, the hammer of the Counter-Reformation, who had defended the fourth-century philosophizing theologians (Hobbes 1994b: 518). Given this context, it is all the more implausible that Hobbes is slipping in some irony. But Curley does not mention this.

My explanation of Appendix i, sections 90–91, makes clear the context of Hobbes's remark in chapter 46: "For at that time philosophers were not a majority of the Fathers" (Hobbes 1994b: 46.10). In the next paragraph of that chapter, Hobbes goes on to criticize the philosophers (philosophizing theologians): "But in explanations of the Nicene creed—and of those whose writings are still extant, there is hardly any doctor of the church in the five hundred years after this council who did not publish some explanation of that creed—not so much concern is shown for the opinion of Scripture." Hobbes is once again criticizing the use of philosophy in religion. He is contrasting the inappropriate philosophizing about doctrine, engaged in by many theologians outside of the Council, with the canonical appropriate biblical investigation, engaged in the by the majority of the Council.

Perhaps Curley would nevertheless insist that *"homoousion"* is a philosophical word and appears in the Nicene Creed and thus ask how this does not taint it with an "admixture of Greek philosophy" (Hobbes 1994b: 46.10).[15] The answer begins with the jejune fact that not every use of a philosophical word is a philosophical use. Think, for example, of *"eidos,"* *"hyle"* and *"pneuma."* More to the point, even words that begin life in philosophy migrate into non-philosophical talk. Think about the use of "transcendental" and "deconstruction" at soirees and barbecues. (Somewhere Bertrand Russell expressed the more extreme view that ordinary language is the graveyard of dead metaphysics.) Now consider the use of *"homoousion"* in the Nicene Creed. Following Eusebius of Caesarea, Hobbes explains in "Historical Narration Concerning Heresy and the Punishment Thereof" that the word *"homoousion"* got into the Creed with the permission of Constantine, who did not mean it in any philosophical sense:

> For this word, *of one substance* . . . was put in as a touchstone to discern an Arian from a Catholic; and much ado there was about it. Constantine himself, at the passing of this creed, took notice of it for a hard word, but yet approved of it, saying that in a divine mystery it was fit to use *divina et arcana verba*, that is, divine words and hidden from human understanding— calling that word *homoousios* divine, not because it was in the divine Scripture (for it is not there), but because to him it was *arcanum*, that is, not sufficiently understood. (Hobbes 1839a: 4: 393)

In short, Constantine used *"homoousion"* simply to distinguish Catholics from Arians. By invoking the name of Constantine, Hobbes is reminding his readers of his doctrine that the sovereign is the head of the Church and the final arbiter in all matters. The word *"homoousion"* is in the Nicene Creed because the sovereign wanted it in, and it meant whatever the sovereign wanted it to mean.[16] Hobbes's *coup de grace* is his observation that the so-called philosophical word was able to be used in the Creed without it having

---

[15] Curley observes that *"ousia"* is also a philosophical word and occurs in the Nicene Creed (Curley 1996b: 287). I think it fair to say that since *"ousia"* is the root of *"homoousion,"* Hobbes would have thought that the meaning of the former word was almost as obscure as the meaning of the latter.

[16] Curley (1996b: 287) thinks that this doctrine does not sit well with Hobbes's profession of the *sola scriptura* principle. If it does not, it is another case of Hobbes's attempt to yoke incompatible elements in his philosophy.

a philosophical meaning because it was obscure, and "the cause of the ob-
scurity of this word, *homoousion*, proceeded chiefly from the difference between the Greek and Roman dialect in the philosophy of the Peripatetics"
(cf. Curley 1996a: 268–9). There is irony here, but not the kind that Curley
thinks there is; Hobbes is calling attention to the irony that a word origi-
nating in philosophy, *homoousion*, can be used with a non-philosophical
meaning precisely because logic-chopping philosophers have obscured its
meaning.

Douglas Jesseph, who in *Squaring the Circle* endorses Curley's position,
fails even more egregiously. He shows that in addition to Hobbes's repeated
futile attempts to give life to monstrous proofs of a squared circle, he came
to doubt both the standard value of pi, substituted another (obviously incorrect) value, and even came to doubt the cogency of the Pythagorean theorem (Jesseph 1999: 273, 287–8). In the light of these facts, Jesseph should
have considered the possibility that Hobbes was just the kind of person who
might hold nonstandard beliefs about religion and not be able to free himself of them even if shown the error of his ways. For Jesseph to conclude that
Hobbes was sincere in mathematics and insincere in his professed religious
beliefs is for him to engage in special pleading. The simpler, more general,
more palpable hypothesis is that Hobbes stubbornly defended mistaken
beliefs and was slow to recognize his mistakes.

The oddity of Jesseph's interpretation is all the more striking when the
shape of his argument for Hobbes's atheism is sketched. He begins: "Both
Wallis and Ward publicly accused Hobbes of being an atheist. . . . I cannot
treat all of the different authors who detected atheistic tendencies in Hobbes's
work and will confine my attention to the writings of Wallis and Ward . . ."
(Jesseph 1999: 309, 321). He then goes on for a dozen pages rehearsing familiar and inconclusive information. From the fact that many people believed
Hobbes to be an atheist, it does not follow that Hobbes was an atheist; and it
is not even strong evidence that he was, as I will show below.

There are other problems with Jesseph's argumentation. After quoting
Michael Hunter as saying "atheists were seen as people who [held such and
such]," he concludes in effect that Hobbes was an atheist (Jesseph 1999: 310,
321). He might just as well have argued: Witches were seen as people who
[were such and such]; therefore, Sarah Good was a witch. Jesseph applies
the same invalid reasoning to the premise: "materialism and atheism were
closely identified in the seventeenth century" (Jesseph 1999: 318). Tell that to
Tertullian and the Mormons.

Sometimes Jesseph uses factive [17] verbs tendentiously in order to make his argument seem to be strong: "Like Wallis, Ward also detected atheistic tendencies in Hobbes's materialism." Jesseph's claim is true in the same sense as this one: "And the theologians of Paris detected heretical tendencies in Thomas Aquinas's Aristotelianism." And he says: "Ward sees anti-Christian tendencies in Hobbes's requirement that [such and such]" (Jesseph 1999: 317). And people see images of Jesus on tortillas, water towers, and their mildewed shower stalls. All that the evidence justifies Jesseph in saying is this: "Ward *thought he* detected . . ." and "Ward *thinks he* sees . . ." Jesseph must have some sense that I am right, because at the end of his litany of witnesses to Hobbes's atheism, he correctly judges, "Thus far the textual basis for any imputation of atheism to Hobbes is hardly overwhelming" (Jesseph 1999: 320).

How does Jesseph then bolster his case? His main line of argument may be laid out as follows:

1. "Hobbes's projects *can* [my italics] be seen . . . as subversive of all religious belief."
2. "Literally dozens of Hobbes's contemporaries took him to be an atheist."
   Therefore, 3. "In light of such facts, it is hardly a great interpretive leap to see the Malmesburian sage as engaged in a sly campaign to discredit the basis for any religious belief."
   Therefore, 4. "I prefer to think of Hobbes as a sly and interesting atheist rather than a confused and bizarre Christian." (Jesseph 1999: 321, 327)

Concerning 1, that something x can been seen as y contributes virtually nothing to the conclusion that x is y, as already shown.

Concerning 2, we are back at the same kind of premise mentioned above. Jesseph may be relying on Quentin Skinner's interpretive principle that, as regards what a great thinker meant, great weight should be given to what his contemporaries believed he meant. I think the principle is too strong and not as helpful as it may seem. Contemporaries are rarely unanimous in their interpretations; what the contemporaries thought is no easier to understand than what the great thinker thought; and a great thinker's explicit denial that he meant what some, many, or all of his contemporaries say he meant should be given great weight (cf. Hobbes 1994a: 77). Further, it is fairly clear that

---

[17] See Kiparsky and Kiparsky 1970, for the term "factive."

Hobbes's contemporaries misinterpreted him on issues that have nothing to do with religion. It is generally accepted today, and I concur in the opinion, that in positing the state of nature, Hobbes is not referring to a historically earliest state and not thinking of the state of nature primarily as a historical condition. Instead, the state of nature refers primarily to a concept, used in a thought experiment, to get people to understand the disastrous condition of anomie (Ryan 1996: 217; Martinich 1997: 30–2). Although he thinks the state of nature is instantiated in certain historical conditions, his point about the state of nature would be no worse off if humans were never actually in the state of nature. But his contemporary critics sometimes understood his state of nature as historical, e.g., Robert Filmer in *Observations on Mr. Hobbes's Leviathan* (1652).

Finally, if the principle were true, Skinner himself would not know what he meant. In his reply to his critics, he rightly laments: "Reading my critics, I am perplexed to learn that I am at once an idealist, a materialist, a positivist, a relativist, an historicist, and a mere methodologist with nothing of substance to say at all. . . . The criticisms they have advanced turn out to be based to a depressingly large extent on a failure to understand what I have said."[18] Certainly some weight should be given to the judgments of a person's contemporaries; but such judgments are just one piece of evidence.

Also, I am dismayed at how little weight the atheist-interpreters give to the opinions of those who did not think that Hobbes was an atheist, especially those who were personal friends. In this regard, defensibility joins hands with completeness. Jesseph does not discuss, among other things, Hobbes's letter to Waller or the supportive letter from the Calvinist Philip Tanny:

> "I confess its [*The Questions Concerning Liberty, Necessity and Chance*] seeming ingenuity hath much swayed me heretofore to think you a good man, and the rather because I observed in it certaine high mysterious speculations, as I thought, the best opened by you, of any man living that I ever yet saw . . ." (Malcolm 1994: 277)

---

[18] Skinner 1988: 231, 268. I sense the same objectionable use of this principle in Overhoff, who makes the following judgments: "Our examination of Luther's treatise *De servo arbitrio* has provided us with good evidence . . . that Hobbes's claim to be in accord with Lutheran or Protestant doctrines was by no means ill-founded. As a matter of fact, most of the theological doctrines developed by Hobbes in his *Questions Concerning Liberty, Necessity, and Chance* clearly corresponded with Luther's own doctrines on these themes" (Overhoff 1997: 618). Shortly later, Overhoff reasons as follows: "the materialist assumptions of Hobbes's Lutheranism were highly offensive to some of his critics. Thus there are good grounds for us to suspect with Cudworth that Hobbes was indeed a materialist fatalist rather than a genuine believer and Lutheran" (Overhoff 1997: 623).

Moreover, Jesseph does not weigh the fact that there is no evidence that Hobbes ever privately wrote that he was an atheist;[19] that none of his friends ever said that he was an atheist;[20] that some, for example, Robert Payne, presuppose that he is not an atheist, and that some, for example, John Aubrey,[21] wrote that he was not one (Martinich 1992: 24; cf. Tuck, 1992). Turning a blind eye to evidence does not make it go away.

Concerning 3, we are comparing the virtues of two theories, and in particular here we are asking, "Which is more defensible?" With respect to this issue, since atheist-interpreters have not adequately defended their theory against the current best counter-arguments, a logical wall prevents atheist-interpreters from taking a legitimate leap of any distance to the conclusion that Hobbes was an atheist. Jesseph's conclusion that "the Malmesburian sage [was] . . . engaged in a sly campaign to discredit the basis for any religious belief" is even less defensible.[22]

Concerning 4, I reply first that personal preferences are irrelevant, and second that his preference presents a false dichotomy.[23] Hobbes is less confused about religion than about mathematics; and even some of those who do not promote the theistic-interpretation think that Hobbes remains interesting, insightful, and innovative (Wright 1999: 428).

Jesseph gives great weight to the fact that "Hobbes's own political theory demands that he never openly profess atheism, regardless of what he actually believed" (Jesseph 1999: 327). He does not seem to appreciate that that fact is no more significant than the fact that Hobbes's own political theory demands that he never openly profess the desirability of suicide, regardless of what he actually believed, or that his own political theory demands that he never urge

[19] I am not arguing that absence of evidence is evidence of absence. Rather, if the particular atheist-interpretation that Hobbes was being deceptive is true, then it is plausible, given the total circumstances of his life, that Hobbes would have written something to this effect and that some of it would have survived.

[20] Cf. Curley: 1996a: 270–1, for a quotation attributed to Edmund Waller that supposedly suggests that Hobbes was an atheist. I think the quotation is too vague to support this judgment. Also, see Malcolm, 1994: 420–2, 785–6.

[21] Curley gives great weight to Aubrey's report that when asked his opinion of Spinoza's *Tractatus Theologico-Politicus*, Hobbes said that "he had outthrowne him a bar's length, for he durst not write so boldly," as evidence of Hobbes's atheism. I give it much less weight because the comment is vague; it is second-hand, and if Aubrey thought it indicated atheism, either he would have noted the fact or would not have categorically asserted that Hobbes was a theist: "For his being branded with atheism, his writings and virtuous life testify against it" (quoted from Curley 1992: 503.)

[22] The atheist-interpretation was more defensible prior to the publication of Lloyd 1992 and Martinich1992.

[23] The Scarecrow preferred to think of himself as having a brain, and I prefer to think of myself as tall, muscular, and with a full head of hair.

revolution, regardless of what he actually believed, and so on ad nauseam. It is not clear to me what force Jesseph thinks the "he-never-openly-professed-atheism" ploy is supposed to have. The following is not a cogent argument: If Hobbes's own political theory demands that he not openly profess atheism and Hobbes does not openly profess atheism, then Hobbes is an atheist. And I cannot think of any cogent argument that does use Hobbes's views about not professing atheism as a premise.

Jesseph says that the "hypothesis of disingenuity is generally a last resort in the interpretation of a philosophical text" (Jesseph 1999: 327). I agree, and do not see that we are anywhere close to the last resort. The theist-interpretation has been rejected, but not refuted.

It is in the nature of interpretation that there will be no end to debate over Hobbes's philosophy. Perhaps some progress will be made if each interpreter reflects on relevant beliefs in her Network and, so far as possible, compares the virtues of her own interpretation with those of others.[24]

[24] I want to thank Sharon Lloyd and Leslie Martinich for helpful comments on an earlier draft of this article.

3

On the Proper Interpretation
of Hobbes's Philosophy

Edwin Curley's article, "I Durst Not Write So Boldly," presents the strongest case for Hobbes's allegedly irreligious views. That is why I devoted an appendix to it in my book, *The Two Gods of Leviathan*. Judging from his article in the *Journal of the History of Philosophy*, I think that the distance between our two views has narrowed considerably (Curley 1996a). Virtually everything he says in the first half of his article is the same as or is compatible with what I maintained in my book. Also, I appreciate his remark that the "great virtue of Martinich's book is that he is very precise about what his thesis entails" (Curley 1996a: 257–8).[1] Nonetheless, he appears to be ironic or sarcastic in the way he expresses the agreement between us. For example, after saying that adherence to the early Christian creeds is an appropriate criterion of orthodoxy, he discusses Hobbes's positions on materialism, the immortality of the soul, the final disposition of human beings, and the nature of the gospel imperatives, and then points out that Hobbes's nonstandard positions on these issues are compatible with the creeds. Because Curley repeats some variation on the phrase, "the early creeds are silent on the questions," there is

---

[1] One reviewer, Richard Greaves, was disgusted by my precision; and offended that I defined my terms. Greaves asked rhetorically: "Does a learned audience need a definition of 'worship'" (*Church History* 62 [1993], 564). (I had used ten words to define "worship.") He did not know that the answer to his question is "Yes." Some Elizabethan and Stuart intellectuals thought that worship was essentially an interior reality. So reporting Hobbes's view was not trivial. Consider simply one example. Locke thought that worship was essentially interior: "More properly, the term 'religious worship' is used to refer to all those actions of the inner virtues of which God is the object, such as the love, reverence, fear, trust of God, etc. This is that inner worship of the heart that God demands, in which the life and breath of true religion consists. Take away this, and all the other activities which form part of religious worship serve merely to provoke God" ("Second Tract on Government," in *Political Writings of John Locke*, ed. David Wootton (New York: Mentor, 1993), 155). Also, Hobbes thought that defining one's terms was the single most important part of a scientific treatment of anything. At the end of a paean to definition, he wrote, "So that in the right Definition of Names, lyes the first use; which is the Acquisition of Science; And in wrong, or no Definitions, lyes the first abuse; from which proceed all false and senslesse Tenets" (*Leviathan* 4.13). Given Hobbes's views about the importance of defining one's terms, it is ironic that a Hobbes scholar would be criticized for defining his terms. Whatever our differences may be, I think that Curley and I are quite close in knowing what is and is not the right way to approach a philosophical text.

Hobbes's Political Philosophy. A. P. Martinich, Oxford University Press. © Oxford University Press 2021.
DOI: 10.1093/oso/9780197531716.003.0004

a hint that Curley thinks that the criterion of the creeds is too weak. There is other evidence of irony, as when, echoing the words of G. E. M. Anscombe, he says, "I will not suggest, as some might wish to do, that Professor Martinich has not done his homework here" (266).[2] The suggestion comes through loud and clear. I feel as Hobbes probably did when John Wallis verbally spanked him for "not saying his lessons correctly." Curley is playing Wallis to my Hobbes.

Notwithstanding the hints of irony, I think that we should take Curley at his word when he says that my definition of orthodoxy is "plausible" (261). After all, it was in fact the criterion used by the Elizabethan and Stuart church. Moreover, it is consonant with the Reformation theme of basing Christian doctrine on understanding the Bible without the fetters of Roman Catholic tradition. So, Hobbes's views are constrained not only by the creeds but also by the biblical text. His novel readings of the Bible are consonant with the view of his associate at Great Tew, the great theologian William Chillingworth, who said that the religion of Protestants was the Bible. Of course, Chillingworth's theological respectability has improved over the centuries to a degree that Hobbes's has not. Finally, Hobbes's reading of the Bible was nonstandard for his times in part because he was much more sophisticated and insightful than all but a few others. Most of his interpretations have been taken over by twentieth-century biblical scholars.

1. *Interpretation.* There is still at least one bar to Curley's acceptance of my entire position: the issue of whether Hobbes should be taken at his word (261). I do not think that this issue will be finally settled. The nature of interpretation is such that, quite aside from the fact that for any text theoretically an infinite number of interpretations can be given, there will almost always be several interpretations that will fit almost all of the evidence, with usually at least some evidence that will need to be forced, shaved, left to the side, or hidden. To drop the metaphor, when evidence does not fit neatly, there are numerous tactics for explaining it away: the text is corrupt; the author was joking; the author was not speaking *in propria persona*; when he or she wrote, the words had a different meaning or implication; the author did not appreciate the consequences of what he or she said; the author was not strongly committed to that view; or the author changed his or her mind. Good interpretations, I believe, are those that make our beliefs fit with our

---

[2] G. E. M. Anscombe, "Mr. Truman's Decree," in *Ethics, Religion, and Politics* (Minneapolis: University of Minnesota Press, 1981), 2: 65.

previous beliefs in the smoothest way. In general, I accept the standards for good interpretations that have been explained in an informal but perceptive way by Quine and Ullian in *The Web of Belief*: conservatism, modesty, simplicity, generality, and refutability. Unlike some contemporary philosophers, I do not believe that the principles of good interpretation can be axiomatized. (I do not know what Curley thinks about this general issue.)

2. *Irony.* The key issue raised by Curley in his article concerns the conditions under which it is appropriate to interpret a text ironically. He is correct in pointing out that I went too far when I said that an ironic interpretation "is acceptable only if the literal interpretation makes no sense." Giving a literal interpretation to a text is the default mode, I believe, but the legitimacy of giving an ironic one can become justifiable long before the literal one makes no sense at all.

Curley thinks that Hobbes is being ironic when he talks about religious issues. But I do not see any irony, for example, when Hobbes presents standard versions of proofs for the existence of God as cogent, extends the theory of personhood that he has crafted to clarify the nature of sovereignty and to explain the daunting theological doctrine of the Trinity, insists that Jesus died only for the elect (as Calvinists hold) and not for all people, professes adherence to the creed, and so on. There may be serious problems with some of these positions—indeed, I think there are—but they are problems that reflect no worse on Hobbes than on others who held either the same view or something analogous. (Virtually anyone's religious credentials can be questioned. I once knew a philosopher who thought that the secret message of Thomas Aquinas's works was that he was an atheist. And there are cogent proofs that some of Aquinas's theological theories were inconsistent.[3]) So if Hobbes is not being ironic on these matters, I think that it is plausible that he intends to be orthodox and in large parts is. (I do not hold that Hobbes was never ironic or sarcastic. The issue is over when he was.) I think that Curley would agree that when a person is being ironic, there must be signs of it. One of these signs, according to Curley, is that Hobbes has contradicted himself on a number of religious issues, "and some would say that this should make us suspicious" (Curley 1996a: 264). In general, this is not a sufficient condition, because many great philosophers have contradicted themselves on some fairly basic issues in their philosophy. In particular, Hobbes contradicted himself on non-religious issues, about which it is clear that he was not being

---

[3] Allan Bäch, "Aquinas on the Incarnation," *The New Scholasticism* 56 (1982), 127–5.

ironic. To focus only on the apparent religious contradictions would be to commit the fallacy of special pleading. I will mention only a few of the apparent non-religious contradictions:

(1) Hobbes sometimes says that a subject gives up his right to the sovereign; and sometimes he says that he does not (*Leviathan* 20.1, 14.8).
(2) He says that in the state of nature everyone is equal, and also gives as an example of the state of nature a condition in which there is a person who is not equal to others (*Leviathan* 13.1–2, 20.2–3).
(3) In one sentence, he both asserts that subjects alienate their rights to the sovereign and implies that they do not (*Leviathan* 17.13).
(4) In many places Hobbes says that sovereignty requires both sufficient power to protect subjects and their consent to be governed by that person, and in another place he implies that power is sufficient (*Leviathan*, "Review and Conclusion," 7 and 17).
(5) Hobbes expresses himself on the nature of law sometimes as a positivist and sometimes as a natural lawyer (*Leviathan* 26.3, 26.8).
(6) Hobbes asserted and purported to have proved that a circle can be squared; yet it is necessarily false that a circle can be squared. So he asserted a contradiction. Hobbes wrote, "Who is so stupid, as both to mistake in Geometry, and also to persist in it, when another detects his error to him?" (*Leviathan* 5.16). Hobbes was. Even when several mathematicians pointed out his errors to him, he could not come to see that he was wrong. So he did not merely assert a contradiction, he tenaciously asserted one.

What are we to make of these contradictions? Concerning (6), should we conclude that Hobbes was being ironic when he purported to square the circle? Was he in fact surreptitiously subverting mathematics as a whole, or at least geometry? Is Hobbes to be interpreted not only as an atheist but as an amathematician also? I do not think so. Hobbes the sincere mathematician made some grievous mistakes. Hobbes the sincere theologian did the same.

I have argued that Hobbes contradicts himself within the space of thirteen words, as when he says, "I authorize and give up my right of governing myself to this man" and conjectured why he fell into it.[4] So, even though I think that one way to explain some of his contradictions, real or apparent, is to

[4] *The Two Gods of Leviathan*, 171–4.

appeal to the distance between passages, I am not wedded to that explanation for all of them. Some of Hobbes's critics claimed that *Leviathan* was replete with contradictions, many of which came within pages of each other. John Whitehall wrote that *Leviathan* was "full of contradictions, execrable, detestable, and damnable Opinions, as a Toad is of Poison."[5]

I agree with Hobbes's principle: "When it happeneth that a man signifieth unto us two contradictory opinions whereof the one is clearly and directly signified, and the other either drawn from that by consequence, or not known to be contradictory to it; then (when he is not present to explicate himself better) we are to take the former of his opinions; for that is clearly signified to be his, and directly, whereas the other might proceed from error in the deduction, or ignorance of the repugnancy" (*Elements of Law, Natural and Politic* 13.9). I think that many, but not all, of the contradictions attributed to Hobbes can be explained away using this principle. It does not explain away (6) above, or (3).

Another reason for not interpreting Hobbes as being ironic when he does or seems to contradict himself or to make an easily detectable mistake in matters of religion is that he made many such errors when it is clear that he is not being ironic. Curley himself points out many of these in his edition of *Leviathan*. Hobbes says that he will discuss *subsistentia* but then does not; rather, he discusses *substantia*. He misrepresents what Queen Elizabeth said and when she said it about her powers as governor of the Church of England.[6] Hobbes was just not as careful as he might have been. In short, his blatant mistakes should not alone move us to think that he had irony on his mind.

For all of his brilliance, Hobbes was sometimes confused and sometimes stubbornly obtuse. I do not think that Hobbes is unique. I believe that I have known two geniuses in philosophy. Each one has had certain blind spots about their philosophical views. Although many people have pointed out what strikes them (and me) as obvious errors, the geniuses simply cannot recognize them. While it is not my intention to see contradictions everywhere, they are much more common than Curley seems to allow; and they are very often not an indication of irony.

Consider the Bible—and we need look no further than *Genesis*. At some point, an editor of some genius cut and pasted together at least three different versions of the early history of the world and mankind. Some of the

---

[5] John Whitehall, *Leviathan Found Out* (1679): 14; see also 4–5, 15, 21, 68.
[6] Hobbes 1994b: 504n17, 547nn25–26.

stories have as many problems with continuity as a film by Edward D. Wood Jr. People now are easily able to see that the resulting stories contradict each other within less than a few hundred words: God created humans after all other creatures, and He created beasts after humans (Gen. 1:24–2:19); Noah took seven pairs of clean beasts into the ark with him and took only two pairs of clean beasts (Gen. 7:2–9); the sun sets twice on the same day as Abraham covenants with God (Gen. 15:9–17). It seems to me that by Curley's principles, the editor should be interpreted as being ironic in juxtaposing such blatantly contradictory passages. But that I think is a method that yields the wrong interpretation of what happened in the composition of *Genesis*, not to mention many other of the biblical books that were put together in the same way.[7] Further, virtually no one before Hobbes recognized many of the internal problems that pervade the Bible. What looks like obvious contradictions to us may not have looked like obvious contradictions to the editor of *Genesis*; and what looks like obvious contradictions to Curley and me may not have looked like contradictions to Hobbes.

There is another problem with the view that Hobbes is being ironic. According to Curley, who is in accord with Strauss on this point, Hobbes expected some readers to recognize that he was being ironic (atheists, agnostics, and/or deists) and other readers not to recognize this (Christians). Oddly, the evidence strongly suggests that those who thought they recognized that Hobbes was being ironic were by and large the Christians. (Charles Blount, an emotionally unbalanced deist, and Daniel Scargill, a callow atheist, probably took Hobbes to be an atheist, but neither was particularly astute nor a friend of Hobbes.)

Curley thinks that I believe that Hobbes lacked the "subtlety" to be ironic in the passages on the trinity at issue (Curley 1996a: 270). That is not my view. Hobbes's cleverness is not the issue; the conditions for meaning something are. As H. P. Grice argued, in order for a speaker to mean that *p*, it is necessary for him to think that his listeners will think that by his utterance he intended them to think that *p* (partly) because they recognize that he intended them to think that. My claim has been that, given what Hobbes would have expected his audience to believe and to think a speaker would mean by writing what he did, he would not expect to be taken ironically. Hobbes put the point this way:

---

[7] The proper explanation would require a great deal of space and is not relevant to my position. Also, the Bible is not special among religious books that are contradictory. In the *Koran*, God allegedly says that everything comes from Him, and then soon afterwards says that bad things do not.

Forasmuch as whosoever speaketh to another, intendeth thereby to make him understand what he saith; if he speak unto him, either in a language which he that heareth understandeth not, or use any word in other sense than he believeth is the sense of him that heareth; he intendeth also to make him not understand what he saith; which is a contradictory of himself. It is therefore always to be supposed, that he which intendeth not to deceive, alloweth the private interpretation of his speech to him to whom it is addressed. (*Elements of Law, Natural and Politic* 13.10)

Certainly some of Hobbes's readers took him as insincere and others as mistaken; but this is not the same thing as taking him as ironic. For example, Whitehall and Clarendon thought that Hobbes contradicted himself but did not maintain that he wrote ironically. Even if some people did construe parts or all his works as ironic, that is no more conclusive than the converse fact that some people took Swift as serious when he was being ironic.

According to Curley, Hobbes "believed revealed religion to be dangerous, not only to the political order, but also to the progress of science" (Curley 1996a: 263). That seems wrong to me. For Hobbes, revealed religion would be dangerous only if its doctrines contradicted good order, such as contradicting the laws of nature, or if not under the control of the sovereign. But Hobbes is quite clear, it seems to me, that the Bible's commands and counsels are consonant with and often the same as the laws of nature (*De cive*, c. 4); and Hobbes's theory of the honorific use of religious language forestalls almost every possibility that science and religion could conflict.

3. *English Calvinism.* Curley is not sure that Hobbes ought to be categorized as a Calvinist. He lists a number of issues on which Calvin and Hobbes differ, but concedes that "perhaps these differences are unimportant by comparison with the similarities Martinich notes" (Curley 1996a: 261n15). While appreciating the concession, I am not sure that Curley understands the sense in which I maintain that Hobbes is a Calvinist. He is not alone. In a review of my book, Johann Sommerville quoted the Dutch Calvinist Gisbert Cocq, denouncing "Hobbes's impious atheisms" as if this were relevant to my thesis (Sommerville 1993: 494). It is not. Sommerville's objection is an instance of *ignoratio elenchi*. In *The Two Gods of Leviathan*, I made clear that I was categorizing Hobbes as a Calvinist in the sense applicable to Englishmen in the seventeenth century. On page 1, I said that he was committed to "the Calvinist Christianity of Jacobean England." Certainly the use of that phrase implies a contrast with other forms of Calvinism, including

seventeenth-century continental Calvinism. On page 15, I said that Hobbes was an orthodox Calvinist in theology, "insofar as it emphasizes that the Atonement is achieved through the mercy, in contrast with the justice, of God."

I went out of my way to distinguish various dimensions of religious attitudes: church government, liturgy, doctrine, and theology.[8] It should have been clear from much of what I said throughout the book that I did not equate (English) Calvinism with Calvin's own view or various types of continental Calvinism. For example, Presbyterians and Theodore Beza were Calvinists, but Hobbes was critical of them, as I noted many times. There are other passages in which I explain the sense in which Hobbes was and was not in agreement with Calvin himself.

As I used the term, Calvinism was a type of theological view that was contrasted primarily with Arminianism, although several other prominent non-Calvinistic theologies could be distinguished. Within England, the salient issue dividing Calvinists and Arminians was that of double predestination. Those who subscribed to that doctrine were counted as Calvinists; those who did not were counted as non-Calvinists, and typically as Arminians. Closely connected with predestination is the issue of whether the universe was completely determined by God's action (Calvinism) or whether the future was causally undetermined to some extent (Arminianism). And there were other marks of English Calvinism such as the belief that Jesus died only for the elect, the belief that salvation (after the fall of human beings) comes from faith alone and that good works do not merit it. On each of these issues, Hobbes takes the Calvinist line.

Within the dimension of church government, the chief contenders in Stuart England were episcopalism versus nonepiscopal views (chiefly, papalism and Independency). Hobbes preferred episcopal church government. Within the dimension of doctrine, I have argued that Hobbes intended to be completely orthodox, and by and large was, even though his theory of the Trinity is Sabellian in my view. By comparison, Milton and Locke were heterodox. On the issue of liturgy, I was not as explicit as I was about the other dimensions, but I in effect maintained that Hobbes was anti-puritan (even Laudian), rather than puritan.

4. *The Trinity and the Latin Leviathan.* Curley places most of the weight for his position on what Hobbes says in the Latin version of *Leviathan* that

[8] Martinich 1992: 333–5.

was published in 1668. It will be helpful to begin with what Hobbes did in the original version. He had contrasted natural with artificial persons and then constructed a technical notion of an artificial person to assist him in establishing the idea of sovereignty. That is why chapter 16, "Of Persons, Authors, and Things Personated," which otherwise would have been intrusive, intervenes between 15, "Of Other Laws of Nature," and 17, "Of the Rights of Sovereigns by Institution." He later applies his novel understanding of personhood to clarify the doctrine of the Trinity. The application does not succeed because it gives results that theologians would find unacceptable.

Now there are two basic ways of interpreting Hobbes's motives here: (1) Hobbes wanted to use his theory of personhood to show (by irony) that the doctrine of the Trinity was absurd or somehow defective. (2) Hobbes wanted to show the power of his novel theory of personhood by using it to explain the doctrine of the Trinity.[9] Curley chooses (1). I think (2) is more likely. Here's why. Given that Hobbes's explanation of the Trinity is defective, is it more likely that a seventeenth-century reader would think (i) that there was something wrong with Hobbes's theory of personhood or (ii) that there was something wrong with the doctrine of the Trinity? I think that most readers would think (i). The Trinity had the status of a fact for most readers; Hobbes's theory did not. He was trying to show that his concept of personhood was worthy of acceptance in general and was not invented merely to help him construct his theory of sovereignty. Showing that his concept of personhood could be used to clarify an issue as difficult as the Trinity would have gone a long way towards doing this. When his theory was shown by some of his contemporaries to give a defective explanation of the Trinity, it was tantamount to failing a critical test. I think that Hobbes would have known that his theory would suffer by comparison.

What was Hobbes's reaction to the criticisms? He did not say or imply, "So much the worse for the doctrine of the Trinity," as one would expect him to do if he was trying to subvert it or had discussed the Trinity ironically. Rather, he engaged in damage control. In the Latin *Leviathan*, he admitted (through the mouths of the characters A and B) that his treatment of the Trinity was mistaken, but he defended himself on the grounds that the intention was "pious" and that the passages "can easily be corrected," and said what he should have (and could have) said that would have made his statements unexceptionable (Hobbes 1994b: 543). Where's the irony?

---

[9] See also Hill 1986: 3: 300–24; and Martinich 1992: 147–50 and 165–6.

The issue is even clearer in "An Answer to Bishop Bramhall," written at about the same time that the Latin *Leviathan* was published. After admitting a defect in his treatment of the Trinity, Hobbes wrote,

> The fault I here made, and saw not, was this; I was to prove that it is not contradictory, as Lucian [the mentor of Arius] and heathen scoffers would have it, to say of God, he was one and three. I saw the true definition of the word *person* would serve my turn in this manner; God, in his own person, both created the world, and instituted a church in Israel, using therein the ministry of Moses: the same God, in the person of his Son God and man, redeemed the same world, and the same church; the same God, in the person of the Holy Ghost, sanctified the same church, and all the faithful men in the world. Is not this a clear proof that it is not contradiction to say that God is three persons and one substance? And doth not the church distinguish the persons in the same manner? See the words of our catechism. (Hobbes 1839a: 4: 316)

If Hobbes is not being ironic here, as I think he obviously is not, why should we think that he is being ironic about the Trinity in other passages that seem to have the same intent, namely, to give a plausible account of the credal understanding of the Trinity? It is simpler and more conservative to maintain that Hobbes had the same conventional intent and succeeded to a greater or lesser degree in various passages than to maintain that he would use the same kind of language about the very same matter seriously in one place and ironically in another.

After the passage quoted above, Hobbes credited John Cosin, then Bishop of Durham and minister to him when he was near death in 1647, with getting him to see that the treatment of the Trinity in the English version of *Leviathan* "was not applicable enough to the doctrine of the Trinity" (Hobbes 1839a: 4: 317) and moving him to modify the Latin translation appropriately.[10]

Curley claims there is an obvious falsehood in Hobbes's statement that "the Nicene Fathers, so many of whom were philosophers, did not bring into the creed itself those terms of art which they used in their explanations" (Hobbes 1994b: 518). Curley maintains that when the Nicene Creed says that Jesus

---

[10] To my knowledge there are no references to Hobbes in Cosin's surviving papers.

was "of the substance of the Father" and "of one substance with the Father," philosophical terms of art are being employed.

I think that Curley's interpretation does not pay attention to the import of the restrictive clause, "those terms of art which they used in their explanations" or to the immediate context of Hobbes's remark. I begin with the latter. Just before the passage quoted by Curley, Hobbes had been criticizing the inappropriate use of philosophical concepts in religion. The character A then contrasts the "published explanations" of the Nicene Fathers with the text of the Creed itself. The published explanations "use definitions taken from the logic and metaphysics of Aristotle;" and A is surprised that "those terms of art which they used in their explanations" do not occur in the creed itself (Hobbes 1994b: 518). Certainly *homoousion* is a term of art and occurs in the creed, but it is the term that necessitates "those [other] terms of art which they used in their explanations."[11] What A is wondering about presumably is why such technical terms as species, genus, essence, hypostasis, hypokeimenon, and similar expressions, do not occur in the Creed.

Hobbes uses the wonderment to allow B, who is the more astute of the two speakers, to make an important point. B says that it is not surprising at all that the technical terms do not appear in the creed. The majority of the members of the synod did not want to include everything in the creed "except what was inferred plainly from Scriptures" (*Leviathan*, ed. Curley, 519).[12] The term *homoousion*, the only nonbiblical term, was added at the insistence of Constantine. Hobbes would have no problem with the sovereign exercising his authority over a church council.

The desire of the bishops to restrict the wording of the creed to biblical language is just what a good Protestant would want. The normativity of the content of the Nicene Creed was not arbitrary. The larger part of the Council of Nicaea resisted the philosophizing tendencies of some of the attendees. There are several stories in the surviving history of the Council that have the impertinence of the philosophers as their moral. According to Socrates Scholasticus, whose history Hobbes would have known, shortly before the

---

[11] *Homoousion* was not a term of Aristotelian philosophy, although Hobbes seems to think that it was. It was rarely used as a philosophical term at all. It is not in F. E. Peters's *Greek Philosophical Terms* (1967). Liddell and Scott's *Greek-English Lexicon* gives some examples of post-Aristotelian uses of it. Certain Fathers of the Church used it with varying significations. See, for example, Wolfson 1970: 332–46; Wolfson 1954: 17–23, 26–8; also Eusebius 1968L 340–54; Kelly 1978: 223–51; Pelikan 1971: 202. Similarly, *ousia* had various senses although again Hobbes seems to think of it as a barbarism of Aristotelian philosophy.

[12] Hobbes 1839b: 3: 536: "praeter ea quae ex Scripturis aperte inferebantur."

Council assembled certain logicians showed off their dialectical skills. An "honest well-meaning" cleric reprimanded them and said that "neither Christ nor his Apostles taught us the art of disputing, nor vain subtleness, nor fallacies, but a plain opinion which is to be guarded by faith and good works."[13] Thereupon the logicians admitted their fault.

Even if we grant that Hobbes said something blatantly false, there is no need to interpret him as speaking ironically. Blatant falsity is not a sure sign of irony. For example, in a letter written shortly after the end of the Council, Constantine said that Arius was the only member who had failed to agree to the resulting creed. Constantine must have known that this was false (since he banished two other bishops for failing to approve the creed) as did all the other members of the Council. I do not know why Constantine made this mistake, but I do not think he was being ironic. Also, Curley points out that I twice say "Apostles' Creed," when "Nicene Creed" was the obviously correct term. *Felix culpa!* My mistake was blatant. I certainly knew better, even though I did not write better (twice!). Yet my blatant falsehood was no sign that I was being ironic. The same may be true of Hobbes, if we want to say that Hobbes was mistaken on the point at all.

Curley says that Clarendon "showed remarkable alertness" in noticing that in one place Hobbes says that "the Egyptian sorcerers performed miracles" and in another place that "no created spirit can perform a miracle" (Curley 1996a: 264n20). This verbal contradiction is less telling than Curley suggests. First, the passage in which Hobbes says that the sorcerers performed miracles occurs as part of a discussion the point of which is to show how easy it is for a false prophet to be mistaken for a true one. So he is not thinking about the niceties of what counts as a miracle and what does not. As he says later, people are "apt to attribute miracles to enchantments" (Hobbes 1994b: 37.10); so people will be inclined to call them miracles, as Hobbes did, when they are not attending closely to that issue. Also, in the same passage, Hobbes quotes Matthew 24:24 in which it is stated that "false Christs and false Prophets . . . shall doe great wonders and miracles" (*Leviathan* 32.7); and there are other biblical passages that say that false prophets perform miracles (Rev. 16:14). So speaking in this way is hardly a serious breach of religion.[14]

---

[13] Socrates Scholasticus: 1739: Book I, c. 8, 216b.

[14] There are two ways of handling such passages. One is to maintain that the author was speaking loosely or imprecisely. The other is to maintain that there are two senses of "miracle." In one sense, a miracle is a causally inexplicable event that severely affects human affairs; the other is similar to Hobbes's, that it is an admirable event, performed by or through God's agency, for some purpose relating to salvation.

Moreover, at this point he had not yet introduced his explicit discussion of miracles. When he did, he disparaged the works of the Egyptian sorcerers by denying that they were genuinely miraculous, and he honored God by saying that only He can work a miracle. Hobbes's explicit treatment of miracles is closer to the concept in a book like *Harper's Bible Dictionary*, which defines miracles as "special interventions by God on behalf of his people,"[15] than it is to Clarendon's. So even if there is a contradiction in the text, I think that Hobbes's considered view is plain, consistent, and consonant with a pious attitude: only God can work a miracle. I do not see any evidence that he is being ironic; and neither did Clarendon.

What about Clarendon's positive view about miracles? He thinks that the sorcerers had performed miracles. He also thinks that the Devil had frequently performed them with God's permission.[16] This certainly suggest that God is in league with the Devil! That's a fine doctrine. (I am being ironic.) Which doctrine would be more subversive of Christianity, Clarendon's or Hobbes's?

Interpretations need to be holistic in the sense of fitting together as many of the author's texts and beliefs as possible. Hobbes puts part of this constraint as follows: "For it is not the bare words, but the scope of the writer that gives the true light, by which any writing is to be interpreted; and they that insist upon single texts, without considering the main design, can derive no thing from them clearly" (Hobbes 1994b: 43.24).[17] I think that Curley's interpretation does not rate highly on this measure. He is on the lookout for prooftexts, but ignores, it seems to me, the thrust of the entire work. So much of the text is obviously Christian and pious in spirit that I cannot hope to quote all of the evidence for it. But here are some examples from the Appendix to the Latin *Leviathan*, the version that is the focus of Curley's article:

> Explain to me, I beg you, the Nicene Creed, not so that I may grasp these matters in my mind, but so that I may understand the words of the faith in such a way that they are consistent with Sacred Scripture. (Hobbes 1994b: 498)

---

[15] Achtemeier 1985: 639.

[16] Clarendon, *A Brief View and Survey of the Dangerous and Pernicious Errors to Church and State, in Mr. Hobbes's Book Entitled Leviathan* (Oxford, 1676), 216–17).

[17] The understanding of the scope of the writer proceeds *pari passu* with an understanding of individual words and sentences. This procedure has been called "the hermeneutic circle." It is also helpful to think of it as dynamic and mutually conditioning.

Certainly [the world was made] from nothing, and not, as Aristotle thought, from preexisting matter. For it is expressly said in Sacred Scripture that all things were made from nothing. (Hobbes 1994b: 500)

Christ was God of God, Light of Light, very God or very God, begotten not made. (Hobbes 1994b: 501)

It is enough for me that he was made my Redeemer. (Hobbes 1994b: 503)

What? Will not God, who made man into an animal from earth, not be able to bring the same man back to life, once he has been reduced to earth? (Hobbes 1994b: 506)

But I, having now the Sacred Scriptures, do not desire the philosophers as my masters. (Hobbes 1994b: 507)

Will not God, who is infinitely merciful, be all the more able, without a violation of his justice, to lessen the permanence and harshness of the punishments which are deserved? (Hobbes 1994b: 507)

It seems to me that, given their due weight, these passages and many others like them forestall the ironic interpretation that Curley has proposed.[18]

---

[18] I want to thank Max Rosenkranz for commenting on this article.

4

The Interpretation of Covenants
in *Leviathan*

Theist interpreters of Hobbes, that is, those who think that Hobbes was a theist, and non-theist interpreters, that is, those who think he was not, agree on at least this: that the most conspicuous difference between *Leviathan* and his other two treatises on political theory is the extensive treatment of religion. While it may appear that they agree about little else, that is not true. They agree about an infinite number of things, to use "infinite" as Hobbes does (3.12).[1] They agree that Hobbes was born in 1588 and attended Magdalen Hall, that he wrote *Leviathan* and many other works . . . , that he was a materialist and determinist, . . . that he engaged in disputes with John Bramhall and John Wallis, among others. (The ellipses indicate that the specification of beliefs common to theist and non-theist interpreters could go on indefinitely.) This is not an idle remark. We could, if it were necessary, state for virtually every sentence in each of Hobbes's published books, or those in Molesworth's edition of Hobbes's works, that it is one that Hobbes authored. We would also agree about the meaning of almost all of the sentences, even though for some sentences we would disagree about what Hobbes meant by them.

I am emphasizing the amount of agreement initially so that we do not in the end exaggerate the difference between my theist interpretation of Hobbes's treatment of divine covenants and many non-theist ones. In sections 1 and 2, I discuss the nature of interpretation, because I think the chances of agreement or disinterested evaluation of the competing views will increase if the nature and standards of interpretation are made explicit. In sections –3–5, I criticize Edwin Curley's non-theist interpretation of Hobbes's doctrine of covenants.

---

[1] References to *Leviathan* within the text will be to chapter and paragraph, and quoted from Edwin Curley's edition (Indianapolis: Hackett, 1994).

Hobbes's Political Philosophy. A. P. Martinich, Oxford University Press. © Oxford University Press 2021.
DOI: 10.1093/oso/9780197531716.003.0005

1. Interpretation and Networks of Belief

Seeing that the disagreements between theist and non-theist interpreters are built upon a broad base of shared beliefs may lead one to wonder what the prospect is for reaching something close to full agreement. My guess is that it is infinitesimally small. The reason has to do with what every interpreter brings to a text, namely, a large and complex Network of Beliefs about the world, built from her own particular experiences.[2] The subnetwork of beliefs that relate to Hobbes's life and philosophy is at most a tiny portion of anyone's Network. Also, even though those subnetworks are very similar, the interpretation of a text is influenced by principles that may be deployed at different times in different ways. But I want to say more about the Network before going on to talk about the principles of interpretation.

The Network has several properties.[3] It seems to be a unity; that is, each belief is or can be related to every other belief. Trivially, they can all be related by conjoining beliefs of the Network. More importantly, many beliefs are logically related to other beliefs. One belief, say "Most people are self-interested," entails others, say, "Some people are self-interested." And some beliefs lend plausibility to other beliefs even if the former do not entail the latter. Second, some beliefs are held more tenaciously or strongly than others. Some are virtually unassailable: the world is very old and most people have lived most of their lives on or very near the surface of the earth. Third, the Network is gappy. Notwithstanding the great number of our beliefs, it is (almost) always possible to add additional beliefs that in effect fill in gaps. For example, the belief that Jones shot Smith has gaps that could be filled in various ways. To take only three dimensions, the shooting could have been done (a) maliciously/accidentally, (b) with a pistol/rifle, and (c) on Sunday/Monday. Fourth, beliefs are added and subtracted in groups rather than individually. A person who comes to believe that Lee has just been divorced also adds at the same time other beliefs, such as that Lee has been unhappy, has hired a lawyer, needs comforting, and so on. Not all of these beliefs may be explicit, but they must be at least implicit.[4] Similarly, when beliefs are deleted, they are subtracted in clusters.

---

[2] My idea of a Network of Beliefs derives from Quine and Ullian (1978).

[3] Only normal Networks (and other concepts) will be described. Diseases and various malfunctions may cause a Network to lose one or more of the described properties.

[4] I hold to a moderate holism, according to which the meaning of any word or sentence depends to some extent on its relation to other words and sentences. It is not possible to have a language in which all the words and sentences are logically independent of each other.

The process of textual interpretation begins when the Network is in effect disturbed by a text. People operate with something like a Principle of Maximum Intelligibility: if something can be understood to have a meaning, it will be understood to have a meaning. The process ends with respect to that text when the Network has been revised in a way that aims at being true.[5] The process of textual interpretation is just a special case of understanding the world in general. The latter principles have proven reliable in the past. They could not be other than reliable, since survival has depended on it. Nevertheless, the process is not obviously mechanical or deterministic. It is partly ad hoc but not predominantly so.

Interpretations are guided by general principles—they might just as accurately be described as maxims or rules of thumb—that are widely accepted, usually without respect to a specific side in a debate. (I will return to this matter below.) My point here is that because interpreters come to a text with a Network of Beliefs, and each person's experience is different from that of every other, it is not surprising that the way one person interprets a significant text will differ from that of another. And it is unlikely that universal agreement can be achieved because one's pre-existing Network will dispose one person to understand it one way and another person to understand it another.

There is something of an irony in the situation within which people try to determine the best interpretation from a class of interpretations. An interpretation can sensibly be judged to be better or worse than another only when an initial Network of Beliefs is the same for both of them. To compare an interpretation I_1 of a text T with respect to a Network N_1 with an interpretation I_2 of T with respect to a Network N_2 is to vary the independent variable. Since better and worse interpretations are always relative to the Network of an interpreter, it may be the case that, according to the maxims of interpretation, relative to N_1, I_1 is a better interpretation than I_2; and relative to N_2, I_2 is a better interpretation than I_1. And given that interpreters have different Networks because of different prior experiences, there may be no way to arbitrate between them.

This, in short, explains why it is highly unlikely that even the best theist and non-theist interpreters could reach a consensus on the crucial issue that divides them: Hobbes's beliefs about revealed religion. To say that each

---

[5] The process of updating the Network in general does not end until death.

interpretation is the "best" is to concede that each uses the broadly shared principles of interpretation in a highly skilled way.

The fact that the chances of complete agreement are remote does not mean that debate is pointless. One interpreter may have made a mistake about some matter that another interpreter can show to be a mistake, for example, about what the evidence is or about how a principle should be deployed. Also, the process of debate often forces an interpreter to clarify the issues and to organize her arguments better. In addition, the fact that there is often not one correct, determinable interpretation does not mean that every interpretation is acceptable. A proponent of one interpretation can recognize that from among the competing interpretations, I_1 is better than I_2, even when I_2 is closer to his own interpretation than I_1.

It must also be noted that just as there may be irresolvable disputes between theists and non-theists, there may be equally irresolvable disputes between the non-theists, for example, the deist and atheist interpretations. And the nomenclature of disputes is always relative to an issue. A theist and non-theist interpreter may agree on some other significant issue, such as Hobbes's belief in absolute sovereignty, that would pit them against interpreters who think that Hobbes was a secret revolutionary and that *Leviathan* was intended as a rebel's catechism.

2. Principles of Good Interpretation

Let's now consider some of the principles of a good interpretation that I alluded to. While philosophers are inclined to be monists or dualists and never, let us say, "trivialists," I think that it is better to begin an inquiry with more principles than ultimately may be necessary rather than fewer. Simplicity is a virtue, but not to the exclusion of others (cf. principle 5 below). At least a dozen principles of interpretation operate, of which I will mention only ten here.

1. Conservatism: A Network should be updated by changing as few of one's existing beliefs as possible. Theories that require enormous changes in the pre-existing Network should be resisted. This property of a good interpretation sometimes interferes with getting the right interpretation. As Hobbes says,

But for those that by Writing or Publique Discourse, or by their eminent actions, have already engaged themselves to the maintaining of contrary opinions, they will not be so easily satisfied. For in such cases, it is naturall for men, at one and the same time, both to proceed in reading, and to lose their attention, in the search of objections to that they had read before. (*Leviathan*, "Review and Conclusion," 13)

Since each principle, if misapplied, can interfere with arriving at the correct interpretation, I will not mention this fact for the others.

2. *Frugality*: Some beliefs are held more strongly than others; so given a choice between deleting a stronger one and a weaker one, the weaker one should go. By "strength" here I mean the quantity of good evidence, not logical strength, which I refer to in the next principle.

3. *Palpability*: A palpable interpretation is the one most obvious or closest at hand. (It may not ultimately be the best interpretation, but it is one that is more likely to be true *ceteris paribus*.) If A is holding a smoking gun and is standing over B, who is prone and bleeding, the interpretation that holds that A shot B is more palpable than the one that holds that C, who is not present, shot B, and that A then took the gun from C.

4. *Generality*: Explanations that apply to a broader range of phenomena are better than ones that apply to a narrower range. The thesis that stock epithets in Homer's work serve the purpose of giving the oral poet an easy way to keep to the meter and time to think about the next line is attractive because of its generality. It is even more attractive because the thesis can be generalized to explain the practice of oral poets in, say, Serbia in the twentieth century.

5. *Simplicity*: The fewer principles or entities required for an interpretation the better. "Ockham's Razor"—entities should not be multiplied unnecessarily—is a corollary of logical simplicity. Misapplications of this principle are both numerous and interesting. The serpent in Eden, Satan, and the devil are traditionally identified with each other. In fact, each has an independent origin and hence different properties.

6. *Coherence*: An interpretation should (be able to) show how each part of the text coheres with the others (horizontal coherence), and how the interpretation coheres with what it is reasonable to hold that the author and his audience believed (vertical coherence).

7. *Completeness*: An interpretation should account for the entire text. What counts as "the entire text" is relative. It could refer to a sentence, paragraph,

or chapter of the whole work. It would be fair, of course, for a critic to object that the interpretation is not acceptable as part of a larger text, several sentences, paragraphs, or chapters.

8. *Consistency*: Propositions added to a Network should be consistent with the existing Network, not necessarily with the statements of the text itself (Skinner 1988: 41–2).

9. *Proportionality*: Each sentence, paragraph, and chapter should be given its appropriate weight. A sentence that looks like a topic sentence should be given more weight than one that appears to be off-hand. Hobbes in effect commented on an aspect of this property when he talked about how to resolve an apparent contradiction in an author's work (Hobbes 1994a: 125). In the so-called "Adulterer's Bible," a typographical error in one occurrence of the seventh commandment was, "Thou shalt commit adultery." If one argued that that text proved that the affairs of David, Solomon, and others in the Hebrew Bible were in fact acceptable, and that the passages that seemed to condemn adultery were ironic, satiric, or hyperbolic, one would be giving undue weight to "Thou shalt commit adultery."

10. *Defensibility*: A good interpretation is able to defend itself against criticisms. This is especially important when one interpretation is competing with another.[6]

These rules are both descriptive and normative. Most interpreters use these principles most of the time; and they ought to apply them, because they are good rules.

3. Hobbes's Theory of Covenants and Its Problems

In "The Covenant with God in Hobbes's *Leviathan*," Edwin Curley argues as part of his general non-theist interpretation that Hobbes's treatment of covenants is designed to show that divine covenants are impossible and that Hobbes expects his audience to infer from this fact that one of the foundations of the Christian religion is destroyed (Curley 2004).[7] Curley rests his interpretation on two main claims. First, Hobbes's doctrine about divine covenants is so ambiguous that it is plausible for a reader to think that

---

[6] There are other principles that do not need to be mentioned here. See chapter 2, "Interpretation and Hobbes's Political Philosophy."

[7] This complex description of Hobbes's intentions is necessary in order to establish that Hobbes meant that divine covenants are impossible. See Grice 1957.

the ambiguity is intended to cast doubt on the possibility of divine covenants. Curley writes:

> Hobbes' Christian critics attacked *Leviathan* both for affirming and for denying the possibility of a covenant between God and man. Filmer attacked Hobbes for affirming that possibility. Clarendon attacked him for denying it. And both writers did this in the name of the Christian religion.
>
> How can this be? Is Hobbes' text really so ambiguous as to permit a doubt about his position? How is it possible that two intelligent readers should have attributed diametrically opposed views to him? (Curley 2004: 199)

Curley thinks the answer to the last question is that Hobbes intentionally made his text ambiguous, so that readers would infer that the idea of divine covenants is incoherent. Curley's second claim is related to the answer just described: Hobbes concocted views about divine covenants so odd that he expected his readers to see that he did not intend them to be taken seriously.[8] So Hobbes must have intended his readers to recognize that divine covenants are impossible, according to Curley.

In this section, I want to cast doubt on both claims by giving a number of examples from Hobbes's political philosophy that show it was ambiguous or otherwise deficient on a large number of issues. Since the ambiguities and other deficiencies infest his general political philosophy, one cannot hold that the ambiguities in his views about religious covenants are proof that he was being non-serious, without holding that he was non-serious about his general political philosophy.

Since the theist interpreter is not committed to any particular interpretation of Hobbes's theory of covenants so long as it is consistent with the theist interpreter's other views, I will not present a separate treatment of Hobbes's theory of divine covenants.[9] I am mainly concerned here with the principle of defensibility, of defending a version of the theist interpretation. More broadly, I am interested in casting doubt on the use of "reading between the lines" when it is not required either by the explicit meaning of the text or the historical context.

---

[8] Curley says that Hobbes's views are "puzzling," "curious," and "peculiar" (Curley 2004: 203, 211).

[9] I think the main lines of Martinich 1992 are correct.

I begin with Hobbes's general understanding of covenants. A covenant is the "mutual transferring of right"[10] (14.9). The most important kinds of covenants are sovereign-making ones, since they provide the stability necessary for the effective use of other covenants. Although in most covenants the only relevant parties are the contracting ones, that is, the persons who acquire an obligation in virtue of transferring their right, it should not be shocking that the most important kind have a slightly different character. As Hobbes explains sovereign-making covenants, in addition to the contracting parties, there is a person who is not a contracting party but has something to gain from the covenant. Borrowing from the law, I will call such a person a "third-party beneficiary." If persons A and B covenant each to transfer their right to $1,000 to be paid to F, then F is the third-party beneficiary. No great importance should be assigned to the meaning of the word "third-party." The logic is the same if A, B, C, D, and E, each with the others, covenant to transfer their right to $1,000 to be paid to F, the third-party beneficiary. Nor need the ordinary meaning of "beneficiary" be taken, if Hobbes is right about the woes of being a sovereign (*The Elements of Law* 24.2).

As applied to sovereign-making covenants, the many prospective subjects are contracting parties and the sovereign is a third party beneficiary. Now this feature strikes many readers as odd or worse. Their reaction is the same as Clarendon's. Intuitively, it seems that the sovereign must have been a contracting party of the covenant with his subjects. If this were not the case, then the following seem to be true:

Absurdity 1: The citizens can release each other from obedience to the sovereign.

Absurdity 2: The sovereign is "at the mercy of his Subjects" (Clarendon 1995: 210).

Absurdity 3: The sovereign does not injure his subjects if he uses his "power wantonly or tyrannically" (Clarendon 1995: 210)

[10] For his own purposes, Hobbes should not have required a "mutual transferring of right," for there are possible cases in which people covenant simply to renounce their right to something. Suppose persons P_1 and P_2 each have rights to something that might injure the other one, say, a bomb. (The bombs could even be ones that could kill both, say, Doomsday Bombs, similar to the one in *Dr. Strangelove: How I Stopped Worrying and Learned to Love the Bomb*.) They might covenant to alienate their rights to use the bomb. So transfer of right should not be essential to covenants. I use "alienate" instead of "renounce" because, for Hobbes, when someone renounces a right, the person "cares not to whom the benefit thereof redoundeth" (Hobbes 1651: 14.6). But in the case imagined, the person does care.

I am using "Absurdity," in an artificially broad sense, to mean a proposition that is intuitively unacceptable, either because it seems to be obviously false as a matter of fact or to contradict some conspicuous element of Hobbes's theory. One of my readers objected that my use of the term "Absurdity" was "absurd." His objection, however, proves the appropriateness of my term, because he naturally used the word "absurd" to express his belief that my use of it was obviously or "intuitively unacceptable."

In order to remind the reader of its technical sense here, and to soften its pejorative connotation, I will capitalize "Absurdity" when I mean it in the sense just described. Notice that for something to be an Absurdity it is sufficient for it to seem to be either unacceptable or false, for we are interested in what the numerous, mutually inconsistent interpretations might indicate about Hobbes's philosophy. That is, I want to show that Hobbes's text is in fact so ambiguous or otherwise flawed that it is easy for multiple interpreters to have contradictory interpretations or for an interpreter to claim that Hobbes's theory is odd, puzzling, or absurd. Consequently, the fact that two seventeenth-century critics interpret a passage or doctrine in contradictory ways or that a philosopher can point out problems with the doctrine does not show that the doctrine is not Hobbes's.[11]

Absurdities 1–3 have nothing to do with "covenants made with God" or religion in general. They are apparent consequences of Hobbes's general theory. I say "apparent" consequences because it is possible that Hobbes or a Hobbesian could show that the alleged Absurdities do not follow from the theory. For example, Hobbes claims, and David Gauthier argues, that his view does not involve Absurdity 1 (Gauthier 1969: 157–60; see 18.3). And although Absurdity 3 seems to entail that there are no constraints whatever on the sovereign, Hobbes himself would argue that the sovereign is bound by the laws of nature (21.7).[12] (Absurdities 1–3 will be used again in the final section of this chapter.)

Other Absurdities follow from other aspects of Hobbes's treatment of sovereign-making covenants. Hobbes says that each contracting party in effect says to every other one, "*I authorise and give up my right of governing*

---

[11] I am not saying that Hobbes did not have a relatively coherent and insightful theory; only that such a theory is highly interpretive. Also, I think that Curley's criticisms of the possibility of divine covenants are (almost) completely correct.

[12] Of course the argument would not rest there. For those who hold that Hobbes's laws of nature are merely prudential, being constrained by them would not be an effective check on sovereigns. Thus, some would consider, "The sovereign is bound only by the laws of nature" to be yet another Absurdity.

myself to this man, or to this assembly of men, on this condition, that thou give up thy right to him, and authorize all his actions in like manner" (17.13). It appears that the sovereign-making formula is contradictory, because one cannot both authorize and give up one's right to something. One can *authorize* someone to do something only with respect to things that one has ownership of or legal control over. A person who owns an automobile can authorize his friend to use it. But once he *gives up* his right to it, he can no longer authorize anyone to do anything with it. A trustee (who herself is authorized) to care for and maintain a property in good condition can authorize someone else to maintain it. But once the trustee's right is given up in some way (say, by termination or removal), she can no longer authorize anyone to do anything with respect to that property. Thus, we propose:

Absurdity 4: One can authorize the use of something the right to which one has given up.

Someone might object that Absurdity 4 is a clear misinterpretation of Hobbes's theory. "Authorize," the objection claims, means the same as "give up." Now this objection will not work, because Hobbes makes very clear that for X to authorize Y to do A is for X to take on the action of A; if Y does A, then X does A. (In fact, this last clause may be imprecise, since Y may not be *doing* A in the proper sense, since Hobbes does not consider Y responsible for A. Y's bodily movements with respect to A are the actions of X.) And it is quite clear that if X has given up X's right to Y with respect to some object O, and Y does something A with O, it is not the case that X does A with O. If Xavier gives or sells his automobile to Yolanda and Yolanda hits a pedestrian, it is not the case that Xavier hits the pedestrian. Hobbes is quite clear that in authorizing the sovereign, subjects take on all the actions of the sovereign: "they are bound, every man to every man, to own, and be reputed author of, all that he that already is their sovereign shall do and judge fit to be done" (18.3; see also 18.4, 18.6).

So there are good grounds for attributing Absurdity 4 to Hobbes's theory. However, that does not mean that the objection considered in the preceding paragraph is completely groundless. If Hobbes's theory is inconsistent, then it may be the case that he says or implies that to authorize someone to do something is also to do something that is incompatible with the idea of authorization. In particular, Hobbes sometimes represents authorizing someone as submitting oneself to that person or putting oneself under the control of that

person. In chapter 21, Hobbes tries to show that his theory of absolute sovereignty affords subjects as much freedom as citizens have according to the
republican or neo-Roman political theory. Many of Hobbes's claims in that
chapter are astounding:

> There is written on the turrets of the city of Lucca in great characters at this
> day the word LIBERTAS; yet no man can thence infer that a particular man
> has more liberty, or immunity from the service of the commonwealth, there
> than in *Constantinople*. Whether a commonwealth be monarchical or pop-
> ular, the freedom is still the same. (21.8)

Hobbes's claim in this passage seems so obviously false that we can add

Absurdity 5: In the seventeenth century, Constantinople was as free
as Lucca.

One might assert in Hobbes's defense that the apparent meaning of Absurdity
5 is not its Hobbesian meaning. In its Hobbesian meaning, Absurdity 5
means that both Constantinople and Lucca were in the state of nature with
respect to all other civil states and in that respect equally free; so, Absurdity
5 is not really absurd. One can grant this defense but then one must observe
that even if Absurdity 5 is a misnomer, Hobbes's claim is open to misinterpretation because its genuine meaning is irrelevant to the issue of whether
republics and their citizens are freer than the civil states governed by absolute
sovereigns. This point suggests that Hobbes's view is committed to a related
absurdity.

Absurdity 6: In the seventeenth century, the citizens of Constantinople
were as free as the citizens of Lucca.

Absurdity 6, it seems, is as false as his claim that there is no difference between monarchy and tyranny except the attitude of the speaker (19.2). Again,
a defender of Hobbes could assert that the apparent meaning of Absurdity
6 is not its Hobbesian meaning, where "Hobbesian" begins to be synony-
mous with "Pickwickian." In its Hobbesian meaning, Absurdity 6 means that
however much political obligation one has in Lucca and however much obligation one has in Constantinople, the obligatoriness (though perhaps not
the amount of obligations) of each is the same. The reply again is that this

defense saves the truth of Hobbes's position by convicting it of irrelevance. Republican theorists never said or implied that in republics obligation is not obligation.[13]

The next absurdity comes from Hobbes's attempt to neutralize neo-Roman or republican theory: "For in the act of our *submission* consisteth both our *obligation* and our *liberty*, which must therefore be inferred by arguments taken from thence . . . ." (21.10). [14] It is not immediately clear, I believe, what Hobbes means by this. Taking "consisteth in" to mean "to have its being in,"[15] one might think that Hobbes is saying in part:

Absurdity 7: Liberty has its being in the act of submission.

This understanding is confirmed by what he says later in the same chapter: "The obligation, and Liberty of the subject is to be derived . . ." The singular number of the verb "is" suggests that obligation and liberty are identical! Hobbes wants the reader to get this impression, because it makes his theory of absolute sovereignty and alienation appear more palatable when compared with the evident liberty in republican theory.[16] However, Absurdity 7 is inconsistent with Hobbes's view that liberty exists in the state of nature and can exist independently of laws and obligations, although it is diminished by them.

Given the main line of argument in chapter 21, my guess is that Hobbes's passage does not in fact mean what Absurdity 7 says. Hobbes wants to show that the act of submission, or at least the words uttered in performing that act, does not limit the natural freedom of a subject. Thus, "consist" probably means "to exist together or alongside of each other as compatible facts." So, he probably means that liberty and obligation can exist together. This notwithstanding, his statement is ambiguous or paradoxical.

[13] One might accuse Hobbes of disingenuousness in asserting Absurdities 5 and 6, but if this is what it is, it does not lend support to those who want to read his text "between the lines." For Hobbes's technique here is to assert his own view in a misleading way; it is not to assert the opposite of his own view with the expectation that the audience will be able to pick out just those assertions from the multitude of sincere ones.

[14] The references of "which" and "thence" in the next clause, "which must therefore be inferred from arguments taken from thence," are clarified by the Latin: "In ipsa submissione consistit tum *obligatio*, tum *libertas*. Itaque ex eadem submissione obligationis, et libertatis argumenta sumi debent" (Hobbes 1839b: 3: 164).

[15] "Consists in," entry 6 under "consists," *Oxford English Dictionary*.

[16] It is no good to object that I am "reading between the lines" here. I have no objection to identifying various implied or covert intentions in a text. I object only to the nonpalpable ones.

In the paragraph containing the passage just considered is another passage that also contains an Absurdity: "And because such arguments [for the origin of obligations] must either be drawn from the express words [of submission] *I authorize all his actions*, or from the intention of him that submitteth himself to his power" (21.19). That is,

> Absurdity 8: The words, "I authorize all his actions," are words of submission.

It is not true that authorizing a person makes one subordinate to that person and makes one submit to him. If a person *P* authorizes a real estate agent *A* to locate and bid on a house, *P* is not thereby subordinate to *A*. *P* is as free as she was before the authorization. If *P* also contracted with *A* not to buy any house during a certain period or to pay a commission to *A* for services rendered, these are obligations that are logically independent of the authorization. If *P* becomes obligated to buy a house because of the "actions" of *A*, it is because these actions are owned by *P* and not because *P* is subordinate to *A*.

Other Absurdities could be drawn.[17] Indeed, it was conventional for Hobbes's critics to accuse him of inconsistency. Bramhall incorporated the claim into the ample subtitle of *The Catching of Leviathan*, which says that *Leviathan* "abound[s] with palpable contradictions." Clarendon gives two lists of Absurdities in *A Brief View and Survey* (190–3, 311–5).[18] And there are others. Some of Hobbes's apparent contradictions are classic, such as the dispute about whether the laws of nature are moral laws, whether moral obligation exists in the state of nature, and whether his treatment of sovereignty by acquisition is compatible with his treatment of sovereignty by institution.[19]

One reason that Hobbesian scholarship has been a growth industry for the last thirty years is that his texts are replete with ambiguities. These ambiguities allow the clever scholar to uncover novel, but textually based,

---

[17] Since subjects own "all the Actions (without exception) of the man or assembly we make our sovereign," when the sovereign kills a person, that person kills himself; that is, every person killed directly or indirectly by the sovereign commits suicide (21.10).

[18] See Lawson 1657: 63; and Pufendorf 1717: 86. Also, in "Hobbes and the Classical Theory of Laughter," Quentin Skinner gives an example of an obviously false statement made by Hobbes. Hobbes claims that his theory of laughter is his own theory, when it was well known to have been expressed by Aristotle. I don't know why Hobbes makes this particular mistake, but I do think he was sometimes sloppy about the facts.

[19] See Moore 1971 and Moore 1972 for a discussion of some contradictions, and Kain 1987 for a discussion of others, plus references to other works.

interpretations of Hobbes's philosophy that run against the conventional, but equally textually based, interpretations. The former include the views that in *Leviathan* he was for toleration, was a utopian (Tuck 1990, 2004), and advocated "autonomous rational action."[20]

In addition to the textual ambiguities, some of the Absurdities arise from the fact that Hobbes's beliefs were odd. He believed that geometric points have extension, that Torricelli and Boyle did not produce good evidence for the existence of vacua, and that he had squared the circle, even after several mathematicians whom he respected pointed out his mistakes to him, sometimes the same mistakes. Rather than admit his own failings, he was flabbergasted that so many intelligent people should be mistaken about his achievements.

My general conclusions are (1) that Hobbes's theory about the nature of covenants is nonstandard insofar as he does not make the sovereign a contracting party; (2) that it is contradictory insofar as by the sovereign-making formula the subject authorizes the sovereign to act for the subject on the very thing that the subject alienates (namely, governing the subject); and (3) that Hobbes often misstates or gives a false impression of what his view is. In short, when Hobbes says something false or dubious about a topic, one palpable explanation is that he or his theory is in some way confused or confusing. There is no need in these cases to attribute to him irony or sarcasm, and no need generally for appealing to the nonpalpable tactic of "reading between the lines" in order to explain them. Of course, it may be appropriate to "read between the lines" in some particular case. So let's see whether Curley has given us reason to do so as regards divine covenants.

4. Opposing Interpretations and Replies

Curley thinks that the contradictory interpretations of Clarendon and Filmer are significant. I do not. Even if Hobbes's views were more conventional in form and substance, the existence of contradictory interpretations would be easy to explain. All that is needed is one correct interpretation and one false one on the very same topic. False interpretations are usually explainable for any number of mundane reasons, such as the inattention, ignorance, stupidity, or personal antipathy of the interpreter, not to mention

---

[20] Quoted from an advertising brochure for Mill 2001.

indeterminate or ambiguous texts. Are any of these possibilities actualized here? Personal antipathy is. Clarendon was alienated from Hobbes around 1650, and the irritation was aggravated in the late 1660s when Clarendon, ever loyal to the Stuart kings, had to live in bitter exile on the Continent, while Hobbes, who had made his peace with the Commonwealth, was safe in England and a friend of Charles II.

As for Filmer, though intelligent, he was not better than a second-rate thinker, one of the last notable defenders of patriarchy. Also, Curley himself thinks that Filmer's interpretation of the Mosaic covenant is suspect: "For Filmer the covenant at Mt. Sinai is an awkward fact, which must be explained away."[21] If Curley is right, we have more reason to trust Filmer less. So both Clarendon, as a hostile interpreter, and Filmer, as possibly a dubious interpreter of Scripture, should not inspire confidence prior to reading their interpretations of Hobbes's text. This does not mean that either or both of them are mistaken in what they say. In fact, I think Filmer is correct in understanding Hobbes to hold that there are straightforward divine covenants, and Clarendon is correct in understanding Hobbes to hold that sovereigns are not contracting parties in sovereign-making covenants. Each can be right because each can emphasize different aspects of Hobbes's account. In short, Curley's strategy of presenting the conflicting interpretations of Filmer and Clarendon as a reason to suspect Hobbes of "writing between the lines" has nothing to recommend it. The way to determine the extent to which the interpretations of Filmer and Clarendon are right or wrong is to read their texts to find out what they say, to read Hobbes's text to find out what he said, and then to compare the two.[22]

But suppose the focus of interest is not the correctness or incorrectness of their interpretations but the meaning of Hobbes's text. How should the process be described? It may initially seem odd that we should do something similar: read Hobbes's text and, as appropriate, read the relevant texts by Filmer and Clarendon and others ("collateral texts"), and compare the tentative interpretations of each to see whether they fit well or not. But it is not. All interpretation involves the same subprocesses,

---

[21] Curley 2004: 212n21. It is not clear to me what Filmer's point is, nor am I sure that he is mistaken. The covenant on Sinai is typically understood as a conditional covenant in contrast with the covenants of Abraham (Gen. 15) and David (2 Sam. 7; Ps. 89:1–38), which are understood as unconditional (Achtemeier 1988: 191).

[22] Curley eventually does this. My objection is to his methodological position that the existence of contradictory interpretations of a certain philosopher gives us a reason to suspect the author of "writing between the lines."

which include the interpreter's having in her Network, either before the interpretation begins or while it is proceeding, nonlinguistic information about who Hobbes, Clarendon, and Filmer were and what their historical circumstances were.[23] The process of interpretation is dynamic, not linear. It requires trying out various conjectures or hypotheses about the meaning of the focal text and the collateral texts and about the beliefs of the authors and audience of each. The process is guided by the principles described in section 2 and ends when the original Network has been updated with the beliefs necessary to understand the text. Let's call "the narrow interpretation" those propositions that state the meaning of the target text, and call "the broad interpretation" those propositions that state the meaning of the target text, the collateral texts, and (putative) facts about the authors and audiences relevant to understanding the target and collateral texts. The broad interpretation may include such propositions as that one collateral text is mistaken about the meaning of the target text; that the interpretation of another collateral text is one-sided, unfair, or uncharitable; and that still another collateral text is meant ironically.[24] Notice that the interpretations of the collateral texts (e.g., Filmer's and Clarendon's) play some role and provide some evidence of what Hobbes meant, but do not provide conclusive evidence.

The mere fact that the interpretations of Filmer and Clarendon are contradictory suggests that the meaning of Hobbes's text cannot be read off from theirs. One or the other may have misinterpreted Hobbes, as Curley realizes. Moreover, the collateral texts are as open to misinterpretation as the target text is. To give more weight to the collateral texts than to the primary text is one way of violating the principle of Proportionality.

This completes my discussion of the merit of Curley's example of having one's own interpretation of an historical text guided by the conflicting interpretations of the author's contemporaries. In the remainder of this article, I want to consider two related matters. One concerns the general strategy of "reading between the lines." The other, which I consider in section 5,

---

[23] My debt to Quentin Skinner's works should be obvious; see his contributions to Tully 1988. My description of the process of interpretation is a simplification. To mention just one additional complexity, the process may require subtracting some of the beliefs that were part of the Network when the process of interpreting began.

[24] I think Clarendon is being ironic when he says, "we may believe that he [Hobbes] doth not himself believe one word in this Book that we find fault with" (Hyde 1676: 254). (I have corrected an obvious typographical error in the original.) And he is being ironic when he refers to Hobbes's geometry as "beloved and justly esteemed" (Hyde 1676: 298).

concerns Curley's use of the strategy in his interpretation of Hobbes's theory of divine covenants.

Concerning the first issue, recall that Clarendon (justifiably) holds that according to Hobbes, no sovereign is a party to a sovereign-making covenant. That is, Hobbes is committed to

Absurdity 9: Sovereigns are not parties to sovereign-making covenants.

This counts as an Absurdity because Clarendon's belief that monarchs are contracting parties accords with the dominant view of the time, against Hobbes's. Clarendon says that because of its "true essential form," a covenant "will never be found . . . [in which] one party covenants, and the other not." Clarendon notes two groups of consequences entailed by Absurdity 9: (1) The sovereign is not obliged to the subjects to "govern righteously"; "the sovereign hath no security for the obedience of his People"; if the people "rebell against him, he cannot complain of injustice don [*sic*] to him, because they have broke no promise to him." These include Absurdities 1–3, mentioned above. In short, the state is less equal and less secure than it needs to be. (2) Hobbes's theory is "destructive of our Religion, and against the express sense of Scripture" (Clarendon in Hyde 1676: 50). Notice that the focus of Clarendon's criticisms is Hobbes's theory of covenants in general. He shows that Hobbes's theory is defective by pointing out that it has (allegedly) false consequences in two realms. As regards the secular realm, Hobbes's theory creates an inequitable and unstable state. As regards the religious realm, Hobbes's theory destroys the Christian religion and does not jibe with Scripture. Clarendon is not saying here that Hobbes had designed his theory of covenants in order to render divine covenants impossible, and to have his readers guess that that was his intention. Indeed, Hobbes appealed to biblical covenants to support his theory (20.16–8). He must have known that if the biblical covenants do not jibe with his theory, it is his theory that will suffer. Moreover, if, based on Clarendon's criticisms, one were justified in holding that Hobbes was using his theory of covenants surreptitiously to subvert revealed religion, then, by parity of reasoning, one would also have to hold that he was surreptitiously subverting the existence of civil states. Hobbes would be both atheist and anarchist.

Rather than asserting that Hobbes is surreptitiously subverting government and religion, Clarendon is observing that the inability of

Hobbes's theory to ground both civil states and revealed religion adequately shows that his theory is fundamentally defective. John Bramhall used the same tactic when he claimed that *Leviathan* should have its name changed to *The Rebel's Catechism*, because "howsoever in words he denie all resistance to the soveraign, yet indeed he admitteth it" (Bramhall 1658: 514). The same kind of reasoning induced him to call Hobbes an atheist. Hobbes objected that it was unfair to draw conclusions from an author's work that the author himself would disavow: "So that his [Bramhall's] atheism *by consequence* is a very easy thing to be fallen into, even by the most godly of men of the Church." Bramhall himself, Hobbes argues, could be accused of atheism by consequence, along with all the scholastic philosophers, even though "they do not say in their hearts that there is no God" (Hobbes 1839: 4: 384). To accept Bramhall's reasoning as it applies to religion but not as it applies to politics is to engage in special pleading.

When Hobbes's readers were forced to choose between, on the one hand, the (assumed) fact that sovereigns actually do covenant with their subjects and that God covenanted with humans, and, on the other hand, Hobbes's nonstandard theory of covenants, they would reject Hobbes's theory and not change their view about the facts. In general, it is a losing strategy to try to subvert belief in some well-entrenched fact by propounding a novel and counterintuitive theory.[25]

None of this is to say that novel and counterintuitive theories never undermine well-entrenched facts; but the process is different from the one to which Curley is committed. When Copernicus advanced the heliocentric theory, he openly explained why the apparent movement of the sun around the earth was not what was actually happening. He did not employ the strategy of "writing between the lines," which would have him try to perform the following bizarre trick: seemingly to assert both (i) the sun moves around the earth and (ii) the sun rises and sets on the earth's horizon, and to expect his readers to infer that he seemed to assert (i) in order to discredit (ii), which he expects his audience to come to think is obviously absurd.[26]

---

[25] This is illustrated in Hyde 1676: 285–6.

[26] Of course there are other ways of getting across a new and controversial position. One might write a dialogue, as Galileo did. But dialogues are not inherently devices for "writing between the lines," and, in any case, *Leviathan* is not a dialogue.

5. The Source of the Mediation Doctrine

Another problem for the strategy of "reading between the lines" is illustrated in Curley's use of it with regard to what he calls "the mediation doctrine": "for there is no covenant with God but by mediation of somebody that representeth God's person" (*Leviathan* 18.3). Curley thinks that what Hobbes means by this, and thus what Hobbes expects his readers to understand, is that there can be no covenant with God *simpliciter*, because it is demonstrable that there can be no mediation between God and humans. Since Curley's interpretation is inconsistent with Hobbes's extended discussion of divine covenants in chapter 35, he concludes that Hobbes did not mean the extended discussion to be taken seriously. That is, Curley is giving the single clause expressing the mediation doctrine more weight than the many paragraphs in which Hobbes discusses something (divine covenants) that readers would have taken as fact. Curley cannot object that what justifies marginalizing the many paragraphs is the fact that Hobbes wants his readers to see that the mediation doctrine expresses his genuine view, for that begs the question.[27]

I think a better interpretive practice is to understand the mediation doctrine in a way that is consistent with other parts of the text, specifically, the extended discussions of divine covenants and consonant with related beliefs of Hobbes's contemporaries. For example: the mediation doctrine occurs in a sentence that begins, "And whereas some men have pretended for their disobedience to their sovereign a new covenant, made (not with men, but) with God, this also is unjust" (18.3). The phrase "some men" suggests that Hobbes is talking about a specific incident (or a few of them). The salient act of disobedience for Hobbes and his readers was that of the Scots and English in the Civil War, the causes of which included the signing of the (Scottish) National Covenant and the Solemn League and Covenant—covenants not authorized by Charles I.[28] Further, Hobbes himself quotes the sentence above in

---

[27] Also, the tactic of privileging the mediation doctrine over the many paragraphs conflicts with Hobbes's own sensible maxim about how to handle apparent contradictions in a text: "For in contradictory significations of the will . . . that which is directly signified, is to be understood for the will, before that which is drawn from it by consequence" (Hobbes 1994: 21.13).

[28] Curley wonders why Hobbes thinks it evident that "if anyone claims to have made a covenant with God without the mediation of his sovereign, he is lying" (Curley 2004: 203). I think the answer is that Hobbes is talking only about the National Covenant and the Solemn League and Covenant. However, one could argue that Hobbes is unfair because the signers of the National Covenant and the Solemn League and Covenant seem to covenant among themselves with God as their witness rather than covenanting with God as a contracting party. Hobbes either did not read the documents themselves or, more likely, read them with prejudice (Cf. Gardiner 1906: 124, 126, 268, 271.)

his "Considerations Upon the Reputation, Loyalty, Manners, and Religion of Thomas Hobbes" (Hobbes 1839a: 4: 432), in order to criticize John Wallis's allegiance during the Civil War to the side that advocated the Solemn League and Covenant.

The proponents of the Solemn League and Covenant believed that, because of sin, human knowledge of God was radically deficient. To get the right kind of knowledge, a covenant between God and man was required; the covenant could be effected only by a mediator, specifically Jesus Christ. The Westminster Confession (1647), which formally expressed the theology of the covenanters, put the point in this way:

> The distance between God and the creature is so great, that ... [creatures] ... could never have any fruition of him ... but by some voluntary condescension on God's part, which he hath been pleased to express by way of covenant. ... It pleased God, in his eternal purpose, to choose and ordain the Lord Jesus ... to be the Mediator between God and man.[29]

These views were not distinctive of the Scottish and English covenanters; they were a prominent part of Reformed theology, as expressed famously by John Calvin in his *Institutes*. One of his favorite titles for Jesus was "Christ the Mediator," based on 1 Timothy 2:5: "One mediator between God and men, the man Jesus Christ." According to Calvin, even the "Old Covenant" depended upon Jesus.[30] In William Ames's *The Marrow of Theology*, Christ is introduced as "the Mediator" and is the person through which God makes "his will known" to humans.[31] So the doctrine of the necessity of a human mediator, of which Christ was the paradigm, was so familiar to his readers and so obviously not satisfied by the Solemn League and Covenant that Hobbes could say, "this pretence of covenant is so evident a lie, even in the

[29] "Humble Advice of the Assembly of Divines ... Concerning a Confession of Faith," 1647: 6.037 and 6.043. The doctrine appeared in other Reformed documents: The second Helvetic Confession (chapter 5) said that the only way to invoke God is "through the mediation of Christ alone." And it is held today: "The Christian faith centres on the person and work of Christ as mediator" ("mediation" in Ferguson 1988: 418–19).

[30] John Calvin 1960. See the Index for references, but especially 1.21, 2.10.1, 2.11.1, 2.12.1, and 3.2.1n5. Calvin's idea of covenants continues to be held by Reformed Christians: see *Eerdmans Dictionary of the Bible*, ed. David Noel Freedman et al. (2000): 878a. That Moses was a mediator between God and the Hebrews continues to be held by biblical scholars. See, for example, the comments on Ex. 20:18, Ex. 34:27–8, and Deut. 5:4–5 in *The New Oxford Annotated Bible*, 3rd ed. (New York: Oxford University Press, 2001).

[31] Ames 1983: chap. 12, sect. 4; see also sect. 9 and chap. 37, sections 2, 6, and 11.

pretenders' own consciences, that it is not only an act of an unjust, but also of a vile and unmanly disposition" (18.3) and expect to be understood.[32]

It was not necessary to take a view of mediation as narrow as the covenanters. A person could have held that there were two covenants (the Old and the New, or the covenant of works and the covenant of grace) or more than two (the covenants with Noah, Abraham, Moses, David, and others). Hobbes favors the multiple covenant view, because it invites the more general principle that "there is no covenant with God but by mediation of somebody that represents God's person" (*Leviathan* 18.3). Given the beliefs of Hobbes's contemporaries, his view that Abraham and Moses mediated the divine covenants was sensible, and not (to his contemporaries) obviously at odds with epistemic or logical principles.

The mediation doctrine occurs in a paragraph devoted to specifying the "rights and faculties of him, or them, on whom the sovereign power is conferred by the consent of the people assembled," in a chapter named, "Of the Rights of Sovereigns by Institution." Hobbes's attention is fixed on protecting the rights of the sovereign against rebellious subjects who might try to undermine the sovereign's authority by claiming an independent covenant with God.

Curley might object that Hobbes makes the same claim against the possibility of covenanting with God without a mediator in his first discussion of the nature of covenants in a chapter that is not explicitly about the rights of sovereigns: "To make a covenant with God is impossible, but by mediation of such as God speaketh to, either by revelation supernatural or his lieutenants that govern under him and in his name; for otherwise we know not whether our covenants be accepted or not" (*Leviathan* 14.23).[33] My reply is based on the same principles and evidence I have presented above. Our interpretation should have the virtue of Proportionality. We need to weigh the evidence of the mediation doctrine against the numerous statements in which Hobbes says or implies that there are divine covenants. We need to consider that Hobbes often misstates or misleadingly states his own views.[34] We need

---

[32] Hobbes has more fundamental objections to the way biblical covenants are understood by Covenant Theology; see Foisneau 2000: 333–58.

[33] I take the "we" in the latter clause to refer to subjects who do not claim a special revelation for themselves.

[34] Examples of his misstatements about his own view of covenants have been given above. Curley also knows that Hobbes misstates some things about divine covenants. Referring to the covenant at Genesis 17, Hobbes says, "In this covenant Abraham promiseth, for himself and his posterity, to obey as God the Lord that spake to him . . ." Curley observes that Abraham did not promise. If we accept Curley's view for the sake of discussion, the importance of this example is that Hobbes misstates facts about religion even when there is no conceivable surreptitious motive. Hobbes was sometimes

to consider what Hobbes plausibly could have meant, given the beliefs of his contemporary readers, especially the beliefs that there have been divine covenants and that any theory that would entail that there could not be any must be false.[35] We need to consider how this passage might fit with other passages, to wit, the similar claim at 18.3 (Coherence and Completeness). And we need to consider the immediate context, two aspects of which are relevant here. First, the marginal summary for the relevant sentence is: "Nor [are there Covenants] with God without Special Revelation." Second, chapter 14 is concerned with the first two Laws of Nature, "Seek peace," and "Lay down your right to all things," which is done through a sovereign-making covenant. In light of all of this, I take Hobbes's comment at 14.23 to be influenced by his view of sovereign-making covenants. When he says, "otherwise we [my emphasis] know not whether our covenants be accepted or not," he is using "we" to refer to those who are not mentioned in the preceding complex phrase, to wit, those who do not receive immediate supernatural revelation and those who are not sovereigns. All of this is evidence that the mediation doctrine in 14.23 is proleptic to the claim at 18.3 and means the same thing. Interpreting the two passages similarly is also justified by their similar wording: "To make covenant with God is impossible, but by mediation of such as God speaketh to (either by revelation supernatural or by his lieutenants that govern under him and in his name)" (*Leviathan* 14.23); and "there is no covenant with God but by mediation of somebody that representeth God's person, which none doth but God's lieutenant..." (*Leviathan* 18.3). That is, the statement at 14.23, like the one at 18.3, must be understood as restricted to those subjects who cannot credibly claim that God appeared to them. That this excludes for practical purposes all subjects does not mean that Hobbes thought that there had never been a revelation, since the ideology of established religions, for example, Judaism, Christianity, and Islam, makes the acceptance of new claims to revelation very difficult.[36]

Curley may say that my interpretation does not take account of the proofs he has produced that show that there are irresolvable epistemological problems with knowing whether a covenant with God has ever occurred

sloppy. So it's a mistake to construe instances of misstatement as prima facie evidence of subversive intent.

[35] See "On the Proper Interpretation of Hobbes's Philosophy," chapter 3 of this volume.
[36] Clarendon too says that God "hath discontinued immediate Communication" with humans after the Bible was completed (Hyde 1676: 235).

(Curley 2004: 203–6). I agree with Curley's arguments.[37] What they show is that Hobbes's theory does not justify the belief that God covenanted with any person, but not what Curley asserts, namely, that Hobbes meant that God never covenanted with any person, that is, that Hobbes *intended* his audience to *recognize* that he *wanted* them to *think* that the belief that God covenanted with any person is false.[38] Showing the latter is much more difficult because of the embedded intentional attitudes. But the latter is required by the concept of meaning something (Grice 1957). The purpose of enumerating the various Absurdities is to show how difficult it is to justify the strategy of "reading between the lines" once the odd consequences of Hobbes's theory, consequences unrelated to divine covenants, are noted.[39]

Perhaps there is some other way to motivate "reading between the lines." Curley quotes this passage:

> God is king over all the earth . . . [and also] king of a peculiar and chosen nation. For there is no more incongruity therein than that he that hath the general command of the whole army should have withal a peculiar regiment or company of his own. God is king of all the earth by his power, but of his chosen people he is king by covenant. (*Leviathan* 12.22)

He then says,

> Can Hobbes seriously think that there is no incongruity, i.e. no contradiction, between God's being king over all the earth by nature and his being king over a particular people by covenant? Or is this an ironic passage, one in which we may reasonably suspect that Hobbes' implicit doctrine is in conflict with explicit doctrine. (Curley 2004: 210)

[37] At one point in his article, Curley says that "According to Martinich, Hobbes could have made his view consistent if he had had at his disposal the fruits of modern Biblical scholarship, and deployed the distinction between parity covenants and suzerainty covenants." In fact, I said that Hobbes "might have found a way around his dilemma" if he had known of the distinction (Martinich 1992: 292). I do not think that Hobbes's view could be salvaged and do think that the Bible contains many internal contradictions and many doctrines that are rationally indefensible.

[38] There are well-known procedures for judging that when someone makes-as-if-to-say that *p* she conversationally implies that *q*. When an interpretation claims that an author made-as-if-to-say-that *p* and in fact meant not-*p* through some nonspecified or unconvincing line of reasoning, as scholars who favor "reading between the lines" usually do in my opinion, the interpretation is dubious. And this is how I judge the non-theist interpretation. See Grice 1975 and Martinich 1984b.

[39] I am tempted to say that it is possible that Hobbes was a non-theist, but we cannot know it. And therefore I resist.

Curley's incredulity is based on the fact that a general of an army might also command a regiment but that this command is not based on a covenant among the soldiers. This is correct but irrelevant. Analogies need to fit only as far as they are intended to fit. What Hobbes wants to show is that something can be F of the whole G and also F of a part of G: king of all people (all over the earth) and king of part of all the people (the chosen people). And his military analogy fits: a general may be general of the whole army and also general of a part of the army. So far from being meant ironically, Hobbes's analogy is clearly correct.

Curley gives another reason for holding that Hobbes knew that his theory of covenants made divine covenants impossible. It is his claim that Hobbes's assertion that God could have a natural kingdom of right and a special kingdom by covenant is so obviously false that Hobbes must have intended his audience to recognize it. Curley says,

> If God has an absolute right of dominion over all men, stemming from his omnipotence, I do not see what rights he might still have to acquire by entering into a covenant with man. What could he have *after* the contract which he did not have before? (Curley 2004: 208)[40]

I think Curley's reasoning is based on a false belief about Hobbesian rights. He seems to think that if someone is a contracting party to a covenant, then that person always ends up with more rights after the covenant is made than he had before; thus, since God always had a right to everything, he could never in fact covenant. That this line of reasoning is unsound can be shown in at least two ways: (i) Suppose A and B covenant to each give C $10 dollars. Then neither ends up with more rights. (ii) In the state of nature, every person has a right to everything; but this does not prevent them from covenanting.[41] They do not get more rights, even when a right is transferred to them. If Adam transfers his right to apple *a* to Eve, she does not get a right she did not have before;[42] rather, one potential barrier to her exercising her right has been removed. Also, when a subject transfers his right to kill his fellow man

---

[40] Richard Tuck in discussion suggested that Hobbes answered the question, "What does God have after the covenant with Abraham that he did not have before?" in *De cive* 16.4. In brief, it is that Abraham acknowledged that the person talking to him was in fact God and not someone or something else.

[41] The case is different when someone has previously given up his right to something. Then that person may reacquire the right to that thing by a transfer of right.

[42] It is not essential to a right that it belongs to a particular person. Although Adam's right to the apple is not Eve's right to the apple, Adam and Eve are equal if both have a right to the apple, and it does not matter who gave the person the right. Even if God gave Adam his right to the apple and Eve

to his sovereign, the subject loses a right but the sovereign does not get a right that he did not previously have. The sovereign already had the right to kill his fellow man in virtue of being in the state of nature (*Leviathan* 28.2).

When Curley says, "If God's omnipotence *entails* that he has those rights, and if his omnipotence is an essential property he has . . . , then God cannot cease to have those rights" (Curley 2004: 208), he seems to be confusing rights with power. God's power would no more be diminished by giving up some rights than a human's power is diminished by giving up rights. A person has as much natural liberty after entering the civil state as he had before (*Leviathan* 14.2 and 21.6), as much power but fewer rights. If Curley were to object that this means that giving up a right produces no effective bond against God, the reply would have to be that that is Hobbes's doctrine: "And covenants without the sword are but words, and of no strength . . ." (*Leviathan* 17.2; see also 18.4; cf. 21.5).

I have been able to defend a theistic interpretation of Hobbes's treatment of divine covenants without mentioning some beliefs that influence my general approach to Hobbes. But it may be helpful if I make these beliefs explicit. Hobbes lays out such distinctions as those between faith and reason, belief and knowledge, immediate and mediate revelation, and applies them ostensibly to solve problems in philosophical theology, often in novel ways. If all of this were a sham, even for the purpose of getting his audience to read between the lines, he would risk looking like a buffoon who has gone to extraordinary effort to construct a philosophical Rube Goldberg machine. Hobbes aspired to construct a science of all things, was proud, and was sensitive about criticism. I do not believe he would adopt an argumentative strategy that would tend to make him an object of ridicule and to persist in it after it caused him to be ridiculed.[43] He wanted

received her right from some other source, Adam and Eve are equal with respect to the apple so long as each has a right to it.

[43] Curley seems to think that Hobbes's misrepresentations of the biblical text are another tactic for discrediting the Bible (Curley 2004: 201). This strikes me as implausible. Wildly wrong, but seriously propounded, interpretations of the Bible are easy to find in sixteenth- and seventeenth-century texts. Hobbes's critic, George Lawson, for example, claims that Jepthah did not sacrifice his daughter (Lawson 1657: 64–5; cf. Judges 11:29–40). Clarendon claims that God was not upset with the Israelites for choosing monarchy (1676: 74; cf. 1 Sam. 8:4–18). In *The Institutes of the Christian Religion*, John Calvin's interpretations, which have Jesus Christ talked about throughout the Old Testament, are replete with mistakes. Without some special background, such as in satire, a misrepresentation of the meaning of a text will not lead the audience to think that there is something dubious about the text, rather than about the representation of it. Of course, I do not think that Hobbes's discussion has the air of satire about it.

his theories celebrated, not laughed at. Given this desire, it was sensible for Hobbes to show that his theory explained the possibility of divine covenants and it was not sensible for him to show that divine covenants are impossible.[44]

[44] I want to thank Jo Ann Carson, Luc Foisneau, Kinch Hoekstra, Leslie Martinich, Neil Sinhababu, Charrisa Varma, and Sharon Vaughan for commenting on this chapter.

5

Four Senses of "Meaning" in the History of Ideas

Quentin Skinner's Theory of Historical Interpretation[1]

In his groundbreaking article, "Meaning and Understanding in the History of Ideas," Quentin Skinner recommends a certain method of historical interpretation, especially for understanding the history of political theory, and probably for the history of philosophy and the history of ideas. Roughly, his position is that in order to understand what a historical text means, it is necessary to know what the author meant or what he or she was doing in writing it; and since the only way to know what the author was doing is to understand his or her context, one must identify the context in order to understand what the author was doing. Although Skinner is right about the necessity of considering context, his theory is untenable as a theory of the proper method of interpretation in the history of ideas, for two main reasons. One is that he builds his case by equivocating on the sense of "mean" and its cognates.[2] The other is that even if he were right about how to identify what the speaker was doing, he would not have described the sense in which historians try to identify the meaning of texts and events.

This article is divided into three parts: (1) An explanation of various senses of "mean." (2) Several examples of Skinner's conflating these senses and the resulting problems of doing so. (3) A statement of the main consequences for the history of ideas.

[1] I want to thank Mark Bevir and Kinch Hoekstra for comments on an early version of this paper, and two anonymous referees for their comments on the penultimate draft.

[2] Hereafter, for the sake of simplicity, in this chapter I omit the phrase "and its cognates."

Hobbes's Political Philosophy. A. P. Martinich, Oxford University Press. © Oxford University Press 2021.
DOI: 10.1093/oso/9780197531716.003.0006

Type	abbreviation	example
Communicative meaning	c-meaning	In uttering, 'The enemy is in sight', the lookout meant that the enemy was in sight.
Significance	s-meaning	For Texans, the Alamo means that tyranny must be resisted at any cost.
Literal meaning	l-meaning	The word 'promise' means *an act that obligates a person to a future action*.
Intention	i-meaning	Lee meant to shoot the deer, but shot the donkey by mistake

Figure 5.1   Four Types of Meaning

1. Four Senses of "Mean"

Equivocating on the word "meaning" is easy, both because that word has several related senses and because understanding the meaning of a text in one of these senses is crucial to understanding its meaning in another sense. For the purposes of this article, it is necessary to distinguish four of these senses (see Figure 5.1).[3] The two most important for understanding Skinner's theory are communicative meaning and meaning as significance. Communicative meaning, roughly what H. P. Grice called "nonnatural meaning"[4] is expressed in (1) and (2):

(1) His hand wave meant that the enemy was in sight.
(2) In uttering, "The enemy is in sight," the lookout meant that the enemy was in sight.

A salient property of (1) and (2) is that they do not entail the statement corresponding to their complement clause:

(3) The enemy was in sight.

I call this sense of the word "communicative meaning," or "c-meaning" for short, because the central uses of this word concern a person's using some

---

[3] "Meaning" has many more senses. In one of them, ideas and concepts are sometimes identified with meanings (and sometimes said to have meaning), for example, Mark Bevir, *The Logic of the History of Ideas* (Cambridge: Cambridge University Press, 1999), 1–2). See also note 5 below.

[4] H. Grice, "Meaning," *The Philosophical Review* 66 (1957), 377–88; and "Utterer's Meaning and Intentions," *The Philosophical Review* 78 (1969), 147–77.

kind of utterance to communicate with another person. The communicative aspect of this sense of "mean" explains why (1) and (2) do not entail (3). Since people can make mistakes or lie when they communicate, a person can mean something that is not in fact true.[5] As (1) and (2) illustrate, explicit cases of c-meaning take the form

Noun + 'mean' + 'that'-clause.[6]

The second sense of "mean" that is relevant to Skinner's theory is best introduced via what Grice called "natural meaning," which he uses as a contrast term for "nonnatural meaning." Sentences that contain "mean," followed by a "that"-clause, entail their complement clause. For example, (4) entails (5):[7]

(4) That smoke means that there is a fire in the hills.
(5) There is a fire in the hills.

Natural meaning is closely connected with meaning as importance or significance ("s-meaning"), as when we ask (6) or (7):[8]

(6) What's the meaning of the Alamo for Texans? (or: What does the Alamo mean to Texans?)

---

[5] Although it is quite possible for a person to mean that p and not to believe that p, there is a close connection between c-meaning and belief. In non-defective cases of a speaker's c-meaning that p, that speaker also believes that p. Although Mark Bevir's focus is more on beliefs than c-meaning, his views are close to my own in several ways (*The Logic of the History of Ideas*, 31–77). For example, his hermeneutic meaning is close to c-meaning (67, 76); and his semantic meaning and literal meaning is very close to l-meaning. However, he, like others, may conflate various senses of "meaning." He sometimes talks about the "meaning an utterance has for its author," "the meaning a text has for us," and "public meanings of greater historical import than the meaning they have for their authors" (69, 116, 72; see also 2, 71, 76), phrases that are more appropriate for s-meaning than c-meaning (or hermeneutic meaning). Bevir has been unfairly criticized by others in a number of ways. Some claim that his emphasis on an author's web of belief ignores the influence of power relations or the rhetoric of texts. But because power relations affect the web of belief, Bevir is not ignoring their effects, just not focusing on them; and to the extent that rhetoric affects content, it is accounted for in the study of the web of beliefs. See the discussions of *The Logic of the History of Ideas* in *Rethinking History* 43 (2000).

[6] Shorter forms are also possible, as in the vague sentence, "By his hand wave, Lee meant something," and in sentences describing sub-propositional meanings: "By 'promise,' Bo meant *an act that obligates a person to future action.*"

[7] For many English speakers, there is no such sense of "mean." For them, the sense closest to natural meaning is one that expresses only a high probability between what is expressed by the subject and what is expressed by the complement clause.

[8] For the purposes of this paper, s-meaning is not numbered separately from Grice's n-meaning.

(7) What's the meaning of 9/11 for Americans? (or: What does 9/11 mean to Americans?)

One difference between natural meaning and s-meaning as importance is that the latter is always relative to some person or group, as indicated by (6) and (7), which contain the prepositions "to" and "for" with a person or persons as the object. The answers to (7) and (8) state the important or significance for the person or persons mentioned:

(8) To/for Texans, the meaning of the Alamo is that tyranny must be resisted at any cost.

(9) To/for Americans, 9/11 means that terrorism is a threat.

Like natural meaning, abbreviated expressions of s-meaning often have a direct object following "mean," as in "The Alamo means resistance to tyranny."[9] But such sentences are expandable into the form

Noun + 'mean' + 'that'-clause.

The fact that c-meaning and s-meaning occur in sentences of the same form facilitates their conflation.

Sentences with "s-mean" in the main clause may seem to entail their complement. For example (8) may seem to entail:

(10) Tyranny must be resisted at any cost.

But it does not. Since trying to defeat tyranny may result in the destruction of all human life,

(11) Tyranny must not be resisted at any cost

is true and contradicts (10). So (8), which is true, cannot entail (10) because (10) is false. In general sentences with "s-mean" in the main clause do not entail the sentences formed from their complement clause. Rather, they entail

---

[9] At one point, Skinner in effect notices that "mean" as it occurs in the phrase, "mean to us" is not the same as c-meaning (Skinner 1988: 272).

a hedged sentence that consists of the complement clause plus the relevant instance of the phrase "for x" or "to x." So (8) entails

(12) For Texans, tyranny must be resisted at any cost,

which is consistent with (11).

The contrast between c-meaning and s-meaning can be drawn in other ways. Sentences using "c-mean" have a passive form while those using "s-mean" do not. So (13) is grammatical, though stilted, while (14) is ungrammatical:

(13) What was meant by his hand wave was that the enemy was in sight.
(14) *What was meant by the Alamo is that tyranny must be resisted at any cost.

The reason that a sentence like

(1) His hand wave meant that the enemy was in sight,

which has "c-meant" as the main verb, can undergo a passive transformation is that c-meaning requires an agent; and the reason that sentences like (14) are unacceptable is that they have s-meaning as the main verb, which does not have an underlying agent. The person or persons to whom something has an s-meaning are indirect objects of that meaning, not subjects.

C-meaning and s-meaning probably would not be confused if texts never had significance or importance. But they usually or always do; and identifying the author's c-meaning is often a clue to its s-meaning: "Part of the s-meaning of Thomas Hobbes's *Leviathan* is that he c-meant that all people are equal." The confusion or conflation of the two senses is abetted by two additional facts. First, "interpretation" is correlative with "meaning," and its sense tracks the sense of the kind of meaning that is in play. So there is c-interpretation and s-interpretation corresponding, respectively, to c-meaning and s-meaning. Second, every case of nontrivial interpretation of c-meaning requires setting it within a more or less complex set of beliefs or facts, and this set either is identical with or is very similar to the kind of situation-setting required for interpreting the significance of something. Understanding the c-meaning of utterances requires making judgments about contextual features, and these contextual features include attributions of belief to the speaker at least in the basic cases.[10]

In addition to the two senses of "mean" already introduced, it is necessary to introduce two more. In the third sense, "mean" is equivalent to "intend,"[11] as a sentence (15) indicates:

> (15) Lee meant [intended] to shoot the deer, but shot the donkey by mistake.

Just as one can c-interpret and c-misinterpret a speaker's c-meaning, one can i-interpret and i-misinterpret i-meaning. So, on the assumption that (15) expresses a truth, either (16) or (17), though stilted, may express a truth:

> (16) Bo (saw Lee shoot the donkey but correctly) interpreted Lee to be meaning to shoot the deer.
>
> (17) Bo mistakenly interpreted Lee to be meaning to shoot the donkey (because she saw Lee shoot it).

The sense of i-meaning is more like c-meaning than like s-meaning. Like c-meaning, one may i-mean something that does not turn out to be true. Also, c-meaning is plausibly analyzed as consisting of embedded intentions to do something, as Grice has shown. Roughly, by an utterance or sentence U, a speaker S means that p if and only if S intends a hearer H to come to believe (alternatively: understand) that p at least in part on the basis of recognizing S's intention to get H to believe that p.[12]

The word "intend" in the analysis above could be replaced by "i-mean" except that it would encourage confusing c-meaning with i-meaning. The word "i-mean" differs syntactically from "c-mean"—syntactically in that "i-mean" takes an infinitive phrase as a complement, and semantically in not requiring embedded intentions.

---

[10] W. Quine, *Word and Object* (Cambridge, MA: MIT Press, 1960), 26–31 and D. Davidson, "Belief and the Basis of Meaning," in *Inquiries into Truth and Interpretation* (New York: Oxford University Press, 1984), 141–54.

[11] C-meaning is more complex than i-meaning in the sense that c-meaning consists of nested intentions; but this fact does not make i-meaning "cruder," as one might say, than c-meaning. Many activities such as downhill skiing require sophisticated intentions that do not include intentions that are communicative.

[12] See note 3.

When utterances, through accepted use or explicit convention, are used by speakers to function in a fixed way, they acquire a conventional or literal meaning. So the fourth sense of "mean" is literal meaning, "l-meaning" for short, as illustrated by the sentence:

(18) The word "promise" means *an act that obligates a person to future action.*

Some device like the italics in (18) is needed in order to avoid false or nonsensical attempts to state the literal meaning of some words, phrases or sentences, such as

(19) The word "nothing" means nothing [that is, has no meaning].
(20) *The word "slowly" means slowly. [Meaning does not have a speed.]

2. Examples of Conflating Two Senses of "Mean"

While it may seem that distinguishing four senses of "meaning" is a lot of machinery for the philosophy of history, it is not too much.[13] Rationality in general requires keeping separate concepts separate. More particularly, the philosophy of history has to be as careful as other disciplines in its technical vocabulary in order to be as rigorous as them. A theory of meaning in the philosophy of history is not defensible if its key term conflates two or more concepts. Skinner's theory of meaning is the case in point. At one place or another, Skinner confuses or conflates three of the four senses in developing his theory of interpretation, as I shall show. Sometimes he writes in such a way that a reader cannot be certain which sense he has in mind. The consequence is that his theory of historical interpretation is either undermined or left without a cogent defense.[14] If Skinner were the only scholar to make this

[13] Skinner distinguishes three senses of "meaning" in "Motives, Intentions, and the Interpretation of Texts," in J. Tully (ed.), *Meaning & Context* (Cambridge: Cambridge University Press, 1988), 68–78. His meaning$_1$ corresponds to l-meaning. His meaning$_2$ corresponds roughly to s-meaning. However, his identification of meaning$_2$ with what the New Critics called "the structure of effects" and Paul Ricoeur's "autonomous space of meaning which is no longer animated by the intention of its author" makes me uncertain whether it is identical with my s-meaning. Skinner's meaning$_3$ is ambiguous between my c-meaning and i-meaning.

[14] Skinner is far from being only theorist to conflate the two senses of "meaning" in ways that undermine their views. To cite only one other example from a distinguished theorist, Joseph Raz begins an article describing a theory that maintains that interpretation is "a process of retrieving and elucidating the meaning the original [text] has ... [t]he role of an author's ... intention." The theory is

mistake, it might not be worth exploring the issue, but in fact the confusion is widespread. I focus on Skinner because of the influence his theory has had.

In "The Practice of History and the Cult of the Fact," Skinner distinguishes between two projects that historians may engage in, explanation and understanding:

[B]y no means all historians are preoccupied with explanation. . . . Some are instead concerned with the provision of interpretations, and thus with the process of placing texts and other such objects within the fields of *meaning* from which their own individual *meanings* can arguably be inferred.[15]

What sense do "meaning" and "meanings" have in this passage? Here is a case for understanding both of them as expressing c-meaning. A standard use of the word "interpretation," is to identify c-meaning; and Skinner's use fits the standard one because he says that historians try to identify the "individual meaning" of texts, and it is texts that have c-meanings. Also, c-meaning depends to a greater or lesser extent on l-meaning, one theory of which considers l-meaning to be a "field."[16]

Here is a case for taking the words "meaning" and "meanings" as expressing s-meaning. Since Skinner says historians deal with the meanings of "objects" in addition to texts, it is unlikely that he is talking about c-meaning, because one can interpret things other than texts (e.g., data). Historians often talk about interpretations of the Thirty Years' War or the English Civil War, and this cannot be a search for the c-meaning of those wars. If Skinner thought that historians were concerned with c-meanings, then he would think that they are no different from historical literary critics. Finally, the phrase "fields of meaning" suggests s-meaning because to give the s-meaning of something is to locate that thing in relation to other objects as if one were locating a flower or rock in a field.[17]

---

obviously talking about c-meaning. Raz then argues that this theory is false because "the meaning of a work [can] change without the work itself changing." But it is clear from his text that he is now talking about s-meaning (J. Raz, "Interpretation without Retrieval," in A. Marmor [ed.], *Law and Interpretation* [Oxford: Clarendon Press, 1995], 155 and 174).

[15] Q. Skinner, "The Practice of History and the Cult of the Fact," in *Visions of Politics*, Vol. I (Cambridge: Cambridge University Press, 2002), 10.

[16] J. Lyons, *Semantics* (Cambridge: Cambridge University, 1977), 250–69.

[17] As T. S. Eliot insightfully explained in "Tradition and the Individual Talent," in *Selected Essays: 1917–1932* (New York: Harcourt Brace, 1934), the meaning (s-meaning) of a literary work changes as its position in literary history changes with the change of time.

Both cases seem pretty strong to me. My guess is that a combination of both parts is correct. It is plausible that Skinner held that historians look for both c-meaning and s-meaning, and that he used the word "meaning" to do double duty. The noun "meaning" can do double duty because, as I mentioned above, every interpretation [c-interpretation] of the c-meaning of a text involves an s-meaning. But Skinner's view would be closer to the truth if he had argued that when the s-meaning of a text is at issue, understanding its c-meaning is often crucial as evidence.

Skinner's ambiguous use of "meaning" seems to be systematic in some of his theoretical work on the nature of interpretation.[18] At one point, he focuses on "the appropriate procedures to adopt in the attempt to arrive at an understanding . . . [of a] a work of literature . . . or on a work of philosophy."[19] He says that the then two prevailing answers were that "the *text* itself . . . [is] the sole necessary key to its own meaning" and that "the *context* 'of religious, political, and economic factors' . . . determines the meaning of any given context."[20] Since a text can never determine by itself its own s-meaning, and since the choice between text and context suggests the debate between textualists, like the New Critics, and contextualists, such as literary historians, both of whom were concerned with c-meaning, Skinner seems to be talking about c-meaning in the passages quoted above. This interpretation of his view is confirmed when he says that according to textualism "the text itself should form the self-sufficient object of . . . understanding," because only c-understanding is relevant to textual meaning. Unfortunately, there is no way to tell either from Skinner's text or context which sense of "mean" he intends; and, if he is conflating the two senses of "mean," we have a good explanation for why we cannot tell.

Historians are interested primarily in s-meaning. They want to know what makes a particular text important or significant. Simply publishing a document or translating a text does not count as history because that alone does not illuminate past events by situating them in an intelligible structure. It is the difference between chronicle and history.[21] Even if one were to make some

---

[18] Coordinate with c-meaning and s-meaning, I will sometimes refer to c-interpretation (and c-understanding) and s-interpretation (and s-understanding).

[19] Skinner, "Meaning and Intention in the History of Ideas," 29.

[20] Skinner, "Meaning and Intention in the History of Ideas," 29.

[21] The issue here is different from the one between analytical and narrative historians. Narrative historians usually convey s-meaning. They are criticized by analytical historians for not explaining why events occurred. This criticism is sometimes put more pointedly: Narrative historians do not give the causes of events.

startling discovery, such as that not Napoleon but Josephine commanded the French troops in Russia, it would not be historically significant if it had no implications for history. Knowing the s-meaning of something requires knowing how it fits into a larger context, either synchronically or diachronically. So, for example, a historian may want to know what importance or significance John Locke's *Two Treatises of Government* had in 1690 or how it changed from 1690 to 1840. In either case, while *Two Treatises of Government* may appear to be the focus, in fact it is the configuration of other texts, beliefs, and events at the relevant time that determine its s-meaning. While this may appear ironic or bizarre, its truth can be illustrated with an example from a novel. In Walter M. Miller Jr.'s *A Canticle for Leibowitz*, a shopping list, which contains the text, "can kraut, six bagels—bring home for Emma," is of great importance for the members of an order of monks who have survived a nuclear holocaust. The members, who know little English, do not realize that its author, I. E. Leibowitz, c-meant that he was to bring his wife a can of sauerkraut and six bagels. This c-meaning is logically independent of the note's s-meaning; the note would have been as significant to the monks if it had been his laundry list or *credo*.[22] Alternatively, an author who was satirizing a certain attitude may have been interpreted by his contemporaries as seriously proposing a government program—something like the initial reception of Daniel Defoe's "The Shortest Way with Dissenters." In this case, the text's s-meaning soon after its publication could be described without asserting anything about what the author actually c-meant. Of course, a scholar could hardly explain how the text was a satire without saying something about what the author c-meant; but merely describing what an author or text c-meant is not to say what the author s-meant.

Let's now consider an example in which Skinner mistakes the relationship between c-meaning and s-meaning. In "The Context of Hobbes's Theory of Political Obligation,"[23] Skinner shows that for most of Hobbes's commentators in the mid-1650s, Hobbes's political theory s-meant that any entity that has the power to enforce the submission of people to its will is a legitimate government (*de facto*-ism). Skinner's evidence is the

---

[22] Skinner says "an understanding of a writer's illocutionary intentions" [roughly, c-meaning] are irrelevant "to understanding the meanings [l-meanings] of texts" (Q. Skinner, "Motives, Intentions, and the Interpretation of Texts," in J. Tully [ed.], *Meaning and Context* [Cambridge: Cambridge University Press, 1988], 75). This is too strong. An interpreter may know the l-meaning of the speaker's word "bank" is *financial institution* only because she sees him looking into his empty wallet and then walking towards *The Bank of America*.

[23] Q. Skinner, *Visions of Politics*, Vol. III (Cambridge: Cambridge University Press, 2002), 264–86.

c-meaning of the texts of those commentators. This inference from what certain commentators c-meant at a particular time to what Hobbes's philosophy s-meant for them at that time is legitimate and shows the historical connection that sometimes holds between c-meaning and s-meaning. Unfortunately, Skinner goes on to conclude that Hobbes himself c-meant that any entity that has the power to enforce the submission of people to its will is a legitimate government.[24] But one cannot always safely infer what an original or controversial author c-meant from what its s-meaning was for his commentators. S-meaning changes as the relevant comparison class changes, while c-meaning remains the same. (Theorists who claim that the meaning of a text constantly changes are talking about s-meaning if what they are saying is true.)[25] Skinner feels justified in inferring Hobbes's c-meaning from the s-meaning of Leviathan even though he quotes only one passage from Hobbes's text, the phrase: "mutuall relation between Protection and Obedience."[26] To argue in this way is to make an author's c-meaning the slave of the audience. A fortiori one cannot always confidently infer what an original or controversial author c-meant from what commentators said that the author c-meant.[27]

[24] Skinner does not consider that original thinkers are often misunderstood in their own time, that the intellectuals he discusses had limited interests in political theory—de facto-ists were hardly likely to discuss Hobbes's views about covenants—and that he puts Hobbes at the mercy of second- and third-rate thinkers and often bigots. Worse, Skinner engages in special pleading. He judges the view that for Hobbes the laws of nature are eternal and unchangeable and that the laws of nature are the commands of God "to stand discredited" (Skinner, "The Context of Hobbes's Theory of Political Obligation," in Visions of Politics, Vol. III, 282). But he does not mention, much less discuss, the evidence against his interpretation. He says nothing about Hobbes's treatment in chapters 14 and 18–21 of covenants, which contradicts the de facto-ist theory; nothing about Hobbes's statements that the laws of nature "are immutable and eternal," that "as delivered in the word of God that by right commandeth all things . . . are properly called laws"; and nothing about his statement that "the precepts by which men are guided by avoid [anarchy] . . . are the laws of nature"—to mention only a few considerations.

[25] For example, H.-G. Gadamer, Truth and Method, 2nd revised ed., tr. J. Weinsheimer and D. Marshall (New York: Crossroad, 1989), 177: "meaning is not fixed."

[26] Skinner, "The Context of Hobbes's Theory," 275. In "Conquest and Consent: Hobbes and the Engagement Controversy," in Visions of Politics, Vol. III, 287–307, Skinner conflates the theory of the de facto-ism, according to which a government is legitimate solely in virtue of having the power to compel compliance with their orders, with Hobbes's theory of political obligation, according to which a person is not a subject until he "consenteth, either by expresse words, or by other sufficient sign, to be his Subject" (Hobbes, 1651: 391/R&C, 7). Skinner ignores the conceptual gap between the conditions for a legitimate government and the action of submitting oneself. As for the former, Hobbes holds that only an irresistible power is legitimate in virtue of its power; and that only God has irresistible power (Leviathan, 187).

[27] In "Law and Self-Preservation: On Misinterpreting Hobbes 1650–1700," in The Persistence of the Sacred, ed. Chris Firestone and Nathan Jacobs (South Bend, IN: University of Notre Dame Press, 2013; chapter 6 in this volume), I argue that Hobbes's political philosophy was largely misunderstood for at least a quarter century after the publication of Leviathan.

My guess is that Skinner thought that his minimalist use of Hobbes's text displayed the power of his method. However, his method of interpreting Hobbes's political thought cannot be considered a confirming case of his theory until it is compared with Hobbes's own text, because a text (understood within its original context) is the single best evidence for what he c-meant. Skinner should accept this principle himself, because he has insisted on identifying what speakers are doing with their words in the sense of what illocutionary acts they are performing; and as all speech act theorists maintain, in saying, "I promise," the speaker promises, and in saying, "I condemn," the speaker condemns, and so on. This principle in no way denies the phenomenon of conversational implication, because what a person implies depends in part on what words the speaker actually uses.[28]

One way to put the problem with Skinner's method is that he is simultaneously committed to identifying the writer's c-intentions, that is, what illocutionary act the writer was performing, and committed to not looking at the most direct evidence of what those intentions and actions were. The direct evidence is the text in its original context. The original context is temporally prior to the context within which commentators write. Skinner looks to a context; but it is the indirect context of commentators. The commentators' context, being subsequent to the performance of the author's illocutionary act, does not make the author's illocutionary act to be the act that it is.[29] Consulting what commentators say that an author c-meant can be valuable evidence about the author's c-meaning. But this evidence is an epistemic element of understanding and does not constitute the author's illocutionary act.

One might object that I am taking Skinner's views too strictly. I hope to show that that is not true. In the second paragraph of "Meaning and Understanding in the History of Ideas," the one that follows his statement about the standard way of identifying "the meaning of any given text," he says that he will argue against both the textualists and the contextualists because both make mistakes about "the conditions necessary for the understanding

---

[28] One might suggest, as an anonymous referee did, that Skinner should be understood to be searching primarily for an author's i-intentions. However, in committing himself to the identification of the illocutionary aspect of a speech act, he has committed himself to the more ambitious project of identifying c-intentions, since the illocutionary aspect is every bit as communicative as the propositional component is. Related to this point, he may be criticized for ignoring or at least underplaying the propositional component of speech acts. See Peter Steinberger, "Analysis and the History of Political Thought," *American Political Science Review* 103, no. 1 (February 2009), 135–46.

[29] Some speech acts following upon other speech acts do help constitute what speech act is performed, for example accepting a bet and reciting marriage vows to a person who has just done the same.

of utterances," and this indicates that he is talking about c-meaning.[30] However, this indication is undermined by his next sentence, in which he says that these mistakes have filled "the current literature in the history of ideas with a series of conceptual muddles and mistaken empirical claims," and shortly later that he's concerned with what is "satisfactory as history."[31] Both the history of ideas and history more generally are concerned primarily with s-meaning, and only secondarily with c-meaning. Again, we cannot always tell for sure whether he intends to be speaking about s-meaning or c-meaning. He may want to explain the nature of c-meaning because of its importance to determining s-meaning. But given what he has said so far, that interpretation has no more going for it than the ones already vetted.

As I have mentioned, historians are not primarily exegetes or chroniclers, but searchers after the s-meaning of events, texts, and objects. A standard objection to narrative history is that it does not present s-meaning. So the significance of Hobbes's political views cannot end with a statement of what he c-meant. Skinner does not use the word "significance" or the word "mean" unambiguously in the sense of "s-mean" in section I of "Meaning and Understanding in the History of Ideas," but "mean" in the sense of "s-mean" becomes prominent near the beginning of section II, and he occasionally uses "significance." This change of language suggests that he thought he was talking only about c-meaning in section I.

In Section II, he says,

> it is rather easy, in considering what significance the argument of some classic text might be said to have for us, to describe the work and its alleged significance in such a way that no place is left for the analysis of what the author himself meant [i.e. intended] to say. . . . [C]onfusions arise most readily, of course when the historian is more interested . . . in the retrospective significance of a given historical work or action than in its *meaning* [s-meaning] for the agent himself.[32]

That "meaning" in the preceding sentence ("meaning for the agent himself") expresses s-meaning is clear from Skinner's example. The "meaning of his [Petrarch's] actual action," of ascending Mt. Ventoux could not have had for

[30] Skinner, "Meaning and Understanding," 29.
[31] Skinner, "Meaning and Understanding," 29, 30.
[32] Skinner, "Meaning and Understanding," 44, my italics.

him the significance and interest that it has for us.[33] The meaning of climbing a mountain can hardly be c-meaning.[34] Petrarch's climb had one s-meaning for him and has another for us. However, Skinner's lack of clarity about the relation between c-meaning and s-meaning is also evidenced by his shift from using "meaning" when he refers to Petrarch's "actual action" to using "significance" when he talks about "us." The comparison of the "meaning" [s-meaning] Petrarch's action had for himself with the "significance" it has for us only makes sense if Skinner thought that c-meaning is identical with significance.

Skinner continues to use the word "significance" when it applies to the historical understanding of an event and the word "meaning" when it applies to the agent, as if a person's actions could not have significance for himself or herself. He refers to "the significance [that] an observer may justifiably claim to find in a given statement or other action, and the meaning [s-meaning] of that action itself."[35] It is plausible that if Skinner were clear that he was now, in section II, using "meaning" in the sense of s-meaning and no longer using it, as he did in section I, in the sense of c-meaning, then he would have used the word "significance" when he referred to the action, just as he had when he referred to the agent. His change of word suggests that he thought he was changing his topic.

In a kind of intermediate summary of section II, Skinner's use of "mean" continues to be susceptible to two different interpretations; but now the options are not between c-meaning and s-meaning, but between c-meaning and i-meaning. He says, "The relevant logical consideration is that no agent can eventually be said to have *meant* or done something which he could never be brought to accept as a correct description of what he had *meant* or done."[36] This interpretation of "meant" as *i-meant* is confirmed by the beginning of his sentence, which is supposed to explain the preceding one: "This special authority of an agent over his intentions . . ."[37] On the one hand, Skinner may be talking about i-meaning, because he is talking not specifically about authors but about agents in general; and, agents sometimes do what they i-mean or intend to do and sometimes i-mean to do something but fail. It is not plausible that Skinner used "mean" with the sense of "c-mean," since

---

[33] Skinner, "Meaning and Understanding," 44.
[34] Of course it could be in other circumstances just as hanging one light in a bell tower can mean the enemy is coming by land and hanging two lights can mean the enemy is coming by sea.
[35] Skinner, "Meaning and Understanding," 44.
[36] Skinner, "Meaning and Understanding," 48, my italics.
[37] Skinner, "Meaning and Understanding," 48.

agents usually or at least often are not performing communicative actions. On the other hand, Skinner may be using the word "mean" with the sense of "c-mean" if, among the class of agents, he wants to privilege speakers who do not simply do things but c-mean things also. The evidence favors the first interpretation, charity the second. But one can't be sure which is right, especially since later in the same paragraph, "meaning" is certainly used once in the sense of "s-meaning" and once in the sense of "i-meaning":

> if a given statement or other action has been performed by an agent at will, and has a *meaning* [s-meaning] *for him* it follows that any plausible account of what the agent meant [i-meant] must necessarily fall under, and make use of, the range of descriptions which the agent himself could at least in principal have applied to describe and classify what he was doing.[38]

The phrase "meaning for him" is a mark of s-meaning. Also, if Skinner were referring to c-meaning, the appropriate phrase would have been "and he (or she) meant it," not "and has a meaning for him." In contrast, an account of what an agent meant is an account of what the agent intended, i-meaning.

In section III, Skinner claims that the textualist methodology for the history of ideas is fundamentally mistaken because it cannot uncover "the relations between what a given writer may have *said*, and what he may be said to have meant by saying what he said."[39] His statement is obscure because of the highly equivocal nature of "saying."[40] My best guess is that he is maintaining that textualism cannot discover the relations between the writer's phatic act (the act of uttering words with l-meaning and as having l-meaning) and the writer's illocutionary act. A charitable interpretation is that he is contrasting the writer's phatic act with what the writer says-that and conversationally implies-that. However, this is problematic because the natural way to take "meant" in "what he may be said to have meant by saying what he said," is not "c-meant" but "i-meant": what he may be said to have *intended* by saying what he said.

Whatever thought Skinner intended to express, he seems to be distinguishing between what a writer may have done in virtue of the l-meaning of

---

[38] Skinner, "Meaning and Understanding," 48, my italics.
[39] Skinner, "Meaning and Understanding," 50.
[40] Austin distinguished at least four senses of "say": phonetic acts, phatic acts, rhetic acts, illocutionary acts. *How to Do Things with Words*, 2nd ed., ed. J. O. Urmson and Marina Sbisà (Cambridge, MA: Harvard University Press, 1975), 92–8.

his words versus what the writer c-meant, notwithstanding the l-meaning of his words. This distinction fits authors who write metaphorically, sarcastically, ironically, or hyperbolically. That Skinner has this distinction in mind is suggested by his use of Daniel Defoe's "The Experiment: or, the Shortest Way with the Dissenters Exemplified." He points out that Defoe is "saying" one thing and meaning something different by what he said because Defoe was writing satire. So Defoe did not say-that what he "said." He contrasts Defoe with John Locke, who "seems to say . . . [something like] what he seems to mean" with the proviso that "even here we might wish (perhaps remembering Swift) to find some means of assuring ourselves that no irony was intended."[41] Skinner's point, in brief, is that speakers often use words in a figurative way, and there is no reliable way of knowing when they are doing so simply by focusing on the words of the text itself. Hence textualism is wrong.

Contextualism is attacked in section IV of Skinner's article on the grounds that its proponents claim to identify the causes of what the author "meant" and thereby to know what the author "meant." His objection is that what the author "meant" does not exhaust what the author was doing. The word "mean" is in scare-quotes because it is not clear in what sense he is using that word at this point. Presumably, it is either "c-mean" or "l-mean."[42] He maintains that what the author was doing in addition to "meaning something" is specified by the illocutionary act that he was performing or by its illocutionary point.[43] His criticism of contextualism is flawed because the distinction between illocutionary point and "meaning," whether "c-meaning" or "l-meaning" is not a proper one. The illocutionary force or the illocutionary point is as much a part of c-meaning as reference and predication is.[44] A speaker who says, "I promise that Lee will be at the party," promises by saying "I promise," refers to Lee by saying "Lee," and predicates future attendance at the party by saying "will be at the party." All three acts are part of one illocutionary act, one act of c-meaning. The single best evidence that a speaker promised something is

[41] Skinner, "Meaning and Understanding," 51.

[42] Occasionally, Skinner explicitly distinguishes between what a text means (l-meaning) and what the speaker means (c-meaning) (Skinner, "A Reply to My Critics," in J. Tully [ed.], *Meaning and Context*, 271).

[43] Skinner, "Meaning and Understanding," 61.

[44] J. Searle, *Speech Acts* (Cambridge: Cambridge University Press, 1969), 42–64. Contrasting the illocutionary force or point of a speech act with some kind of meaning is a pervasive problem to which Searle's theory of speech acts is not susceptible. If a speaker says, "I promise that I will be at the party," "I promise" contributes to the l-meaning of the sentence in the same sense that "that I will be at the party does" and a complete statement of what the speaker c-meant includes both the illocutionary force and the propositional content: the speaker promised that he would be at the party.

his or her use of the phrase, "I promise," because of that phrase's l-meaning. The illocutionary act that is performed depends on the l-meaning of the words uttered even when the words are used metaphorically. The c-meaning of the metaphor, "My lover is a red rose," is what it is because of the l-meaning of "My lover is a red rose," and could not be conveyed by "My lover is a diesel engine." As for "l-meaning" itself, it does not express an action at all. It is a property of certain sounds, marks, and gestures.

From the evidence of a later article, " 'Social Meaning' and the Explanation of Social Action," we can infer that Skinner was confusing s-meaning with c-meaning. There Skinner at first identifies "social meaning" with the "meaning [an action has] for the agent performing it."[45] This identification of social meaning with s-meaning is acceptable. However, he later removes the social meaning from the agent performing the action and places it in the agent who understands the action; and hence he changes the nature of the meaning. He holds that "the meaning [s-meaning] of an action seems . . . to be equivalent to gaining uptake of the nature of the illocutionary act performed [c-meaning] by the agent in issuing this particular utterance."[46] To use Skinner's example, the social meaning of a policeman's warning a skater about the danger of thin ice is, according to Skinner, the skater's understanding that the policeman was warning her. Following Grice, he calls the policeman's meaning "nonnatural," which is equivalent to my c-meaning.[47] But for the skater S to understand that the policeman is warning S is for S to understand what the policeman c-meant. It is not to understand the social meaning of the action, the s-meaning. (The s-meaning may be that the policeman was doing his duty, or exercising his authority, or showing off.) In short, Skinner conflates c-meaning with s-meaning.

Perhaps sensing the strangeness of equating social meaning (s-meaning) with nonnatural meaning (c-meaning), Skinner tries to shore up his view by appealing to the fact that Grice held that "the criteria for judging linguistic intentions are very like the criteria for judging non-linguistic intentions."[48] This appeal is much too weak, because Grice's point relates only to the evidence for intentions and not to the nature of the states or actions that require

[45] Skinner, " 'Social Meaning' and the Explanation of Social Action," in J. Tully (ed.), *Meaning and Context*, 79.

[46] Skinner, " 'Social Meaning' and the Explanation of Social Action," 84.

[47] Skinner, " 'Social Meaning' and the Explanation of Social Action," 84; see also Skinner, "A Reply to My Critics," 261.

[48] Grice, "Meaning," quoted by Skinner, " 'Social Meaning' and the Explanation of Social Action," 85.

intentions. It is as if Skinner observed that the criteria for judging that humans are mammals are very like the criteria for judging that nonhumans are mammals, and thus inferred that humans are nonhumans. Skinner's invalid reasoning that s-meaning is equivalent to c-meaning leads him claim that Yoruba tribesmen, who carry a box covered with shells that they believe contains their souls, are performing the illocutionary act of protecting their souls.[49] He also holds that a girl who obsessively reads books is performing the illocutionary act of "taking refuge":

> Again it seems that the crucial question to ask is what the girl may be doing in performing just this action. The answer is that she is "taking refuge" and preventing what she takes to be "intrusions" by an overdemanding family. And again it seems that to ask and answer this question about the illocutionary force of the action is equivalent to asking about the girl's intentions in acting this way.[50]

That "protecting one's soul" and "taking refuge" are not illocutionary acts is obvious and evident from their failure to pass any of the standard tests for being an illocutionary act verb.[51] The most reasonable explanation for Skinner's mistake here is that he conflated s-meaning with c-meaning.

This conflation is similar to Skinner's failure to distinguish i-meaning from c-meaning in a crucial passage near the end of "Meaning and Understanding":

> But to be able to characterize a work in such a way, in terms of its intended illocutionary force, is equivalent to understanding what the writer may have meant[1] by writing in that particular way. It is equivalent, that is, to being able to say that he or she must have meant[2] the work as an attack on, or a defense of, as a criticism of, or as a contribution to, some particular attitude or line of argument, and so on.[52]

---

[49] Skinner, " 'Social Meaning' and the Explanation of Social Action," 85. See also M. Hollis, "Reason and Ritual," *Philosophy* 43 (1968), 231.

[50] Skinner, " 'Social Meaning' and the Explanation of Social Action," 85.

[51] Z. Vendler *Res Cogitans* (Ithaca: Cornell University Press, 1972), 6–10.

[52] Skinner, "Motives, Intentions, and the Interpretation of Texts," 1988: 76: numerals inserted by me. An anonymous referee suggested that Skinner's emphasis on "intended illocutionary" has the consequence that he treats illocutionary acts as a form of i-meaning. Assuming here for the sake of discussion that no illocutionary acts are purely conventional, it is true that illocutionary acts have an intentional dimension. That follows from their being communicative acts. This fact does not change the fact that Skinner focuses on the relation between c-meaning and illocutionary acts.

"Meant[2]" in the above passage cannot have the sense of c-meant. "C-meant" would need to be followed by a "that"-clause in this context. Because "meant[2]" is followed by a noun phrase, it must have the sense of "intended."[53] This judgment is supported by the fact that taking it in the sense of "intended" yields a very smooth reading.

3. Conclusion

The obvious conclusion of my analyses of Skinner's "Meaning and Understanding in the History of Ideas," is that failure to distinguish various senses of "mean," familiar from the philosophy of language, undermines Skinner's theory of historical interpretation. In particular, his belief that identification of the s-meaning will yield the speaker's c-meaning turns on his conflation of s-meaning and c-meaning. Also, his overreliance on contextual information to the neglect of a close reading of the text is incompatible with his privileging of the writer's illocutionary act.

Two other conclusions are even more important. First, identifying a speaker's or author's c-meaning is not peculiar to the history of ideas or the history of philosophy. Identification of c-meaning is the default mode of interpretation. (Special circumstances permit other modes of interpretation.) So to the extent that Skinner is right in believing that identifying what illocutionary act the author performed, it does not identify anything characteristic of historical interpretation. Second, since historians characteristically are interested primarily in the s-meaning of texts, not to mention events and objects, Skinner's theory that historical interpretation is the identification of c-meaning is both misleading and mistaken.

---

[53] In still another sense of "mean," the word has the sense of "refer to," as in "When she said, 'My friend from Atlanta,' the speaker meant Lee." But it is obvious that it does not have that sense here.

6

Law and Self-Preservation in *Leviathan*

On Misunderstanding Hobbes's Philosophy, 1650–1700

> Let him go with this Elogy, That he was a Man much blam'd, but little
> understood.
>
> —*Mercurius Anglicus**

Thomas Hobbes's philosophy was by and large misunderstood by his critics in the second half of the seventeenth century.[1] In this chapter I explain some of the principal sources for this misunderstanding and then give three substantive examples of it. Of these three examples, the third, Hobbes's grounding of obligation in the irresistible power of God, is both the most important one for philosophy and the one that most affected later thought about revealed religion. Hobbes, I shall argue, attempted to preserve a religion and politics of the early seventeenth century with methods that would become characteristic of the Enlightenment.

1. Hobbes's Jacobeanism

Hobbes was once described as a "radical in the service of reaction."[2] The accuracy of that description has not been sufficiently appreciated. He was

---

* The epigraph from *Mercurius Anglicus,* a short-lived seventeenth-century newspaper, is taken from Jon Parkin, *Taming the Leviathan* (Cambridge: Cambridge University Press, 2007), 346.

[1] Showing that several of Hobbes's contemporaries misunderstood his philosophy is not the same as showing that most did, but producing all the evidence for my view is not possible within the limits of this chapter. I am illustrating my point by producing representative examples of the misunderstanding. Also, I am indebted to Parkin's *Taming the Leviathan,* an impressive work of scholarship, for leading me to many of the works cited here. His interpretation of the evidence greatly differs from mine.

[2] John Tulloch, *Rational Theology and Christian Philosophy in England in the Seventeenth Century,* 2nd ed. (Edinburgh: William Blackwood and Sons, 1874), 26.

Hobbes's Political Philosophy. A. P. Martinich, Oxford University Press. © Oxford University Press 2021.
DOI: 10.1093/oso/9780197531716.003.0007

a reactionary in the sense that he defended a form of Jacobeanism in the third quarter of the seventeenth century when already that view had largely disappeared by the beginning of the English Civil War. Thus, we need to understand what Jacobeanism consists of in order to understand Hobbes's philosophy. It has two parts: subscription to absolute sovereignty and English Calvinism.

Absolute sovereignty is the view that the sovereign (1) has all political power in the state; and (2) has authority over (virtually) every aspect of life. For Hobbes, the "virtually" condition is needed in order to exempt the sovereign from authority over the steps a subject may take to avoid imminent death. As regards English Calvinism, it consists roughly of being (1) orthodox in doctrine,[3] (2) Calvinist in theology, (3) preferring an episcopal and Erastian church government, (4) non-puritan in liturgy, and (5) professing the Bible to be the "true religion of Protestants," to use William Chillingworth's phrase.[4] Each of these latter elements deserves some explanation.

Regarding orthodoxy, one criterion was acceptance of the decrees of the first four ecumenical counsels; and Hobbes did accept them. Another criterion for being orthodox during most of the seventeenth century in England was profession of the Thirty-Nine Articles. One might argue that Hobbes could not have professed all of them because some of his teachings are inconsistent with some of them, for example, that the monarch had priestly powers, and the Thirty-Nine Articles denies this. But that Hobbes had a different understanding of Christianity than some of the doctrines in the Thirty-Nine Articles is not relevant. What was required was profession of them, and that could be done in good conscience even if one disagreed with or did not understand part of their content. The phrase, "implicit faith," was used to describe the faith of people who had an imperfect or incomplete

---

[3] Hobbes's orthodoxy is the most controversial of the elements listed. If private individuals make judgments about orthodoxy, then very often one person's orthodoxy is another person's heresy. If someone with authority to make judgments about orthodoxy judges someone's doctrine to be heterodox, then that person's doctrine is heterodox, relative to the community that accepts that judge's judgment. But no such authoritative person made such a judgment about Hobbes's doctrine; and it is unlikely that someone could, since Hobbes satisfied the criterion for orthodoxy in seventeenth-century England. I distinguish between orthodox and standard views. Of course, many of Hobbes's religious views were nonstandard, as were many of his political and mathematical ones; and he prided himself on holding paradoxical views.

[4] Although James I was more interested in dogmatic theology than the Bible, his commitment to the Bible is indicated by his support for a new translation of the Bible into English, the Authorized Version of the Bible, and more commonly known as, the King James Bible. His Bible-oriented Protestantism is also indicated by his preference for sermons in church services since sermons were always based on biblical texts.

understanding of Christian doctrine; and an implicit faith was sufficient. Also, all of Hobbes's Arminian opponents, notably Bishop John Bramhall, did not accept some of the articles, specifically the ones on predestination.

Regarding *Calvinist theology*, it is important to distinguish between beliefs in propositions and the theories that are used to explain, account for, or fill out that belief. Augustinianism and Thomism in the fourteenth century and Arminianism and Calvinism in the seventeenth century were competing Christian theologies. People could be orthodox in the sense described above and yet hold different theologies. In the late sixteenth and early seventeenth centuries, the dominant theology was Calvinism, in contrast with Lutheranism and Thomism. Hobbes, whose formative years were precisely in this period, was a Calvinist, and not just any kind of Calvinist, such as a Dutch or Swiss Calvinist, but an English Calvinist, like his monarch, James I. To point out that some Calvinists outside of England held theological views opposed to those of Hobbes is as irrelevant as pointing out that during the middle of the twentieth century a communist in the Soviet Union had different beliefs from those in the People's Republic of China. Even to point out that some Calvinists in England had some views different from Hobbes would not alone prove that Hobbes was not an English Calvinist. Characteristic elements of the theology of English Calvinism were that God is incomprehensible and the cause of all things, that God predestined the elect to heaven and the damned to hell, that Jesus died only for the elect and not for all human beings, and that the work of redemption was wholly a work of mercy and contained no element of justice (*Leviathan* 41.2).[5]

The first element I mentioned, that God is incomprehensible, calls for a special comment. God is radically unlike human beings or anything else of which they can have sense experience. His nature is "capable properly of no definition . . . God is an incomprehensible, first, and absolute Being."[6] Not only was it impious to try to speculate about God's nature, it could not yield anything that could be known. Perry Miller summarized his belief in this way: "God is not to be understood, but to be adored. This supreme and awful essence can never be delineated in such a way that He seems even momentarily to take on any shape, contour, or feature recognizable

---

[5] All citations to this work are by chapter and paragraph number and are taken from Thomas Hobbes, *Leviathan*, rev. ed., ed. A. P. Martinich and Brian Battiste (Peterborough, ON: Broadview Press, 2011).

[6] John Preston, *Life Eternall, or, A Treatise of the Knowledge of the Divine Essence and Attributes* (1631), 94. See also, William Ames: "what God is, none can perfectly define, but that hath the Logicke of God himselfe," *Marrow of Sacred Divinity* (1643), 11. Cf. *Leviathan* 34.4.

in the terms of human discourse, nor may His activities be subjected to the laws of human reason or natural plausibility."[7] Substantive beliefs about God beyond, say, that he exists and is omnipotent, the two things Hobbes said could be known about God, could be had only from revelation—thus the importance of biblical interpretation. This explains why Hobbes in fact does not speculate about the nature of God. His view of God fits the character of modern thought if we accept, as I think we should, Alexander's Pope's attitude:

> Say first, of God above, or man below
> What can we reason, but from what we know?
> Of man, what see we but his station here [?]
> ...
> Know, then, thyself, presume not God to scan.
> The proper study of mankind is man.
>
> *Essay on Man* 1.17-19, 2.1-2.

Hobbes's modesty about the scope of human knowledge included the sensory world: "the principles of natural reason . . . are so far from teaching us anything of God's nature, as they cannot teach us our own nature, not the nature of the smallest creature living" (*Leviathan* 31.33). In contrast, Arminian theologians thought that natural theology could discover a great deal about God. And although they may have said that God is incomprehensible, since this was a standard view, their philosophical starting point was that God was good. From this premise they argued that since a good person would not condemn people to hell unless they were responsible for their actions and since responsibility requires free will, people had free will. The attitude of at least many Calvinists was that free will presupposed that God was not the cause of everything and not the single ultimate cause of reality, two propositions at variance with the long tradition of Christianity. As for the relationship between free will and responsibility, Calvinists thought that it was either a mystery or, like Hobbes, thought that human responsibility was consistent with God's causality.

Hobbes showed a *preference for an episcopal and Erastian church government* over other forms. He thought that Independency, essentially congregationalism, was acceptable, especially in the confused circumstances

---

[7] Perry Miller, *Errand into the Wilderness* (Cambridge, MA: Harvard University Press, 1984), 51.

shortly after the Civil Wars (*Leviathan* 47.20). So he was not as adamant about the issue as James I, who said "No bishop, no king." What he detested was Presbyterianism, according to which the church had authority over everyone, including the monarch.

Concerning *liturgy*, Hobbes thought that it should consist of "words and phrases not sudden, nor light, nor plebian, but beautiful and well composed; for else we do not give God as much honour as we can" (*Leviathan* 31.34). For him, this described the liturgy of the Church of England before the Independents and Presbyterians took control of the Church. It largely explains why he attended worship services conducted according to the rights of the Church of England during the Commonwealth, even though they were officially banned.[8]

The last element, *professing the Bible to be the "true religion of Protestants,"* is consonant with Calvinist modesty about the limits of human reason. Because God is incomprehensible, he had to reveal to human beings the things that they needed to know for salvation. If human reason were sufficient for knowledge of God, the Bible would be otiose. It is no good to object that only the weak of mind need the Bible to achieve heaven, because that position denies the inherent need for revelation.[9]

The reason for introducing the issue of Hobbes's Jacobeanism is twofold. First, typically when people add new beliefs to their system of beliefs, they are unlikely to change basic beliefs of that system; and religious propositions—for Hobbes, Jacobeanism—are usually part of the basic ones. Second, because Jacobeanism was passé in the second half of the seventeenth century, many of his critics were unable to understand what Hobbes was holding and why, because they were ignorant of his religious and political foundations. It should be remembered that Hobbes was about two decades older than some of his critics, such as John Wallis, Seth Ward, Ralph Cudworth, and Thomas Pierce, and more than three decades older than many others, such as John Tillotson, Thomas Tenison, and Samuel Parker. All of these critics achieved their success either as part of the anti-Calvinist, Laudian clergy, as part of the subsequent Laudian

---

[8] A. P. Martinich, "Thomas Hobbes's Interregnum Place of Worship," *Notes and Queries* 252 (2007), 433–6.

[9] For more about Hobbes's Calvinism and the proper way to interpret him, see A. P. Martinich, *The Two Gods of Leviathan: Thomas Hobbes on Religion and Politics* (Cambridge: Cambridge University Press, 1992); and chapters 2 and 3 of the present book, which also contain references to works by my critics.

generation of Restoration clergy, or as opponents of absolute sovereignty. Robert Filmer, who shared Hobbes's commitment to absolutism, and John Bramhall, a Laudian and Arminian, were two of the few critics who were also roughly his age.

At least three other elements contributed to Hobbes's alienation from the prevailing views of the latter half of the seventeenth century. One is that he was committed to the new science, which seemed to be inconsistent with traditional doctrine. Another is that his particular version of that new science was unique.[10] Still another is that Hobbes was familiar with and accepted much of the latest biblical scholarship of the time, and his critics were not or did not. (Most of these views are accepted by theistic biblical scholars today.) In short, rather than rejecting the basic beliefs he held as a young adult during the reign of James I, Hobbes tried to reconcile Jacobeanism with the new science. This reconciliation consisted in large part of working in the spirit of Enlightenment thinking. The new science could be put to work to solve longstanding religious and political issues.

My interpretation of Hobbes, as a philosopher trying to reconcile traditional religious content with the new science, is consonant with interpretations that have been given of his friends and colleagues, Marin Mersenne, Pierre Gassendi, Thomas White, Kenelm Digby, and, more generally, a large part of the early modern period.[11] Scholars who do not attend to these aspects of religion are prone to be mistaken about the nature of his project, his beliefs, and the significance of the opposition of his contemporaries. The attacks by Presbyterians, Independents, and certain members of the Church of England may lead one to think that no space remains on the spectrum of Christian beliefs for Hobbes to stand on. I contend that such space exists, but, unfortunately for him, this space was sparsely populated during the second half of the seventeenth century.

[10] See, e.g., Steven Shapin and Simon Schaffer, *Leviathan and the Air-Pump* (Princeton: Princeton University Press, 1985).

[11] Margaret Osler, *Divine Will and Mechanical Philosophy: Gassendi and Descartes on Contingency and Necessity in the Created World* (Cambridge: Cambridge University Press, 1994); Beverley Southgate, *"Covetous of Truth": The Life and Work of Thomas White, 1593–1676* (Dordrecht: Kluwer Academic, 1993); Peter Dear, *Mersenne and the Learning of the Schools* (Ithaca: Cornell University Press, 1988); and Steven Gaukroger, *The Emergence of a Scientific Culture* (Oxford: Oxford University Press, 2006).

2. Eleven Charges against Hobbes and Their Relation to Hobbism

Because Hobbes's actual views are so different from the views attributed to him, we need to distinguish between Hobbes's actual views and Hobbism, the distorted set of doctrines that were attributed to him from at least the Restoration onwards. Hobbism consists in large part of eleven propositions, which are tantamount to charges against him. His critics claim that he held the following:

1. There was a time when the state of nature was universal.
2. Self-preservation is a law of nature.
3. The most important obligation human beings have is the obligation to preserve themselves.
4. An entity that has power over a group of people is a legitimate government (de facto-ism).
5. Sovereigns have absolute authority.
6. Subjects are permitted to rebel against their sovereign.[12]
7. The foundation of all political authority is a contract.
8. Property rights do not exist prior to the establishment of a civil state; they are granted by the sovereign.
9. The laws of nature are not commanded by God.
10. God does not exist because only bodies exist.
11. No religion is true.

Of these charges Hobbes holds only 5 and 8, neither of which is anti-religious.[13] Many of Hobbes's critics themselves assert 5. To us, it may look as if the large majority, 1 through 8, are about politics alone, 10 and 11 are about religion, and 9 is about both. However, for Hobbes's contemporaries, all except perhaps 8 are about religion; and for John Locke even 8 is squarely about religion. God commands humans to preserve themselves and they cannot do this very well without property.[14]

---

[12] One might notice that 5 and 6 are either contradictory or almost so. This does not indicate a mistake on his critics' part. If Hobbes's theory is contradictory, then both complaints would be correct.

[13] As regards 10, many scholars think that Hobbes was an atheist.

[14] John Locke, *Two Treatises of Government*, ed. Peter Laslett (Cambridge: Cambridge University Press, 1967), 286–8.

The apparent discrepancy between the way we see these eleven propositions and the way seventeenth-century intellectuals did may be explained by their belief that politics and religion were inextricably connected. This point can be illustrated by considering propositions 1–3. Both 1 and 2 were thought to be inconsistent with the goodness of God, who commanded that people love one another. According to Jesus, the fundamental law of human relations is "Love your neighbor as yourself" (Mark 12:28–30). Concerning 3, some of Hobbes's critics objected that his political theory makes sovereigns as powerful as God, and that his statement that leviathan is a mortal God is blasphemous. But it is not, judged by the standards of Jacobeanism. Referring to Psalm 82, James I, in his *Speech to the Lords and Commons of the Parliament at White-Hall*, says,

The state of monarchy is the supremest thing on earth, for kings are not only God's lieutenants upon earth, and sit upon God's throne, and even by God are called Gods. Kings are justly called gods for that they exercise a manner or resemblance of divine power upon earth. For if you will consider the attributes to God, you shall see how they agree in the person of a king. God has power to create, or destroy, to make, or unmake at his pleasure, to give life, or send death, to judge all, and to be judged nor accountable to none; to raise low things, and to make high things low at his pleasure, and to God are both soul and body due. And the like power have kings: they make and unmake their subjects; they have power of raising and casting down, of life and of death; judges over all their subjects, and in all cases, and yet accountable to none but God only.[15]

In the rest of this chapter, propositions 1 through 3 will be considered in some detail and shown to be false generalizations of Hobbes's actual position.

[15] James I, *The Political Works of James I*, ed. Charles Howard McIlwain (Cambridge, MA: Harvard University Press, 1918), 307. James had said "kings are in the word of GOD it selfe called Gods, . . . and so adorned and furnished with some sparkles of the Diuinitie" (James I 1918: 281). Even at mid-century, some of Hobbes's critics believed that sovereigns had something akin to divinity. Eutactus Philodemius, the pseudonym of a defender of the Commonwealth, acknowledged that the "best of Magistrates . . . are called Gods" (Eutactus Philodemius, *An Answer to the Vindication of Doctor Hammond, Against the Exceptions of Eutactus Philodemius. Wherein is Endeavored to be Cleared What Power Man Hath* [1650], 18). See Stephen Baskerville, *Not Peace but a Sword* (London: Routledge, 1993), 5, 103, 118, for other examples.

Charge 1: There Was a Time When the State of Nature Was Universal

Most of those who criticized Hobbes's conception of the state of nature thought he was making a historical claim about primeval times. Robert Filmer begins with God and the first humans: "If God created only Adam and ... the woman ... ; if also God gave to Adam not only the dominion over the woman and the children that should issue from them, but also over the whole earth to subdue it, ... I wonder how the *right of nature* can be imagined by Mr Hobbes, [to be] 'a condition of war of everyone against everyone.'"[16] Filmer realizes that Hobbes acknowledges that the state of nature "never generally" existed over the entire world but does not stop to consider that such an acknowledgement might indicate a misinterpretation of Hobbes's position. Nor does Filmer consider that Hobbes's supposition of people "sprung out of the earth like mushrooms without any obligation one to another," might mean that Hobbes was not talking primarily about history.[17] I'll return to this point in a moment. Bramhall, Seth Ward, William Lucy, and Edward Hyde, the Earl of Clarendon, are other good examples of famous critics who criticized Hobbes's use of the state of nature on the grounds that it was not a historical condition.[18]

When Hobbes's concept of the state of nature was accepted, it was interpreted as the condition of people after the fall of Adam and Eve. In *Killing is Murder, and No Murder*, Michael Hawke writes, "[F]or after the fall of our first Parents the natural State of men, before they were setled in a Society, as Master *Hobbs* truely sayeth, was a meer Warre."[19]

The principal reason that Hobbes's critics did not understand the character of the state of nature[20] was that for them the origin of things had to be

---

[16] Robert Filmer, *Patriarcha and Other Writings* (Cambridge: Cambridge University Press, 1991), 187; originally published in 1652.

[17] Thomas Hobbes, *On the Citizen* 8.1; translation from *On the Citizen*, ed. and trans. Richard Tuck and Michael Silverthorne (Cambridge: Cambridge University Press, 1998). Subsequent citations to this work, abbreviated *OC*, are given in the text by chapter and section number.

[18] John Bramhall, *The Catching of Leviathan, of the Great Whale* (1658a), 567–8; Seth Ward, *In Thomae Hobbii Philosophiam* (Oxford, 1656), 287; William Lucy, *Observations, Censures and Confutations of Notorious Errours in Mr Hobbes His Leviathan* (1663), 147–8; and Edward Hyde, *A Brief View and Survey of the Dangerous and Pernicious Errors of Mr. Hobbes His Leviathan* (1676), 28.

[19] Michael Hawke, *Killing is Murder, and No Murder* (1657), 7.

[20] An intellectual who did understand Hobbes on this point was Matthew Wren, who in *Monarchy Asserted*, wrote: "Originally every man had Right to every thing. ... There was no settled Propriety before the Establishment of Propriety; ... I must alwayes assert, That though Originally in the state of nature... every particular Man had Right to prosecute his own Advantage, though to the Ruine of other Men" (Matthew Wren, *Monarchy Asserted* [1660], 18–19, 48–9).

explained in terms of the history that they believed was reported in the book of Genesis. But Hobbes's approach to origins is completely different. His political philosophy is not historical but scientific. In *De corpore* (OL 1: [cv]), Hobbes brags that political science is no older than he.[21] For him, science consists of definitions and the consequences of these definitions. As such, all the propositions of science are necessary and a priori. This is how Hobbes thinks that he avoids skepticism. (Not, "I think; therefore, I am," but "I define x as y; therefore, x is y.") Scientific propositions are universal but also necessarily true; and as a priori, they are non-empirical. In contrast, experience is always of the particular and always empirical. Some propositions that express experience may be universal in form, but they are not scientific because they are not necessarily true. Hobbes says that the proposition, "Every crow is black," is universal and true, but contingent because while true today it may happen to be false at another time (*"hodie quidem contingere potest ut sit vera, alio tempore ut sit falsa"* [OL 1: 33–4]). According to Hobbes's understanding of philosophy, "[I]t is evident that we are not to account as any part thereof that original knowledge called experience, in which consisteth prudence, because it is not attained by reasoning, but found as well in brute beasts as in man" (*Leviathan* 46.2).

Understanding Hobbes's approach is made more difficult by the fact that his idea of science is unusual. His paradigm is geometry, and his understanding of it non-standard. Points actually have length and width and lines actually have width in addition to length.[22] Also, Hobbes conceives geometry as generative or constructive. In *Leviathan*, he says, "By PHILOSOPHY is understood *the knowledge acquired by reasoning, from the manner of the generation of anything, to the properties; or from the properties, to some possible way of generation of the same"* (*Leviathan* 46.1; see also OL 1: 2).

When it is systematized, a science like geometry begins with the simplest elements and builds on them: "So the geometrician, from construction of figures, findeth out many properties thereof, and from the properties, new ways of their construction by reasoning" (*Leviathan* 46.1). In geometry, one begins with a definition of a point and then a straight line; ideally these definitions are formulated in terms of how to construct them. One then proceeds to

---

[21] *De corpore*, in Thomas Hobbes, *Opera Latina*, ed. Molesworth (London: John Bohm, 1839–45), 1: [cv]. Subsequent citations to the work, abbreviated as OL, are given in the text with volume and page numbers.
[22] Thomas Hobbes, *English Works*, ed. William Molesworth (London: John Bohm, 1839–45), 7: 211.

deduce whatever follows from these definitions. One then defines a plane figure and does the same for it; and then one defines various kinds of plane figures, and so on. The analogous operation in political philosophy is to begin with the simplest case, that is, the condition of human beings in which no laws exist. For expository purposes, I call this the "primary state of nature."

After drawing the appropriate conclusions, such as that war is generated by competition, diffidence (that is, distrust of others), and the desire for glory, one then adds the definition of a law of nature. The deductions resume. The specific laws of nature are deduced from the definition of a law of nature, plus other definitions that he had supplied, notably, the definitions of a human being and the right of nature. This yields what I call the "secondary state of nature." It is a state of nature because the civil state has not yet appeared, but it is not the primary state of nature because it contains the laws of nature.[23] In *On the Citizen (De cive)*, Hobbes described his general procedure by saying that he began "with the matter of which a commonwealth is made," that is, people in the state of nature, and then went on to describe how the civil state "comes into being and the form it takes, and to the first origin of justice" (Preface, 9).

I have already mentioned that Hobbes's contemporary critics did not appreciate the geometric and generative character of Hobbes's scientific method. Hyde cannot understand how Hobbes could hold that it is "unavoidably necessary for every man to cut his neighbour's throat."[24] He cannot see how people could fall "into that condition of war" if "Nature hath thus providently provided for the Peace and Tranquility of her Children, by Laws immutable & eternal, that are written in their hearts."[25] What Hyde does not understand is that the laws of nature cannot be appealed to in the primary state of nature. (I will return to this theme of science as deduction from definitions in the next section, in which the second charge against Hobbes is at issue.)

Strategically and perhaps rhetorically, Hobbes wants to begin only with the state of nature because he wants to show how horrible the condition of human beings is without government. Having discussed the concept of the state of nature in science, I can now describe its empirical application. Hobbes thinks that it exists in three kinds of situations: during civil war, in highly primitive conditions, and in international relations. But these

---

[23] Martinich, *Two Gods of Leviathan*, 76–86.
[24] Hyde, *Brief View and Survey*, 37.
[25] Hyde, *Brief View and Survey*, 38.

empirical applications do not change the character that the concept of the state of nature has in Hobbes's science of politics.

In short, the state of nature, for Hobbes, is primarily a concept in a thought experiment. For my purposes, what is important about the groundlessness of charge 1 is that it illustrates how feeble the understanding of Hobbes's philosophy by some of his critics was. They did not appreciate his aspirations to develop a science of politics as rigorous as Galileo's physics and Euclid's geometry, even though *De cive* had been published five years before *Leviathan*.

Charge 2: Self-Preservation Is the Fundamental Law of Nature

Like the first, this proposition, the second charge made against Hobbes, is false. In *Leviathan*, the first law of nature is "to seek peace" (*Leviathan* 14.4), and the law is similar in *De cive* (*OC* 2.3).[26] Rather than being a law, self-preservation is the object of the dominant desire of human beings and a concept in the definition of a law of nature. As Hobbes states, "A Law of Nature (lex naturalis) is a precept or general rule, found out by reason, by which a man is forbidden to do that which is destructive of his life, or taketh away the means of preserving the same, and to omit that by which he thinketh it may be best preserved" (*Leviathan* 14.3). But the definition of a law of nature is not a law any more than the definition of a horse is a horse. Nonetheless, the reason his critics made the mistake they did is understandable. In *Leviathan*, Hobbes says that the general rule of reason is "*that every man ought to endeavor peace, as far as he has hope of obtaining it; and when he cannot obtain it, that he may seek and use all helps and advantages of war*" (*Leviathan* 14.4). If the reader is not attentive to the slight changes of wording, she might identify the general rule of reason with the first law of nature; and since the general rule of reason contains what Hobbes describes as "the sum of the right of nature" (that is, "the liberty each man hath . . . for the preservation of his own nature" [*Leviathan* 14.4, 14.1]), she might conclude that self-preservation is a law of nature.[27] However, both this identification and the slide from the sum

---

[26] Somewhat confusingly, Hobbes says, "The first *of the Natural Laws* derived from this fundamental natural law [the first one]" is "*that the right of all men to all things must not be held onto; certain rights must be transferred or abandoned*" (Hobbes 1998: 2.3). So the first *law of nature* (the foundation) is "to seek peace when it can be had; when it cannot, to look for aid in war" (Hobbes 1998: 2.2).

[27] The mistake of identifying self-preservation with the first law of nature is abetted by the text of *De cive*, which includes the right of war in the first law of nature: "*to seek peace when it can be had; when it cannot, to look for aid in war*" (*De cive* 2.3).

of the right of nature to a law of nature are illegitimate. The first law of nature is only the "first branch" of the general rule of reason, not the whole of it. And while the rule of reason contains the right of nature, containing something is not identical with being it. The right to self-preservation is the "second" branch of the general rule of reason and is no part of the first law of nature (*Leviathan* 14.4).

As with the first charge, many critics leveled the second charge against Hobbes.[28] In *A Discourse of Ecclesiastical Politie*, Samuel Parker writes that for Hobbes, "[s]elf-preservation [is] the first and fundamental law of nature" and self-interest and self-preservation is an obligation; and thus when the "Tye [of self-interest] happens to cease, their Obligation becomes Null and Void."[29] Writing about the same time as Parker, Thomas Tenison implies that for Hobbes self-preservation is the most "ancient" law.[30]

One of the most interesting critics who charged that, for Hobbes, self-preservation is a law is the anonymous author, supposedly one J. Shafte, of *The Great Law of Nature, or Self-Preservation, Examined, Asserted, and Vindicated from Mr. Hobbes his Abuses* (1673).[31] The title tells the story, but the point is reinforced in the text, where Shafte wrote that, for Hobbes, "that Great Law of Nature [is] Self-preservation."[32] He assumes that "the Law of Nature" is operating as soon as Hobbes introduces the state of nature. He says that if the right of nature permitted a person to do things that actually led to his destruction, then "the Law of Nature will *re vera*, really and truly be broken, contrary to design and apparence."[33] As this quotation indicates, Shafte repeats the mistake that critics made with respect to charge 1. He illicitly uses propositions that are not yet in play. Writing about the state of nature, which occurs in chapter 13 of *Leviathan*, Shafte tries to use propositions

---

[28] In order to broaden the historical scene, my examples will focus on authors writing after 1669.

[29] Parker, *Discourse of Ecclesiastical Politie*, 120–1, 116.

[30] Thomas Tenison, *The Creed of Mr. Hobbes Examined* (1670), 147. John Cosin was unhappy with Hobbes for holding that "God's dominion is founded in his power" (Parkin, *Taming the Leviathan*, 63). Also, Skinner quotes a seventeenth-century commonplace book that says that for Hobbes, "the prime law of nature in the soul of man is that of temporal self-love" (Quentin Skinner, *Visions of Politics: Hobbes and Civil Science* (Cambridge: Cambridge University Press, 2002), 283).

[31] The identification of Shafte occurs in Early English Books Online. His book is interesting because, though he is virtually unknown, his description of Hobbes's views is more accurate than most of Hobbes's critics.

[32] J. Shafte, *The Great Law of Nature, or, Self-Preservation Examined, Asserted and Vindicated from Mr. Hobbes his Abuses* (1673), A2r–A2v; see also 19.

[33] Shafte, *The Great Law of Nature*, 5. There is one place where Shafte's language accurately captures Hobbes's view: "the rules of reason, [are] grounded upon Equality and Self-preservation" (Shafte, *The Great Law of Nature*, 15). It is possible of course that Shafte's wording is correct because he is using a shorthand expression for "law of Self-preservation."

that are introduced only in chapter 14, "Of the Laws of Nature." Given the logical resources in chapter 13, nothing yet can be just or unjust, as Hobbes says (*Leviathan* 13.13).

Another problem with Shafte's interpretation is that he seems to think of the right of nature as a claim right, "granted [to a human being] . . . by God." This is the reason he thinks that the right of nature and the equality of men entail that each person has a right to "a just and equal portion" of all things: "Seeing men are equal by Nature, one man ought not to take to himself a greater liberty in his actions, which respect or concern another man."[34] But obviously, for Hobbes, the right of nature does not give people the right to an equal share of things, only an equal right to compete for whatever they desire.[35]

The misunderstanding that self-preservation is a law of nature for Hobbes is still alive in 1683 when Oxford University, which wanted to support the claim of James, the Duke of York, to succeed Charles II, condemned various propositions by such diverse thinkers as the Presbyterian Richard Baxter, the republican John Milton, and the Independent John Owens. Proposition 7 is directed against Hobbes: "Self-preservation is the fundamental law of nature, and supersedes the obligation of all others, whenever they stand in competition with it (*Hobbes de Cive, Leviathan*)."[36] Motivated by the Oxford Judgment, several sermons further spread the idea that that self-preservation was a law of nature according to Hobbes, such as one given by James Brome, a royal chaplain, who condemns "our Republican *Leviathans*."[37] Brome's

[34] Shafte, *The Great Law of Nature*, 13.

[35] There are other problems with Hobbes's account of rights. In the primary state of nature, a person is supposed to have a right to everything, that is, an absence of external impediments to do whatever he or she likes. However, other people in the state of nature often are external impediments to a person—I owe this point to Kevin Smith—and so, as a matter of logic, there is no right to everything in the state of nature, given that there is some density of population that forces people to interact with others. Also, even if one person were in the state of nature, she would not have a right to everything according to Hobbes's definition if something were inaccessible because mountains, valleys, or quicksand are often external impediments to objects. One reason that it is important to realize that the rights in the state of nature are liberty rights is that Hobbes claims that a certain principle applies to them, when in fact that principle is not true of liberty rights. The principle, which I call "The Principle of the Right to the Means Necessary to an End," is "Whoever has a right to an end has a right to the means necessary to achieving that end." Hobbes clearly holds the Principle (Hobbes 2002: 18.8). He thinks it allows him to argue that sovereigns are absolute, that is, since sovereigns have the right to govern his subjects and one of these rights is to judge what means are necessary to achieve that end, the sovereign can judge that he needs all the rights of his subjects (except for the right of self-preservation and related ones). In short, he is an absolute sovereign.

[36] *The Judgment and Decree of the University of Oxford Past [sic] in their Convocation July 21, 1683, against Certain Pernicious Books and Damnable Doctrines Destructive to the Sacred Persons of Princes, their State and Government, and of all Humane Society* (Oxford, 1683), 3.

[37] See Parkin, *Taming the Leviathan*, 374–5. Skinner has incisively discussed Hobbes's philosophy within the context of republicanism, more precisely, the differences between Hobbes's philosophy and

misunderstanding is about as perfect as one might hope to imagine.[38] Roman Republicanism is the view that a healthy state is one in which the citizens participate in governance, while Hobbes's view is that the sovereign decides who participates and to what extent. Chapter 21 of *Leviathan* is a relatively explicit attack on Roman Republicanism.[39]

During the Exclusion Crisis (1678–81), some intellectuals began to accept a role for Hobbes's concept of self-preservation in political philosophy. For Locke, people have an obligation to defend themselves because God commanded human beings to multiply and fill the earth: "Everyone is . . . *bound to preserve himself*, and not to quit his Station willfully.[40] Although Locke prefers to talk about the law of the Preservation of Society, that obligation, it seems, gives way to the obligation of self-preservation if one's own life is endangered.

Like the de facto controversy, the Allegiance Controversy of 1689–90 concerned the problem faced by people of conscience who had sworn allegiance to one monarch and were then pressured to swear allegiance to the person or persons who displaced that monarch. In 1688, James II had left England for the safety of France because William of Orange had come from the Netherlands, ostensibly to observe the election of a new parliament. But in the absence of James, William was made monarch, even though he was not the next person in the line of legal succession. Those who refused to swear allegiance of William were called nonjurors.

William Sherlock began as a nonjuror and defended Charles and his brother James after the Rye House Plot in his pamphlet, *The Case of Resistance of the Supreme Powers Stated and Resolved*, in which he presented "ways of proving and confirming *the Doctrine of Non-resistance, or Subjection to the Sovereign Princes*."[41] When he decided to swear allegiance to William, he felt the need to explain his reasons. In *The Case of Allegiance Due to Sovereign Powers*, Sherlock argues that an obligation to obey *de facto* powers is created

republicanism. See, e.g., Quentin Skinner, *Hobbes and Republican Liberty* (Cambridge: Cambridge University Press, 2008).

[38] Parkin may be subject to this judgment when he says, "In some ways Hobbes's own project might be regarded as a highly original variant of conservative republican themes" (Parkin, *Taming the Leviathan*, 179; cf. 178).

[39] See Skinner's *Hobbes and Republican Liberty* and the literature referred to there; as well as A. P. Martinich, "Hobbes's Reply to Republicanism," in Luc Foisneau and George Wright (eds.), *New Critical Perspectives on Hobbes's Leviathan* (Milano: FrancoAngeli, 2004).

[40] Locke, *Two Treatises*, 2:6; see also Jeremy Waldron, *God, Locke, and Equality* (Cambridge: Cambridge University Press, 2002), 157.

[41] William Sherlock, *The Case of Resistance of the Supreme Powers Stated and Resolved* (1684), 2.

by the fact that they are ordained by God. So it seems possible to have obligations to two sovereigns, to the *de facto* sovereign and to the deposed sovereign, who retains his political legitimacy. He supports his view by citing Canon 28 of the Church of England, as set down in Bishop John Overall's *Convocation Book* of 1606. That canon declared that it was a mistake to think that the authority in "new Forms of Government, begun by Rebellion, and after thoroughly settled, . . . [are] not of God."[42] Sherlock takes this to be an endorsement of de facto-ism.[43]

Sometimes acceptance of one of Hobbes's central concepts was combined with an important misunderstanding of his theory. For example, Sherlock appeals to the "inward principle of Self-Preservation."[44] It is not clear what status this "principle" is supposed to have, whether a psychological law, normative law, or something else. Whether he would want to maintain this at all costs or not, at one point Sherlock does say, "Self-Preservation is as much a Law to Subjects, as to the Prince."[45] And one of Sherlock's critics, Thomas Browne, understands Sherlock to be asserting that "*Hobbs's Self-preservation* [is] . . . the *primary Law of* Nature."[46] In any case, Sherlock appeals to self-preservation to justify the view that whatever "settled" entity is in control of a person's life is a legitimate government in the sense that it has "God's Authority, and must be obeyed."[47] This is a version of the de facto theory of legitimacy espoused by some thinkers during the Engagement Controversy. (It is connected with charge 4 above.) For Sherlock, a usurper on the throne is owed as much obedience as a rightful ruler is, even if consent is not given. So, while he helps himself to Hobbes's concept, he does not end up with Hobbes's view.

As for the possibility that Sherlock may be committed to holding that a subject could have a double allegiance, one to the *de jure* sovereign, who is legitimate, and one to the *de facto* one, who is illegitimate, he denies it. A person owes allegiance only to the person who has power over his life; and this is often the *de facto* sovereign, who has authority from God. The de jure sovereign might have the right to the government, but not the authority of the government. That is, right and authority, and hence right and allegiance, are pulled apart. Since authority is given by God alone, not by the consent

[42] John Overall, *Bishop Overall's Convocation-Book* (1690), 59.
[43] Parkin, *Taming the Leviathan*, 382–4.
[44] William Sherlock, *The Case of Allegiance Due to Soveraign Powers* (1671), 3.
[45] Sherlock, *The Case of Allegiance*, 42.
[46] Thomas Browne, *An Answer to Dr. Sherlock's Case of Allegiance to Sovereign Powers* (1691), 17.
[47] Sherlock, *The Case of Allegiance*, 5.

of the subjects or any other fact or property, God sometimes ignores what is right; but Sherlock does not consider this consequence. At the end of 1688, James II had possession of "Legal Right," but not the authority of government. At the same time, William III had the authority of government, but not the legal right. According to Sherlock, both nonjurors and most jurors made the same mistake, namely, in thinking that Legal Right was the only ground for allegiance. Sherlock's identification of a supposed error common to both jurors and nonjurors is clever, if not convincing; so, it is not surprising that he shores up his position by appealing to principles of the Church of England and the Bible. One of the biblical texts is Daniel 4:21, "[H]e [God] taketh away Kings, and setteth up Kings." Sherlock understands this passage to have the consequence that God removed James II via William's invasion. However, another possible interpretation is exploited by one of Sherlock's critics. Browne uses the same quotation plus a similar one, "He removeth Kings, and setteth up Kings" (Daniel 2:21), on the title page of his An Answer to Dr. Sherlock's Case of Allegiance to Sovereign Powers.[48] The implication that Browne intends the reader to draw is that only God removes kings, not human beings. Since James II was not removed by God, he remains king.

A non-biblically based objection to Sherlock's views was that, for him, "Strength always has Right" and that the source of that strength is of no importance. For him, "Strength, or Power, still carries right from God inseparably along with it. . . . And Right always carried by Power is not a Right to settle Peace but to make War. . . . So his Power carrying Right, throws all into a state of War, as much, I conceive as Mr. Hobbs's Power giving it."[49] Sherlock replies by denying that his views were the same as Hobbes's. The key difference between them, Sherlock claims, is that he held that "no Man is a Subject, without his own Consent, or Submission. . . . The greatest Conqueror cannot Compel us to be his Subjects without our own submission."[50] And he says: "[W]e do not Assert, with Mr. Hobbs, That as soon as any Prince or Rebel has got Possession of the Throne, we immediately thereby become his Subjects."[51] Sherlock's defense against the charge is ironic, since at this point it looks exactly the same as Hobbes's view, and it is not de facto-ism. Sherlock's use of the claim, "no Man is a Subject, without his own Consent,"

---

[48] Browne, An Answer to Dr. Sherlock's Case.

[49] John Kettlewell, The Duty of Allegiance Settled upon its True Ground (1691), 53.

[50] William Sherlock, Their Present Majesties Government Proved to be Thoroughly Settled (1691), 14, 16.

[51] Sherlock, Their Present Majesties Government, 19.

echoes Hobbes's claim that there is "no obligation on any man which ariseth not from some act of his own" (*Leviathan* 21.10).[52] As for the claim of Sherlock's opponent that Hobbes holds that "Strength always has Right," it is simply false. Only irresistible power, which belongs to only God, always has right (*Leviathan* 31.5).[53] For human beings, "right" in the sense of authority requires the consent of the subjects.

Charge 3: The Most Important Obligation Human Beings Have Is the Obligation to Preserve Themselves

One reason that Hobbes's critics recoiled from the idea that self-preservation could be a law of nature or in some way be obligatory is that such a connection undermined the traditional view that obligation is opposed to self-interest. They feared something like this Hobbist line of reasoning:

1. All acts of self-preservation are acts of self-interest. (Analytic)
2. If self-preservation is a law of nature, then all people have an obligation to preserve themselves. (Analytic)
3. Self-preservation is a law of nature. (Hobbism)
4. Therefore, all people have an obligation to preserve themselves (perform acts of self-preservation). (From 2 and 3)
5. Therefore, all people have an obligation to perform acts of self-interest. (From 4 and 1)

According to ordinary morality, obligation and self-interest are largely incompatible. So, if the above argument stands, the ordinary sense of obligation seems to be destroyed. And since this ordinary sense was thought to prevent society from falling into chaos, the Hobbist argument seems to be "destructive to all Society."[54] Hobbes's critics were especially worried about the obligation to keep oaths and covenants. (This is related to charge 6 above.)

[52] One difference between the two philosophers is that Hobbes thinks that human authority arises when subjects consent to be governed by a sovereign and Sherlock holds that human authority is given by God. The submission of the subjects is "the Visible Evidence, that such a Prince has receiv'd his Authority from God" (Sherlock, *Their Present Majesties Government*, 7; see also 14).

[53] When Sherlock supported Charles II and his brother after the Rye House Plot, he wrote, "*God himself set up a Soveraign and Irresistible Power in the Jewish Nation*" (Sherlock, *The Case of Resistance*, 3). This suggests that he had read Hobbes by this time.

[54] Daniel Scargill, *The Recantation of Daniel Scargill* (Cambridge, 1669), 6.

If Hobbes's critics had not thought that he had made it the first law of nature, they probably would have accepted self-preservation as an obligation.[55] After all, as Locke argues, people are created by God, and hence are God's property; and each person has an obligation to protect God's property from destruction.[56] If some other law had been first, say, "Love your neighbor as yourself," then the obligation of self-preservation would not have trumped all other obligations. However, if self-preservation is the first law of nature, then it seems to be logically prior to all other obligations, and hence the highest obligation. As mentioned above, the Oxford Condemnation expresses its opposition to this.

Although they were mistaken to think that self-preservation was an obligation according to Hobbes, they were right in sensing that his project threatened one of their central beliefs, namely, that reality contains goodness and value as an essential part. The striking refrain of the first creation story in Genesis is that what God created was "good" and that the entire creation was "very good." Even more important than the belief that creation is good was their belief that God was inherently good. The premise that creation is good, combined with the principle that nothing can give what it does not have, entails that God the Creator is inherently good. Hobbes thinks that to attribute properties like mercy and goodness to God is engage in anthropomorphism. Only beings that have feelings can be merciful and God does not have them. Most philosophers in the Judeo-Christian tradition would have agreed with Hobbes that God does not have feelings. However, they would contest the claim that no account of mercy and goodness can be given independent of feelings. No such option is available to Hobbes, for whom to be good is to be desired (*Leviathan* 6.7). It is appropriate for humans to say that God is good and merciful, as well as that he sees and understands, because such statements are "signs of honor" and show honor to God that is owed to him, not because he is the Creator, but because he is sovereign over humans by nature in virtue of his irresistible power (*Leviathan* 31.5–6). Because Hobbes eliminates inherent goodness from both the world and from God, the traditional foundation of morality is undermined. His own account of the source of morality is supposed to show how moral obligation is generated from or grounded in something that is not obligation and does not have inherent normative value. To do this, he of course cannot include or

---

[55] See, e.g., Parker, *Discourse of Ecclesiastical Politie*, 122; and William Barclay in Locke, *Two Treatises*, 420.
[56] Locke, *Two Treatises*, 271.

presuppose the existence of obligation in the state of nature. (To understand the force of this condition, consider the treatment of the state of nature by Locke, who assumes that it contains laws, obligations and values.)[57] Thus, Hobbes begins his account of obligation with a condition that contains no obligations, that is, a condition in which there are no laws at all. One sees this clearly at the end of chapter 13 of *Leviathan*, "Of the Natural Condition of Mankind," where he says that in the condition of "mere," that is, pure, nature, "The notions of Right and Wrong, Justice and Injustice have there no place" (*Leviathan* 13.13).

Now Hobbes gives the impression that obligation arises in the state of nature only when the laws of nature have been added to it, the secondary state of nature, because he first explains the origin of obligation in chapter 14, "Of the Laws of Nature," after the first law of nature has already been proved. He says, "And when a man hath . . . abandoned or granted away his right, then is he said to be OBLIGED or BOUND, . . . and that he ought, and it is DUTY, not to make void that voluntary act of his own" (*Leviathan* 14.7). What Hobbes means is that obligation is nothing more than "a declaration or signification by some voluntary and sufficient sign or signs," that he no longer has his right (*Leviathan* 14.7). The consequences of giving up a right are solely behavioral. People will say that the person *P*, who gave up the right to do *A*, is obliged or has an obligation not to do *A*. If someone asks *P* to do *A*, *P* may say that he cannot because he is obliged or has an obligation not to do *A*. If *P* subsequently acts as if he still had the right to do *A*, other people will object or may interfere with his attempt to do *A*.

It is difficult to explain what Hobbes means because he is saying something so new that it is difficult to express using our ordinary words. No matter how his point is stated, it is subject to being misunderstood as meaning something relatively conventional. This problem notwithstanding, it is necessary to try to convey his point as precisely as possible. He means that an obligation is not a new entity in the world. The world continues to consist of nothing more than bodies in motion. What is different is that the speaker, in uttering some words, has indicated his intention to other people that he will not to exercise his right to *O*. The obligation of the speaker consists of nothing extra. To use some contemporary terminology, it is not correct to quantify

---

[57] In general, Locke helps himself to too many concepts. For example, he assumes that the world is common property and then explains how private property comes about. It would have been more interesting if he had begun from a state in which there was no property and explained the origin of property.

over obligations. It is not the case that once one has laid down a right, there now exists an X such that X is an obligation. There are no nonnatural properties in the sense that G. E. Moore believed there were. Hobbes's view about obligations may be helpfully contrasted with his view about the civil state. Although Hobbes generally does not want to be committed to any entities other than bodies in motion, he seems to commit himself to the existence of artificial persons such as the civil state when he says that it is a "real unity" (*Leviathan* 17.13).

I said above that Hobbes gives the "impression" that obligation arises only when the laws of nature have been added to the state of nature because he introduces the concept of obligation along with the laws of nature. However, it might seem that, given his principles, obligations should be able to arise in the pure or primary state of nature because "a declaration or signification by some voluntary and sufficient sign or signs" that a person no longer has a right does not depend on the existence of any law of nature. One way to remove this appearance of obligation in the state of nature is to appeal to a principle used above. One cannot infer propositions from definitions that have not yet been introduced. Since Hobbes does not define "laying down of right" when he discusses the mere state of nature, one cannot infer that one can lay down a right in the mere state of nature.

If certain empirical changes in behavior are the only consequences of acquiring an obligation, then obligations seem to be rather weak. This is exactly Hobbes's view of them: the words and actions that signify the laying down of a right are "the BONDS, by which men are bound and obliged, bonds that have their strength not from their own nature (for nothing is more easily broken than a man's word), but from fear of some evil consequence upon the rupture" (*Leviathan* 14.7). Obligations without fears of not fulfilling them are empty. This is a wholly naturalistic account of human obligation. But it is not a complete account of human obligation or of obligation in general.

In addition to saying that obligation arises from laying down a right, Hobbes speaks of the laws of nature as obliging: "From that law of nature by which we are obliged to transfer to another such rights as, being retained, hinder the peace of mankind, there follows a third, . . . *that men perform their covenants made*" (*Leviathan* 15.1); "The laws of nature oblige *in foro interno*" (15.36); and "The same laws . . . oblige only to a desire and endeavor" (15.39). That he is speaking of moral obligation is indicated by his table of sciences, where the laws of nature are named moral laws; and he says that "the true doctrine of the laws of nature is the true moral philosophy" (15.40).

These quotations raise the question of whether Hobbes thinks the obligation that attaches to the laws of nature is grounded in something more basic. Most Hobbes scholars think that Hobbes's laws are merely prudential and not moral, and not genuine laws. For them, the laws of nature are dictates of reason—full stop. If this interpretation of the laws of nature is correct, then Hobbes has completely separated the foundations of obligation and morality from God. That's what many of Hobbes's contemporaries thought. I hold a contrary view, that for Hobbes the laws of nature are genuine laws,[58] because he says that in doing science one must speak literally, because he holds that all laws are the commands of someone, and because he sometimes asserts that the laws of nature are God's commands. The law of nature, which "dictateth to men that have no civil government what they ought to do, . . . dictateth the same . . . to the consciences of sovereign princes . . . where not man, but God reigneth, whose laws, such of them as oblige all mankind in respect of God, as he is King of kings" (*Leviathan* 30.30; see also 40.1 and 42.37). This quotation from chapter 30 occurs in Part 2 of *Leviathan*, which applies to commonwealths in general. The special treatment of Christian commonwealths has not yet begun. A sticking point for philosophers who believe that the laws of nature are commands of God is how to explain how one knows that God does command them. Hobbes says that one way that God speaks to people is through reason, that the laws of nature are discovered by reason, and that "our natural reason" is "the undoubted word of God" (*Leviathan* 32.2). Hobbes, like almost all intellectuals in the seventeenth century, thought this last point was obvious.

Granted that the obligation attached to the laws of nature is grounded in their being commands of God, we can ask, "In virtue of what are God's imperatives commands?" This is to ask, "In virtue of what does God have authority to command anything?" Most seventeenth-century English intellectuals gave one or both of two standard answers. One is that God has authority over humans in virtue of being their creator; the other is that God has authority over humans in virtue of being good. Sherlock opted for creation grounding authority in order to avoid being convicted of Hobbism.[59]

Hobbes rejects both. He is right to say that creating something does not give one authority over that thing. A workman who makes something, say, a

---

[58] For a full defense of my view, see *The Two Gods of Leviathan*, and also chapters 3 and 7 in this volume.

[59] Sherlock, *The Case of Allegiance*, 15.

bowl, does not have "authority" over that bowl, if he is employed by someone else. The employer has the authority or control over it. Since it is odd to say that anyone has authority over a bowl, let's change the example. A slave who creates a child does not have authority over that child. The owner of the slave has authority over the child. The owner may authorize the slave parent to care for the slave child; but the authority remains in the owner. The reason is that the owner has power over the slave. (Shortly, we shall see what lies at the foundation of this.) It is also incorrect to say that God has authority over humans in virtue of his goodness. The best person in the world does not have authority over anyone in virtue of her goodness. Goodness is logically irrelevant to authority.

Therefore, Hobbes's answer to the question, "In virtue of what d Leviathan does God have authority to command anything?" is different. He says, "The right by nature whereby God reigneth over men and punisheth those that break his laws is to be derived, not from his creating them, as if he required obedience as of gratitude for his benefits, but from his *irresistible power*" (*Leviathan* 31.5). Many of Hobbes's critics thought that locating the source of authority in God's irresistible power was religiously suspect.[60] However, it was an idea that many intellectuals were themselves committed to because it is the straightforward interpretation of a famous text in the epistle to the Romans: "Let every soul be subject unto the higher powers: for there is no power but of God" (Romans 13:1, Authorized Version).[61] "Power" (ἐξουσία) here has the additional sense of authority. It is a concept that others made use of at the same time. In *Killing Is Murder, and No Murder*, Michael Hawke writes, "The Power of all Kings, Princes, and Rulers, immediately proceeds from God . . . there is no power but from God."[62] In his pamphlet, *Transcendent and Multiplied Rebellion and Treason Discovered*, Hyde writes, "*Political Authority, is the power which the Supreame Magistrate hath over men's Persons and Estates . . . The original thereof is from God; who is the only Potentate,* The King of Kings, and Lord of Lords, 1. Tim. 6, 15, *and from none other, Men or Angells.*"[63]

In short, Hobbes first says that human obligation arises from their laying down of rights. He then connects the laying down of rights to the second law

---

[60] Parkin, *Taming the Leviathan*, 57.

[61] Hobbes uses this text in his argument against Robert Bellarmine's case for the indirect temporal authority of the Pope (Hobbes 2002: 42.10). He also uses other biblical texts with the same force (e.g., Colossians 3:30, 3:22; 1 Peter 2:13–5, and Titus 3:1).

[62] Hawke, *Killing Is Murder, and No Murder*, 10, 11.

[63] Edward Hyde, *Transcendent and Multiplied Rebellion and Treason Discovered* (1645), 1.

of nature and maintains that all the laws of nature oblige. Ultimately, they are obligatory because of the irresistible power of God. Although obligation is grounded in a kind of power, that power can only be divine.

· · ·

Hobbes's views look particularly odd for several reasons. He was defending a religious and political view that had gone out of style at least two decades before *Leviathan* appeared. He tried to reconcile traditional Christian doctrine with the new science, which would dominate Enlightenment ideology before the seventeenth century ended. His own version of the new science was eccentric. His biblical understanding was more sophisticated than those of almost all of his critics. Given these elements, it is not surprising that his contemporaries largely misunderstood him on a number of basic issues. I illustrated this point by considering and disarming three of the most common and volatile charges made against him. We thus have good reason to look with suspicion at the caricature of Hobbes in Hobbism and take seriously the uniquely theological and indeed Christian character of Hobbes's thought, even if his particular brand of theology is thought, even by those in his own time, to be somewhat passé.

7

The Laws of Nature Are the Laws of God
in *Leviathan*

The most difficult issue to resolve with respect to the correct interpretation of Hobbes's view about the laws of nature in *Leviathan* is their relation, if any, to the commands of God. I think that Hobbes's considered view is that the laws of nature are genuine laws and impose obligations because they are commanded by God. Let's consider what Hobbes says about laws in general. All laws consist of two aspects (Hobbes 1651a: 26.2/137; references to *Leviathan* are to chapter and paragraph number, followed by the page number of a 1651 edition). The first and more salient component is the content of the law. Hobbes usually expresses the content of the laws of nature in the indicative mood, such as "You lay down your right to all things" and "You keep your covenants." Expressing laws in the indicative mood may seem odd because Hobbes thinks that laws are commands and commands are often expressed as imperatives; and he himself sometimes formulates laws as imperatives, such as, "Make peace." However, formulating laws in the indicative mood is not odd; many contemporary jurisdictions formulate laws in just this way. Here's a randomly selected law:

THEFT.
(a) A person commits an offense if he unlawfully appropriates property with intent to deprive the owner of property.
(b) Appropriation of property is unlawful if:
  (1) it is without the owner's effective consent;
  (2) the property is stolen and the actor appropriates the property knowing it was stolen by another; or
  (3) property in the custody of any law enforcement agency was explicitly represented by any law enforcement agent to the actor as being stolen and the actor appropriates the property believing it was stolen by another. (Texas Penal Code: Section 31.03)

Hobbes's Political Philosophy. A. P. Martinich, Oxford University Press. © Oxford University Press 2021.
DOI: 10.1093/oso/9780197531716.003.0008

Given the propensity to think of laws as commands, I think it is amazing that Hobbes so rarely slips into the imperative mood.

One place where he does use the imperative is in his explanation of the distinction between commands and counsels. He gives, "Do this," as an example of a sentence that may be a command or counsel, depending upon who said it and with what intention. If a person with authority said it to a subordinate and expects the subordinate not to have any reason for obeying other than that the authority wants it done, then "Do this" is a command. If the person does not have authority over the addressee and intends to direct the addressee to perform an action beneficial to the latter, then a primary desire is counsel.[1] My guess is that Hobbes chose the underdetermined sentence, "Do this," because he did not want his readers to form a judgment about whether the sample utterance was a command or counsel on the basis of its content. If Hobbes had chosen, "Do not take the belongings of other people without their permission," his readers may have thought, "This is a command," and if he had used, "Get an education," his readers may have thought "This is counsel." Yet, for Hobbes, each of these latter examples could be command or counsel. A more unfortunate aspect of his selection of "Do this"—and the same would hold if he had chosen either of the other two examples I suggested—is that he does not clearly enough communicate the idea that these utterances can be made explicit commands or counsels by prefixing them with a performative phrase, "I command" or "I counsel."

The upshot of this discussion is that a command, like other illocutionary acts, has two elements, a propositional content and a force, and that often the force is fully expressed only when an illocutionary act verb in performative form prefixes the content of the law. However, sometimes the words expressing the force should not be expressed. This is especially true when the laws of nature are to be proved using only a logic that applies to sentences in the indicative mood, as was the case in the seventeenth century. There was no logic of imperatives or performative utterances at that time. So, while "You lay down your right to all things" and "You keep your covenants" can be proved straightforwardly, "Make peace" cannot. In order to make it provable, it has to be paraphrased as, "You make peace." Here's a proof briefly

---

[1] Hobbes does not point out that, given his characterization of command and counsel, something can be both: Suppose there is a good God, a sovereign by nature, who wants to nudge human beings toward conduct that will benefit them, and so directs the laws of nature to human beings, which he expects them to understand through reason as his mode of promulgation. The omission does not surprise me. Hobbes was a fallible philosopher, as are we all.

stated: (1) You act to satisfy your desire to preserve yourself. (2) If you do not make peace, then you do not act to satisfy your desire to preserve yourself. Therefore, (3) You make peace.

Well, precisely what expression is supposed to express the force of the laws of nature? I think there are only two plausible possibilities: Either reason commands them or God commands them. In favor of the former is the fact that Hobbes sometimes says that reason commands. However, Hobbes should not think that reason has any *authority* over human beings; and it is easy to use synecdoche without realizing that the statement is not strictly true. Consider the slogan "Guns kill people." Since both John Deigh and I believe that Hobbes's explicit view of reason is that it is only instrumental by suggesting means to given ends, I will not discuss the possibility that reason commands the laws of nature further. That leaves the disjunct that God commands the laws of nature.

There are positive reasons for holding that God commands the laws of nature. Hobbes says they are. They are the "the undoubted word of God" because God speaks to human beings through reason. Hobbes knows that human psychology makes people prone to act on dangerous desires. So fear of death and hope for a comfortable life may not be sufficient to preserve them. Fear of the punishments of God, an invisible power, helps people obey them. The legal (forensic) character of the laws of nature make people more inclined to obey. Many scholars think that Hobbes's definition of religion as fear of invisible powers is part of Hobbes's surreptitious campaign against theism. That is highly implausible. Christians understood fear of God to be of the essence of their religion. The beginning of wisdom is fear of the Lord. After Adam and Eve sin, they are afraid of God. When God wants to make a covenant with the Israelites, they are afraid of him, and plead with Moses to intercede for them. Martin Fotherby, bishop of Salisbury, wrote:

> Religion itselfe is a kind of fear. Religion is nothing else, but the fear of some God: as the Creator himself hath expressly defined it. . . . Religion is an affection, which begetteth a care of worshipping a certain superior Nature, which is commonly called God. (Fotherby 1622: 122)

We may find religions of fear repulsive, but the seventeenth-century English did not. So it would be absurd for Hobbes to try to get people to understand that there is something wrong with Christianity specifically, and religion generally, by "writing between the lines."

A vivid example of divine fear is the Engagement Controversy. Thousands of the English balked at taking the Engagement for fear of violating the third law of nature: "You keep your covenants." In the state of nature, the fear of God inclines people to obey the laws of nature because God is "the revenger of their perfidy" (Hobbes 1651a: 14.31/70). God is doing his job only if he is taking revenge for violation of his laws. This is only to say that fear of God's power helps motivate people to obey the laws of nature, not that it is sufficient to get everyone always to follow them.

I believe that Deigh accepts at least the spirit of what I have said about the laws of nature with respect to how they can be proved. What he does not accept is that for Hobbes the laws of nature are commands of God (Deigh 2016a: 304–7). He, like most nonlaw theorists, quotes Hobbes's comment at the end of chapter 15: "These dictates of reason men use to call by name of laws, but improperly; for they are but conclusions or theorems concerning what conduceth to the conservation and defence of themselves" (Hobbes 1651a: 15.41/80). Deigh maintains that since Hobbes had been proving laws of nature for two chapters, he must mean that the laws of nature are identical with the dictates of reason. But if that were true, why didn't Hobbes say that? Why doesn't he use the phrase, "the laws of nature," one more time if his position is that the laws of nature as such are not laws? That would eliminate any idea that those "laws" were laws. One explanation is that he did not want to be saddled with the paradoxical sentence, "The laws of nature are not laws." Counting against this explanation is the fact that Hobbes embraced paradox (see Parkin 2016). A different explanation, one that has some force with me, is that, as great a stylist as he was, Hobbes sometimes phrased his points sloppily. But there is a better explanation. He shifts to a different locution, "dictates of reason," precisely because he wants to indicate what part of a law of nature is provable, namely, the propositional or action-guiding part, and what part makes it a command. Propositions when proved by reason and commanded by God are laws. Until the end of chapter 15, he could not discuss these propositions as commanded because he could not prove sentences of the form, "I, N.N., command that p." As theorems, the laws of nature have to be formulated without a performative prefix. In order to convey that the laws of nature are laws only insofar as they are commanded, as he intends to do in this context, Hobbes adopts the phrase, "dictates of reason." So now, having proved what he wanted to prove, he takes the next step and reports what makes them laws: "if we consider the same theorems as delivered in the word of God that by right commandeth all things, then they are properly called *laws*" (Hobbes 1651a: 15.41/80). This statement is not an "inconvenient aside" (Deigh 2016a: 309).

One might ask, "Why God?" I have already explained why it could not be reason. And there does not seem to be any alternative. Holding that God commands the laws of reason is, given the background assumptions of seventeenth century intellectuals, inference to the best explanation. When Anglo-American philosophers describe their methods, they often say that they are argument and analysis. If they think about Kierkegaard and Nietzsche, they may think of insight as another method. But one of the most powerful and pervasive methods is inference to the best explanation. God's command is a better explanation than anything else Hobbes had available.

Nonlaw interpreters think that when Hobbes says, "men use to call [the theorems] by the name of laws, but improperly," he is including himself in the "men." But if he were including himself, he is using an odd locution. When a person refers to a group indefinitely—that is, without a quantifier—and says something critical of it, the implication is that they do not include themselves in the group unless they go out of their way to include themselves. When I say, "Professors do not help students enough with their writing," I'm not talking about myself. I mean professors for the most part, not universally. So if Hobbes wanted to include himself among the people who use the name of laws improperly, he should have said so: "Men, including me, use to . . ." It would have been very odd for Hobbes to admit that he uses one of his technical terms improperly. If "laws of nature" was used by him improperly, one may wonder why he did not preface his proofs of those "laws" by saying something like this: "men use to call [the theorems I am about to prove] by the name of laws, but improperly. I will use the appropriate term 'dictates of reason,' and because they are deducible from the definition of 'law of nature,' I will also refer to them as theorems."

The apparent oddity of the passage, "men use to call," is removed if we take it in the most straightforward way, given that he says (1) that God is a sovereign by nature; (2) that reason is one of the ways by which "God declareth his laws" to human beings; and (3) that the laws of nature are found out by reason (Hobbes 1651a: 31.2/186; 31.3/187; and 14.3/64). It is no good to object that (1) and (2) are expressed long after, in chapter 31, for that chapter belongs as much to Part Two, "Of Commonwealth," as any of the earlier chapters; and its position at the end of Part Two is appropriate since it aids the transition to Part Three, "Of a Christian Commonwealth." Few Hobbes interpreters accept (1) and (2). But that is not pertinent. The pertinent point is that his formulation of his theory includes the laws of nature as laws.

In philosophy, of the making of many objections, there is no end. Deigh recently devised a new one that I consider ingenious. It consists of three components. The first is Hobbes's insistence that definitions are "the starting points of the reasoning, which is to say, the adding and subtracting of words, that yield the theorems of science" (Deigh 2016a: 309). The second is that the nonlaw interpretation "conforms . . . more closely" to Hobbes's method of science (Deigh 2016a: 306). The third is that, taking Hobbes's definition of "law of nature" strictly, one will see that it entails that laws of nature are not laws.

I accept the first component but not the second or third. Concerning the second, one problem is that Hobbes's practice does not always conform to his official method. He does not invariably deduce conclusions from definitions, although terms that have been defined may occur in the premises. It is fortunate that Hobbes would not invariably follow his explicit method, because much of his philosophy would then disappear. Also, whether he is conscious of his lapse or not, he does not follow his explicit method with respect to his assertion that God commands the laws of nature. Near the beginning of chapter 31, Hobbes says, "There wants onely, for the entire Knowledge of Civill duty, to know what are those Lawes of God" (Hobbes 1651a: 31.1/186). Hobbes knows that a political philosopher in the seventeenth century has to deal with the issue of the relation of God's laws to civil laws. Heck, we need to do that in the United States in the twenty-first century!

Also, I think that Deigh places too much weight on "assessing *Leviathan* as a work of philosophy" when it comes to "evaluating the competing interpretations" (Deigh 2016a: 305n29). For any given doctrine, almost any philosopher may have made a mistake, even a demonstrable one. Hobbes thought no one could be "so stupid as both to mistake in geometry and also to persist in it when another detects his error to him" (Hobbes 1651a: 5.16/21). Yet he was. I also do not agree with Deigh's claim that law interpreters are committed to the proposition that "the source of the obligation to which those [sovereign-making] contracts give rise is the third law of nature" and not "the contracts on which a commonwealth is founded" (Deigh 2016a: 305). I don't think law interpreters are so committed. The laws of nature and sovereign-making covenants are two different kinds of things. So nothing stands in the way of holding that obligation comes from different sources. The laws of nature bind simply because God is a natural sovereign with irresistible power who promulgates them through reason. Covenants bind when people mutually lay down some rights by their voluntary actions. To say that there are two sources for some object with the name N is not to say that N is ambiguous. For example, one source of wealth is inheritance and another is industriousness; one source of obligation is the laws of nature and another is covenanting. If "obligation" were ambiguous, then the sentence, "The laws of nature are a source of obligation and so is covenanting," would be semantically defective. But it is not.

Deigh's remark that Hobbes uses, not a categorical statement, but a hypothetical one to explain when the dictates of reason are laws—"if we consider the same theorems as delivered in the word of God that by right commandeth them, then are they properly called laws" (Deigh 2016a: 306; Hobbes 1651a: 15.51/80)—is also not probative. Even beside the fact that the logical form of scientific statements is hypothetical, I want to point out that all sorts of true philosophical propositions can be expressed as hypotheticals, such as "If we consider the proposition expressed by, 'Study mathematics,' as advice, then it is counsel."

I now turn to the second part of Deigh's argument that the laws of nature are not laws because "law" in "law of nature" does not mean *law*. He says,

> when a term consisting of two names joined together is defined, the definition preempts the use of the definition of either name whenever that name occurs as a component of the term. Likewise, it preempts the use of either name with some undefined meaning whenever the name occurs as a component of the term. The preemption is necessary to prevent the term from having two distinct extensions and thus being ambiguous. (Deigh 2016a: 310)

Deigh's description of Hobbes's view of definitions has to be too strong, for it has the consequence that "right" in "right of nature" does not mean *right*; "commonwealth" in "commonwealth by acquisition" does not mean *commonwealth*; and "laws" in "civil laws" would not mean *laws* because each of these technical terms are multi-name scientific ones (cf. Hobbes 1651a: 20.1/102; and 26.1/136). What is true is the weaker proposition that component "words" of a multi-name technical term may not have the same meaning that they have outside of that technical term (hereafter: "ordinary meaning"). With this proposition, Deigh could go on, as he does, to assert that it is plausible that "law" in "law of nature" does not have its ordinary meaning, just as "liberty" in "civil liberty" does not have its ordinary meaning. Deigh says:

> In chapter 21, for instance, he defines "liberty of subjects" after first defining "liberty." His definition of "liberty" is the absence of external impediments to motion. His definition of "liberty of subjects," is the absence of laws forbidding action. Hobbes, however, also observes that laws in themselves are not external impediments to action and hence that one speaks absurdly in holding that a law deprives one of liberty. "Liberty," therefore, when it occurs in "liberty of subjects," does not have the meaning with which Hobbes defines it. As Hobbes puts the point, in such occurrences it is not used with its proper sense. (Deigh 2016a: 310)

In other words, "law of nature" is a multi-name, technical term and should be understood as a unity as if it were a fused expression, "law-of-nature" (like "morning glory," which is sometimes written "morning-glory"), or as if it were spelled without intervening spaces ("lawofnature," like "butterfly"). Deigh alludes to Hobbes's statement that only natural liberty is "properly called liberty" (Hobbes 1651a: 21.4/108). So, Deigh infers, for Hobbes, civil liberty is not liberty.

In chapter 21, the division of liberty into natural and civil strongly suggests that each is a kind of liberty because each signifies the absence of a relevant kind of "Opposition" or "external impediment" (Hobbes 1651a: 21.1/107). That "liberty" in "civil liberty" is a genuine kind of liberty is suggested by Hobbes's claim that the "*Liberty* of *Subjects*" extends to "all kinds of actions, by the laws praetermitted" (Hobbes 1651a: 21.6/109). In the Latin *Leviathan*, Hobbes says, "a citizen is said to have liberty for those actions about which nothing is laid down in the laws, and these things alone" (Hobbes 1668: 105: "*Libertatem* habere Civis dicitur illas actiones de quibus in Legibus nihil definitur, & ad eas solas"). If civil liberty were not a kind of liberty, then Hobbes's saying that a citizen has "liberty" would be analogous to saying that a morning-glory is a glory or a butterfly is a fly. (It is also no good to argue that a citizen "is said" to be free but is not really free, just as calling a tail a leg does not mean that dogs have five legs, because Hobbes often uses "is said" when the way things are said is the way they are.)

The civil laws themselves are "Artificiall Chains," which subjects "have fastned [*sic*] at one end, to the lips of that Man, or Assembly, to whom they have given the Soveraigne Power; and at the other end to their own Ears"

(Hobbes 1651a: 21.5/108–9; cf. Hobbes 1668: 105). Of course, if one switches from the category of civil liberty to natural liberty ("corporall Liberty"), then subjects have "freedom from chains, and prison," and it is absurd for them to "clamor as they doe, for the Liberty they so manifestly enjoy" (Hobbes 1651a: 21.6/109). Hobbes then returns to the category of civil liberty and points out that it is equally absurd for subjects to complain about their artificial chains and "a Sword in the hands" of the Sovereign, for without those things, "all other men would be masters of their lives" (Hobbes 1651a: 21.6/109). In other words, they would be slaves, unfree persons.

I don't think Hobbes would accept the objection that artificial chains cannot be impediments because they are artificial, for if he did, then sovereigns, who are artificial persons, would not be persons; and it is crucial to Hobbes's theory of authorization to have artificial persons who can represent their subjects. Again it would be absurd for him to divide persons into natural and artificial, as he does (Hobbes 1651a: 16.2/80).

How then should Hobbes's claim that only "natural *liberty* . . . is properly called *liberty*" and his claim shortly later that "we take liberty in the proper sense, for corporal liberty" be taken (Hobbes 1651a: 21.4/108, and 21.6/109)? (In the Latin *Leviathan*, the second occurrence of "proper" is not translated.) "Proper" may mean applicable to only one thing. But it does not always have that narrow meaning. It can also mean more appropriate or strictly applicable to one thing than any other, as when someone says, "The proper part of the U.S. Constitution excludes its Preamble." My friend Jonathan has told me that my fedora is a proper hat, unlike my "gimme cap." (Caps are hats, as a person wearing a cap would quickly discover in a courtroom with a sign saying "No hats.") From "Natural liberty is proper liberty," one is not justified in inferring "Civil liberty is improper liberty," or "Civil liberty is nonproper liberty." Nonproper liberty could be "liberty" in a derivative or broader sense. Deigh should not put too much weight on the word "proper" because Hobbes did say that when the theorems of chapters 14 and 15 are delivered in the word of God, they are "properly called Lawes" (Hobbes 1651a: 15.41/80).

There are three positive reasons for holding that natural laws are laws. First, Hobbes divides laws into two kinds in chapter 26, one of which is natural law (Hobbes 1651a: 26.36/147-8). If natural laws were not laws, then it would be absurd for him to make this division, similar to dividing horses into two kinds, equine and saw. The second reason is the way Hobbes explicates his definition of "law of nature." He begins by saying that law is inconsistent with right, where right is liberty, Rights are contrasted with laws: "Law, and

Right, differ as much, as Obligation, and Liberty; which in one and the same matter are inconsistent" (Hobbes 1651a: 14.3/64). If a law of nature were not a law, then it would be pointless or misleading for Hobbes to use the concept of law and its contrary "liberty" to explain his definition. Hobbes is not using the words "law" in "law of nature" metaphorically or as part of a fused expression.

The third reason is Hobbes's idea, explained above, that a complete law consists of two parts, the action-guiding propositional part and the force-indicating part.[2] Most philosophers say that sentences with the main verb in the indicative mood are assertions; but there are reasons to think that view is wrong (Martinich 1984: 72–6). In any case, if Hobbes knew speech-act theory, he might have said that a sentence such as, "You do not drive faster than 20 mph in a school zone," is indeterminate with respect to its force since none is expressed.

As I said above, the propositional part of a law of nature can be proved by reason from the definition of "law of nature." But who is the authority or sovereign who commands these laws? Hobbes says it is God, who is sovereign in virtue of his irresistible power. And God promulgates the content of the laws through reason, which is "the undoubted word of God" (Hobbes 1651a: 32.2/195). Since no one in seventeenth-century England doubted that God commanded the laws of nature, Hobbes did not need to produce a proof.[3] Richard Cumberland complained that Hobbes did not prove that God commanded them and attempted to do so in the 400 substantial pages of De Legibus Naturae (1672). Though he labored mightily, I see nothing in that book that would count as a demonstration. Later, John Locke tried and failed to prove that the laws of nature were commanded by God; and he knew that he had failed. But he did not give up his belief that they were.

When Hobbes is talking only about the propositional part of a law, the part that can be proved by reason, he says that the laws of nature are not laws and sometimes signals this narrow reference by using the term "dictate of reason." Why should he use a different term unless he wanted to mark a difference? And when he says that the laws of nature are laws, he often makes clear who the authority is who makes the propositions laws: God.

---

[2] This two-fold structure is familiar from speech act theory. See Searle 1969 and Martinich 1984.
[3] My guess is that, given Hobbes's epistemological views, a person could never have more than empirical evidence for a belief that God commanded the laws of nature.

8

Leo Strauss's Olympian Interpretation

Right, Self-Preservation, and Law in *The Political
Philosophy of Thomas Hobbes*

Leo Strauss's early book, *The Political Philosophy of Thomas Hobbes* (Strauss
1936), remains important for at least three reasons. First, it is Strauss's most
complete and textually based treatment of Hobbes.[1] Since Strauss insisted
on close readings of texts, it is worth seeing how accurate his own reading
is.[2] Second, some accomplished scholars think that Strauss has proven some
of his central theses in it. Robert Kraynak writes, "As Strauss has shown,
Hobbes's whole system rests on the antithesis of vanity and fear"[3]; and, "as
Strauss has shown . . . Hobbes's whole political science rests on a prescientific
moral attitude"[4] Gregory Vlastos said that it

> ranks with the finest work on Hobbes produced in my lifetime. Its schol-
> arship is solid from beginning to end, daring and provocative, but never
> eccentric. . . . I trust that . . . this first, powerful and eminently sane contri-
> bution to the history of ideas . . . may win for it many readers both in and
> outside the ranks of true believers.[5]

Included in the books that Vlastos refers to are those by Gauthier (1969),
Peters (1956), Reik (1977), and Watkins (1973)—a distinguished set of
books. He wrote this in the same year that Gregory Kavka's (1986) *Hobbesian
Moral and Political Philosophy* and Jean Hampton's (1986) *Hobbes and the
Social Contract Tradition* were published. Allan Bloom (1974) said Strauss's
book was "well argued," "the one most reputed and uncontroversial in the

---

[1] Strauss had not yet developed his theory of reading between the lines when he wrote *The Political
Philosophy*. For a decisive refutation of that method, see Blau 2012.
[2] Stauffer (2007: 224) calls Strauss's treatment of Hobbes in *The Political Philosophy* "a rigorous
analysis." That is not quite the same thing as an accurate one.
[3] Kraynak, *History and Modernity in the Thought of Thomas Hobbes*, 106.
[4] Ibid., 197.
[5] Vlastos, Sunstein, and Gordis, "Further Lessons of Leo Strauss."

Hobbes's Political Philosophy. A. P. Martinich, Oxford University Press. © Oxford University Press 2021.
DOI: 10.1093/oso/9780197531716.003.0009

scholarly community," and its conclusions do not appear to be "outrageous."[6] One of the earliest reviewers, Michael Oakeshott praised the book:

> I must express at once my admiration for the book as a whole, for the careful scholarship which has gone to make it, for the great subtlety of its argument, and for the brilliance of his exposition. It has the rare quality of presenting an original thesis and supporting it with an apparently conclusive argument, and . . . its ingenuity is stimulating and never misleading.[7]

While it reportedly became Strauss's least favorite book, he did not indicate any reservations about what he said was the basis of Hobbes's philosophy in the preface added to the American edition of 1952.[8] However, he is not completely silent about its origin in "On the Basis of Hobbes's Political Philosophy," where he implied that Hobbes's political philosophy is based on his moral view and "not . . . his natural science," for which there is no need.[9] Third, the book remains the object of important discussions of Strauss's philosophy and has been described as "an excellent entryway into his thought"[10].

Strauss had two main goals for *Political Philosophy*, goals that are indicated in its subtitle: *Its Basis and Its Genesis*. Of these two goals, I will say a little about the genesis before moving onto my main topic. According to Strauss, Hobbes rejected the method of philosophy by the time he left Magdalen Hall. While he retained the traditional moral and political philosophy of the ancient world, especially that of Aristotle, he adopted history as his method for discovering the nature of human beings. The reason for the methodological switch was Hobbes's realization that the Aristotelian theory, especially as it had been modified in the sixteenth century, could not be "applied." My guess as to what Strauss meant by the inapplicability of the theory is that Hobbes discovered that given what Aristotelians said about human nature and reason, there was no way to get people to act in ways that would establish a healthy polity. Aristotle's theory fails because human passions move

---

[6] Bloom, "Leo Strauss: September 20, 1899–October 18, 1973," 383.

[7] Oakeshott, "Dr. Leo Strauss on Hobbes," 133; see also Devigne, *Recasting Conservatism: Oakeshott, Strauss, and the Response to Postmodernism*, 190–3.

[8] Bloom, "Leo Strauss: September 20, 1899–October 18, 1973," 383; see also Stauffer, "Reopening the Quarrel between the Ancients and the Moderns," 224, for references to Strauss. However, he did express some reservations about his interpretation of Hobbes's anthropology in Strauss, *Hobbes' politische Wissenschaft in ihrer Genesis*, 8.

[9] Strauss, *What Is Political Philosophy?*, 179; also 180; for more on Strauss's attitude about *The Political Philosophy*, see Heinrich Meier in Strauss, *Hobbes' Critique of Religion*, 8–9.

[10] Stauffer, "Reopening the Quarrel between the Ancients and the Moderns," 224b.

people to act, not reason. Hobbes, Strauss goes on, discovered this during his study of history. Strauss indicates that Hobbes's introduction and translation of Thucydides' *History of the Peloponnesian War* is decisive evidence for his hypothesis about the importance of history for Hobbes. Strauss was tempted to believe that there was more evidence for his view, namely the manuscript "Essayes," which later appeared in *Horae subsecivae*, especially the essay on Tacitus.[11] He did not discuss the *Essayes* in any detail because he could not prove that they were authored by Hobbes. For Hobbes, the way to get a polity established is to exploit the desire for self-preservation. All of this was discovered before 1628; and Strauss proposed that this origin of Hobbes's beliefs caused Hobbes to make them the basis of his moral philosophy.

In 1629, Hobbes supposedly discovered Euclid's geometrical method for the first time. In the 1630s, he met with Galileo and became committed to the resolutive-compositive method of the new science. Since the moral basis for Hobbes's philosophy had been discovered before the discovery of natural science, and since the resolutive-compositive method does not entail anything about the nature of human beings, Strauss concluded that that method contributed nothing to Hobbes's political philosophy. Moreover, the method of the new science actually obscured the historical and humanist foundation of Hobbes's theory; so at least in that way, it was pernicious.[12]

I now turn to the other goal of Strauss's book, the philosophical basis for Hobbes's political philosophy. My thesis, baldly stated, is that Strauss's view is fundamentally mistaken about the foundational concepts of Hobbes's political philosophy.[13] The easiest way to show this is to discuss three concepts that are central to Hobbes's political philosophy, concepts that Strauss thinks are interlocked: right, self-preservation, and law.[14] The first of these, right, is supposed to be the most important element. Its general importance for Strauss is evidenced by the title of what many consider his best book, *Natural Right and History*. So I will begin with Hobbes's conception of right and then take up self-preservation and law.[15]

---

[11] Strauss 1952: xii–xiii n1.

[12] Strauss, *What Is Political Philosophy?*, 179–81.

[13] Adrian Blau has appropriately pointed out that the standards of Hobbes scholarship were not high in the 1930s, and Strauss deserves credit for inspiring better work on Hobbes.

[14] Strauss thinks that a fourth element, vanity, is central to Hobbes's philosophy. For the purposes of presentation, I need only the three mentioned. Vanity will be discussed in connection with self-preservation.

[15] Blau thinks that Strauss's misreadings are not restricted to *The Political Philosophy of Thomas Hobbes*; and that Strauss is not a reliable interpreter (Blau 2012: 144–5).

1. Rights

In the Preface, Strauss makes a claim that will be important to him for the next forty years: modern natural law is grounded in natural right as "an absolutely justified subjective claim" or in rights as "subjective claims," which are "the justified claims (of the individual)."[16] Strauss's construal of Hobbesian rights as claim rights comes out clearly when he says that what the fear of death justifies is "a right, a claim." He then explains this idea in a footnote:

> The right is the minimum claim which as such is fundamentally just and the origin of any other just claim; more exactly, it is unconditionally just because it can be answered for in face of all men in all circumstances. A claim of this kind is only the claim to defend life and limb. (Strauss 1936: 155n2)

Setting aside for now precisely what sense "subjective" has, I want to show that Strauss is wrong to think that Hobbes's rights are normative.[17] While claim rights, not to mention other kinds which confer institutional powers, are normative, they have nothing to do with the foundations of Hobbes's philosophy. Normativity does not enter his philosophy before the introduction of the laws of nature, which comes after the discussion of the nature of rights in each of Hobbes's presentations of his political philosophy.[18]

Rights in the state of nature are liberty rights. They make no demands on other people and do not limit their liberty. They are liberty rights because they are not constrained by any law and hence are nonnormative. In the natural condition, rights do not give any human being any claim against anyone else. If a person destroys or eliminates someone's rights in what has been called the "primary state of nature,"[19] that person has not done anything unjust because that person's liberty rights are unlimited, except by one's own physical ability.[20] The other person has had her rights diminished, but that no

---

[16] Strauss, *The Political Philosophy of Thomas Hobbes*, viii and 156.

[17] In "On the Basis of Hobbes's Political Philosophy," Strauss reports Raymond Polin's view that Hobbes denied "all moral or juridical significance to the right of nature." (Strauss, *What Is Political Philosophy?*, 175). Relevant to the point, he says that "Hobbes has recourse to the state of nature in order to determine not only the status or manner of being of justice or natural right, but its content or meaning as well natural right as determined with a view to the condition of mere nature, is the root of all justice" (ibid, 190; also 191). The "right of nature [is] . . . a 'subjective' right" (ibid., 191).

[18] Part II, chapter 16 of *The Elements of Law, Natural and Politic*; chapter 2 of *De cive*; and chapter 14 of *Leviathan*.

[19] Martinich, *Two Gods of Leviathan*, 74–9.

[20] More precisely, one's liberty rights are limited by one's power.

more involves an injustice than does one's beating another person in a race. All have the right to win, and none of the losers is wronged. Terminating the liberty rights of others is not unjust. Injustice is acting as if one has a right when one does not have it. Injustice is not defined in terms of obligation. Obligations arise when a person lays down one or more of their rights. An action in the primary state of nature cannot and need not be justified because justification can occur only within a normative system.[21]

The absence of justice and injustice is not the absence of good and bad as Hobbes understands those concepts. One of the striking features of Hobbes's moral philosophy is that "good" and "bad" (or "evil") are not moral terms.[22] In The Elements of Law, Hobbes says that every "man, for his own part, calleth that which pleaseth, and is delightful to himself, GOOD; and that EVIL which depleaseth him."[23] In the diagram of sciences in Leviathan, ethics, the science of good and bad, is the study of the "consequences from passions of man" and separated from the science of unjust and unjust.[24] What is good is what is desired to happen. What is desired not to happen is bad. This is a wholly naturalistic analysis of good and bad. All chosen actions are good on Hobbes's account—they are at least good in the near—or short-term—because every such action proceeds from a desire; and what is desired is good. The action A of a person P_1 may be bad from the point of view of another person P_2 if P_2 desires that P_1 not do A.

Good and evil acquire a tincture of morality in the civil state. When subjects create their sovereign, they commit themselves to desiring the same things the sovereign desires for the sake of salus populi. Consequently, not to do what the sovereign requires breaks the third law of nature, "Keep your covenants."

Strauss's attempt to begin modern political philosophy with Hobbes's view about rights is misguided, I think, for two reasons. First, many

[21] Martinich, Two Gods of Leviathan, 74–9. Hobbes usually talks as if not fulfilling an obligation requires laws. However, technically a person can have a Hobbesian obligation without any laws at all, by gift. Gifting a right to do an action A has the consequence that if the gift-giver does A, then the gift-giver would be not fulfilling her obligation because she would be acting without right.

[22] In De cive, Hobbes uses "boni" and "mali" to denote good and bad human beings, respectively (De homine, in Hobbes 1972: 47; OL 1839b 2: 147; Hobbes, Philosophical Rudiments Concerning Society and Government, 100).

[23] Hobbes, The Elements of Law, Natural and Politic, 7.3.

[24] Hobbes, Leviathan, insert between p. 40 and 41; see also De homine, 11.4, in Hobbes 1972: 47. It is a vexed question whether Hobbes should have divided science into three parts, as indicated by his tripartite work, Elementa Philosophica, or into two parts, as indicated by the two-fold division in the diagram in Leviathan (see, for example, Sorell 1986, 24–8).

modern theorists ultimately cared more about liberty or freedom than they did about rights. Rights are taken seriously because they are instrumental for ensuring liberty or freedom. If freedom could not be ensured by rights but could be ensured by something else, say, the existence of conscience or the greater happiness of everyone, then they would have been. Other modern philosophers take the happiness of the greatest number of people as their goal; and talk about rights is considered nonsense. Second, Hobbes is a not a champion of either rights or freedom. Rights cause conflict. He thinks that only a few rights can be exempt from possible prohibition in a civil state. Even when rights are not explicitly transferred to the sovereign, the sovereign has the authority to quash them by using the principle that whoever has right to an end has a right to the means to that end.[25]

If freedom is more highly valued than rights, then the first modern would be someone who challenges an institution that restricts freedom. An obvious candidate, more obvious than the author of *The Prince* or the English apologist for property, is Martin Luther, because he successfully challenged the authority of the Roman Catholic Church. Of course, Luther did not want people to have unbridled personal freedom. Since the will is in bondage to sin, individual freedom has to be bridled by the Holy Spirit; and his criterion for being bridled by the Holy Spirit was in effect agreement with his views.

Catherine Zuckert gives the impression that Strauss later recognized the close connection between rights and liberty in Hobbes. Explicating Strauss's lecture, "Progress or Return?," she writes that Strauss saw that for Hobbes, " 'rights' were . . . seen to consist, fundamentally, in liberties."[26] It is not clear to me what her basis for saying this is. In the same paragraph, she quotes Strauss as saying that for moderns "freedom gradually takes the place of virtue" and that "Man has no nature to speak of," and then "He makes himself what he is."[27] But while freedom may be necessary to make oneself what one is, this does not justify attributing to Strauss the idea that Hobbes saw a close connection between freedom (or liberty) and rights.

---

[25] Hobbes, *Leviathan*, 18.8/90. References to *Leviathan* are to a 1651 edition with chapter and paragraph, followed by a slash and then the page number in a 1651 edition.

[26] Zuckert, "Strauss's Return to Premodern Thought," 98.

[27] Strauss. "Progress or Return," 244–5; quoted by Zuckert, "Strauss's Return to Premodern Thought," 98.

2. Self-Preservation

Let's now consider Strauss's interpretation of self-preservation in Hobbes's philosophy. For Strauss, it is closely connected with reason. His most direct and extended discussion of self-preservation occurs in his explication of Hobbes's claim, in the Dedication of *De cive*, that human nature can be summed up in "two most certain postulates."[28] The first postulate is natural appetite (*cupiditatis naturalis*); the second is natural reason (*rationis naturalis*). If a mathematician or philosopher sums up something in two postulates or principles in the right way, then those two principles are separate and do not mingle. One will not need or depend on the other. And there is every reason to think that Hobbes intends his two postulates to be separate. Just before asserting the two postulates, Hobbes explains how he came up with each of them. The postulate of natural appetite came from the fact that "from a community of goods there must needs arise contention, whose enjoyment should be the greatest."[29] Competition, not vain-glory, Hobbes indicates, is the origin of the postulate of natural appetite. Hobbes does not bring vanity into the account, and he does not need to.

The second postulate, natural reason, came from his realization that justice comes to exist when property comes to exist; and property comes to exist "not from nature, but consent."[30] The first postulate denotes something that is common to human and nonhuman animals, namely, competition for goods that cannot be shared. It also is the source of human misery. When "men . . . have an appetite to the same thing; which very often they can neither enjoy in common, nor yet divide it," they are at war.[31] What is important here is, again, that contrary to Strauss's interpretation Hobbes does not bring vanity into the account and does not need to.

As for the second postulate, it is supposed to solve the problem caused by the first postulate: "when I applied my thoughts to the investigation of natural justice, I was presently advertised from the very word *justice* (which signifies a steady will of giving every one his *own*), that my first enquiry was to be from whence it proceeded that any man should call anything rather his *own*, than *another man's*."[32] There is no obvious logical connection between natural

---

[28] Strauss, *Natural Right and History*, 8; and Hobbes 1972: Ep. Ded.; see also Cooper, "Reason and Desire after the Fall of Man."
[29] Hobbes, *Philosophical Rudiments*,1.6.
[30] Ibid., 92–3.
[31] Ibid., 1.6.
[32] Ibid., 92–3.

justice, property, and reason and there need not be, because Hobbes is reporting the psychological sequence of how he discovered the two postulates.
The postulates themselves are not to be proved; they are postulated. What is
clear from Hobbes description of the genesis of the two postulates and the
postulates themselves, natural appetite and reason, one principle of human
nature causes a problem; the other one can solve that problem.

Strauss interprets the two postulates very differently. When explaining the
first postulate, natural appetite, he claims that it is reducible to predation and
ultimately to vanity. While natural predation exists in the nonhuman animals, it alone is not sufficient according to Strauss to generate the war of all
against all. Lions, for example, kill other animals within the strict limits of
what satisfies their hunger. He says that Hobbes needs something else, another principle, in order to transmute the many natural appetites for finite
things, into one infinite appetite.

In order to establish his point, he introduces the concept of reason: "the
specific difference between man and all other animals is reason," because he
wants to say that man is "the most cunning, the strongest, and most dangerous animal"[33] and "Human appetite is . . . different from animal appetite . . . by the fact that in the case of man appetite has reason at its service."[34]
The cause of the "boundless desire" for unlimited power is that man comes to
know by reason that he cannot preserve his present power "and the means to
live well, without the acquisition of more," in particular, without an infinite
amount of power.[35] According to Strauss, Hobbes believes that all humans
want "absolute rule over the whole world."[36] Although Strauss sometimes
denies that Hobbes ultimately relies on reason to generate the infinite desire
for power, we have just seen that it is central to his explanation of the first
postulate.

Strauss's belief that Hobbes appeals to the second postulate of human nature is a mistake. As our paraphrase indicated, Hobbes does not draw on
reason for the first postulate at all. It would be wrong for him to do so because reason plays the central role in his discussion of the second postulate.
Natural predation alone can generate a war of all against all for lions and
other carnivores. If several hungry carnivores were placed in a small enclosed
space with only a half-pound of meat, a war of all against all would break out.

[33] Strauss, *The Political Philosophy of Hobbes*, 9.
[34] Ibid., 9.
[35] Ibid., 10, and quoting Hobbes.
[36] Strauss, *The Political Philosophy of Hobbes*, 10.

What is salient here is a moderate amount of population density and moderate scarcity, two elements that may be presupposed to exist in Hobbes's state of nature. One might object that this criticism is ineffective if Hobbes made a mistake when he was elaborating his view about the two postulates. What is needed, Strauss's defender may say, is a criticism of Strauss's reasoning employed in the process of interpreting. However, my criticism is not that Strauss presented a fallacious argument, but rather that his interpretation simultaneously does not fit Hobbes's text and needlessly attributes to Hobbes a confused and philosophically defective understanding of his own two postulates. Hobbes said he discovered two postulates and introduced each separately. And there is nothing in his text to justify introducing the second one in order for the first one to do its work.

It is no good to object that Strauss is reading between the lines, for two reasons. First, he had not yet adopted the tactics of reading between the lines when he wrote *The Political Philosophy*. Second, he held that those tactics were to be initiated only when the text itself involved some defect such as an inconsistency or a dangerous doctrine. But neither condition applies to this case. In particular, we shall see that even if all human beings were vain, Hobbes could have asserted this without danger.

Perhaps Strauss realized at some level the importance of keeping the first postulate free of reason. This would explain why he calls that supposed desire of human beings "the irrational striving after power." That is, reason breeds irrationality. Strauss may have been attracted to understanding Hobbes's philosophy as a Hegelian dialectic. He often uses Hegelian language to explain Hobbes's view. For example, he says that Hobbes's "turn to history is 'sublated' in Hobbes's later 'unhistorical,' 'rationalistic,' politics" and that the "significance of the antithesis between naturalistic and anthropological political philosophy . . . becomes fully apparent if one grasps that this antithesis is only the abstract form of a concrete antithesis in the interpretation of and judgement on human nature."[37] He appeals to Hegel's authority for his claim that Hobbes's moral view is "specifically bourgeois."[38] Aristocratic virtue and bourgeoisie virtue interact and give rise to a new virtue, which nonetheless retains the name "aristocratic." Strauss holds that Hobbes creates something new by taking the human fear of death and making it self-conscious: people become reflectively conscious that they fear death.[39]

[37] Ibid., 8.
[38] Strauss, *Hobbes's Critique of Religion*, 162.
[39] Strauss, *The Political Philosophy of Thomas Hobbes*, 127–8.

Sometimes the transmutation of a concept occurs within Hobbes's philosophy: "In the movement from the principle of honor to the principle of fear, Hobbes's political philosophy comes into being."[40] Strauss certainly enjoyed transmuting one concept into another, for example, natural appetite to vanity and, as we shall see, reason to self-preservation. Finite passion becomes infinite passion through the mediation of reason. Reason becomes irrational because it frustrates the desire of self-preservation, the desire it was supposed to satisfy. Reason, which the Western philosophical tradition had almost always treated as good, becomes bad. The dialectic can continue by detaching reason from vanity and transmuting it into to self-preservation to make reason good.

While Strauss's judgment that natural appetite plus reason produces irrational striving may be attractive as part of a Hegelian dialectic, it not true to Hobbes's text. The paradox is completely avoided by a straightforward interpretation of Hobbes's text. Another way that Strauss may be hiding his use of the second postulate in his explanation of the first is by describing the infinite desire as "spontaneous" and as arising "out of the depths of man himself." But spontaneity and the depths of human nature are not in Hobbes's text; and Strauss did not use them when he argued for his interpretation.[41]

Strauss wants Hobbes's natural appetite to be only one appetite because he wants it to be just one particular thing, vanity, rather than a variety of passions: "man's natural appetite . . . has its basis in the pleasure which man takes in the consideration of his own power, i.e., vanity."[42] "The origin of man's natural appetite is . . . not perception but vanity."[43] He does not even *try* to explain how there could be a desire for infinite power before anything is perceived, before there is any perception of one thing moving another. While Strauss wants to place all the blame for war on vanity, he cannot legitimately infer that that was Hobbes's theory as regards the first postulate. Hobbes always gave multiple causes for war in each of his political works. He presents at least three causes of war in the state of nature in his three great political works. In *The Elements of Law, Natural and Politic*, the first cause of war, as mentioned above, is that "some are vainly glorious" and others are "moderate, and look for no more but equality of nature."[44] The second cause of war

---

[40] Ibid., 128.

[41] Ibid., 11.

[42] Ibid.; see also Strauss, *Spinoza's Critique of Religion*, 89–90.

[43] Strauss, *Natural Right and History*, 11.

[44] Hobbes, *The Elements of Law, Natural and Politic*, 14.3; see also Strauss, *Spinoza's Critique of Religion*, 93.

is the tendency of people to act badly when they do not like something about other people; mixed in with this cause is the propensity of people to compare each other's worth and think that they are the best.[45] The third cause is that "many men's appetites carry them to one and the same end; which end sometimes can neither be enjoyed in common, nor divided."[46] In *De cive*, they are: (1) "vain-glory"; (2) "the need [of a man who practices equality in nature] to defend his property and liberty against the other;" (3) the desire to want something that other people want "at the same time"; and possibly, (4) the desire for others to "form a high opinions of oneself."[47] I am not sure whether (1) and (4) are separate causes or not. In any case, (2) and (3) do not depend on vanity, and (3) is "the most frequent cause" of war. Independently of this issue, Hobbes introduces the issue of conflict in the state of nature by saying that men come into conflict in the state of nature "but not for the same reason"[48] In *Leviathan*, the causes of war are competition, distrust of others, and the desire to seek fame (*ad famam spectat*) and the love of glory, not specifically vain-glory or vanity.[49] So it is not true that according to Hobbes only vanity was in Pandora's box.

When Strauss indicates that "in the three presentations of his [Hobbes's] political philosophy," vanity is the only cause of war, Hobbes supposedly identifies vanity with "man's very nature."[50] Strauss thinks that Hobbes made this clear in *Leviathan* when he wrote that "*Pride* and other passions" cause human beings to need government.[51] Strauss simply ignores the phrase "other passions" and has pride, interpreted as vanity, do all the work. Strauss says that Hobbes decided to not "explicitly . . . take as his departure the reduction of man's natural appetite to vanity."[52] Again, the text gives the lie to this interpretation. Hobbes explicitly does not take universal vanity as his departure in any of his political works. In *Elements of Law*, only *some* men suffer from vanity; others are moderate. In *De cive*, everyone is at war, but for different reasons. One man, "according to that natural equality which is among us, permits as much to others as he assumes to himself; which is an argument of a temperate man, and one that rightly values his power."[53] But "the most

[45] Hobbes, *The Elements of Law, Natural and Politic*, 14.4.
[46] Ibid., 14.5.
[47] Hobbes, *On the Citizen*, 26; see also Hobbes, *De cive*, 114; see also Hobbes, *Leviathan*, chapter 13.
[48] Hobbes, *On the Citizen*, 26.
[49] Hobbes, *Leviathan*, chapter 13.
[50] Strauss, *The Political Philosophy of Thomas Hobbes*, 12.
[51] Ibid., 13.
[52] Strauss, *Natural Right and History*, 12.
[53] Hobbes, *On the Citizen*, 1.4.

frequent cause why men want to hurt each other arises when many want the same thing at the same time, without being able to enjoy it in common or to divide it."[54] In *Leviathan*, as I said, the third cause of war is the love of glory and the desire to seek fame.[55] Not all glory is vanity. Glory proceeds from "the imagination or conception of our *own power* above the power of him that contendeth with us."[56] Someone who does not agree with one's estimate of one's own power refers to it as pride. The difference between glory and pride, Hobbes suggests, is merely one of attitude. False glory is the kind of glory that "depends on one's trust in the opinion of others . . . whereby one may think well of himself, and yet be deceived."[57] Vain-glory in a person is built on "the flattery of others or only supposed by himself for delight in the consequences of it." It is characteristic of "young men," and, like dejection of mind, does not move a person to action.[58] So in his explicit treatment of vain-glory, it is not dangerous to others.

Strauss claims that in *Leviathan*, "Hobbes could not make up his mind to treat the view which is in reality conclusive for him, that man's natural appetite is vanity, unequivocally as the basis of his political philosophy," because if he had said that, then people would know that he believed that "man is by nature evil."[59] This is supposedly why Hobbes "in the final pre-sentation [of human nature] puts vanity at the end."[60] He was trying to hide vanity. Just so.

Since the vanity of some people is presented as the first cause of war in *Elements of Law* and *De cive*, it is odd that Strauss thinks that Hobbes felt he needed hide vanity in his third treatment. Even if he wanted to hide vanity, it would not be because a belief in human evil was inflammatory. If Hobbes had had any worries about what seventeenth-century Christians would think, he could have said that he was taking the actual fallen condition of human beings as his starting point, since all men are sinful. Moreover, in the guise of a Calvinist, a view shared during the Commonwealth by Presbyterians and Independents alike, he could have said that human beings were totally

---

[54] Ibid., 1.7.

[55] Hobbes, *Leviathan*, 26–7, 61–2; Hobbes *Latin Leviathan* in *Leviathan*, ed. Malcolm, 193.

[56] Hobbes, *The Elements of Law, Natural and Politic*, 9.1.

[57] Ibid.

[58] Hobbes *Leviathan*, 27, 49.

[59] Strauss, *The Political Philosophy of Thomas Hobbes*, 13.

[60] Ibid. Later, Strauss implies that a person who kills someone in the state of nature is a murderer" (Strauss, *The Political Philosophy of Thomas Hobbes*, 17).

corrupted by the original sin.[61] As for the likelihood that it was part of Hobbes's philosophy that human nature was sinful, he explicitly denied it for good reasons, one of which is this: "the afflictions of the mind, which arise only from the lower parts of the soul, are not wicked in themselves."[62] Strauss was well aware of Hobbes's denial; so he had to explain it away. His explanation depends on quoting part of the relevant text. But he omits quoting the part that undermines his interpretation:

> Some object that this principle [that except they be restrained through fear of some coercive power, every man will distrust and dread each other] being admitted, it would needs follow, not only that all men were wicked . . . but also wicked by nature, which cannot be granted without impiety. But this, that men are evil by nature, follows not from this principle. For though the wicked were fewer than the righteous, yet because we cannot distinguish them, there is a necessity of suspecting, heeding, anticipating, subjugating, self-defending, every incident to the most honest and fairest conditioned. Much less does it follow, that those who are wicked, are so by nature. For though from nature, that is, from their first birth, as they are merely sensible creatures, they have this disposition, [to] . . . do whatsoever is best pleasing to them; . . . yet are they not for this reason to be accounted wicked. For the affections of the mind, which arise only from the lower parts of the soul, are not wicked themselves; but the actions thence proceeding may be so sometimes, as when they are either offensive or against duty. (Hobbes 1972: 99–100)[63]

---

[61] For the sake of argument, I am assuming here that Hobbes's view of human beings originated from history or empirically. In fact, I think that the issue of the historical fall of human beings is irrelevant to Hobbes's scientific presentation of human beings.

[62] Hobbes, *Philosophical Rudiments*, "Preface"; Strauss, *What Is Political Philosophy?*, 175.

[63] Objectum porro a nonnullis est, quod, admisso hoc principio, continuo sequatur homines omnes non modo malos, quod forte, etsi durum, concedendum tamen est; cum id clare dictum videatur in Scripturis sacris; sed etiam, quod concede sine impietate non potest, natura malos esse. Illud vero, homines natura malos esse, ex hoc principio non sequitur. Nam etsi pauciores essent mali quam boni, quoniam tamen bonos a malis internoscere non possumus, necessitatis diffidendi, cavendi, anticipandi, subjugandi, quoquo modo se defendendi, incumbit perpetuo etiam bonis et modestis Minus vero sequitur eos ipsos, qui mali sunt, ita factos esse a natura. Quamquam . . . a natura, hoc est, ab ipsa nativitate, ex eo quod nascantur, *animalia* hoc habeant, ut statim omnia quae sibi placent, cupiant faciuntque quantum possunt, ut quae impendent mala, aut metu fugiant, aut ira repellant, non tamen ob eam causam mala censeri solent: nam affectus animi qui a natura *animali* proficiscuntur, mali non sunt ipsi, sed actionaes inde provientes . . . confitendum est, posse homines a natura cupitatem, metum, iram, caeteros affectus habere *animales, ut tamen mali facti a natura non sint.* (Hobbes 1972: "Preface," LW 147; cf. Strauss 1936, 13–4)

Hobbes gives here two reasons why he is not committed to the sinfulness of human nature. First, he does not need the strong premise that all people are sinful and therefore dangerous; he needs only the two modest and plausible premises that some people are dangerous and that we can't always know which ones they are. Second, human nature would not be sinful even if every human being was actually vain because passions are not sins; only actions are. Hobbes says this in the Author's Preface to the Reader of *De cive* (100). It is particularly odd to make vain-glory the appetite that causes human problems, for vain-glory is not a strong motivator those who suffer from it: "Vain-glorious men . . . are enclined to rash engaging; and in the approach of danger, or difficulty, to retire if they can; because not seeing the way of safety, they will rather hazard their honour, which may be salved with an excuse; than their lives, for which no salve is sufficient."[64] Vain-glory is the cowardly lion of passions.

I have just now been discussing vanity in explaining why Hobbes does not believe that human nature is evil. But, as Strauss correctly points out, in this context Hobbes "does not mention vanity at all."[65] Strauss is again not reading between the lines. He is looking at the black ink of the text and saying that Hobbes does not say what one should expect him to say if Strauss's interpretation is correct. How then does he justify his interpretation that Hobbes puts everything on vanity? His evidence is the absence of evidence: "Natural vanity disappears in the *caeteros affectus*. It must vanish into them, it must be hidden by them, if man's natural innocence is to be asserted."[66] Although it is not clear to me whether Strauss is alluding to the position of vanity in Hobbes's treatments of passions in chapter 6 of *Leviathan* or in his treatment of the state of nature in chapter 13, it does not matter which is the case. If it is the former treatment, then Strauss is mistaken about Hobbes's purpose in analyzing so many passions. He wants to show that his metaphysics of motion is able to explain the most varied and complex of human phenomena. Vanity or vain-glory is not hidden. In addition to being discussed as others are, "Vain-glory" is noted in the margin. Hobbes had no reason to hide it because vanity is all too commonly observed. If, instead, Strauss is alluding to its treatment in

[64] Hobbes, *Leviathan*, 49.
[65] Strauss, *The Political Philosophy of Thomas Hobbes*, 14.
[66] Ibid.

chapter 13, vanity is not hiding. Vain-glory is a variant of glory; and glory is mentioned.

Almost any other explanation would be more plausible than Strauss's. We recently saw that Hobbes relies on various causes to explain war in the state of nature; and when he does mention vanity, he claims and needs to claim only that some people are vain. Some or many men may be vain all the time; but it is not part of human nature.[67]

Let's now focus more narrowly on Strauss's discussion of the second postulate of human nature. Strauss says that reason is "reduced" by Hobbes to the desire for self-preservation.[68] In this case, a non-passion supposedly becomes a passion. My guess is that Strauss wanted to convert Hobbes's second principle, reason, into a passion because he thinks a thick conception of reason is characteristic of ancient thought. A thin conception of reason is characteristic of modern thought because, according to Strauss, modern political philosophy valorizes will. For Hobbes, the last passion or desire before action is will. So, since vanity is a passion, Strauss has confirmed his view that Hobbes's philosophy is basically a philosophy of will if by "reason" Hobbes means the desire for self-preservation. For Strauss, the deep reality of the dichotomy of appetite and reason is the dichotomy of the passion of vanity and the passion for self-preservation.

Strauss moralizes both vanity and self-preservation.[69] He claims the two postulates are "not the naturalistic antithesis of morally indifferent animal appetite (or of morally indifferent human striving after power), on the one hand, and morally indifferent striving after self-preservation, on the other, but the moral and humanist antithesis of fundamentally unjust vanity and fundamentally just fear of violent death."[70] If Strauss's interpretation were right, then Hobbes would be a less impressive philosopher than he is generally credited as being, for part of the genius of his system is that he generates moral and political normative entities, laws and obligation, from nonnormative ones, appetites and reason.

I do not doubt that one can selectively harvest parts of Hobbes's philosophy and end up with the philosophy Strauss attributes to Hobbes. But what one would have is not Hobbes's philosophy but Strobbes's.

---

[67] Hobbes, *The Elements of Law, Natural and Politic*, 14.3; and *Philosophical Rudiments*, 1.4.
[68] Strauss, *Natural Right and History*, 15.
[69] Strauss, *The Political Philosophy of Thomas Hobbes*, 14–5.
[70] Ibid., 27.

3. Law

Let's now focus on the last of the three concepts, law. Let's suppose with Strauss that medieval natural law theories make law independent of the human will.[71] Hobbes's natural law theory is the same. For Hobbes, the natural laws are independent of the will also. They are discovered by reason, not invented or created. They are eternal and unchanging. They always bind *in foro interno* no matter what an individual person should want or "wills" with respect to when they bind *in foro externo*.

If the laws of nature are in fact the commands of God, as Hobbes sometimes says, then there is an even stronger sense in which the laws of nature do not depend on human will.[72] Strauss, along with a majority of scholars, may find my claim wholly unconvincing. According to Strauss, "The law of nature or the moral law as Hobbes conceives of it is not by itself . . . a law properly speaking."[73] Typically, supporters of this position quote the following passage as if it were an explicit statement of that view:

> These dictates of reason men use to call by the name of laws, but improperly; for they are but conclusions or theorems concerning what conduceth to the conservation and defence of themselves; whereas law, properly, is the word of him that by right hath command over others.[74]

In reply, I'll make only three points. First, dictates of reason are not strictly identical with laws because counsels may be dictates of reason too.[75] Second, laws have to be commanded by someone with authority; so considered in abstraction from the command, the propositional contents are not laws; and, as theorems of reason, they are not laws. But from this, it does not follow that they are not laws simpliciter. Hobbes says that these dictates are "the undoubted word of God,"[76] and that one of the ways that God speaks to humans is through reason.[77] Hobbes's use of the phrase "dictates of reason" makes clear that he is talking about the propositional content, independently

---

[71] Ibid., viii.

[72] Hobbes, *Leviathan*, 30.

[73] Strauss, *What Is Political Philosophy?*, 193.

[74] Hobbes, *Leviathan*, 15.41.

[75] Hobbes *Leviathan*, 25.1–16, 131–6.

[76] The phrase "undoubted word of God" and similar phrases referring to the same thing were not unusual from 1600-1650. But they always referred to the Bible.

[77] Hobbes, *Leviathan*, 32.2/195; 31.3/187, and 36.5–6/224.

of the force that it has as a law. If Strauss is right about the laws of nature, then Hobbes contradicted himself several times over. If I am right, he is saying what he ought to say. While Hobbes did contradict himself on several occasions, his contradictions should not be multiplied unnecessarily. It is no good to say that Hobbes was speaking metaphorically when he called the dictates of reason "laws," for then he would be violating one of his basic principles of science: "metaphors and tropes of speech" can never be "true grounds of ratiocination."[78]

Even if my reply is not accepted, there are other reasons for holding that it would not be important if the laws of nature are not genuine laws. The science of the laws of nature is the "true moral philosophy."[79] Since these so-called laws are independent of human will—they are deduced by reason—Hobbes's morality is not based on will. Strauss presumably would accept my premises but deny my conclusion, because he conceded that the sovereign "does not . . . determine the content of the moral law. . . . [T]he moral law essentially precedes the sovereign: the obligation to obey the sovereign is a natural law obligation."[80] As I understand Strauss's comments on these latter quotations, he thinks that Hobbes's doctrine is contradictory and that we need to choose which one is closest to his intentions. Because Strauss thinks that Hobbes is a modern and therefore someone who privileges will, he thinks that "the demand of civil obedience necessarily takes precedence" over objectivity, that is, that the sovereign's will trumps everything else.[81] I don't see this. And I find his paradoxical comment that "by trying to give reasons for unqualified submission to authority Hobbes makes impossible unqualified submission to authority" at best mystifying. There is definitely a problem with Hobbes's philosophy here: the inalienable right of self-preservation can and does sometimes conflict with the commands of the sovereign.[82] I believe he should have simply admitted this fact. No sovereignty is so absolute that a subject never has a right to disobey a command. But this is a problem with absolute sovereignty. Proponents of limited sovereignty freely acknowledge that the individual and the sovereign may sometimes come into conflict.

It is not accurate to say that the civil laws begin with a human being, if this is taken in the sense of a natural human being. Laws are commands of an

---

[78] Ibid., 25, 131–6.
[79] Ibid., 15.40.
[80] Strauss, *What Is Political Philosophy?*, 193–4.
[81] Ibid., 194.
[82] See Sreedhar 2013 for a discussion.

artificial person. The sovereign is not identical with any human being or set of human beings. When it is said that Elizabeth Tudor or Charles Stuart was the sovereign, "was" has the sense of constitution. The female Elizabeth and male Charles constituted the sovereign, just as gold constituted the ring of Gyges and bronze the shield of Achilles. So law as law is not to be identified with any natural human being's natural will. The law is causally dependent on human beings, in that no sovereign can will anything unless at least one human being wills something. But it is a misleading oversimplification to say that civil law depends on the will of a human being.

What I have said so far is consistent with a sense of "law" in which the laws of nature depend on human nature. The laws of nature have the content that they do because of the way human beings are. It would be absurd for there to be laws applying to human beings at the most basic level if they were not connected in the right way with human nature. Think about why "Every human being has to master every theorem of mathematics before the age of five," and "Every human being has to kill every other human being as soon after it is born as possible" cannot be laws of nature.

How does what I am saying fit with the claim of many scholars that Hobbes is a voluntarist (or a legal positivist)? The answer depends on the interpretation of voluntarism. If a voluntarist is any philosopher who believes that law is command, Hobbes is one. But such voluntarists can consistently hold that genuine natural law is not arbitrary. Hobbes sometimes says that God commands the laws of nature. But that voluntaristic element is not the whole story about natural law as the original law. The command of law is not the content of the law; and the content is proved by reason, "the undoubted word of God," as mentioned above.[83]

What God says in virtue of reason is constrained by what reason yields. Reason cannot yield contradictions. They are the opposite of reason, namely, absurdity and irrationality. Reason cannot even yield contingent truths such as that monarchy is better than democracy or perhaps that democracy is better than monarchy, because reason always expresses what is necessary and the negation of a necessary truth is a contradiction. But the negation of a contingent truth is not a contradiction but another contingent proposition.

The laws of nature speak through reason in this way: Starting from the natural desire of self-preservation, reason calculates how self-preservation is necessarily achieved. Will only comes into Hobbes's story when he gives his

---

[83] Hobbes, *Leviathan*, 32.2; see also 31.3.

theory of action. Every act is caused by some desire; a will or a willing is the last desire before the action occurs. An act of will is part of the causal chain that ends in an action (that is not a passion). Will itself does not determine the content of a human being's desires. The desire has a certain content: to live, to feed, to have shelter, to be not too hot and not too cold. But neither the desire nor the will determines the content in the relevant sense in which to determine something is to cause it. The connection between a desire and its content is a logical relationship. Most desires do not have self-preservation as their content because self-preservation is the dominant desire that requires many other desires as means to that end. The desire for self-preservation does not, however, attach immediately to many actions or even attach at all to some, such as eating, drinking, or injecting known harmful substances.

Strauss might object that there is a significant difference between ancient and modern natural law, because Hobbes's laws of nature are not genuine laws.[84] But that is beside the point. Strauss wanted to show that the foundation of law for Hobbes was subjective and based on will; and the laws of nature are neither. If one objects that I have not gone back far enough or deeply enough to identify the foundation of law or that the laws of nature are deduced from self-preservation, my reply may begin by pointing out that the laws of nature in fact are deduced from the definition of "law of nature," of which self-preservation is a part, and not self-preservation itself. A stronger reply may be that if self-preservation is the foundation of law, then the foundation of baptism or (the sacrament of) penance is sin, and the foundation of the American Revolution was tyranny.

For Hobbes, civil law cannot contradict natural law, and the content of natural law is proved by reason, and a fortiori consistent with reason. Of course, no one has the right to judge that a putative command of the sovereign is in fact inconsistent with the laws of nature. The logic of sovereignty prohibits citizens from interfering with the sovereign's job of governance. Here is a paradox in Hobbes's theory: a sovereign's putative command may not be a law in fact; but no citizen has the right to act on the belief that it is not.

4. Conclusion

Strauss was wrong to think (i) that for Hobbes rights in the state of nature are claim rights; (ii) that the two postulates of human nature are vanity and

[84] Strauss, *What is Political Philosophy?*, 193.

self-preservation; (iii) that reason is reducible to self-preservation; (iv) that vanity is the only cause of war in the state of nature; and (v) that laws for Hobbes are fundamentally subjective and grounded in will.[85]

Why did Strauss go so far wrong in his interpretation? My guess is that such big mistakes are the result of his desire to confirm a big theory, the theory that modern political philosophy is significantly different in specific ways from the theory and practice of ancient political philosophy. Although he did not have the grand theory of *Natural Right and History* completely worked out in 1936, the last chapter of *The Political Philosophy of Thomas Hobbes* sketches a general theory of history, in which Hobbes, the representative of modern philosophers, is contrasted with Plato and Aristotle, the representatives of classical philosophy. I think that Strauss's desire to get Hobbes's philosophy to fit his general theory caused him to misunderstand that philosophy.

An alternative way for me to put the point is that Strauss's interpretation of Hobbes and other political philosophers is Olympian. Seeing philosophical texts from a great height, he thought he saw a large pattern; but the pattern required adjusting some details in order to fit and taking little or no account of others. The god on high has favorites and enemies, and makes judgments about them accordingly.[86]

---

[85] Among the important, correct, and relatively novel claims that Strauss makes are that the "fundamental distinction of bodies is that into bodies natural and bodies politic" (1959, 175). This implication is that Hobbes never should have made *De homine* separate from *De corpore*. Second, Hobbes's emphasis on self-preservation and a thin conception of reason greatly contrasts with the assumptions of classical philosophy.

[86] I want to thank Devin Stauffer for discussing my views about Strauss's interpretation of Hobbes at an early stage; Kody Cooper and Eva Odzuck for their helpful comments; and Adrian Blau, whose comments were invaluable.

9

Hobbes on Sovereignty by Acquisition in *Leviathan*

1. Introduction

In *Leviathan*, Hobbes gives the impression that his treatment of sovereignty by acquisition will show that it is in all essentials the same as sovereignty by institution. In his explicit treatment of sovereignty by acquisition, he says that it "differeth from sovereignty by institution only in this, that men who choose their sovereign do it for fear of one another and not of him whom they institute; but in this case, they subject themselves to him they are afraid of" (20.2/102).[1] What is essential is that those who choose their sovereign "do it for fear" (20.2/102). He underlines the similarity by saying "the rights and consequences of [sovereignty by acquisition] . . . are the very same with those of a sovereign by institution, and for the same reasons" (20.14/104; see also 20.3/102). Each kind of sovereign is the same because "the sovereign is absolute over both [kinds of subjects] or else there is no sovereignty at all" (20.14/105). A consequence of the same authority being in both kinds of sovereign is that subjects are no freer in one kind of government, whether it be democracy, aristocracy, or monarchy, than they are in another (21.8/110).

The neatness of this account is disrupted by the actual words that Hobbes uses when he describes the process of sovereign acquisition. More precisely, he seems to say that the conquering sovereign becomes a covenanting party in sovereignty by acquisition. In other words, his account of sovereignty by acquisition in *Leviathan* seems to be inconsistent, as this set of propositions indicates:

1. Sovereignty by institution and sovereignty by acquisition differ in only a minor way, namely, with regard to the cause of the fear, that moves the prospective subjects to covenant.

---

[1] References to *Leviathan* are to chapter and paragraph number, followed by the page number of a 1651 edition. Spelling and punctuation are modernized.

Hobbes's Political Philosophy. A. P. Martinich, Oxford University Press. © Oxford University Press 2021.
DOI: 10.1093/oso/9780197531716.003.0010

2. In sovereignty by institution, the sovereign cannot be a party to the covenant.

3. In sovereign by acquisition, the sovereign is a party to the covenant.

The evidence for (1) has already been given. He commits himself to (2) by his reasoning that a sovereign by institution cannot be a party to the covenant because it does not exist prior to the covenanting but is the product of it (18.4/89). Most of the passages supporting (3) are in chapter 20 and in the "Review and Conclusion"; they will be discussed below. The main goal of this chapter is to explain how the passages that support (3) can be interpreted as consistent with (1) and (2), and why such an interpretation makes Hobbes's position philosophically more attractive than saddling him with a contradiction.

I begin by giving an account of sovereignty by acquisition that is consistent with what he says about sovereignty by institution.

2. Sovereignty by Acquisition

Hobbes defines sovereignty by acquisition as follows:

> A commonwealth *by acquisition* is that where the sovereign power is acquired by force; and it is acquired by force when men singly, or many together by plurality of voices, for fear of death or bonds, do authorize all the actions of that man or assembly that hath their lives and liberty in his power. (20.1/101–2)

Before discussing the paradigmatic cases of sovereignty by acquisition, I want to say something about the fact that he treats parental authority and despotism as instances of sovereignty—unwisely, I think (20.14/104). Parents have authority or control over children who are incapable of making a covenant due to immaturity; so even if we assume that parents have "absolute authority" over their children, it cannot be political authority (16.10/82). And parental authority cannot be grounded in genetics, since adults who take charge of foundlings have the same authority as biological parents. As for children old enough to covenant, the first child or two cannot create a commonwealth because they are too few (cf. 16.4/102 and 20.5–6/103). My conjecture is that Hobbes's desire for a comprehensive theory construed parental authority as a kind of sovereignty because other theorists did, such as patriarchal theorists, similarly for despotism.

Even if despotism is a form of sovereignty, his treatment of it in terms of dominion was a mistake. Dominion was originally an absolute property right that did not arise from contract or consent. A *dominus* had absolute control of a household (*domus*), which included women, children, and slaves who lacked legal standing. If it is essential to a theory of sovereignty, it is in competition with social contract and consent theory. If despots rule in virtue of dominion, they are not sovereigns (20.4/102). As a political concept, dominion misdescribes the political relationship among sovereigns and their subjects, or is at best a metaphor.

A final defense of Hobbes's position may be that "despotism" is a kind of sovereignty as stipulated by his definitions. But in that case, what he says is trivial and does not describe political reality. I do not want to beg the question against Hobbes. He thinks that his theory can account for the authority of despots. But even if I concede this for the sake of argument, despotism is not more closely attached to sovereignty by acquisition than it is to sovereignty by institution. An instituted sovereign can become a despot by treating his subjects harshly; and an acquiring one can cease being a despot by treating his subjects well.

I will now discuss proper sovereignty by acquisition. It typically arises after a war between two commonwealths, in which one is victorious and the other one destroyed. While occasionally a conqueror will kill every member of the defeated people or the vanquished will commit suicide, usually some or even most of the members of the destroyed commonwealth survive. The survivors have one live option according to Hobbes, namely, to take the conquering sovereign as their new sovereign. However, he actually describes two options, A and B. In A, the conquering sovereign adds the conquered survivors to his commonwealth. In B, the conquering sovereign requires the survivors to create a different sovereign to rule them, and hence a different commonwealth.

In option A, the conquering sovereign allows the survivors to become subjects of his commonwealth[2] by directing them to incorporate themselves

---

[2] A technical qualification. In the case of a democracy, the survivors covenant to make the assembly of all subjects their sovereign.

into his commonwealth. This occurs through a covenant made among both the survivors and the existing subjects of the conquering sovereign. All of them together authorize the conqueror to be the sovereign of them all. The covenanting may be thought of as a "renewal" of the original covenant of the conquering sovereign or an expansion of the covenanting population. Since the ordinary maturation of children in commonwealths requires them to covenant when they come of age, Hobbes's theory would have fit the facts of political life more clearly if he had said that covenanting was a recurring process. This position would also have strengthened the idea that covenants are directed at the future.

Hobbes could have explained sovereignty by acquisition in a way that would have made the essential similarity of them to covenants by *institution* clear. The survivors of a war could simply become additional members of the covenanting population of the conqueror. Since both the sovereign's original subjects and the additional survivors authorize the same one person to be their sovereign, they all become equal members of the same commonwealth. That is Hobbes's point in this passage:

> [F]or a man that is monarch of divers nations, whereof he hath in one the sovereignty by institution of the people assembled, and in another by conquest, that is, by the submission of each particular to avoid death or bonds, to demand of one nation more than of the other, from the title of conquest, as being a conquered nation, is an act of ignorance of the rights of sovereignty. (20.14/104)

The covenant that the existing subjects of the conquering sovereign make with the survivors is consistent with their original sovereign-making covenant because, in making it, they are obeying the command of their sovereign to covenant with the survivors (14.28/69). In his discussion of the Old and New Covenants of the Bible, Hobbes says that the covenant originally involving God and Abraham is later "renewed" with his son Isaac and still later with others, and finally renewed with the disciples of Jesus (e.g., 35.4/216–7, 40.5/250, and 40.14/256). Nothing about this option of sovereignty by acquisition precludes it from being an act of renewal like the biblical covenants just alluded to.

The fact that most of the subjects of the conquering sovereign usually will not be in the presence of the survivors is no obstacle to the covenanting. Either the sovereign will be present, possibly as commander-in-chief, and will represent the absent members; or the sovereign's representative will be present, and so, by the transitivity of representation, will represent those subjects.[3]

If the conquering sovereign is a monarchy, then the person constituting the monarch remains the same.[4] If the conquering sovereign is an aristocracy, then the persons constituting the aristocracy may remain the same or change in number as the conquering sovereign chooses (19.23/101). If the conquering sovereign is a democracy, the persons constituting the sovereign increase by the number of survivors. This first way of handling survivors of a conquest is straightforward. The second option for sovereignty by acquisition that Hobbes describes is not.

My account of option B will explain a view that Hobbes could have expressed clearly. In this option, the conquering sovereign directs the survivors to create a *new* sovereign *who is constituted by the conquering sovereign*. That is, the new sovereign consists of the conquering sovereign, who is an artificial person (17.13–4/88). The new sovereign is unusual in that the person who constitutes this artificial person is himself an artificial person. But the important point is that the new sovereign of the survivors is not identical with the conquering sovereign. The structure of this new sovereign of the survivors may seem to be counterintuitive. Yet it is important at least insofar as it illuminates this obscure passage:

> Whereas heretofore . . . the Roman people governed the land of Judea . . . yet was not Judea therefore a democracy, because . . . they [the Judean survivors] were governed by one person, which though as to the people of Rome was an assembly of the people, or democracy; yet as to the people of Judea, . . . was a monarch. (19.13/99)

---

[3] Hobbes never says that when persons create the sovereign, they become artificial persons themselves. But they do. When a natural person covenants and thereby creates a sovereign, that person also creates a subject. Subjects are relative to a sovereign and the creature of sovereign-making. This fact about the creation of artificial or institutional persons holds generally. When the natural person Sophocles created the artificial person of Oedipus for *Oedipus Tyrannus*, Sophocles became the artificial person of a dramatist. And when a particular natural person, say, Alvin Actor, plays the character Oedipus, he becomes the artificial person of Oedipus and an actor. Most commentators approve of Hobbes's position in *De homine*, according to which Agamemnon is the agent of the action and the person playing Agamemnon is the actor. But Hobbes leaves out the relationship of the dramatist to Agamemnon and the actor.

[4] This person is usually a natural person; but we will see that an artificial person can be the person constituting the monarch.

Hobbes's position in the above passage may be illustrated by describing a series of historical or quasi-historical events that have the same logic as Hobbes's Rome-and-Judea one. I begin with a case in which the conquering sovereign is a monarchy. Cyrus is a natural person, and that natural person constitutes the King of Persia. The title, "King Cyrus of Persia," like all other such designations, denotes ambiguously. Speakers sometimes use it to refer to the natural person Cyrus and sometimes to the artificial person of the king (who is constituted by Cyrus). Sometimes it refers to both, as in the sentence, "As King Cyrus of Persia ate his breakfast, he commanded his troops to attack the Babylonians." The natural person Cyrus was eating breakfast at the same time as the artificial person of the king was commanding his troops.

When Persia conquered Babylon, the King of Persia (the conquering sovereign) directed the surviving Babylonians to take a new sovereign to replace their old one. Let's call the new sovereign the "King of the Survivors of Babylon." This sovereign was constituted by the King of Persia, who of course is an artificial person. Although both Persia and the Kingdom of Babylonian Survivors are monarchies, they are constituted by different monarchs. The natural person Cyrus constitutes the person of the king of Persia; and the artificial person, the king of Persia, constitutes the artificial person of the King of the Survivors of Babylon. Several figures picture the situation:

In Figure 9.1, the curly brackets around the trunk of a person signify an artificial person. It turns out, as Hobbes indicates in the quotation above, that the new sovereign of the survivors of a conquest will always be a monarch under option B (19.10/98).

The person who constitutes the sovereign of Persia	The sovereign (monarch) of the conquering commonwealth	The sovereign of the survivors of Babylon

Cyrus, a natural person	The King of Persia, an artificial person	The king of the survivors of Babylon, an artificial person, consisting of the King of Persia

Figure 9.1 A natural person who constitutes the artificial person of a monarch, which constitutes the artificial person of a monarch of newly conquered individuals.

1	2	3
The natural persons constituting the conquering aristocracy	the aristocratic sovereign of the conquering commonwealth	the monarchic sovereign of the conquered survivors
$P_1, P_2, ..., P_i$	$\{P_1, P_2, ..., P_i\}$	$\{\{P_1, P_2, ..., P_i\}\}$

Figure 9.2 Natural persons constituting the artificial person of an aristocracy, which constitutes the monarch of newly conquered individuals.

3. Artificial Persons as Persons Constituting a Sovereign

We have just seen how a conquering monarch directs survivors to create a new monarch, with himself as the artificial person who constitutes the new sovereign. I will explain why conquering aristocracies and democracies also have monarchs as their new sovereigns. When the conquering sovereign is an aristocracy, the single artificial person is the aristocracy itself; and the persons who constitute the aristocracy are individual aristocrats. When the conquering aristocracy directs the survivors to make their sovereign to be the sovereign constituted by the aristocracy, that new sovereign is a monarch because the aristocracy is one (artificial) person. The aristocrats themselves are not identical with the sovereign of the survivors. Hobbes's view may be clearer if it is put abstractly (see Figure 9.2). Let the persons of the conquering commonwealth be persons $P_1, P_2, ..., P_n$ (not shown in Figure 9.2); let the natural persons constituting the conquering aristocracy be $P_1, P_2, ..., P_i$ (column 1); let the artificial person of the aristocracy be $\{P_1, P_2, ..., P_i\}$ (column 2); and let the sovereign who is the monarch of the conquered survivors be $\{\{P_1, P_2, ..., P_i\}\}$ (column 3):[5]

The new sovereign of the survivors is a monarch, $\{\{P_1, P_2, ..., P_i\}\}$. The conquering sovereign is an aristocracy, $\{P_1, P_2, ..., P_i\}$; and it consists of individual aristocrats, $P_1, P_2, ..., P_i$.

I would not have gone through all of this if it were not necessary to explain what Hobbes said in the difficult quotation above about the Romans and the Judeans. Hobbes takes Rome to be a democracy because it was supposedly ruled by the people of Rome (*Populus Romanus*). In Figure 9.3, column 1 represents the individual citizens of Rome; and column 2 the sovereign of Rome, the artificial person constituted by the members of 1. When Rome

[5] I am assuming that individual aristocrats are also subjects of the aristocracy. If one objects to this assumption, the specification of the subjects of the commonwealth changes to $P_j, P_k, ... P_n$.

1	2	3
The individual citizens of Rome	The sovereign of Rome	The sovereign of the surviving Judeans
$P_1, P_2, ..., P_n$	$\{P_1, P_2, ..., P_n\}$	$\{\{P_1, P_2, ..., P_n\}\}$

Figure 9.3 The natural persons, who constitute the Roman republic, which constitutes the monarch of the newly conquered Judeans.

conquered Judea, it directed the Judeans to make (the artificial person of) the people of Rome to constitute their new sovereign, represented by column 3:

Since Rome is a democracy, the sovereign of Rome is the artificial person constituted by the natural persons who are Romans. That artificial person is one person, indicated by the brackets of $\{P_1, P_2, \ldots P_n\}$. And since that conquering sovereign directs the surviving Judeans to make their new sovereign to consist of the conquering sovereign, namely, the people of Rome, the new sovereign of the Judeans is an artificial person itself consisting of an artificial person. In the quotation above about the Judeans, there are four sets of ellipses. They mark the places where Hobbes misstates the reason why the Judean survivors have a monarch for a sovereign.[6] Here is the quotation again with previously omitted text restored and in boldface:

> whereas heretofore the Roman people governed the land of Judea, **for example, by a president;** yet was not Judea therefore a democracy, because **they were not governed by any assembly into which any of them had right to enter, nor by an aristocracy, because they were not governed by any assembly into which any man could enter by their election;** but they were governed by one person, which though as to the people of Rome was an assembly of the people, or democracy; yet as to the people of Judea, **which had no right at all of participating in the government** was a monarch. (19.3/99)

The reason that Hobbes gives for denying that Judea could be democracy, namely, that the people of Judea "had no right of participating in the government," is misleading or false. In no other place in *Leviathan* does Hobbes say that the form of a commonwealth depends on whether any particular subject

---

[6] Rather than in chapter 20, Hobbes gives this example in chapter 19, which is about the three kinds of commonwealth.

or group of subjects are possible constituting persons of the sovereign. Nor would it fit his theory if he had said this. The fact that no commoner can be a person constituting a monarch (because they do not have royal blood) is not what makes a commonwealth a monarchy; it is the fact that the person constituting the sovereign is only one person. The same should be said about aristocracies and having noble blood mutatis mutandis. The relevant fact about an aristocracy is that the persons constituting it are more than one and fewer than all of the subjects.

Hobbes does not make explicit that "the people of Rome" denotes one artificial person. But it is has to be one (artificial) person because the persons of sovereigns always are unitary.

Hobbes wrote as if there were no other possible outcomes of a conquest with respect to a new sovereign (20.2/102; see also Hobbes 1650a: 20). But there were and are. Here is an intuitive and historically based one: The natural person Edward Longshanks constituted the artificial person King Edward I of England. In the late thirteenth century, he conquered Wales. In doing so, Edward Longshanks became or constituted the king or prince of Wales in addition to constituting the king of England. The king of England and the prince of Wales were similar, but different. Two deep differences between the two sovereigns are that they had different subjects at the same time and that the two groups of subjects had different laws. A deep similarity is that the same natural person constituted each sovereign. That the king of England on formal occasions wore different robes than the king of Wales is not a superficial fact. It helped the subjects know which sovereign was acting. The example of Edward Longshanks is a case of conquest, in which one natural person who is a king of one state becomes a king of another state: one natural person, two distinct artificial persons.

4. Sovereignty by Substitution

Another historical example similar in some ways to the one discussed in the preceding paragraph is different in others. The natural person, James Stewart (aka Stuart), constituted the artificial person of the sovereign of Scotland from infancy until his death in 1625. He constituted also the artificial person of the sovereign of England from 1603 until his death (19.23/101). The desire of the natural person James to constitute one artificial person of a United Kingdom of England and Scotland failed because neither the Scots nor the

English liked the idea. This example shows that the same natural person can come to constitute an additional sovereign without the conquest of a commonwealth and without the institution of a new commonwealth. The natural person James succeeded the natural person Elizabeth Tudor as the artificial person of the monarch of England, who never dies by law.

The examples of Edward Longshanks and James Stuart have been explained in terms of conquests and sovereign-making covenants. Hobbes should have recognized a third and possibly a fourth type of origin. In the third type of sovereignty, the sovereign of the survivors is neither the conqueror nor the other survivors. There are some historical or nearly historical examples that illustrate what I mean. The first is a slightly altered history of William of Orange's defeat of King James II of England in the Glorious Revolution of 1688. In this world, William does not become king of England—he is too concerned with politics on the continent—but directs the surviving English to make Mary Hyde (née Stuart) their sovereign. (It is not germane to my altered history that Mary was actually William's wife and King James II's daughter.) The English consequently covenant to make Mary their sovereign because they fear William, not Mary and not each other. That is, the survivors covenant among themselves to make their sovereign a person that the conqueror instructed them to choose. Call this "sovereignty by substitution."

One might object that his scenario is either a case of sovereignty by institution or sovereignty by acquisition. Since it cannot be sovereignty by acquisition, because Mary did not conquer them, it must be sovereignty by institution. I have two replies. The first is the more important one. The objection presupposes that sovereignty by institution and by acquisition are the only two kinds of sovereignty; and I am challenging that presupposition. The second reply reiterates the process of creating the new sovereign of the English survivors. They fear William because he conquered them; but they do not make him their sovereign. And they do not fear each other. So their action must be a different kind of sovereign origin.[7] What about Mary? She is not an object of fear because the survivors know that she is committed to

[7] The English in the scenario do not fear each other; they fear their conqueror; and one reason they do not fear each other is that an insufficient time has elapsed for them to resume their fear of each other. People have to observe the bad behavior of human beings without government and then to reason about that bad behavior, the possible way to defeat that behavior, and then to get others to agree to make a sovereign. Hobbes's account of the original condition of human beings is a construction that is not true to the empirical facts. It has illustrative value as a rational reconstruction, but not as a universal condition, as he sometimes admits. In the Glorious Revolution scenario, because Mary becomes sovereign hard on the heels of William's victory, neither sovereignty by institution nor sovereignty by acquisition describes it.

English political traditions, is familiar with governance, has a good disposition, and, last but not least, is a Protestant.

It is easy to think of or imagine other examples of sovereignty by substitution, for example, in stories or variations on those stories in the Old Testament, one of Hobbes's main sources for historical examples. To avoid unnecessary multiplication of kinds of sovereignty, I will not require that a conqueror dictates who the substituted sovereign will be. A sovereign by substitution is a person who becomes the sovereign of persons who lose their preceding sovereign whether by force, by choice, or by other adverse circumstances; and that sovereign is not an object of fear. Here are four examples: Around 1030 BCE, the Israelites, who had God as their sovereign, chose to change their sovereign and select Saul to be their sovereign king. In short, they substituted Saul for God. This is not a case of sovereignty by institution, because they already had a sovereign, nor by acquisition, because Saul did not conquer them. The biblical account indicates that the substitution goes smoothly. While God did not choose Saul to be king initially, he came to approve it (1 Samuel 9:15-6). Hobbes incorrectly describes this example in chapter 20 as if it were a case of sovereignty by acquisition. One might say that Hobbes wanted monarchy to be unappealing because of England's recent troubles with Charles I. But in other places in *Leviathan*, he says he prefers monarchy over any other form of government (19.4/95-6). So it is unclear why he treats this as sovereignty by acquisition.

The second example derives Assyria's conquest of the northern kingdom of Israel in 722/721 BCE. Some of the survivors fled to Judah where they became incorporated into that kingdom.[8] The third example occurs supposedly in the sixth century BCE. The pharaoh of Egypt, who deposed the king of Judah, directed the survivors to make the brother of the deposed king their new king (2 Chronicles 36:1-4). Finally, in a variation of an earlier example, King Cyrus of Persia (Isaiah 45:1)[9] conquered Babylon. Among Babylon's subjects were Judahites. Cyrus directed the surviving Judahites to make Nehemiah their sovereign, under the title "governor" (2 Chronicles 36).[10]

---

[8] Adrian Blau points out that on my account, "any case where someone moves country—even temporarily, but definitely permanently—is also sovereignty by substitution."

[9] I am describing a possible world that is close to the world of 2 Chronicles 36.

[10] There is another kind of case in which an artificial person becomes the person constituting another artificial person. Trying to explain how God can be both the god of the entire world and also the special god of Israel, Hobbes compares the situation to a commander in chief who has authority over many commanders and is also one of those commanders (12.22/57-8; see also chapter 4 in this volume). I want to change his example somewhat for my purposes in this chapter. Suppose that, by tradition, the general of the Army of Northern Virginia was also the highest general, the commander-in-chief of the Confederacy. Then the artificial person of the commander-in-chief of

Oddly, Hobbes does not mention a fairly frequent way that a new sovereign arises: palace coups. For example, Claudius in effect murdered Caligula and consequently became the emperor of Rome. It is not idiomatic to say that Claudius conquered Rome; and maybe Claudius did not conqueror Rome in Hobbes's technical sense, because the Romans never had a chance to fear Claudius. The Romans simply accepted Claudius. I suppose Hobbes might have said that upon the death of Caligula, the Romans feared Claudius (although they did not know it) and implicitly covenanted among themselves to make Claudius their sovereign. But this is not plausible, and this kind of case will lead me to distinguish ways that sovereignty arises that Hobbes did not countenance in his theory in section 6.

5. On a Sovereign's Retaining All Rights

No matter how many kinds of sovereignty there are in addition to sovereignty by institution, they are all consistent with the essential elements of sovereignty by institution in chapter 17 of *Leviathan*: natural and artificial persons, authorization, representation, and covenant. In addition, they are all consistent with Hobbes's claim that the sovereign does not covenant either with his prospective subjects or with anyone else. One reason this is important is that if he were a covenanting party, then he would have to give up some right to someone. That is part of Hobbes's concept of covenant.[11] But if the sovereign gave up any right, then it would not be "as great as possibly men can be imagined to make it" (20.18/106).

Laying down a right, no matter how trivial it appears, may be disastrous for the sovereign. The Foole of chapter 15 thinks that the probability of his being discovered to have violated a covenant is inconsequentially small. But probabilities are not relevant to Hobbes's project of a scientific politic that deduces only necessary propositions. The tactic of calculating the probability of a contingent event is not part of Hobbes's science. For him, the Foole is not acting rationally because it is possible that his violation of a covenant will be revealed. One never knows how a secret will out. This cautionary

---

the Confederacy would have as its constituting person the general of the Army of Norther Virginia, who is itself an artificial person. The person constituting the general of the Northern Army of Virginia was the natural person Robert E. Lee.

[11] In the ancient Near East, some covenants were unilateral. But that is not relevant here.

tale was told to Roman Catholic children in the 1950s in order to emphasize the absolute privacy of the confessional. A priest was lecturing seminarians on this very point when he said, "I would never reveal the name of the very first person whose confession I heard. That person confessed to killing his or her father." At the next moment, a person walked into the room and said, "You don't remember me, Father, but I was the first person whose confession you heard." Although this example does not involve laying down a right, it shows how an unlikely trivial action can cause a disastrous result. In particular, the action of laying down an apparently trivial right can have a disastrous result. Consider a slightly revised description of the story of King Eglon of Moab and the Israelite Ehud. Suppose that a salient right of the king was that no subject had the right to be alone with him. After conquering Israel, the Israelite Ehud comes before Eglon and pays tribute. Eglon is so pleased with the tribute that he agrees to Ehud's request to meet with Eglon alone in his chamber in order to give him secret information. Eglon's decision to lay down his right not to be alone with Ehud seems safe enough. The king's well-trained guards would be just outside the door and Ehud ostensibly would not have a weapon on him. Unfortunately for Eglon, during the private meeting, Ehud pulled a sword from under his clothes and plunged it deep into the king's belly (Judges 3:12–3). This example shows how dangerous it is for a sovereign to give up any right. Consequently, if a conquering sovereign had to give up any right, as Hobbes seems to suggest, his reign would be slightly more vulnerable than otherwise. The assassination of Ehud illustrates that fact that no matter how trivial a right may seem, specifying that a sovereign by acquisition needs to give up some right to the survivors is not justified by Hobbes's criterion for sovereignty—that the sovereign's power be as great as imaginable (20.18/106–7).

6. Passages about Sovereignty by Acquisition that Are Apparently Inconsistent with Sovereignty by Institution

My view about what Hobbes could and should have said about sovereignty by acquisition is consistent with chapter 20, even those passages that appear at first sight to say that a conqueror is a party to covenants with survivors. Here is an example:

Dominion [is] . . . acquired to the victor when the vanquished, to avoid the present stroke of death, covenanteth either in express words or by other sufficient signs of the will that so long as his life and the liberty of his body is allowed him, the victor shall have the use thereof at his pleasure. (20.10 / 104; see also 17.13/87; and 18.8/90–1)

This passage neither says nor entails anything about a sovereign covenanting or laying down any rights. In particular, the clause, "so long as his [the survivor's] life and the liberty of his body is allowed him [by the victor], the victor shall have the use thereof at his pleasure," does not. The time referred to by "so long" is important to both the survivors and the conqueror in different ways: the survivors keep their life and the sovereign can use their bodies. While Hobbes does not mention it in chapter 20, a sovereign by institution has the same right to use the bodies of his subjects as a sovereign by acquisition does. Both kinds of sovereign have the right to use the bodies of their subjects whether they are the survivors of a conquest or subjects of the conquerors. The limit of a sovereign's use of their subjects' bodies is their self-destruction:

No one is bound by the words themselves [of a sovereign-making covenant] either to kill himself or any other man; and consequently, . . . the obligation a man may sometimes have, upon the command of the sovereign, to execute any dangerous . . . office, dependeth not on the words of our submission. (21.15/112)

Hobbes does not mention the possibility of conflict between a subject's "liberty of his body" and the sovereign's use of it "at his pleasure." That is simply a flaw in his treatment of sovereignty by acquisition. The phrase, "the victor shall have the use [of the survivor's body] at his pleasure," is also consistent with sovereignty by institution, in which a party gives up his right of "governing himself," thereby putting the subject's body under the sway of the sovereign's decisions.

Someone may object that it is necessary to distinguish between a sovereign's having the right to a subject's body insofar as the sovereign believes that the subject's body is necessary for the defense of the subjects, and the right to "the use [of the survivor's body] . . . at his pleasure." I concede this. But it is a distinction without a practical difference, since subjects do not have the right to judge whether the sovereign is using their bodies for their proper purposes or simply at his pleasure. The difference is analogous to the difference between the rights people have in the state of nature and their right of nature.

A different objection is that the "dominion" passage does not fit my interpretation of sovereignty by acquisition because the subjects of the conquering sovereign are not mentioned or alluded to. My reply is that the presence of those original subjects is implied since the conquering sovereign (or someone it authorizes) *represents* those subjects. I am not asserting that Hobbes had my interpretation in mind when he wrote about sovereignty by acquisition, only that he could have and should have.

A stronger bit of evidence against my position that, for Hobbes, a sovereign by acquisition should not be a party to a covenant occurs in this passage:

> *Seeing sovereignty by institution is by covenant of every one to every one, and*
> *sovereignty by acquisition by covenants of the vanquished to the victor* [my
> italics] *or child to the parent;* it is manifest that every subject has liberty
> in all those things the right whereof cannot by covenant be transferred . . .
> (21.11/111)

The phrases, "of every one to every one" and "of the vanquished to the victor," are parallel, as they should be. However, their content is dismayingly different. The latter phrase says or suggests that the sovereign is a party to the covenant, something that Hobbes should not mean. By parity of grammatical form, "to the victor" in the latter phrase indicates that the vanquished (the survivors) are covenanting with the victor (the conqueror). But if this is what Hobbes meant, he has made the sovereign vulnerable to violating his part of the covenant and thereby being open to criticism from the other covenanters, who may consider themselves freed of their obligations. If this interpretation is correct, then the way he goes on next is odd. He says that "a child [may covenant] to the parent" (21.11/111). On the one hand, if a child is young, it is unable to covenant. And on the other hand, if the child is old enough to covenant, and the parent is a party to that covenant, then they are in the state of nature in which each is afraid of the other. This is a case of sovereignty by institution. It is not a case of conquest because the child did not vanquish the parental sovereign. Rather, the parent's "authority" over the child has lapsed, and some new arrangement has to be agreed to. But, if only one or two parents are involved and one child, they cannot create a commonwealth, because three

persons are too few to constitute a commonwealth. To end this line of reasoning quickly, Hobbes's theory cannot handle the actual situation of children becoming competent according to the laws of nature and sovereignty.
Hobbes could have handled this situation with other resources that he has.
He could have said that the child of age authorizes the parent to represent
her to keep her safe, and she gives up certain rights to help the parent do
this. This would not be a political arrangement; but that is as it should be,
since families are not commonwealths.

This way of handling the child-to-parent relationship suggests an alternative way of interpreting the phrase, 'by covenants of the vanquished to the
victor,' namely, that the victorious subjects covenant with the vanquished
through the person of their sovereign, who represents them. The presence
of the victor at a covenanting ceremony should not be taken to involve the
person of the sovereign as a party to the covenant. The victor represents those
who had much earlier authorized him to represent them. My interpretation
of the child-to-parent covenant and the vanquished-to-the-victor covenant
requires some pulling and tugging on the text. But it results in a consistent
theory of sovereignty.

The final difficult passage about sovereignty by conquest occurs in the
"The Review and Conclusion":

> Conquest . . . is the Acquiring of the Right of Sovereignty by Victory.
> Which Right is acquired by the people's Submission, by which they contract
> with the Victor, promising Obedience, for Life and Liberty. ("Review and
> Conclusion," 7/391)

What Hobbes should be taken to mean is similar to the meaning
I recommended for passages above. The conquering sovereign acquires the
right to govern the survivors and to be obeyed by them because they submit
themselves in the same way as the sovereign's original subjects submitted
themselves, namely, by covenanting to make it their sovereign.

7. Conclusion

Only one significant problem with Hobbes's account of sovereignty by acquisition has been the topic of this chapter. There are others. For example, even
if one accepts that the sovereign by acquisition is not a party to a covenant

with the survivors, it is not certain that the survivors covenant with anyone. Consider this brief passage:

> the point of time, wherein a man becomes subject to a Conquerour, is that point, wherein having liberty to submit to him, he consenteth, either by expresse words, or by other sufficient sign, to be his Subject. ("Review and Conclusion," 6/390)

The passage says that a survivor *submits* to the conqueror and *consents* to be his subject. But neither submitting nor consenting requires a covenant. To submit to an authority is simply to yield or accept it. Each conquered person can submit unilaterally. If the authority accepts the submission, the act is successful but no covenant or contract is involved. Consenting in itself does not create an irrevocable obligation. Recent institutional policies in the United States that allow either party to withdraw consent to sexual relations shows that consent is revocable, unlike a sovereign-making covenant. If consent seems to create obligation, it is because something more accompanies the consent, something not articulated. If a landowner consents to allow a neighbor to cross his land for some purpose, the landowner retains the right to withdraw the consent at will, unless some social or contractual norm applies, such as the neighbor's incurring some expense because she was acting on the consent. But then we are no longer talking about consent.

The set of inconsistent propositions listed early in this chapter is resolved by replacing (3) with this:

> In sovereign by acquisition, the conqueror represents his conquering subjects in a sovereign-making covenant among them and the survivors of the conquest.[12]

[12] My thanks to Adrian Blau, Leslie Martinich, and Shane Wagoner for comments on earlier drafts.

10

Natural Sovereignty and Omnipotence in Hobbes's *Leviathan**

The relationship between omnipotence and natural sovereignty is discussed in chapter 31 of *Leviathan*, "Of God's Natural Kingdom," the last chapter of Part Two, "Of the Commonwealth." That is an appropriate place for it because the natural kingdom of God belongs in the philosophical part of *Leviathan* precisely because it is natural. Also, God's natural sovereignty is relevant to the matter of the laws of nature being his commands, known by reason, as he sometimes says they are.[1] In addition to these timeless reasons, there was at least one time-bound reason for discussing the issue. A standard under-standing of the authority of kings, or of any absolute human monarch, was modeled on divine sovereignty. The sovereign's properties represented or resembled God's properties. While it was possible to question whether any monarch was an absolute sovereign or ought to be one, it was not practi-cally possible to question that God was an absolute sovereign. God's abso-lute sovereignty is asserted as a matter of course in books of the 1630s and 1640s.[2] The properties of the sovereign God could be used to figure out the

* I want to thank Laurens van Apeldoorn, Robin Douglass, Jake Galgon, Leslie Martinich, Johan Olsthoorn, two anonymous readers for Oxford University Press, and the participants at the European Hobbes Society Meeting, April 8, 2015, King's College, London, for their comments on earlier versions of this chapter. In this chapter, *Leviathan* is referred to as L, followed by the appropriate chapter and the page number in Hobbes 2012. *Questions Concerning Liberty, Necessity, and Chance* is referred to as QLNC, followed by the page in the edition of 1656. References to *De cive* are referred to as DCv, followed by the chapter and section number.

[1] L, 15, p. 242. On the issue of the laws of nature being commands, see chapter 6, "The Laws of Nature are the Laws of God in *Leviathan*," and John Deigh, "Reply to Martinich," European Hobbes Society, http://www.europeanhobbessociety.org/newpublications/debate-martinich-deigh-on-law-2-deigh/, accessed June 16, 2017.

[2] Another reason to discuss God's natural sovereignty is to fill out Hobbes's position that subjects have no right to rebel. In a sovereign-making covenant, subjects transfer their right of governing themselves to the civil sovereign. They might have an excuse to disobey if they could argue that God desires disobedience. But they cannot argue that way if God is a natural sovereign and if a law of na-ture, in particular, the law that enjoins keeping one's covenants, is a genuine law. See L, 31, p. 570; see also L, 43, pp. 928–9 and 950–4.

properties of an absolute human sovereign or those of the human sovereign to get a better idea of the sovereignty of God. Sometimes it is hard to know which direction the comparison is going. Thomas Adams seems to reason from God's sovereign properties to those of human sovereigns, although he indicates that he will proceed by "comparing earthly things with heavenly" ones. Notice in the following passage how the properties of God are passed down to human sovereigns:

> the king eternall, immortall, invisible . . . All inferiour kingdomes are de-
> rived from him . . . he doth not take away temporall kingdomes, that gives
> an eternall kingdome. He who is the blessed and only Potentate, the king
> of kings, and Lord of Lords; is content to distribute some honour among
> certaine men. Of [human kings it is] . . . presumptuous to say, *Divisum
> imperium cum Iove Caesar habet*: but *Imperium summum sub Iove Caesar
> habet.*[3]

Caesar has the highest authority under God. Shortly later Adams continued in the same vein:

> There is *Deus naturaliter*, a God by nature, the one only God himselfe. . . .
> *Deus est immortalis Rex, Rex est mortalis deus*: God is an immortal king,
> the king is a mortall god. . . . We distinguish betweene the eternal GOD, and
> the temporal LORD : but we obey the temporall LORD, for his [God's] sake
> that is the eternall God. And certainely he that refuseth obedience to the
> temporall King, hath yet made no gracious entrance into the everlasting
> kingdome of Iesus Christ.[4]

For Adams, too, there can no conflict between the commands of God and the commands of a Christian king.

Hobbes and Adams are also alike in calling the human sovereign "a mortal god" in a favorable sense.[5] The concept of a human sovereign as a "mortal god" is suggested by the famous line, "I [God] said, 'you are gods.'" Adams

---

[3] Thomas Adams, *Commentary or, Exposition upon the Divine Second Latin Epistle General, Written by the Blessed Apostle St. Peter* (London, 1633), 239. The first Latin sentence at the end of the quotation above was attributed to Virgil and appears in his biography by Aelius Donatus. See Virgilius Maro, *Opera P. Virgilii Maronis* (Cambridge, 1632). Adams corrects the thought of that sentence in the next clause.

[4] Adams, *Commentary*, 239–40.

[5] L, 17, p. 260.

mentions this text and refers to the reader to the Gospel according to John, chapter 10, verse 34, rather than the original source, Psalm 82:6. Adams had used the phrase, "mortal gods," twenty years before the publication of *Leviathan*.[6] He and Hobbes wrote in the same spirit because both were non-puritan, episcopal, Calvinist, anti-Catholic supporters of King James I.[7]

The properties of the human sovereign mirror God's because he was God's representative or vicegerent.[8] In short, an investigation of God as the natural, absolute sovereign is instructive with respect to the properties of the human, absolute sovereign. Near the end of this chapter, I will describe how the properties that Hobbes attributes to human sovereigns are properties traditionally attributed to God.

Since the Christian conception of God as an absolute sovereign was rooted in favored texts from the Bible, it is important to study these texts. Such a study complements what Hobbes says as a philosopher.[9] The similarity between the properties of a civil sovereign and the Lord God psychologically reinforces belief in the authority of the sovereign. To paraphrase the adage, "like father, like son," like sovereign, like God.

In the first paragraph of chapter 31, Hobbes wrote:

Subjects owe to Sovereigns simple Obedience in all things wherein their obedience is not repugnant to the laws of God. . . . There wants only for the entire knowledge of Civil duty to know what are those laws of God. For without that, a man knows not . . . whether it be contrary to the law of God or not: and so, either by too much civil obedience offends the Divine Majesty, or through fear of offending God, transgresses the commandments

[6] To my knowledge, the only favorable use of "mortal God" earlier than Adams's is that of John Bill, printer to the king, in his preface to William Camden in *The Abridgment of Camden's Britania* (London, 1626), [1]. Earlier uses of the phrase, "mortal god" are unfavorable.

[7] I have argued for this understanding of Hobbes in various places, first in *The Two Gods of Leviathan: Thomas Hobbes on Religion and Politics* (Cambridge: Cambridge University Press, 1992), and later several times, for example in chapter 3, "On the Proper Interpretation of Hobbes's Philosophy." On Adams's beliefs, see J. Sears McGee, "On Misidentifying Puritans: The Case of Thomas Adams," *Albion* 30, no. 3 (1998): 401–18, and J. Sears McGee, "Thomas Adams," in *The Dictionary of National Biography*, http://www.oxforddnb.com.ezproxy.lib.utexas.edu/view/article/131?docPos=3, accessed July 15, 2016.

[8] This idea can be found in other thinkers of the time, for example, Edmund Hall, *Lazarus's Sores Licked* (London, 1650), 17, and [Anon.], *Discourse Presented to those Who Seek Reformation of the Church of England* (London, 1642), 116. See also, Camden, *The Abridgment*, [1].

[9] For the purposes of this discussion, we can put aside the issue of whether Hobbes genuinely believed what he wrote. I want to explain how he represented his position and suggest that it is inspired by the Bible. Also, I am not precluding other influences on Hobbes's views.

of the Commonwealth. To avoid both these rocks, it is necessary to know what are the Laws Divine.[10]

A century earlier, John Calvin had raised the same issue of whether people should obey God or their human sovereign in case their commands conflicted. His view is unsurprising, "Obedience to man must not become disobedience to God." He went on: "How absurd it would be that in satisfying men you should incur the displeasure of him for whose sake you obey men themselves!"[11] If we momentarily think about the human predicament from a Christian perspective, Hobbes's answer is better than Calvin's because his forestalls the difficulty of figuring out exactly when God's commands might conflict with those of the secular sovereign. That is, subjects are never faced with the hard choice of choosing between God and their sovereign because God commands people to obey their earthly sovereigns.[12]

Hobbes's use of "the Divine Majesty" suggests what his audience presupposed: God is a natural sovereign and had a law from the beginning. Seventeenth-century texts are replete with the phrase "Lord God" and variations on it, such as "Lord Almighty" and "Almighty God." Early English Books Online cites almost two thousand works that use "Lord God" in the thirty years between 1620 and 1650. The other two phrases are also used regularly. As the context of the use of these phrases by English divines shows, the phrases are closely connected with biblical texts, especially some of the psalms, as we shall see. These phrases are never or virtually never used to explain the relation between God's almightiness or omnipotence and his sovereignty, probably because the connection is too close to require explanation. Also, many divines, especially Laudian ones, preferred to relate God's sovereignty to his justice and goodness.

Hobbes asserted the connection between sovereignty and omnipotence in a marginal note in chapter 31: "The right of God's sovereignty is derived from his omnipotence." The paragraph adjacent to the note says, "The Right of Nature whereby God reigneth over men and punisheth those that break his

---

[10] L, 31, p. 554.

[11] John Calvin, *Institutes of the Christian Religion*, ed. John T. McNeill, trans. Ford Lewis (Philadelphia: Westminster Press, 1960), 1520.

[12] If one doubts that choosing between God and one's sovereign can ever be a hard choice, consider that that situation involves a judgment about what God commands, what the sovereign commands, and whether there is a genuine conflict. Also, for Hobbesian humans, there is the conflict between the desire to avoid death or pain relatively soon versus the desire to avoid long-term pain in the relatively distant future.

Lawes is to be derived . . . from his *Irresistible Power*."[13] According to Hobbes, the criterion for irresistible power is power that can "never [be] taken away."[14] Because we know that the power of human beings can be taken away, we know that human sovereigns do not have irresistible power.[15]

Although people in the state of nature have unlimited rights, no one is sovereign because the right to rule "could not be obtained by force." No one has omnipotent power. If anyone had "Power Irresistible; there had been no reason, why he should not by that Power have ruled, and defended both himselfe" and others. And "consequently it is from that Power, that the Kingdome over men, and the Right of Afflicting men at his pleasure, belongeth Naturally to God Almighty . . . as Omnipotent."[16] In *De cive*, Hobbes momentarily gives the impression that a human being could theoretically be a natural sovereign because he discusses natural sovereignty as it might occur in the state of nature: "in the natural state of men, *sure and irresistible power gives the right of ruling and commanding those who cannot resist*."[17] However, the next clause cancels the suggestion, so that "the right to do anything whatsoever is an essential and direct attribute of omnipotence."[18] But why should "sure and irresistible power" ("*potentiam certam et irresistibilem*") be equated with omnipotence? I believe that Hobbes intuited that anyone who had such power would be the sovereign only as long as that irresistible power lasted, since no one had authorized the sovereign to represent them or transferred their power to him. Since the strength of every human being begins to fail, a group with a natural sovereign would be inherently unstable. But God's strength and hence his authority never fails because he is omnipotent.

It is easy to interpret the opening verse of the Bible as evidence for and an expression of God's omnipotence: "In the beginning, God created the heavens and the earth."[19] To create is to make something from nothing.

---

[13] L, 31, p. 558; see also QLNC, 111. Most likely, Hobbes did not believe that "God is omnipotent" is literally true. But he writes as if it is in chapter 31. See Thomas Holden, "Hobbes's First Cause," *Journal of the History of Philosophy* 53, no. 4 (2015), 647–67.

[14] L, 31, p. 558.

[15] Hobbes considers the sense in which human beings have dominion over lions and bears and lions have dominion over individual people. It concerns which thing has more physical power. But whichever has dominion in this sense, "it may be called dominion, . . . [but] properly it cannot," QLNC, 141–2. In *De cive*, 8.10, Hobbes says that people have right and dominion over beasts.

[16] L, 31, p. 558; also EL, 14.13–4.

[17] DCv, 1.14.

[18] DCv, 1.14.

[19] Genesis 1:1. God's sovereignty, based upon his creating the world, is described as "the intuitive logic of monotheism." See Roy Rosenberg, "Yahweh becomes King," *Journal of Biblical Literature* 85, no. 3 (1966), 297; see also 302.

To bring something from being nothing to being something is, metaphorically, to traverse an infinite metaphysical distance, which can be accomplished only by an infinite, that is, an omnipotent, power. Scholastic and scholastically trained philosophers often explained God's omnipotence in connection with his creating: "From him, through him, and in him are all things."[20] His creating "pertains to God's essence . . . [as] his omnipotence."[21] Almost all early modern theists thought that the opening chapter of Genesis would confirm their view that the efficient cause of everything is a creative cause. Omnipotence is tied to God's sovereignty when, near the end of the end of the first creation story, God gives human beings dominion over the other animals.[22] An axiom of Western medieval and early modern philosophy was that a thing cannot give what it does not have.

Hobbes's view contrasts with three of the standard accounts of God's sovereignty, each of which he rejects. One is that God is sovereign because he is good.[23] Evidence of God's goodness is reported in the first creation story. At the end of several of the days of creating, God sees that what he has made is good; and at the end of the sixth day, the end of his creating, he says that what he had made was "very good."[24] Hobbes could have explained the goodness of creation in two ways. One is that the things of creation are desired by human beings, namely, light, air with birds, water with fish, and land with plants and beasts. The other is that creation was good because God desired it, as evidenced by his creating.[25] The second way is not literally true, because God does not literally have desires according to Hobbes. In any case, neither explanation of the source of goodness is relevant to God's sovereignty. There is also no logical connection between making good things and obligation. And there is no connection between creation, gratitude, and obligation: "The right of nature whereby God reigneth over men . . . [comes] not from his creating

[20] William Ames, quoting Romans 11:36, in *The Marrow of All Theology* (Durham, NC: Labyrinth Press, 1968), 91; see also 90, 94, 100. On the general issue of the relevance of the Bible to political theory in the seventeenth century, see Eric Nelson, *The Hebrew Republic* (Cambridge, MA: Harvard University Press, 2010).

[21] Ames, *Marrow*, 92. Ames supports his view with various quotations from such diverse texts of the Bible as Isaiah 9:6, Jeremiah 32:18, 2 Chronicles 20:6, Luke 1:37, Philippians 3:21, 1 Timothy 6:15.

[22] See also Robert Filmer, *Patriarcha and Other Writings*, ed. J. P. Sommerville (Cambridge: Cambridge University Press, 1991), 7.

[23] See, for example, Gottfried Leibniz, "The Common Concept of Justice," in *Political Writings*, 2nd ed., ed. Patrick Riley (Cambridge: Cambridge University Press, 1988), 45–7, 57–9.

[24] Genesis 1:31.

[25] L, 6, p. 80.

them, as if he required obedience as of gratitude for benefits."[26] Owing a debt of gratitude to someone does not make that person a sovereign. Few saints were sovereigns; and no one became sovereign by doing good works.

A second explanation for the natural sovereignty of God comes from considering only God's making of the world. The opening chapter of Genesis can be interpreted as indicating that God was sovereign of the world because he made it.[27] A third explanation is that God was sovereign because he owned the world. If God owns the world, then there is no mystery about how he can give Adam dominion over the animals. The second and third explanations sometimes go together: God owns the world because he made it. Psalm 24 begins: "The earth is the Lord's, and the fullness thereof; / the world, and they that dwell therein. / For he hath founded it upon the seas, and established it upon the floods."[28] Hobbes did not deny Yahweh's ownership; he simply thought that ownership was not the foundation of sovereignty.[29] George Lawson, one of Hobbes's earliest critics, combines the two explanations:

> Dominion in general is twofold: . . . of possession or government. That of possession we call propriety: in which respect God is absolute Lord of all his creatures, because he createth and preserveth them, so that their very being is more his then theirs.[30]

[26] Hobbes may have conflated the arguments from ownership and gratitude, because at the end of the discussion he says that God's sovereignty does not depend on his being "Creator and gracious," as if these amounted to the same thing (L, 31, p. 558). Other philosophers and divines distinguished between the creator and ownership arguments and the gracious and goodness arguments, as we shall see.

[27] The biblical author may well have thought that God's sovereignty was based in his making; see, e.g., John Gibson, Genesis, vol. 1 (Edinburgh: The St. Andrew Press, 1981), 5.

[28] Psalm 24:1–2, The Bible, King James Version, with the Apocrypha (London: Penguin Classics, 2006), 695. The New Revised Version translates these verses as: "The earth is the Lord's and all that is in it, / the world, and those who live in it; for he has founded it on the seas, / and established it on the rivers." The New Oxford Annotated Bible, College 3rd ed. (New York: Oxford University Press, 2001), 794. Cf. Luc Foisneau, Hobbes et la Toute-Puissance de Dieu (Paris: Presses Universitaires de France, 2000), 29.

[29] Because the biblical authors conceived of God in various ways, the texts are not always consistent. Some passages suggest that God does not bestow dominion but only something more like stewardship. Even if that is true, God's sovereignty is implied by passages such as "all the earth is mine" (Ex. 19:5; see also Ps. 89:11). Although human ownership of property depends on the existence of sovereigns who protect the property of their subjects, if the entire earth is said to belong to one person and that person has the power to control it, the fair inference is that the "owner" of the earth is its sovereign. The fact that Yahweh's ownership seems to be even more restricted in other passages— He owns Canaan or Israel and not necessarily other places (Gen. 14:19, 22; L, 35, p. 634)—is also not a viable objection to God's sovereignty. God's special kingship is compatible with his universal kingship See chapter 4, "The Interpretation of Covenants in Leviathan."

[30] George Lawson, Examination of the Political Part of Mr. Hobbs his Leviathan (London, 1657), 150. The second element, "government," is not relevant to my discussion.

Neither the making nor the owning explanations are cogent according to Hobbes. It is evident that making something does not confer ownership of it. Parents make children and have authority over them, but they do not own them. Hobbes's explanation for parental authority is complicated and possibly inconsistent. In any case, he does not connect parental authority with either making or owning.[31] Unless a person has sold or contracted out their labor, it is plausible that a person owns what he makes. God was in that position at creation. Hobbes does not give any reasons for holding that making is logically independent of owning. Nor does he explain why owning does not confer sovereignty. However, it is not hard to think of a Hobbesian explanation. Ownership is correlative with property; and property presupposes sovereignty. It is the sovereign's commands about what people may do or not do with respect to things that constitutes property. Property owners as such do not have any authority to command others. Hobbes's attribution of omnipotence to God may seem somewhat odd, for he sometimes says that the only thing that human beings can know of him is that he exists.[32]

Arash Abizadeh has argued that God is an artificial person by fiction for Hobbes. In brief, his argument is this: When Hobbes discusses representation "by fiction," he discusses five groups, in five successive paragraphs, (1) inanimate things, (2) children and madmen, (3) idols, (4) God, and (5) a sovereign. Concerning the first three types, Hobbes says that the things represented are not authors. But Hobbes does not say this about God (4).[33] Abizadeh claims that Hobbes implies that the reader should add "and God can be no author." While space does not allow me to explain the problems with Abizadeh's position in detail, some of them can be stated briefly. One concerns his claim that because Hobbes says of the examples in the first three groups, that they cannot be authors, and because he does not say that God can be an author, he expects the reader to supply the proposition that God cannot be an author. Abizadeh thinks that Hobbes can expect his reader to provide the extra proposition because it is required by "the rhythm already set in motion by Hobbes's prose."[34] But there is no such rhythm. Each

---

[31] The ability of a parent to kill an infant or young child is tantamount to omnipotence. But Hobbes cannot make this explicit without giving the impression that human sovereignty does not depend on a covenant. In fact, he is often interpreted as holding that sovereignty by acquisition does not depend on a covenant. Cf. A. P. Martinich, *Hobbes* (London: Routledge, 2005), 125–8.

[32] Hobbes 1976, 36.16.

[33] Arash Abizadeh, "The Representation of Hobbesian Sovereignty," in *Hobbes Today*, ed. S. A. Lloyd (Cambridge: Cambridge University Press, 2013), 137–9.

[34] Ibid., 139. Cf. L, 22, pp. 386–7.

paragraph contains a slightly different structure, as demanded by group of examples being discussed. Also, there was no need to say that God was an author, since that was the presupposition of his readers. My guess is that if Hobbes had written, "Of course, God is an author," a just-so story would be told to explain why Hobbes meant it as sarcasm. Another problem is that, as the fifth group of examples shows, a person by fiction can have authors. So it is not necessary to think that Hobbes is implying that God cannot be an author. Yet another problem is that Abizadeh's position does not fit with the Latin version of *Leviathan*. The relevant passage is, "Etiam Dei veri Persona geritur, & gesta est. Mundum enim in propria Persona creavit. In redimendo genere Humano Personam Dei gessit Iesus Christus" ("Also, the Person of the true God is borne and has been borne. For in his own person, he created the world. In redeeming human kind, Jesus Christ bore the Person of God.").[35] God the Father acts "in propria Persona," and "Persona *Propria*" is Hobbes's term for a natural person.[36] Finally, a general problem is that Abizadeh does not consider all the relevant evidence. His interpretation cannot accommodate straightforward statements by Hobbes such as that Leviathan is the "*Mortall God,* to which wee owe under the *Immortall God,* our peace and defence,"[37] although Abizadeh quotes it.

In one place, Hobbes implies that his proof for the existence of God is a proof that something that is "eternal, infinite, and omnipotent" exists.[38] About eternity, he may think that he has to assert it of God because if God began to exist at some particular time, there would have to be some moving body that caused God to come to exist; and so God would not be the first cause. About infinity, Hobbes may have thought that he could assert it because he was not committing himself to very much. God is infinite because everything that human beings sense is finite. God, who cannot be sensed, is

---

[35] Hobbes 2012, c. 16, p. 249, my translation.

[36] Hobbes 2012, c. 16, p. 245. In a later, formidable article, Abizadeh claims that Hobbes changed the wording in the Latin translation in order "to avoid the charge of heresy." (Arash Abizadeh, "Hobbes's Conventionalist Theology, The Trinity, and God as an Artificial Person by Fiction," *The Historical Journal* 60, no. 4 (2017): 915–41). This assertion seems to be made only to neutralize contrary evidence. Abizadeh's main position in the later article is that Hobbes is a theist, whose God of course acted in history, as narrated in the Bible, and is "constructed artificially by human convention" (ibid.) His thesis is paradoxical according to Hobbes's standards. In nontechnical language, this makes Hobbes's God both fictive and a fictional character. Cf. Roy Sorenson, "Fictional Theism," *Analysis* 75 no. 4 (2015): 539–50. Limitations of space preclude the full answer that Abizadeh's article deserves.

[37] L, 17, p. 260.

[38] L, 12, p. 166. But cf. Holden, "Hobbes's First Cause."

not finite, and so is infinite. It was easier for a seventeenth-century geometer like Hobbes to have a deflationary idea of infinity than an arithmetician.

Because God's natural sovereignty is grounded in his omnipotence, he enjoys carte blanche in his treatment of human beings:

> To those therefore whose Power is irresistible [omnipotent], the dominion of all men adhereth naturally by their excellence of Power; and consequently it is from that Power that the Kingdome over men, and the Right of afflicting men at his pleasure belongeth Naturally to God Almighty ... as Omnipotent. And though Punishment be due for Sinne onely, because by that word is understood Affliction for Sinne; yet the Right of Afflicting, is not alwayes from men's Sinne, but from Gods Power.[39]

One benefit of Hobbes's position is that it provides a straightforward solution to the problem of evil:[40]

> This question, *Why Evill men often prosper; and Good men suffer Adversity,* has been much disputed by the Ancient, and is the same with this of ours, *by what Right God dispenseth the Prosperities and Adversities of this life;* and is of that difficulty, as it hath shaken the faith, not onely of the Vulgar, but of Philosophers, and which is more, of the Saints, concerning the Divine Providence. *How Good,* (saith *David*), *is the God of Israel to those that are Upright in Heart; and yet my feet were almost gone, my treadings had well-nigh slipt; for I was grieved at the Wicked, when I saw the Ungodly in such Prosperity.* [Ps. 72:1–3] And *Job,* how earnestly does he expostulate with God, for the many Afflictions he suffered, notwithstanding his Righteousnesse? This question in the case of *Job,* is decided by God himselfe, not by arguments derived from *Job's* Sinne, but his own Power. For whereas the friends of *Job* drew their arguments from his Affliction to his Sinne, and he defended himselfe by the conscience of his Innocence; God himselfe taketh up the matter, and having justified the Affliction by arguments drawn from his Power, such as this, *Where wast thou when I layd the foundations*

---

[39] L, 31, p. 558. Hobbes's view that nothing that God can do to creatures can be an injury was a mainstream view. See, for example, Arthur Hildersam [aka Hildersham], *CLII Lectures upon Psalme LI preached at Ashby-Delazouch in Leicester-shire* (London, 1635), 520.

[40] The book of Job proposes many solutions to the problem of evil. Hobbes's preferred solution might be called "The God-Above-Justice Solution." As almighty, God has a natural authority over humans, that is, is sovereign over them and hence cannot be unjust to them.

of the earth,[41] [Job 38:4] and the like, both approved *Job's* Innocence and reproved the Erroneous doctrine of his friends. Conformable to this doctrine is the sentence of our Saviour, concerning the man that was born Blind, in these words, *Neither hath this man sinned, nor his fathers; but that the works of God might be made manifest in him.*[42] And though it be said, *That Death entered into the world by sinne,* (by which is meant that if *Adam* had never sinned, he had never dyed, that is, never suffered any separation of his soule from his body,) it follows not thence, that God could not justly have Afflicted him, though he had not Sinned, as well as he afflicteth other living creatures, that cannot sinne.[43]

Hobbes's solution is true to part of the book of Job.[44] In reply to one of his friends' speeches, Job says,

> He is not a man as I am, that I can answer him
> Or that we can confront one another in court.
> If only there were one to arbitrate between us
> And impose his authority on both.[45]

Job is oblivious to the irony of his comments. Indeed, no one can arbitrate between him and God because God is not on the same legal or moral level as human beings. God is not subject to any laws, and hence cannot be just by following them or unjust by breaking them.[46] Hobbes could have quoted another part of Job in support of his view. The passage, "And God appeared to Job out of the whirlwind" may be interpreted as referring to God's power. Similarly, human sovereigns cannot be just or unjust with respect to the laws of their commonwealth. It was part of the common law that the king could do no wrong. Human sovereigns approach omnipotence as much as a nondivine person can insofar as they have all the political power in a

---

[41] This verse contains a solution to the problem of evil that may be called "The Unanswerable-Question Solution." Humans do not have enough information to be able to answer the question. This solution is different from The God-Above-Justice Solution.

[42] This verse from the gospel of John 9:3 expresses still another solution, different from those mentioned above. It does not occur in Job.

[43] L, 31, p. 560; see also QLNC, 102, 104–5.

[44] There are at least seven solutions proposed in the book of Job. Most of them are obviously unacceptable such as that Job is not good and that he is rewarded in the end.

[45] Job 9:32–3; see also 9:2–4, 9:15–9, 13:3, 13:15, 16:21, 23:3–5, 31:35–7.

[46] Thomas Aquinas wrestles with the issue of God's justice at *Summa theologiae* I, Q. 21, art. 1.

civil state. However, I think that Hobbes's considered view is that absolute sovereigns are above justice and injustice because they make laws, not because they approximate to omnipotence.

Hobbes's view that God is a natural sovereign in virtue of his extraordinary power was not peculiar in the mid-seventeenth century. People as distant from Hobbes politically as the Leveller John Lilburne conjoined power and kingship:

> God, the absolute sovereign Lord and King of all things in heaven and earth, the original fountain and cause of all causes, who is circumscribed, governed, and limited by no rules, but doth all things merely and only by his sovereign will and unlimited good pleasure.[47]

The connection between omnipotence and obedience is implicit in some of the work of William Ames. His answer to the question, "by what motives a man may be stird up to embrace the call of God," is that he is called by "an omnipotent God, to whom we ought to hearken and give eare."[48] The idea goes back to the Fathers of the Church. Saint Ambrose wrote, "you Princes, and Potentates of the earth, yee ought your selves . . . live under the command, and obedience of the omnipotent God."[49] God's absolute sovereignty immunizes him against criticism about predestination. Arthur Hildersham wrote: "God had done no wrong, if in his eternall decree he had chosen no man unto life but reprobated all men unto destruction. For he is our absolute soveraigne Lord as we have heard; and it was lawfull for him, to doe with his owne what himselfe pleased."[50] The reasons that God cannot injure any creature are divided into two by Hildersham:

---

[47] John Lilburne, *The Free-man's Freedom Vindicated* (London, 1646). Lilburne does not use the word "omnipotence." But omnipotence is suggested by the phrase "fountain and cause of all causes" and more particularly, "cause of all causes," which imitates other biblical phrases applied to God such as "lord of lords" and "king of kings." Only God is lord and only God is king; and only God is cause of causes. The connection between unlimited power and kingship seems to supervene on the clustered ideas of absolute sovereignty, lordship, universal kingship, being cause of causes, being absolutely unlimited, and legitimately arbitrary. The glue holding them together is psychological association. Neither Lilburne nor the other seventeenth-century intellectuals who string together some or all of these ideas analyzes their logical relationships. More important than the fact that they were not philosophers is the fact that these ideas occur together in the Bible without analysis. Concerning Lilburne's statement that God's "will is the rule of all righteousness," see also Hildersam, *CLII Psalms*, 520: "the only thing that justifies God is his 'will and good pleasure.'"

[48] William Ames, *Conscience with the Power and Cases thereof Divided into V books* ([Leyden and London], 1639) 11–12.

[49] Ambrose, *Christian Offices Crystal Glass* (London, 1637), 1.

[50] Hildersam, *CLII Lectures*, 249.

1. In regard of his Soveraignty, and Supreame, and undependent power he hath over all things that he hath made, even as the potter hath over his clay. . . . In respect of this Soveraignty, and Supreame power of God, *Elihu* saith, *Iob 33.13.* that *God giveth no account of any of his matters.* . . . 2. In regard of his will, it is not possible he should wrong any of his creatures, for his will is the rule of all righteousnesse, and every thing is therefore just &, because his will is so.[51]

To say that God may treat people in whatever way he sees fit, as Hobbes and others say or imply, is not to deny that he treats most good people well.[52] In fact, an important part of the biblical conception of the divine king is that he uses his strength to protect his people. The moral of the Deuteronomistic history, which covers the history of the Israelites in the desert after the Exodus up to the Babylonian Captivity, is that Yahweh protects Israelites and they prosper when Yahweh is obeyed; and they suffer when they disobey.[53] This reciprocal relationship between protection and obedience is similar to Hobbes's "protection and obedience" formula, in the "Review and Conclusion" of *Leviathan.*

Returning to the separation of power from goodness, we should consider the biblical passages in which Yahweh behaves abominably, as when he orders the slaughter of the inhabitants of Jericho, Ai, Hazor, and other cities:

Joshua said, "The city and all that is in it shall be devoted to the Lord [Yahweh] for destruction. Only Rahab the prostitute and all who are with her in her house shall live" . . .

Then the Lord [Yahweh] said to Joshua, "do not fear or be dismayed . . . You shall do to Ai and its king as you did to Jericho and its king" . . . When Israel had finished slaughtering all the inhabitants of Ai . . . and when all of them to the very last had fallen by the edge of the sword, all Israel returned to Ai, and attacked it with the edge of the sword. The total of those who fell that day, both men and women, was twelve thousand—all the people of Ai.

---

[51] Ibid., 248. See also John Arrowsmith, *Armilla Catechetica. A Chain of Principles* (London, 1659), 345; Christopher Cartwright, *A Practical and Polemical Commentary or Exposition on the Whole Fifteenth Psalm* (London, 1658), 50; and Henry Church, *Miscellanea Philo-theologica. Or, God, & Man* (London, 1637), 107.

[52] Hildersam, *CLII Lectures,* 249.

[53] Although early modern intellectuals did not use the term "Deuteronomistic History," they believed that the Bible taught that good behavior was rewarded and that bad behavior was punished.

For Joshua did not draw back his hand, with which he stretched out the sword, until he had utterly destroyed all the inhabitants of Ai . . . according to the word of the Lord [Yahweh].[54]

Joshua might have said about Yahweh what several American politicians have reportedly said about one or another dictator, "He's a son of a bitch, but he is our son of a bitch."[55] If we think that these tales of slaughter in the name of God must have been so abhorrent to Hobbes that he could not have accepted them, recall that both sides in the English Civil War justified or excused their barbarities because they were fighting on the side of God. General histories typically mention that "God's Englishman," Oliver Cromwell, killed the inhabitants of Drogheda and Wexford after those cities surrendered; but the killing of non-combatants, including women and children, occurred on a smaller scale during most of the war. The "godly" soldiers on the parliamentary side believed that they were slaughtering Catholics, who corrupted Christianity, and atheists.[56] Christians accepted that some horrific behavior was approved of or performed by God (see, e.g., Genesis 22). While we may not like Hobbes's view about God's sovereignty and his solution to the problem of evil, the discrepancy in attitude is due in large part to the deep differences between his moral world and our own.

Hobbes does not have to show that God's apparently bad behavior is incompatible with his goodness, because he, like other negative theologians, does not think that God is literally good.[57] In saying this, Hobbes is not contradicting anything in the three most important creeds of the Christian Church. The Apostles' Creed begins, "I believe in God the father Almighty, creator of heaven and earth." It says nothing about his supposed goodness. The Nicene Creed begins, "I believe in one God, the Father Almighty, Maker of heaven and earth, and of all things visible and invisible." Again, nothing about goodness. While it takes some time for the Athanasian Creed to get to the properties of God, when it does, the first property attributed to him is being almighty, and it never adds that God is good. Rather, since human beings consider calling someone good to be a way of honoring a person, they

---

[54] Joshua 6:17; Joshua 8:1–2; Joshua 8:24–7, in *The Bible* 2006: 217, 279, 280, respectively.

[55] For other stories about Yahweh's horrific commands, see Joshua 10:16–11, 23.

[56] Diane Purkiss, *The English Civil War* (New York: Basic Books, 2006), 288–99.

[57] L, 31, p. 566. That is Hobbes's official position. In other places, he explains God's goodness as if it were literally applied to him. In his debate with John Bramhall, he holds that God's goodness is a consequence of his irresistible power (QLNC, 159).

ought to call God "good." Hobbes's position does seem to be incompatible with the Thirty-Nine Articles, but they, undergoing various revisions, have an unusual status in English history; and have much less weight than the early creeds. Bishop John Bramhall wrote of them:

> Some of them are the very same that are contained in the Creed; some others of them are practical truths, which come not within the proper list of points or articles to be believed; lastly, some of them are pious opinions or inferior truths, which are proposed by the Church of England to all her sons, as not to be opposed; not as essentials of Faith necessary to be believed by all Christians *necessitate medii*, under pain of damnation.[58]

One apparent problem with Hobbes's treatment of God's being a natural sovereign is that it does not fit the definition of a sovereign that he gave in *Leviathan*. A sovereign is

> *One Person, of whose Acts a great Multitude, by mutuall Covenants one with another, have made themselves every one the Author, to the end he may use the strength and means of them all as he shall think expedient for their Peace and Common Defence.*[59]

In *Leviathan*, Hobbes never said that God was a party to a sovereign-making covenant involving Adam and Eve.[60] The text of Genesis 3 and 4 presupposes that God's authority was independent of any covenant. It would have been absurd to interpret "Do not eat of the tree . . ." as counsel. As shown by their behavior after disobeying God and the punishment they receive from him, they were commanded—given a law—not to eat of the tree of the knowledge of good and evil. The easiest way to explain the discrepancy between Hobbes's definition and what he said about God's sovereignty is that Hobbes intended his definition to define only human sovereignty. This interpretation is made plausible by two things. One is the context in which it appears. Hobbes is beginning to explain how human sovereigns are created by a covenant. The other is that it is plausible that a sovereign is a person who has the right to command, that is, the right to have people obey simply because

---

[58] John Bramhall, *Schism Guarded and Beaten Back upon the Right Owners* (London, 1658), 200.
[59] L, 17, p. 260.
[60] Cf. Martinich, *Two Gods*, 147–9, 277–8, 286–7, 291–2, 383–4.

the person desires it.[61] Also, whoever has a right to the end has a right to the means. And both a human sovereign in virtue of a covenant, and the natural, divine sovereign in virtue of his power have that right.

About the fact that God does not have to act for the safety and defense of his subjects, as a sovereign does, one might begin by saying that it is "God's prerogative,"[62] as a natural sovereign, and then go on to say that as a matter of fact God typically saves those who obey him.

Hobbes's discussion of the nature of God's sovereignty prepares the reader for the main point he wanted to make in chapter 31:

> It remaineth therefore that we consider, what Praecepts are dictated to men, by their Naturall Reason onely, without other word of God, touching the Honour and Worship of the Divine Majesty.
>
> Honour consisteth in the inward thought, and opinion of the Power, and Goodnesse of another: and therefore to Honour God, is to think as Highly of his Power and Goodnesse, as is possible. And of that opinion, the externall signes appearing in the Words, and Actions of men, are called Worship.[63]

Although goodness does not literally apply to God, literal power irresistible does. Hobbes likely first learned about the unique power of God by hearing and having explained to him the opening chapter of the Bible, as suggested above. In any case, for more than a millennium before, philosophers had thought that creation required omnipotence. So the commitment to God's omnipotence comes from (representing oneself as) accepting the Bible.[64]

The Old Testament expresses some ambivalence towards monarchy. However, the history of Israel from the latter part of II Samuel to the end of II Kings and in the two books of Chronicles is a history of government by kings. Both King David and King Solomon are among the most admired figures in the Old Testament. It is much easier to see one's god reflected in a "unitary executive" than it is to see it reflected in a council: "The kingship of YHWH has its

---

[61] See L, 25, p. 398. For almost all seventeenth-century thinkers, to have sovereignty over a person would mean that the person has an obligation to obey the sovereign's commands. Hobbes's comment that God is a natural sovereign in virtue of his omnipotence, but that human beings have an obligation to obey him in virtue of their weakness may be odd. However, he gives an argument for his view. Suppose two beings were omnipotent. Then neither would have sovereignty over the other because neither could compel the other. Also, neither would have an obligation towards the other. So obligation has to arise from strength that is less than omnipotent; see DCv 15.7.

[62] Decades ago, a philosopher and theist told me this.

[63] L, 31, p. 560. See also AW, 35.16.

[64] Biblical scholars recognize that God does not actually create the world from nothing, since primeval water and a formless earth are present before creation begins.

earthly counterpart in the rule of the Davidic dynasty . . ."[65] Hobbes's practical commitment to monarchy is strong enough that he interprets the key antimonarchical passage in the Old Testament as endorsing absolute sovereignty:

> *This shall be the Right of the King you will have to reigne over you. He shall take your sons, and set them to drive his Chariots and to be his horsemen, and to run before his chariots; and gather in his harvest; and to make his engines of War, and Instruments of his chariots; and shall take your daughters to make perfumes, to be his Cookes, and Bakers. He shall take your fields, your vine-yards, and your olive-yards, and give them to his servants. He shall take the tyth of your corn and wine, and give it to the men of his chamber, and to his other servants. He shall take your man-servants, and your maid-servants, and the choice of your youth, and employ them in his businesse. He shall take the tyth of your flocks; and you shall be his servants.*[66]

Hobbes's interpretation of this passage has at least this much sense. Both he and its author thought of God as a king.

God as king is the dominant representation of him in the Psalms and other books. The second paragraph of Hobbes's discussion of omnipotence and natural sovereignty begins with two quotations from Psalms: "*God is King, let the Earth rejoyce*, saith the Psalmist. And again, *God is King though the Nations be angry; and he that sitteth on the Cherubims, though the earth be moved.*"[67] Hobbes is translating from the Vulgate. And his translation is a bit free. Twice, he puts "God is King" for "Dominus regnavit."[68] Hobbes's use of these passages is appropriate because the theme of God's kingship and his power are closely associated: "The central image used to portray God is that of kingship, and the emphasis is on . . . power."[69] More of Psalm 97 supports Hobbes's view:

> Clouds and darkness are round about him;
> righteousness and judgement are the habitation of his throne.
> A fire goeth before him,
> and burneth up his enemies round about.
> His lightnings enlightened the world:

---

[65] John Collins, *Introduction to the Hebrew Bible* (Minneapolis: Fortress Press, 2004), 477.

[66] 1 Samuel 8:11–7; quoted in L, 20, p. 316.

[67] L, 31, p. 554. Because natural sovereignty depends on omnipotence and only God is omnipotent, sovereignty by acquisition cannot depend on power alone.

[68] See L, 31, p. 555.

[69] Collins, *Hebrew Bible*, 475.

the earth saw, and trembled.
The hills melt like wax at the presence of the Lord [Yahweh],
at the presence of the Lord of the whole earth.[70]

The same is true for Psalm 99. After saying that Yahweh has been enthroned, the psalmist says, "The Lord [Yahweh] is great in Zion: / and he is high above all people. / Let them praise thy great and terrible name."[71] Divinity, power, and kingship are inseparable for the psalmist:

The Lord [Yahweh] reigneth, he is clothed with majesty;
the Lord is clothed with strength, wherewith he hath girded himself:
the world also is established, that it cannot be moved.
Thy throne is established of old:
thou art from everlasting.[72]

The psalmist often expressed power figuratively, especially in terms of storms and water. And so Psalm 93 continues:

The floods have lifted up, O Lord, the floods have lifted up their voice;
the floods have lifted up their waves.
The Lord on high is mightier than the noise of many waters,
yea, than the mighty waves of the seas.[73]

Another powerful natural phenomenon associated with God was thunder and lightning on mountain tops. Certain mountains were associated with the Israelite God. Just as Zeus lived atop Mt. Olympus and Baal on Zaphon, Yahweh lived on a mountain.[74] One of the earliest epithets of Yahweh, "El Shaddai," is usually translated as "God Almighty" and is understood as referring to a mountain god.[75] Because the concept of omnipotence is more sophisticated than great power, older parts of the Bible associated kingship with

---

[70] Psalm 97:1–5, in *The Bible* (2006) 767.
[71] Psalm 99:2–3, in *The Bible* (2006) 768.
[72] Psalm 93:1–2, in *The Bible* (2006) 764.
[73] Psalm 93:3–4, in *The Bible* (2006) 764. Also: "The voice of the Lord [Yahweh] is upon the waters: / the God of glory thundereth . . . / The voice of the Lord [Yahweh] is powerful; / the voice of the Lord [Yahweh] is full of majesty" (Psalm 29:32, in *The Bible* (2006) 699). And: "Thou rulest the raging of the sea" (Psalm 89:9, in *The Bible* (2006) 759).
[74] Cf. Harold Attridge, ed., *HarperCollins Study Bible* (New York: Harper One, 2000), 804n89.12.
[75] Although the literal meaning is conjectural, most scholars believe that El Shaddai means *God of the Mountain*.

a power less than omnipotence. The paradigm of a powerful leader was the warrior-king, for example, the first two kings of Israel. Since a nation's God was supposed to protect the people from its enemies, God was portrayed as a warrior.[76] One of the oldest passages in the Bible is a song to Yahweh as a warrior:

> I will sing unto the Lord [Yahweh], for he has triumphed gloriously:
> The horse and his rider hath he thrown into the sea.
> . . . The Lord is a man of war:
> The Lord [Yahweh] is his name.[77]

Divinity, kingship, and the power of a warrior occur together in this passage:

> Who is this King of glory?
> The Lord, strong and mighty,
> the Lord, mighty in battle. . . .
> Who is this King of glory?
> The Lord of hosts, he is the King of glory.[78]

And Hobbes could have referred to passages in other books of the *Bible*, for example, Isaiah 3:1 and 42:13.

The concept of a warrior God and the fact that king was preceded by tribal chiefs who established their authority through military prowess may raise the question of which came first: warrior chief or warrior god? My guess is that each concept reinforced the other. Kings liked to represent themselves as having divine qualities. In defense of his claim to absolute sovereignty in a speech to Parliament (1610), King James said, "even by God himself they [kings] are called gods."

I began this chapter by discussing Hobbes's belief that omnipotence is sufficient for sovereignty; I then discussed how having great power, more precisely, more power than one's enemies, is sufficient for being a sovereign, divine or nondivine. I now want to point out how Hobbes may assert the properties standardly attributed to God to sovereigns in an attenuated sense.

---

[76] The idea of a warrior king in the ancient Near East goes back to the third millennium BCE. See Steven Garfinkle, "Ancient Near Eastern City-States," in *The Oxford Handbook of the State in the Ancient Near East and Mediterranean*, ed., P. Fibiger Bang and W. Scheidel (New York: Oxford University Press, 2013), 94–120.

[77] Ex. 15:1, 3, in *The Bible* (2006) 85.

[78] Psalm 24:8, 10, in *The Bible* (2006) 695.

The sovereign approaches omnipotence with respect to its subjects,[79] as alluded to above, in that they have transferred their rights of government to the sovereign, and by the principle that whoever has a right to an end has a right to the means, they have potentially transferred all their power to him.[80] The sovereign approaches omniscience in that whenever a dispute arises about a matter of fact or science, he has the right to decide what the truth shall be taken to be.[81] The sovereign approaches omnibenevolence in that he can do no wrong and what he desires is good, and the sovereign is just in the sense that he is the judge of all disputes, and above justice and injustice in that he cannot break any law since he makes the law.[82] Finally, the sovereign is the redeemer because he saves his subjects from the impending death of the state of nature.

Hobbes's view can be considered an answer to those enemies of Charles I, who would have denied that kings are like gods, for example, Henry Parker who wrote that those who look upon the king as "the efficient . . . cause, and the Subject of all power" and "maintain, That all Kings are in all things and commands . . . to be obeyed, as being like Gods, unlimitable, and as well in evil, as in good unquestionable" are "sordid flatterers."[83]

Because of his historical situation, Hobbes thought that the proper understanding of Christianity should be biblical.[84] The biblical conception of God that prevailed from at least the fourth century on was the conception of an omnipotent and sovereign God; and that conception was salient because it appears at the beginning of the Bible. Another part of that conception, or another conception that was not distinguished from the first, was that God, as king, was a great warrior because he had great power. This God punished the Israelites and human beings generally when they disobeyed him; and he protected people when they obeyed him. This reciprocal relationship between protection by and obedience to God was understood as being essential. Goodness had little to do with it.

---

[79] I will not repeat the phrase "with respect to his subjects" for the other properties.

[80] See A. P. Martinich, "Authorization and Representation in Hobbes's *Leviathan*," in *The Oxford Handbook of Hobbes*, ed. A. P. Martinich and K Hoekstra (Oxford: Oxford University Press, 2016), 315–38

[81] L, 18, pp. 268–74.

[82] L, 18, pp. 270, 272–4.

[83] Henry Parker, *Observations upon Some of his Majesties Late Answers and Expresses* (London, 1642), 44, spelling modernized.

[84] Hobbes may have thought biblical religion was important because Christianity does not challenge the established government, and because, in Israelite religion, the king was the head of the religion, as much as anything else.

11

The Author of Sin and Demoniacs

Two Calvinist Issues in Thomas Hobbes and Some Contemporaries

1. English Calvinism and Hobbes

In *The Two Gods of Leviathan* and other works, I argued that Hobbes was
an English Calvinist and that his Calvinism was an important part of religious and political views he shared with King James I. Like James, Hobbes
was a Calvinist in theology, and supported episcopacy in ecclesiology and
absolute sovereignty in political theory. One might think that Calvinism and
episcopacy are strange bedfellows, but two of the great sixteenth-century
archbishops of Canterbury, Edmund Grindal (1519–1583) and John Whitgift
(1530–1604), were Calvinists.

English Calvinist theology consists of these propositions:

(a) From all eternity, God determined both who will go to heaven
and who will go to hell independently of their behavior (double
predestination).
(b) Redemption was purely an act of mercy on God's part.
(c) Jesus died for the elect only, not for all people.
(d) God's nature is incomprehensible.
(e) God is absolutely sovereign.

Something should be said about (d) and (e). Virtually all seventeenth-
century Christians would have accepted them. But they often give them only
lip service. It was not usual for non-Calvinists to assert (d) and then to write
at great length about God's nature. (See Jackson 1628: sig. B2^r and 234; and
also Hutton 1978: 639 and 645.) In contrast, Calvinists emphasized them in
the sense of using them to develop their own positions and to criticize their

Hobbes's Political Philosophy. A. P. Martinich, Oxford University Press. © Oxford University Press 2021.
DOI: 10.1093/oso/9780197531716.003.0012

opponents. For example, William Twisse, prolocutor of the Westminster Assembly, criticized the Arminian Thomas Jackson for claiming that the nature of God can be partially understood through comparison with creatures:

> I should rather think, the incomprehensible nature of God is not to be manifested by way of resemblance, drawn from inferior things.... For comparison hath place only between things agreeing in kind, or in proportion. But God and his creatures in neither . . . (Twisse 1631a: 19; see also 9–10, spelling modernized).

A favorite passage of the English Calvinists, chapter 95 of Augustine's letter to Laurentius, *Enchiridion on Faith, Hope and Love*, concerns the fact that God's judgments are opaque to humans: "when of two infants, whose cases seem in all respects alike, one by the mercy of God chosen to Himself, and the other is by His Justice abandoned (wherein the one who is chosen may recognize what of justice due to himself, had not mercy intervened); why, of these two, the one should have been chosen rather than the other, is to us an insoluble problem" (Cf. Twisse 1631: 626).

As for (e),[1] emphasis on it led to this summary of the English Calvinist view of what people need to enter "the Kingdome of Heaven": faith and obedience. Obedience is acting in accord with what authority commands, and what an authority commands is a law. It follows that obedience is acting in accord with the law. In short, his view consists of three elements: (a) two things are required: faith and obedience; (b) obedience is following the law of God; and (c) the faith that is required is belief that Jesus is the Christ. These same three elements are asserted to be the essence of the ways God taught people how to get to heaven by Twisse: (a) God specified two ways a person could get to heaven, "The Law and the Gospel" (Twisse 1632: A2^r). (b) By the law, he means what God commands, as indicated by his reference to Deuteronomy 30:16: the law says "Doe this [what God commands] and thou shalt live" (Twisse 1632: A2^r). If we equate sin with disobedience, as we should, given the moral of the story of the first sin, then we will say with Twisse that the "Law require[s] . . . That wee should bee without sinne" (Twisse 1632: A3^r). (c) If everyone "were righteous, that is, without sinne; we should have no neede of Christ Jesus" (Twisse 1632: A2^v–A3^r). But because everyone sinned,

---

[1] See Calvin 1559: I.17.2; and I.17.5

the gospel provided another way to salvation: "Believe in Jesus Christ, and thou shalt be saved" (Twisse 1632: A2 ᵣ).

It should not be surprising that Hobbes embraced and persisted in adhering to English Calvinism. It was the official theory of the monarch during Hobbes's formative years, and he was stubborn, loathe to give up an opinion he firmly held, much less admit a mistake. One of my favorite anecdotes about Hobbes is that he once went to a social gathering, sat down, and began expounding his views. Although he replied to some comments and questions, when he sensed they were objections, he stood affronted, said "I come to instruct, not to dispute," and left in a huff.

I now proceed to the main part of this chapter, which concerns whether God is the author of sin and whether demoniacs in the Bible are madmen. I believe that a study of these issues provides further evidence of Hobbes's Calvinism.

2. The Author of Sin

The first issue concerns whether God is the author of sin or not. It is helpful to discuss this issue with respect to three propositions:

(1) God is the cause of everything.
(2) God is the cause of sin.
(3) God is the author of sin.

Almost all theists unreflectively assent to (1).[2] Philosophical theists in the Judeo-Christian tradition accept (1) because God is the ultimate explanation for everything. He is the creator of all things. If anything other than God was a creator, then the Judeo-Christian tradition would not be a monism but at least a dualism.

Proposition (2) seems to follow from (1). Sin seems to be a thing because murder, mendacity, and theft seem to be things that are almost everywhere. But most theists balk at (2). They hold that God is good, even all-good; consequently, they believe that it is impossible for (2) to be true. Eager to prevent a good god from being connected to sin, they try to reconcile (1) and

---

[2] Paul of Tarsus at Ephesians 1:11, says, "we have our inheritance, being predestinated according to the purpose of him who worketh all things" (Authorized Version).

(2) by holding that God is the author only of the good things and that the devil and individual sinners are the cause of sins. The Arminian Thomas Pierce (1622–91), who will be discussed below, is a good example of this tactic (Pierce 1655: 11; cf. Pierce 1658a: *6ʳ). That God only creates what is good is evidenced by the biblical story of creation, which emphasizes that what God made was good: "*God saw everything that he had made, and behold it was very good*" (Pierce 1655: 15). Their view that God does not create everything abandons monism. The devil and people sin, on this view, because they have free will. The actions of free will initiate actions but are not themselves caused by any preceding cause. Free-will actions are the source of something new in the world. They are mini-acts of creation. Pierce says this explicitly: "We see the things that are made by the *Fiat* of our *will*, and behold they are very *evil*. This *Creative power* of *ours* we justly reckon as the sequel of *humane weaknesse*" (Pierce 1655: 15). An often unnoticed consequence of this view is that, contrary to standard Christian teaching, God is not strictly "the creator of heaven and earth," but the creator of heaven and earth, minus the free actions of persons (Pierce 1655: 17; see also 21).

Some Christian philosophers, trying to be true to God's exclusive role as creator but also committed to the creativity of human action, suggested that God is only the cause of a creature's existence and not what it does.[3] But this move lands one back in the same logical place as before: it means that God may be the ultimate cause of the things that exist but not the ultimate cause of everything, in particular, not the cause of what they do. One must create a thing in a specific condition, with its properties. A creature can't be, say, Fido, without being a dog that is either standing, sitting or lying down, and scratching or not scratching, and so on. Hobbes expresses this position when he mocks the view that God is not the cause of the "particular and determinate act of killing Uriah." There cannot be "a power that were not the power to do some particular act, or a power to kill and yet to kill nobody in particular. If the power be to kill, it is to kill that which shall be by that power killed, whether it be Uriah or any other" (Hobbes 1656: 108).[4] His point was that any exercise of a power is always the cause of a fully particular event. For him, God caused David to send Uriah to the front lines, and David's sending

---

[3] Cf. William Perkins, a Calvinist, wrote: "God hath most certainly decreed every both thing and action . . . Yes, he hath most directly decreed the wicked workes of the wicked. For if it had not so pleased him, they had never been at all" (Perkins 1592: 18).

[4] Anselm of Canterbury was also clear that "God causes both the 'natures of all things' and also 'the singular actions that come from the bad will'" (Anselm, *De casu diaboli*, sec. 20).

Uriah to the front lines kills Uriah, and hence God killed Uriah. This is what Hobbes meant by the phrase, "the giving of that power is the application of it to the act" (Hobbes 1656: 108).

Another way of trying to reconcile propositions (1) and (2) is to hold that sin is nothing. As Bishop John Bramhall wrote, "sin . . . [has] no true entity or being in it" (Hobbes 1656: 98). Hence it is not something that needs to be or even can be created. If sin seems to be a thing, it is partially the fault of natural languages, which give names to sins as if they were things. While "murder" and "lying" are names of sins, the sins themselves or sins qua sins are not things. One way to see this is to separate two semantic aspects of many value-judgment words. One element describes the act, and the other expresses a moral or legal evaluation of that act. So the descriptive element of "murder" is roughly *causing the death of a human being* and the evaluative element is *unjustly*. The descriptive element of "lying" is roughly *intentionally saying what is false to someone* and the evaluative element is *unjustly*. The word "unjustly," at least as it applies to sin, does not describe a real or internal property of a thing; it expresses an evaluation based upon violation of a law or command of God (Twisse, quoted in Pierce 1658a: 136–7). The evaluation involves no new entity. The only entities are the killing and the false telling. In other words, "is a sin" should not be considered a genuine predicate. Hobbes obliquely refers to this dual-aspect semantics when he explained that God's power causes only "those motions and present acts from which the act that is not now, but shall be hereafter, necessarily proceeds" (Hobbes 1839a: 5: 142). The killing of Uriah is a complex motion, and the sinfulness of the motion is not itself a motion.

Calvinists also explained the dual aspect of concepts like murder by using the matter/form distinction of Aristotelian philosophy. God is the material cause of murder but not the formal cause. That is, God caused the event of the killing of Uriah (the matter) but he did not cause the event as a sin (the form) (cf. Pierce 1658a: 136–7). Hobbes seemed to reject this kind of move when he criticized those who held that God is "the prime cause of the law and also the prime cause of . . . all other actions, but no cause at all of the injustice."[5] He said it is like saying that "one man maketh both a straight line and a crooked, and another maketh their incongruity" (*Leviathan*, 46.31).

---

[5] Hobbes's comment seems to imply that God is the cause of injustice. But he does not draw this inference.

The dual-aspect semantic explanation may not be so obvious for the word "sin" because its descriptive element is minimal. But this analysis, the predicate "x is a sin" is equivalent to "x is an action and x breaks a command of God" satisfies the requirements of the dual-aspect view. So (2) may be represented as

(2a) God is the cause of some actions and these actions violate God's commands.

(2a) does not entail that God performed any action that violated God's commands. God never commanded himself not to cause Uriah's death. Rather, God commanded David not to murder. So it was only David who violated God's command.

Now, these observations may only delay an objection. Underlying the complaint against or the worry about (2) is the belief that if one causes a sin, then one is culpable for the sin whether one is explicitly commanded not to cause the sin or not. So, the proponent of (2) needs to show that one can be the cause of sin without being culpable. This can be done. Suppose that A is a good person and B is such a bad person that A's goodness makes B want to do something evil. Since A loves C, B kills C. In this case, there is a sense in which A is the cause of C's death. If A were not so good, B would not have killed C. B in fact may say and believe that A is the cause of B's behavior. Many guilty people pass off the blame to some object by irrelevantly citing that object's presence in an earlier part of the causal chain. This is nicely illustrated by the story of the first act of disobedience. When God asks Adam whether he has eaten the forbidden fruit, Adam says, "The woman, the one you gave me . . ." The point of Adam's remark is that Eve is the cause of Adam's action, and so is God, since God gave Eve to Adam. But Adam is conceptually confused. He is conflating a cause of an action with the person culpable for an action. B does the same.

One might object that a being that has irresistible power, as God does, is responsible for all that happens. Paradoxically, Hobbes uses this fact to immunize God against any moral criticism. Irresistible power justifies everything; hence all of God's actions are justified. Thus, Hobbes says, "This question in the case of Job is decided by God himself, . . . by arguments drawn from his power, such as this, *Where wast thou when I laid the foundations of the earth*" (Hobbes 2002: 31.6/558). His view may even be considered moderate if compared to that of Twisse who wrote in *The Riches of Gods Love*:

[God has no need] of any pretext of justice to take a man's life from him . . . God can annihilate the holiest Angel by power absolute. . . . *Tiberius* commanded the Virgins to be deflowered, that they might be strangled. . . . If God were disposed to strangle any, certainly he hath no need to have them deflowered first. . . . God can lawfully annihilate the holiest creature that lives, and that without all respect to sin . . . Tiberius willed that the Virgins should be deflowered and impiously he willed it. God willed that David's Concubines should be deflowered, and holily he willed it. (Twisse 1653: 21, 23, 25, spelling modernized)

Let's now consider proposition (3). Its relation to (1) is difficult to state because it is not immediately clear what "author of sin" may mean. Anti-Calvinists in seventeenth-century England usually did not explicate it and often used it as if it were equivalent to (1). Pierce lists a number of different senses of "author," including "the first *beginner* of a work, sometimes him who doth *help advance* it; . . . sometimes only a *persuader;* sometimes a *sole cause;* . . . sometimes he that *shews the way*" (Pierce 1658a: 188). None of these senses seems to be as strong as that intended by the anti-Calvinists. One difference between "cause" in (1) and "author" in (3) is that "author" strongly connotes that God is morally responsible for sin; as such (3) is inflammatory in a way that (1) is not. Bramhall knew that Hobbes endorsed (1) and hence thought he was justified in attributing (3) to him. He wrote, "to charge the true God to be the proper cause and the true author of all the sins and evils which are in the world," is worse than being an atheist, a Manichee, or a heathen (Bramhall 1655: 61). "I hate this doctrine from my heart. . . . It destroys liberty, and dishonours the nature of man" (Bramhall 1655: 60).

Hobbes denied (3) in two ways. The first way depends on the claim already discussed, that irresistible power justifies absolutely: "what he doth, his doing maketh just" (Hobbes 1839a: 5: 138). It was mentioned earlier that Hobbes used this idea to explain and justify God's behavior towards Job (Hobbes 2002: 31.6/558; see also Hobbes 1998: 15.5). A related point is that God cannot sin because sin requires breaking a law and breaking a law requires being subject to the law but God is "not subject to another's law, and that therefore it is blasphemy to say that God can sin" (Hobbes 1839a: 5: 138). The second way of denying that God is the author of sin depends on Hobbes's theory of authorship. To be the author of an action is to own that action, and to own an action can be the result either of one's own behavior or of the behavior of another. When subjects authorize a sovereign to govern them, the sovereign's actions are owned by his subjects and not by him. The sovereign is in effect the tool of the subjects. About the author of sin, Hobbes says, "it cannot be said that God is the author of sin, because not he that necessitateth an action, but he that doth command and warrant it, is the author" (Hobbes 1839a: 5: 139; cf. Pierce 1658a: 210–11). This may seem to be a poor way for Hobbes to explain why God is not the author of sin. It seems to suggest that the sinner commands or warrants the sin. But that does not make sense. People have no authority with respect to sin. In fact, Hobbes's point is probably that God only causes the action and does not command or warrant it.[6] However, even if God were to warrant an action, it would not be a sin: "if God own an action, though otherwise, it were a sin, it is now no sin" (Hobbes 1839a 5: 139). Why is it not a sin? Hobbes's answer is an appeal to the first way of denying (3): because *what he doth his doing maketh just*" (Hobbes: 1656: 105).[7] Hobbes's explanation is very close to that expressed by John Calvin in his *Sermons on the Psalms*:

That when God *makes* an *Angel* or a *Man* a *Transgressor*, he himself doth not transgress, because he doth not break a law. The *very same sin*, viz. *Adultery* or *Murder*, in as much as it is the work of *God* the *Author, mover,* and *compeller*, it is *not* a *crime*; but in as much as it is of *man*, it is a *wickedness*. (quoted in Pierce 1655: 10, spelling modernized)

In addition to the two ways of responding to Bramhall just discussed, Hobbes had another. At one point Bramhall wrote: "It [the doctrine that God is the cause of evil] makes the first cause, that is, God Almighty, to be the introducer of all evil and sin into the world, as much as man, yea, more than man, by as much as the motion of the watch is more from the artificer, who did make it and wind it up" (Bramhall 1655: 60). Hobbes pointed out that Bramhall was contradicting Paul of Tarsus: "Thou wilt say then unto me, 'Why doth he [God] yet find fault? For who hath resisted his will?' Nay but, O man, who art thou that repliest against God? Shall the thing formed say to him that formed it, 'Why hast thou made me thus?' Hath not the potter power over the clay, of the same lump to make one vessel unto honour, and another unto dishonour?" (Romans 9:21, Authorized Version). Bramhall replied that the

[6] I owe this point to Brian Battiste.

[7] It is important that Hobbes explicitly denies that God can commit a sin because if Hobbes did not, then it might suggest that God is the author of sin.

"clay" people being referred to are sinners, and they have no right to complain (Hobbes: 1656: 98; cf. Calvin 1559: III.23.4). It is implausible that Paul thought the reply applied only to sinners qua sinners, but Bramhall probably had no better reply available to him.

3. The Debate between Thomas Pierce and William Barlee

Just as nothing was settled in the debate between Bramhall and Hobbes, nothing was settled in other debates between Calvinists and Arminians, for example, one that overlaps the Hobbes/Bramhall one. In *A Correct Copy of Some Notes Concerning Gods Decrees, Especially Reprobation* (1655),[8] Pierce claimed that Calvin and Barlee held that God is the author of sin. Early in his book, Pierce quoted a number of passages from *Institutes of Christian Religion* and other works without naming Calvin as the author. The first, as he rendered it is:

> That *all things* happen, not only by God's Prescience, but by his express *order* and positive *Decree*. Whereby many from the *womb* are devoted to certain and *inevitable Destruction*, that by their misery God's Name may be glorified. (Pierce 1655: 9; cf. *Institutes* III.23.6, spelling modernized)

A second passage from the *Institutes* he rendered as follows:

> That God directeth his *voice* to some men, but that they may be so much the *deafer*; he gives *light* unto them, but that they may be so much the *blinder*; he offers them *instruction*, but that they may be the more *ignorant*; and he useth a *remedy*, but to end they may *not* be *healed*. (Pierce 1655: 9; cf. Calvin 1634: 480 or *Institutes* III.24.13)

From these and other passages Pierce concluded that Calvin held (3), that God is the author of sin. It is plausible that from (3), Pierce infers (4):

(4) God is culpable for causing people to sin.[9]

---

[8] Barlee's version of the origin of the dispute is in Barlee 1656: 4–5, 9.

[9] In one passage, Pierce says that the question is not "*Whether God doth sin*" but "whether he *willeth* the *sins of his Creatures, and impels them to wicked acts*" (Pierce 1657: 38).

Pierce may have felt justified in drawing the inference because Calvin wrote, "God was the authour of that triall of Job, whereof Satan and the wicked theeves were ministers." Here the inflammatory word "author" appears although Calvin was not saying that God is the author of sin. Calvin held that "It was Gods will to have the false King Achab [sic] deceived," but from this it does not follow that God was the author of sin (Calvin 1634: 98; see also Calvin 1960: I.18.1).[10]

Because neither the passage about Job nor the one about Ahab says or implies (3), they do not seem to provide any evidence that Calvin thought (3). As regards Ahab, since he was evil, one can maintain that he got what he deserved. As for Job, one would need to prove that causing Job's suffering was a sin. Notwithstanding the absence of direct evidence, Pierce takes it as evident, based upon the quotations presented above and others, less telling, that Calvin holds (3).

Pierce's positive position consists of the denial of (2)–(4), and a weakening of (1):

(1') God is the cause of all good things
(2') God is not the cause of sin.
(3') God is not the author of sin.
(4') God is not culpable for causing people to sin.

(1') is the crucial proposition. If he can establish that, then, assuming God is all good, he is justified in holding (2')–(4'). (1') is supported by the book of *Wisdom* 1:13–14, "God made not death, neither hath he pleasure in the destruction of the living: for he created all things that they might have their being" (Pierce 1655: 21), and also by Ecclesiasticus 15:12, "Say not thou, 'He hath caused me to err' / for he hath no need of the sinful man" (Authorized Version). (Pierce 1655: 23).[11] The causes of sin are wicked angels and men (Pierce 1655: 31).

In holding (1'), Pierce is following Augustine of Hippo, who in *De Libero Arbitrio* had made the same claim. The cause of evil is each person who wills to do something evil. If one asks why people will to do something evil, Augustine says that there is no answer (*De Libero Arbitrio* II.18; cf. Calvin

---

[10] "*Colligemus, eius probationis cuius Satan & scelesti latrones ministri fuerunt, Deus fuisse authorem*" (Calvin 1559: I.18.1; see also III.23.3).

[11] Asserting that God was the cause only of good things was a standard Arminian claim; for example, Bramhall made it (Hobbes 1656: 97–8).

1554: III.23.4). Augustine was aiming to counteract Manicheanism, so he did not want the cause of evil to be anything ultimate or divine (*De Libero Arbitrio* II.17): "since, moreover, every defect comes from nothing, see where this movement belongs: you may be sure it does not belong to God" (*De Libero Arbitrio* II.20).

Barlee answered Pierce in *Praedestination . . . defended against Post Destination. In a Correptorie Correction* (1656). His main line of defense against Pierce is that neither Calvin nor Twisse ever said in so many words that God is the author of sin. According to Barlee, by relying exclusively on inference, Pierce violates a central principle of interpretation. One may never use the consequence of that person's words to charge them with a pernicious doctrine:

> the very first *element* and rudiment of all *moderation & pacification . . . viz:*
> That only must be taken to be the express positive opinion of any which he
> holds forth everywhere to be so in the most significant terms he can express
> himself in . . .: Every *man must be allowed to be the best interpreter of his
> own mind*. Direct positions must be produced to prove what other men's
> judgements are in any matter . . . : And if this be true, as it is most true, [do
> you not] ... know that the men you speak of . . . deny God to be the *author
> of sin*, whilst they repeat it at every turn that sin hath no efficient cause."
> (Barlee 1656: 55, spelling modernized)[12]

Pierce is unfair, according to Barlee, to claim that Barlee said that God is the author of sin, because Barlee "nowhere says, either in express terms, or in any *equipollent*, that God . . . is the *Fountain* or *Cause of sin*" (Barlee 1658: 54, spelling modernized). As for those places in the Bible that appear to say that God is the author of sin, Barlee interprets them "in a *figurative sense*" (Barlee 1658: 55). Pierce takes quotations out of context, "without any due regard to the scope of the words, or the authors explained meanings" (Barlee 1656: 52; cf. Hobbes 1651a: 43.24).

If it were fair to make inferences to a person's beliefs, then, Barlee claims, he could conclude that Pierce is an atheist (Barlee 1656: 55; see also 69; cf. Pierce 1658b: sig. *4[v] and **1[r]). In his subsequent book, Barlee says that

---

[12] Compare Barlee's interpretive principle with Hobbes's: "When it happeneth that a man signieth unto us two *contradictory* opinions, whereof the *one* is *clearly* and directly *signified,* and the *other* either *drawn* from that by consequence, . . . then . . . we are to take the *former* for his opinion; for that is clearly signified to by his, and directly" (Hobbes 1994a: 13.9).

Pierce's doctrines are "next door to down-right *Atheisme*" (Barlee 1658: 54 of chapter 3; see also 57 of chapter 3). He dismisses the accusation that he had said that Pierce was in the "State of Damnation" (Barlee 1658: 12; see Pierce 1658a: 45; and 1658c: A3^{r-v}). He only indicated that Pierce was like the "raging waves of the sea, foaming out their own shame, wandering stars, to whom is reserved the blackness of darkness for ever."[13] And he did not call Pierce a Socinian, only that his doctrine was a "Consequentiall *Constructive Socinianisme*" (Barlee 1658: 12).

The main justification for the assertion that God can cause the actions that are sins as performed by humans and not be culpable for them depends upon the weight Calvinists give divine sovereignty and omnipotence (Barlee 1656: 27, 58, 63, 66, 82, 85; and 1658: 2; for Whitfield, see Pierce, 1658a: 1–2). While omnipotence and sovereignty are usually not separated, if one had to order them according to rational priority, Hobbes and possibly other Calvinists would put omnipotence first. God is sovereign because he is omnipotent. One reason for saying this is that Hobbes attributes God's goodness and justice to his "power," that is, omnipotence (Hobbes 1839a: 5: 212). Also, God's power determines the character of his justice. Divine justice, rather than being giving each what is owed to him, as it is for humans, is simply God's distribution of "blessings and afflictions," however he chooses this: "Justice is not in God as in man, the observation of laws made by his superiors" (Hobbes 1839a: 5: 212).

A corollary of God's omnipotence is that some of his intentions, not to mention his nature, are mysterious: "poor orthodoxe *Ignaros*, wee think it the highest perfection of our *sober wisdome*, not to be wise above what *is written & so* we give no other causes of *predestination* then what the Scriptures do" (Barlee 1656: 16). For Hobbes, God's wisdom, mercy and justice derives from "an incomprehensible attribute given to an incomprehensible nature" (Hobbes 1839a: 5: 212; see also Hobbes 1839a: 4: 313).

Although Barlee regularly denies that Calvin or Twisse ever said that God is the author of sin (e.g., Barlee 1656: 74), he makes a limited concession on that matter at least once. He concedes that they "maintaine God to will sinne, but only in the sense in which Augustine of Hippo did, namely, that "nothing fals out but what God wils shall be, either by his reall effecting of it, or his

---

[13] Barlee 1658: page 12 of chapter 2 (the pagination of this book begins several times anew); cf. Barlee 1656: 43, 174); cf. Jude 13.

voluntary permission of it for his own glory" (Barlee 1656: 71; see also 72–3, and 89).[14]

One argument against Calvinistic predestination depends on its supposed inconsistency with free choice or free will. While Hobbes simply denied that the concept of a will that is free of efficient causation makes sense, Barlee asserts that they are compatible. He latches on to Pierce's assertion that it was necessary for him to publish his *Correct Copy* and observes that that necessity was "no waies opposite to your *Liberum Arbitrium*, or *free will*" (Barlee 1656: 9; see also 28–9; cf. Pierce 1657a).

Barlee often appeals to authority for his views. In addition to Augustine, Calvin, and Twisse, he sometimes appeals to the Lambeth Articles and Council of Dort; the English representatives were "the visible lawful *Representers of our Mother English Church there*" (Barlee 1656: 18). So there is a political aspect to correct Christian belief. This point is reinforced by Barlee's occasional appeals to the views of King James, to whom he refers on one occasion as "the then Learned Supreme Politicall Governour of the Church of England" (Barlee 1656: 17). On this latter point, Pierce had an excellent rhetorical reply against Barlee's and Edward Reynolds's use of the authority of James I. As Pierce points out, James was a Calvinist in his youth but "in his *riper and wiser years* he found so great reason to *retract* and *abjure his former error*, that he readily accepted of *Bishop Mountagues appeal*" (Pierce 1657b: 7). The Calvinists' commitment to the early views of James I and the late views of Augustine pose a dilemma for English Calvinists, as Pierce points out. Either a person's later opinion is better than his earlier opinion or it is not. If it is, then Calvinists cannot appeal to the authority of James I; if it is not, then they cannot appeal to the later opinion of Augustine. So Calvinists either abandon the beliefs of their King James or the beliefs of the great theologian Augustine. A similar dilemma might have been possible to direct against Pierce himself. Either he accepts that a person's later opinion is better than an earlier opinion or it is not. If the later opinion is better, then Pierce is committed to Augustine's "Calvinist" view of predestination. If the later opinion is not, then Pierce is committed to King James's Calvinism (Pierce 1657b: 7–8). However, Pierce is clever enough to say that he presents the dilemma against Barlee merely to show that the latter's appeal

---

[14] Barlee refers to chapter 95 of Augustine of Hippo's *Enchiridion on Faith, Hope and Love*. See also Calvin 1554: III.23.8.

to authority is ineffective and that he does not appeal to the authority of either James or Augustine.

Pierce constructs another dilemma for Presbyterians like Barlee and Reynolds. Either the judgment of King James has authority or it does not. If it has authority, then Presbyterianism is unacceptable. If it does not, then Barlee and Reynolds hold a treasonous view. Pierce quotes James's "Answer to Dr. *Reynolds* at *Hampton Court*, where the *Doctor* had seemed to plead for something like a *Presbyterie*. '*A Scottish Presbyterie, said the King, as well agreeth with Monarchie, as God and the Divel*'" (Pierce 1657b: 8).

Sometimes Pierce deals with Barlee, "Doctor *Twisse* and Master *Hobbs*" together, all of whom he thinks are "frequently *condemned* out of their own *mouths*" (Pierce1658a: 210). He refers to various passages in which Hobbes says that sins are actions, that God is the cause of all actions, and that God is "*a Principal Agent in the causing of all actions*." He then reports incredulously that Hobbes then "*denies* him [God] to be the *Author* of the *actions*" (Pierce 1658a: 211; cf. Hobbes 1656: 105–7). Being paired with Twisse would have been an honor for any English Calvinist, and Pierce says that Hobbes is "as able a *Calvinist* as their party hath lately had" (Pierce 1658a; 138 of chapter 3). Barlee, of course, does not want to be linked with the anti-presbyterian advocate of absolute sovereignty and refers to Hobbes as "*Monstrous Leviathan Hobbs*" (Barlee 1658: 7 of chapter 3). Although Barlee does not like being associated with Hobbes, he advocated the same position with similar arguments.

4. William Twisse and Thomas Jackson

The two debates already discussed—one between Hobbes and Bramhall and the other between Barlee and Pierce—were preceded by a similar one between Twisse and Jackson earlier in the century. Twisse believed the underlying problem with Jackson's position rested on two facts: one was his reliance on pagan philosophy and the other was his inability to refute the pagan views when they conflict with Christianity. According to Twisse, Jackson needlessly introduced problems that would not otherwise exist. Jackson began from the proposition of Hermes Trismegestus that "God is a sphere, whose Centre is everywhere, whose circumference is nowhere" (Jackson 1628: 55). The proposition is not obviously intelligible. How can a center, which is defined as a point in Euclidian geometry, be everywhere, when it would seem to require at least a solid figure to have any chance of being true? And how can a circumference be nowhere? If it is nowhere, then it has no dimension at all, and this seems to contradict the idea that a circumference is the diameter times π. Twisse's point was that none of these problems would arise if one had not introduced pagan philosophy in the first place, from an "Egyptian Priest," as the anonymous author of the preface to Twisse's book says (Twisse 1631a: sig. (*.*)ʳ). Such borrowing makes Twisse think that Jackson was "more foul than Arminius himselfe" and "espouses a corrupt Divinitie" (Twisse 1631a: sig. A2ʳ and 55).

In the same spirit, Twisse opposed Jackson's comparisons of created substances to God. He objected to comparing God's duration to the flow of a *"fountayne or Ocean,"* from which time and duration *"perpetually flow"* (Twisse 1631a: 139). He says that the "phrase, *to flow*, favoureth of a natural and necessary emanation" especially when "it is resembled by the flowing of water from a founteyne" (Twisse 1631a: 139). That is, Twisse thinks that God is so unlike his creatures that comparisons between God and creatures almost always fail. Hobbes shows the same sensibility when he says that it is absurd to say that *"faith* is *infused* or *inspired*, when nothing can be *poured* or *breathed* into anything, but body" (*Leviathan* 5.10; see also 46.18). Hobbes's debunking of language derived from created reality and inappropriately applied to God is consonant with Calvinist attitudes.

It would be a mistake to think that Twisse was not well versed in pagan and scholastic philosophy. He deployed and sometimes approved of views held by Thomas Aquinas[15] and discussed the views of Giles of Rome, Cajetan, Capreolus, Durand of St. Pourçain, Gabriel Biel, and many others (e.g. Twisse 1631a: 10, 82, 108–9, and 118). His dispute with Jackson was not due to a "want of profound knowledge in Metaphysicall speculations" among Calvinist divines (Twisse 1631a: sig. (*.*)ʳ). Indeed Twisse proved to be a formidable opponent on Jackson's own ground. Twisse's accusation that Jackson wanted "All Christians . . . [to be] called back" to the doctrine of "Plato and Plotinus . . . as if by the Prophets and Apostles they [Christians] had been carried too far" is not implausible (Twisse 1631a: (*.*) 2; cf. Perkins 1597: 17). Criticizing the use of pagan philosophy in Christian theology was standard Protestant practice, as Hobbes's complaint against John Wallis indicates, "And would you learn Christianity from Plato and Aristotle?" (Hobbes

---

[15] A notable example is what Thomas says at *Summa Theologiae* I, Q. 14, art. 8: "Seeing the will of God is most effectuall, it followeth not only that those thinges come to passe, which God will have come to passe, but also that they come to passe after the same manner that God will have them come to passe" (quoted from Twisse 1631a: 10–1; cf. Pierce 1657b: 33–4).

1839a: 4: 426). Indeed, a regular refrain in Hobbes's reply to Bramhall's book attacking *Leviathan* is that it is not in scripture or is contrary to Scripture.

5. Demoniacs

The second issue I want to discuss concerns the compatibility of Christian belief with the view that the people possessed by demons in the New Testament were actually madmen. Hobbes indicates that they are. According to him, the belief in demons originates with the pagan Greeks, whose natural philosophers did not know the physics of the brain and vision. In particular, they often confused visual illusions with true vision. The images seen in dreams were mistakenly interpreted as veridical perceptions of real things composed of "subtle or ethereal matter" (Hobbes 2002: 45.2/ 352). These supposed things were called demons, and get their first important literary treatment in Hesiod's *Theogony* (Hobbes 2002: 45.3/353). From Greece, these doctrines spread to Asia, Egypt, and Italy. The Jews picked them up in Judaea and Alexandria during the Diaspora (Hobbes 2002: 45.4/353).

Hobbes anticipates the objection that the idea that people possessed by demons were merely madmen seems implausible because if this were true, then Jesus would have known it, and if he had known it, he would not have spoken to the demons. Hobbes's reply is that Jesus's address to the demons is no stranger than his address to the sea, which he surely knew was not a person. More particularly, just as one might order a fever to leave someone who is sick without believing that the fever is a person, Jesus ordered demons, the madness, to leave madmen (Hobbes 2002: 45.5/354).

Someone may ask why Jesus did not correct the Jewish false beliefs about demons. Hobbes calls this question "more curious than necessary for a Christian man's salvation," just as curious as asking why all men are not saved, why God left it to men to use their "natural reason and industry" to figure out natural causes (Hobbes 2002: 45.8/355), or as curious as why Moses did not set down the "time of the creation" of earth, sea, men, beasts, and demons (Hobbes 2002: 45.8/355).

Taking "demon" and its related word "devil" figuratively also allows one to make sense of other biblical passages. When the New Testament says that Jesus was "*carried thence by the devil in an exceeding high mountain, who showed him thence all the kingdoms of the world,* wherein we are not to believe he was either possessed or forced by the devil, nor that any mountain is high enough according to the literal sense to show him one whole hemisphere" (Hobbes 2002: 45.6/354).

When I talk about the compatibility of the view that people are possessed by demons and Christian belief, I mean more than logical consistency. The issue involves the psychological compatibility of equating demons with madmen and seventeenth-century Calvinism or some other seventeenth-century religious sensibility. One reason for thinking that they were compatible is that Hobbes acknowledged that he was indebted for his view to Joseph Mede, who had a great reputation for piety (Hobbes 1839a: 4: 327).

Mede was often said to be a Calvinist. Calvinists, more than non-Calvinists, studied the Book of Revelation, and Mede was one of the great scholars of that book. Also, his failure to be elected a fellow of Christ's College was attributed to the animosity of the anti-Calvinist and vindictive Valentine Carey (d. 1626), who thought Mede "looked too much towards Geneva" (Mede 1664: LXV; Mede 1677: XXXVI). One of Mede's best friends was Twisse, who wrote that Mede's view about demons as having given him the "greatest content" in a laudatory Preface to Mede's The Apostasy of the Latter Times (Twisse 1641: a2^r). Further, the Presbyterian Stephen Marshall was particularly happy with Mede's view. This evidence, however, is not sufficient to declare Mede a Calvinist because the anti-Calvinist Thomas Jackson was also a friend. It is also reported that when asked whether he was a Calvinist or anti-Calvinist, he said that he avoided "being taken to be of a side" (see Jue 2006: 29–30).

In either case, Mede was an ardent Christian whose argument that demoniacs are madmen is especially intriguing because it is surprisingly modern. It relies on the premise that nature is uniform and requires uniform principles of explanation. His argument begins by interpreting John 10:20, "He hath a Devil, and is mad," as saying simply that the person is mad, just as saying, "He is mendacious and a liar" is to say that he is a liar (Mede 1642: 87).

Mede then appeals to two uniformities of nature, synchronic and diachronic. As for the former, he observes that while the "People of God" had demoniacs, other nations seem not to have had them (Mede 1642: 123; cf. 127–8). It is implausible, he says, that one nation would have demoniacs and not others, for what befalls the people of one nation befalls the people of other nations. If the Jews had demoniacs, other nations must have had demoniacs too, but they may have been called by a different name (Mede 1642: 127–8). Other nations had madmen, and John calls the demoniac a madman, so according to the principle that what befalls one nation befalls another, it is plausible that demoniacs are simply madmen.

One might object that it makes sense that only Jews had demoniacs, because they are a special people. Mede would reply that the Jews do not seem to think demoniacs are "any strange or extraordinary thing, but as a matter usual" (Mede 1642: 123). This does not exactly answer the objection, but this is what Mede says.

As for the diachronic uniformity, there were madmen before New Testament times and madmen after New Testament times. So it is plausible that there were madmen during New Testament times. Since demoniacs do not seem to exist before New Testament times or after, it is plausible that demoniacs were madmen under another name. It is good not to multiply kinds of entities without necessity. In short, the simplest way to understand the biblical references to demoniacs is to identify them with what "we call *mad-men,* and *Lunaticks*" (Mede 1642: 123).

How is it that no one earlier figured out that demoniacs were madmen? Mede's answer is philosophically quite sophisticated. He says that when the same things are "presented to us under different notions," they are often not recognized to be the same (Mede 1642: 120). To use the classic example from contemporary philosophy of language, it took people a very long time to figure out that the evening star is the morning star. Mede uses this general fact about names to explain another oddity in the Bible. Comets are seen by all nations, but the Bible appears to contain no reports of them. But this is implausible. The reasonable explanation is that the biblical authors used a different name for comets, to wit, signs of "Divine power":

> Should a man therefore think, there never appeared any of them in those times, or to those Countries? It is incredible: Or that the Jews were so dull and heedless as not to observe them? That is not likely neither: What should we say then? Surely, they conceived of them under some other notions than we do, and accordingly expressed them in some other way: As what if by a *Pillar of fire,* such a one perhaps as went before the Israelites in the Wilderness? Or by a *Pillar of fire and smoke?* As in that of *Joel, I will shew wonders in the heavens, and in the earth, Blood, and Fire, and pillars of Smoke:* Or by the name of an *Angel of the Lord,* whereby no doubt they are guided? (Mede 1642: 122, spelling modernized)

Mede gives other examples, such as the angel of the Lord who appeared just before the Israelites passed through the Red Sea. He concludes, "These, I say, or some of these may be descriptions of those we call *Comets*; which because they are disguised under another notions, and not denominated from *Stella*, or *Coma*, hence we know them not" (Mede 1642: 122).

What Mede did by understanding signs of divine power as comets was to reconcile one kind of miraculous event with natural science. I have argued that this was one of Hobbes's main projects in *Leviathan*. His explanation of Noah's rainbow, presumably the first one ever seen, is particularly important in this respect. Noah had no knowledge of the laws of nature and could not have conceived of how anything physical could have caused it. It was, then, a miracle, according to Hobbes's definition (Hobbes 2002: 37.2/233). So, rather than violating one or more of the physical laws of nature, Noah's rainbow is consistent with them. Faith and reason are reconciled. It is worth noting that Twisse also thought investigation of rainbows was a way of discovering "a secret of nature, very curious and nothinge vain . . . for it is the glory of God to hide a thinge" (Twisse 1631a: 20).

Mede's reconciliation of astounding biblical events with natural science is even more fine-grained than Hobbes's. He apportions different kinds of demoniacs into various subgroups of madmen: "Masters of Physick tell us of two kindes of *Deliration*, or alienation of the understanding." One kind is "*sine Febre* [without fever], when a man, having no other disease, is crased and disturbed in his wits," of which there are two types, "*Melancholia* and *Mania*" (Mede 1642: 86). Further, people who suffer from "*morbus Comitialis* or falling sicknes [probably epilepsy], and whatsoever is properly called *Lunacy*" are also demoniacs. Similarly, Saul's "Melancholy" was demonic (Mede 1642: 86).

Naturalizing demoniacs in order to bring the Bible into conformity with modern science was not Mede's primary purpose. He wanted to show that the concept of daemons is connected with Gentile religion, which perverted Christianity in the form of Roman Catholicism. He tells the full story in great length and detail in his book, *The Apostasy of the Latter Times, in which, (according to divine predication) the world should wonder after the Beast, the Mystery of Iniquity should so farre prevaile over the Mysterie of Godlinesse, whorish Babylon over the virgin-Church of Christ; as that the visible glory of the True Church should be much clouded, The True unsustained Christian Faith corrupted, the purity of true worship polluted. Or The Gentile's Theology of Daemons, etc.* (1641).

6. Conclusion

The upshot of this history of some arguments about Calvinist views about the authorship of evil and demoniacs is that Hobbes is an integral part of it. He represents himself as adhering to the doctrines of King James I. Of course, as regards some aspects of his religious and political views, he is more original and exciting. He is head and shoulders above his contemporaries in many ways. But beneath the shoulders, he is an English Calvinist fighting some of the same battles as others were fighting against anti-Calvinists.[16]

---

[16] I want to thank Ivan Heyman for his comments.

12

Hobbes's Erastianism and Interpretation

1. Introduction: Independency and Evidence

Recent work by Jeffrey Collins throws into high relief many of the most disputed issues concerning how evidence about religious beliefs ought to be interpreted in Thomas Hobbes's philosophy, and in early modern philosophy more generally. In the *Allegiance of Thomas Hobbes*,[1] Collins argues that Hobbes was strongly Erastian, enthusiastically favored Independency during the Interregnum, and was generally anti-religious. Although we agree about Hobbes's Erastianism, I maintain that Hobbes tepidly endorsed Independency in the early 1650s but preferred theological Calvinism, then out of favor, as a form of Christianity, adhered to by King James VI and I, episcopacy as an adjunct to absolute sovereignty, and a high liturgy.[2]

Our respective treatments of the following brief passage from *Leviathan* illustrate some of our differences: "And so we are reduced to the independency of the primitive Christians to follow Paul or Cephas or Apollos, every man as he liketh best. Which [is] . . . perhaps the best" (Lev. 47.20).[3] Collins takes these words to be an enthusiastic endorsement of Independency, that Hobbes believed "that Independency was the church model most likely to secure religious peace and protect the ecclesiastical supremacy of the state."[4] He tries to buttress his position by saying that Hobbes "concluded that only gathered, voluntary congregations enjoyed church authority."[5] But the phrase "gathered, voluntary congregations" is tendentious language, and Hobbes never used the phrase to my knowledge. Collins is right in holding

---

[1] J. R. Collins, *The Allegiance of Thomas Hobbes* (Oxford: Oxford University Press, 2005).

[2] "Theological Calvinism" is understood here as profession of double predestination, unqualified acceptance that God is the cause of all things, denial of free will, and restriction of the work of redemption to the elect alone.

[3] Thomas Hobbes, *Leviathan*, ed. A. P. Martinich (Peterborough, ON: Broadview Press, 2002), 47.20. References from *Leviathan* are to chapter and paragraph number.

[4] Collins, 129.

[5] Ibid., 125.

Hobbes's Political Philosophy. A. P. Martinich, Oxford University Press. © Oxford University Press 2021.
DOI: 10.1093/oso/9780197531716.003.0013

that Hobbes was virtually alone in holding that the sovereign had both the power of jurisdiction and the power of ministry. But Hobbes justified his position by appealing to the Bible and early church history. Both Moses and David had both secular and priestly authority; Constantine summoned the Council of Nicaea; and he was called a "bishop."

On my view, both the words themselves and their immediate context show that Hobbes did not enthusiastically endorse Independency. The first clause, "And so we are reduced to the independency of the primitive Christians," is a statement of fact. Independency was the established church in 1651. Further, while the reference to "primitive Christianity," may suggest some approval, because as a good Protestant Hobbes thought the early church was best, the allusion to Paul, Cephas, or Apollos suggests restraint or disapproval for two reasons. First, the differences between the people mentioned were the cause of dissension in the Christian community in Corinth.[6] Second, Hobbes's use of the hedge word "perhaps" mitigates his endorsement of Independency, and this hedge is strengthened by the two qualifications he immediately adds: "if it [Independency] be without contention and without measuring the doctrine of Christ by our affection to the person of his minister." The fact that the primitive church did not satisfy these qualifications Hobbes added suggests that he thought it would not be long before the Commonwealth's Independency also caused contention. This is confirmed by his comment that "if pastors be not subordinate one to another, so as that there be one chief pastor, men will be taught contrary doctrines, whereof both may be, and one must be, false."[7] Hobbes seems not enthusiastic, but wary. In other words, Hobbes seems to have thought that Independency was at the time the least bad option available because episcopacy had been abolished and Presbyterianism was infected by a pernicious democratic element.

In any case, Hobbes did not think Independency was right for him. One of the few direct facts we have of his religious preference in the early 1650s is his own testimony that he attended the services of "a good and learned man" ("*vir bonus et doctus*"),[8] who conducted them according to the rubric

---

[6] See 1 Corinthians 3:22.

[7] *Leviathan* 39.5.

[8] Thomas Hobbes, *English Works*, ed. William Molesworth (London, 1839), I, xvii: The phrase occurs in a passage that may be translated: "Returning to England, he [Hobbes] indeed found preachers in churches, but seditious ones, also extemporaneous, bold, and sometimes blasphemous prayers; moreover, no creed and no Decalogue. So for three months, he did not find any worship services in which he could participate. Finally, a friend led him to a church, more than a mile from his residence, where the pastor was a good and learned man, who administered the Lord's Supper according to the rite of the Church, and with whom he participated in the worship services."

of the Church of England, even though it had been outlawed. His attendance is confirmed by Aubrey, who mentions that Hobbes received the sacrament from John Pearson, later the bishop of Chester; and I have argued in another place that Hobbes's learned divine is Pearson.[9] Collins dismisses Hobbes's testimony on the grounds that White Kennett claimed that Hobbes went to church only for show and that Hobbes never attended services in the city.[10] But Kennett did not have first-hand knowledge of Hobbes's religious practice during the Restoration, since he was born in 1660 and wrote about Hobbes in 1708,[11] more than twenty-five years after his death and when Hobbes's views were conflated with eighteenth-century Hobbism.

In the passage just considered, Collins and I disagree at one level about internal criticism: What did Hobbes mean and what significance should be attached to it? But deeper than this disagreement are two more important aspects of interpretation. One is the interconnectedness of evidence. Neither view depends on one or a few isolated facts. The alleged facts are interconnected. The other aspect of disagreement concerns the weight that should be given to certain facts, both testimonial and nontestimonial. In the example just discussed, the weight of the testimony of Aubrey, Hobbes, and Kennett is at issue. But we also disagree about nontestimonial facts such as Hobbes's taking the Engagement upon his return to England. Collins thinks that this weighs heavily as evidence of Hobbes's commitment to the Commonwealth and, by implication, to Independency. To me the fact has little relevance or weight, both because of at least two related facts. Thousands of royalists took the Engagement, and Charles II in exile allowed his supporters "what liberty their consciences shall give them to do, to preserve themselves for the King's service."[12] The most plausible explanation for Hobbes's return to England in my opinion is straightforward. After a decade in exile he had a mind to go home, as he told Clarendon; he saw some risk from the French Roman Catholic clergy; and he was out of favor with influential members of the English court in exile. On my view, Hobbes was always an Erastian, as

---

[9] "Hobbes's Interregnum Place of Worship," *Notes and Queries* 54 (December 2007), 433–6.

[10] Collins, 245.

[11] White Kennett, *Memoirs of the Family Cavendish* (London: printed and sold by H. Hills, 1708). Kennett probably did not associate with the Cavendishes until the eighteenth century, so he was in no position to know what tales about Hobbes were true. Kennett was an opportunist, described by his sympathetic biographer as "Eager to advance his career," "angling for the deanery of Peterborough," and as having a "reputation for sycophancy exemplified by the flattering eulogy he delivered at the funeral in Derby of William Cavendish, 1st Duke of Devonshire" (DNB, vol. 31, 285a).

[12] *Calendar of State Papers Domestic* 1650, 89–9; quoted from Edward Vallance, "Oaths, Casuistry, and Equivocation: Anglican Responses to the Engagement," *Historical Journal* 44 (2001), 64.

most politicians and English intellectuals were for most of the sixteenth and seventeenth centuries. As for his practical political decisions, Hobbes was a loyalist ("one who supports the existing form of government," *Oxford English Dictionary*).

2. Interpretation as Inference to the Best Explanation

In my view, interpretation is a kind of inference to the best explanation. As such, it employs inductive reasoning. Given a set of facts, one proposes the hypothesis that best explains those facts. A basic characteristic of inductive reasoning is that while an inference to some hypothesis may be justified by some set of facts {f1, f2, ... , fn}, increasing the set with additional facts may falsify or disconfirm the hypothesis. So the hypothesis that all the marbles in a jar are black is justified by the facts that the first five marbles drawn from the jar are black. However, if the fact that the sixth marble is white is added, then the original hypothesis is falsified. As a form of inductive reasoning, the more evidence the better.

Here are four examples in which Collins omits some of the evidence. First, Collins thinks that Hobbes's odd religious views are evidence of esotericism. He does not discuss the following part of Hobbes's letter to Edmund Waller of July 1645:

> My odd opinions are baited. But I am contented with it as believing I have
> still the better, when a new man is set upon me that knows not my paradoxes
> but is full of his own doctrine, there is something in the disputation not
> unpleasant. He thinks he has driven me upon an absurdity when t'is upon
> some other of my tenets and so from one to another till he wonder and ex-
> claim and at least finds I am of the antipodes of the schools.[13]

The key word in Hobbes's letter is "paradoxes," by which he means "A statement or tenet contrary to received opinion or belief; often with the implication that it is marvelous or incredible; sometimes with unfavorable connotation, as being discordant with what is held to be established truth, and hence absurd or fantastic; sometimes with favorable connotation, as

---

[13] Hobbes, *The Correspondence of Thomas Hobbes,* ed. Noel Malcolm (Oxford: Clarendon Press, 1994), 124.

a correction of vulgar error" (*Oxford English Dictionary*). Hobbes continued this theme of paradoxes in his debate over free will with Bishop John Bramhall:

> The Bishop speaks often of paradoxes with such scorn or detestation, that a simple reader would take a paradox either for felony or some other heinous crime, or else for some ridiculous turpitude; whereas perhaps a judicious reader knows what the word signifies; and that a paradox, is an opinion not yet generally received. Christian religion was once a paradox ... Insomuch as when a man calleth an opinion [not his own] a paradox, he doth not say it is untrue, but signifieth his own ignorance; for if he understood it, he would call it either a truth or an error. He observes not, that but for paradoxes we should be now in that savage ignorance, which those men are in that have not, or have not long had laws and commonwealth, from whence proceedeth science and civility.[14]

The straightforward interpretation of Hobbes's espousal of odd views is that he held odd views. For Hobbes, a geometrical point has extension and a geometrical line has width. That's odd. He believes that the qualitative experience people have of the world is nothing but motions in them; and he feels no need to explain how these motions could be a feeling. That's odd too. Charles II, as Collins knows, called Hobbes "the oddest fellow I've ever met." Being odd and having odd views is no evidence of an intention to subvert revealed religion, just as it is no evidence of an intention to subvert mathematics or materialism.

Second, as regards state control of the Church, Collins does not mention the favorable treatment that Christians gave to the reign of David, who was both the secular and religious sovereign of Israel. Nor does he discuss John Foxe's praise for Constantine, "a second Moses sent and set up of God, to deliver His people out of their so miserable captivity into liberty most joyful. Constantine .... established the peace of the Church."[15] What Collins argues is an exclusively pagan view of religion is one that was and is held by many Jews and Christians. In the late twentieth century, the Christian Coalition wanted a Christian federal government. A third example concerns the relation between Hobbes's Erastianism, humanism, and commitment to religion.

---

[14] Hobbes, *The Questions Concerning Liberty, Necessity, and Chance* (London, 1656), 239.
[15] John Foxe, *Foxe's Book of Martyrs*, abridged ed. (Springdale, PA: Whitaker House, 1981), 42 and 47.

His Erastianism lends itself to the construction of a syllogism: all Erastians are Protestants; Hobbes is an Erastian; therefore, Hobbes is a Protestant. It then follows that Hobbes is a Christian. Sometimes Collins represents Protestantism and humanism as antagonistic to each other[16] and says that Hobbes's Erastianism is "superficial" and that he is even more a humanist; for he thinks that Hobbes's pagan view of the world is grounded in his humanism:

> If Hobbes displayed some affinity with Protestant Erastianism, his religious thought was animated by a religious skepticism that rendered this affinity superficial. Furthermore, his deference to the religious authority of the state did not follow from a sincere concern for Godly reform, but from a realist's sense of the political dangers of religious feeling. . . . Hobbes developed this psychological understanding of religious belief . . . not within a Protestant context.[17]

Collins emphasizes Hobbes's knowledge of Cicero, Tacitus, Plutarch, and other ancient pagans, who thought that all religion was superstition and should be controlled by the state. But reading the views of pagans does not mean that one accepts the views of those pagans.

Even if everything Collins writes about the influence of humanist scholars on Hobbes were true, it would not prove his conclusion that "Hobbes's humanism trumps his Protestantism," since humanism and Protestantism are not contraries.[18] Collins does not mention the fact that many sixteenth- and seventeenth-century humanists were Christians, for example, John Calvin, whose humanism was "crucial to his thought."[19] More generally, the humanists did not just return to Greek and Latin pagan writings, they returned to the Bible. One of Erasmus's greatest accomplishments was to prepare Greek and Latin editions of the Bible.

The absence of information about Knox, Calvin, Erasmus, and many others gives the impression that Collins is engaged in special pleading. He claims that such scholars as Gerardus Vossius,[20] John Selden, and Hugo Grotius, all of whom talked about pagan religion and the political use of religion,

---

[16] Collins, 37.

[17] Ibid., 26.

[18] Ibid., 57. Collins in effect sees this when he is not promoting his thesis that Hobbes is irreligious; see, e.g., 207.

[19] William J. Bouwsma, *John Calvin* (New York: Oxford University Press, 1988), 113.

[20] Collins, 49.

influenced Hobbes; but he does not mention that the lives and writings of these three men make it evident that they were sincere Christians, albeit sometimes critical of certain forms of it. There was a rumor that Selden was an atheist. Brian Duppa, bishop of Salisbury and a friend of Selden, denied it. Selden and Hobbes were friends and thought to have similar views about religion. I think they were similar. Collins represents Duppa as a great enemy of Hobbes.[21] But I do not see this animosity in Duppa's correspondence. Reporting his meeting with Hobbes in 1656 at Roehampton, Duppa does not denigrate Hobbes at all but says that he "brought away . . . his *Elements of Philosophy*, translated into English," no doubt a present from Hobbes.[22] About *Leviathan*, Duppa is ambivalent: "And yet as in the man so there ar [*sic*] strange mixtures in the book; many things said so well that I could embrace him for it, and many things so wildly and unchristianly, that I can scarce have so much charity for him, as to think he was ever Christian."[23] Just as Duppa denied the rumor that Selden was an atheist, the same should be denied of Hobbes.

Since Vossius, Selden, and Grotius did not abandon Christian belief, given all they knew about pagan religions, we have no reason to conclude that Hobbes did, based upon similar evidence. This point can be generalized. Hundreds of professional Jewish and Christian scholars alive today know everything that Hobbes knew about pagan writings about religion and yet do not give up their faith. Obviously, knowledge of this material does not logically or psychologically compel intelligent people to conclude that revealed religion is false.

A fourth example of omitting relevant evidence concerns the relation between belief in a revealed religion and skepticism in early modern Europe. Since Hobbes is skeptical about most claims to revelation and miracles and skeptical that revelation or miracles are objects of knowledge, Collins thinks Hobbes is skeptical of any revealed religion. If Collins were right, then, in addition to Hobbes, Erasmus, Montaigne, and Kierkegaard would not believe that revealed religion is true. Now of course one can say that all of these thinkers were irreligious. But one ought not to ignore the evidence presented by Richard Popkin, whose work does not appear in Collins's bibliography, that skepticism was used by Roman Catholic thinkers against Protestants,

---

[21] Ibid., 245, 255–6.
[22] *The Correspondence of Brian Duppa and Sir Justinian Isham, 1650–1660*, ed. Gyles Isham (Northamptonshire: The Northhamptonshire Record Society, n.d.) , 119.
[23] Ibid., 41.

Protestants against Catholics, Protestants against Protestants, and Catholics against Catholics. Skepticism can just as easily be used in defense of revealed religion as against it. I might also mention that the Roman Catholic Church is skeptical of every alleged revelation and miracle that might threaten its authority.

Collins does not discuss a different and more plausible explanation for Hobbes's skepticism. Writing at the beginning of the scientific revolution, he recognized, as many other intellectuals did, that the new science and Christianity seemed to be inconsistent with each other. So it seemed that one had to choose between them. Some intellectuals, such as Hobbes's friends Marin Mersenne, Pierre Gassendi, Thomas White, and Kenelm Digby, wanted to reconcile science and revealed religion. They wanted to embrace natural science without rejecting revealed religion. Hobbes's solution was to explain why the two could not contradict each other. Faith and reason belong to different realms.

Thus, both can be embraced. Hobbes was not even the first to propose this. The Roman Catholic Cesar Cardinal Baronius, famously quoted by Galileo, wrote that the Bible does not teach how the heavens go, but how to go to heaven. In my experience this continues to be one of the most popular defenses of revealed religion, among intellectuals and nonintellectuals alike. My complaint is that Collins does not discuss the evidence for this interpretation of Hobbes's philosophy. The point of these examples can be generalized. To prove one's position, it is not sufficient to produce only the evidence in favor of it. It is also necessary to present the evidence against it.

In criticizing Collins for not providing all the evidence, I am not assuming that scholars ever have access to all the facts; they could not discuss them all if they did. What's required roughly is a treatment of all the relevant evidence. I say "roughly" because often all the evidence is neither necessary nor practicable to set out. In practice, the display of evidence is dialectical with one scholar adducing what she takes to be the weightiest and most salient evidence, and then another scholar countering with evidence to the contrary, supplemented with criticism of the first scholar's interpretation of her evidence; and when the first scholar is unconvinced, as is likely, she replies and supplies more evidence and counter criticism; and so on. So there is no way to enumerate the relevant evidence in a reasonable space. Moreover, scholars will disagree about what is relevant and how much weight should be given different evidence, unlike the case of the black and white marbles.

Here's an example of a dispute over the weight and relevance of a piece of evidence. Collins thinks that Hobbes's comment that "*ecclesia*, in ancient Greece, signified 'a Congregation or an Assembly of Citizens, called forth to hear a Magistrate speak unto them'" shows that he favors Independency.[24] I think the weight and relevance of the definition is minimal. Notice first that Collins ignores the force of his own phrase "in ancient Greece," which accurately captures Hobbes's point that he is talking about the meaning of the phrase about two thousand years earlier in the Peloponnesus. He is not talking about seventeenth-century Independent congregations. Since a king is a magistrate, the comment about *ecclesia* applies as much to episcopal churches as any other kind. Moreover, Hobbes shortly later defines a church as "a company of men professing Christian religion, united in the person of one sovereign; at whose command they ought to assemble and without whose authority they ought not to assemble."[25] There is no hint that he is talking specifically about Independent congregations. The phrase, "united in the person of one sovereign," applies more saliently to the Church under Charles I and his representative William Laud than it does to the Rump Parliament, the presumptive sovereign in 1651, or to Triers and Ejectors. Also, Collins's use of Hobbes's comment about "*ecclesia*" is not relevant to his thesis because Hobbes did not maintain that individual Independent congregations were churches in the proper sense. They did not have the power "to command, to judge, absolve, [or] condemn."[26] When Hobbes goes on to say that such "a Church . . . is the same thing with a civil commonwealth consisting of Christian men, and is called a *civil state*, for that the subjects of it are *men*, and a *Church*, for that the subjects thereof are *Christians*,"[27] he is reporting what had been the law of England under the Stuarts and earlier monarchies, namely, that the entire people of England were members of the Church, no matter what the form of ecclesiastical government.

Collins unreasonably privileges Hobbes's comment about "*ecclesia*," which is merely one item in a list of several items relevant to understanding what a church is, briefly: a building, a congregation or assembly of citizens, "the whole multitude of Christian men," "the elect only," a congregation of Christians having the "power to will, command, to be obeyed, to make laws, or to do any other action whatsoever," and then Hobbes's own

[24] Collins, 125.
[25] *Leviathan*, 39.4.
[26] Ibid., 39.5.
[27] Ibid., 39.5

definition, mentioned above.[28] In short, I see no grounds for Collins's claim that Hobbes's statement of the meaning of the ancient Greek word "*ecclesia*" "normatively privileged gathered congregations, and handicapped more universal models of the church."[29]

Although Collins does not discuss Hobbes's alleged atheism, that topic is relevant to the general issue of evidence being considered here. The direct evidence that survives does not support the view that he was an atheist. John Aubrey, who knew Hobbes well, explicitly considered the issue of Hobbes's alleged atheism, and denies its truth: "For his being branded with atheisme, his writings and virtuous life testifie against it. . . . To prevent such false and malicious reports, I thought fit to insert and affirme as abovesaid."[30] Furthermore, Hobbes left nothing in his two autobiographies, written in the 1670s when he had little to fear, to suggest that he was irreligious; and there is no other documentary evidence to that effect. Nor did any of his personal friends ever claim he was an atheist. The account of Hobbes's death by James Wheldon supports Hobbes's claim to have been a good member of the Church of England. Finally, if the Cavendishes thought Hobbes was irreligious, they shouldn't have had him buried inside the parish church. The maxim, "Absence of evidence is not evidence of absence," needs to be qualified to read, "Absence of certain evidence is evidence of absence, because sometimes the absence of evidence that it is reasonable to expect to have if something is a fact is evidence against the existence of the alleged fact: no victim, no motive, no opportunity, no murder."

3. Suspicion and the Enlightened Reader

Collins may find the two-realm solution to the problem of faith and reason "highly suspicious." He thinks that Christian belief has to be knowledge, not just belief.[31] However, since it is faith and not knowledge that is a theological virtue, it is not clear why this should be so. Jesus said, "Blessed are they who believe and have not seen,"[32] not blessed are they who present cogent arguments for the existence of God. Moreover, the pertinent issue is not

---

[28] Ibid., 39.3–4.
[29] Collins, 125.
[30] Aubrey, *Brief Lives*, 1:353.
[31] Collins also thinks that if miracles exist, they have to be objects of knowledge (29).
[32] John 20:29. When Collins later discusses Hobbes's views about faith, he says they are "significant," but I'm not sure what Collins thinks the significance is (124).

whether Collins or Thomas Aquinas or John Calvin wants Christian belief to be knowledge but whether Hobbes thought belief was sufficient and whether this was a plausible way to treat Christian dogmas.

Collins's threshold of suspicion seems to me to be too sensitive. He says that the "gap between the composition of the books of the New Testament and their reception by the Church as canonical" is "suspicious."[33] The suspicion is that of Collins, not Hobbes. Again hundreds, if not thousands, of educated Christians and Jews know that many centuries separate the writing and canonization of many of their books of revelation; yet that fact should not be the basis for suspicion of their faith.

Being overly suspicious allows one to judge any view a person might espouse as disingenuous; it is to commit the "damned-if-you-do, damned-if-you-don't fallacy," as when Collins says that Hobbes was not concerned about "the evidentiary value of miracles . . . but their utility."[34] He thinks it highly suspicious that Hobbes says that miracles were "for the procuring of credit to Gods Messengers, Ministers, and Prophets."[35] If Hobbes had not said that miracles had a religious purpose, Collins could have judged it "highly suspicious" that Hobbes would allow things tantamount to magic tricks to count as miracles. Hobbes is damned if he does specify a religious purpose for miracles and damned if he doesn't. To me, it would be suspicious if miracles had no religious purpose. Given that they should have a purpose, what is a better purpose than the one that Hobbes attributes to them?

Collins says that my interpretation, in *The Two Gods of Leviathan*,[36] of Hobbes as a religious thinker "assumes the complete sincerity of his [Hobbes's] often highly dubious scriptural interpretation and appeals to patristic authority."[37] I did not assume it. Knowing what the standard view of Hobbes was, I devoted a large part of *The Two Gods of Leviathan* to rebutting the standard interpretation that Hobbes is insincere precisely because I took that view seriously. I showed that, given the cultural context of early and mid-seventeenth century England, Hobbes's own upbringing, his actual religious practice and his writings, the more plausible interpretation is that he was sincere. As for Hobbes's allegedly dubious scriptural interpretation, Collins gives no examples; and in fact most of Hobbes's interpretations

---

[33] Collins, 29.

[34] Ibid., 28.

[35] *Leviathan*, 37.6; Collins, 28.

[36] Martinich, *The Two Gods of Leviathan: Thomas Hobbes on Religion and Politics* (Cambridge: Cambridge University Press, 1992).

[37] Collins, 27.

of the Bible are now adopted by almost every academic biblical scholar. At least since the seventeenth century, any critical investigation of the Bible has induced some nervous believers to accuse the critic of being irreligious. For example, Brian Walton (1600–61), bishop of Chester, the chief editor of a Polyglot Bible,[38] had to put up with the fulminations of the Independent divine, John Owen.

When Collins argues that the assumption of Hobbes's sincerity has "been undermined by scholarship convincingly demonstrating the highly rhetorical nature of Hobbes's religious writing,"[39] he refers to David Johnston's book, published six years before *The Two Gods of Leviathan*, and Skinner's *Reason and Rhetoric in Hobbes's Leviathan*, which hardly mentions my book and certainly does not consider my evidence or arguments, much less refute them. Sometimes Collins refers to Paul Cooke's *Hobbes and Christianity*.[40] But Cooke focuses on refuting Howard Warrender's view, not mine. To paraphrase a quip of G. K. Chesterton, my thesis has not been refuted; it has not been seriously considered.

In order to justify the low threshold of suspicion, many scholars press into service the distinction between exoteric and an esoteric teaching. Exoteric doctrine is understood by unenlightened readers while only enlightened readers understand, indeed, even notice the esoteric doctrine. According to Collins, Hobbes's *Leviathan* was written for enlightened readers, "particularly sovereigns."[41] But while he calls James I wise,[42] Hobbes nowhere claims that sovereigns are inherently wise or enlightened.[43] His discussion of the first cause of the dissolution of commonwealths, namely, "*that a man to obtain a kingdom is sometimes content with less power than to the peace and defense of the commonwealth is necessarily required*," alludes to Charles I's "Response to the Nineteen Propositions."[44] One reason he would not want

[38] The edition published during the Commonwealth was dedicated to Oliver Cromwell. This dedication was replaced with one to Charles II after the Restoration. This kind of side-switching was relatively common and not surprising, given human nature.

[39] Collins, 27.

[40] David Johnston, *The Rhetoric of Leviathan* (Princeton: Princeton University Press, 1986); Quentin Skinner, *Reason and Rhetoric in Hobbes's Leviathan* (Cambridge: Cambridge University Press, 1996); Paul Cooke, *Hobbes and Christianity* (Lanham, MD: Rowman & Littlefield, 1996).

[41] Collins, 33.

[42] *Leviathan*, 19.23.

[43] Hobbes said, "those persons, that for the most part can give no other proof of being wise take great delight to show what they think they have read in men by uncharitable censures" (*Leviathan*, Introduction, 3).

[44] *Leviathan*, 29.3.

to identify sovereigns with the wise is that if a sovereign had to be enlightened in order to be the sovereign, then his status would depend on a natural quality, or at least a natural quality that was enhanced in a particular way. This obviates the necessity of the social contract. Also, if the sovereign's position depended on being enlightened, then the sovereign could be deposed if it could be shown that the sovereign were not enlightened. Hobbes does not want to trust in people's judgment on this kind of matter. Hobbes's sovereign is a judge and makes the legally correct judgment in virtue of his office, not some supposed wisdom.

As for the supposed unenlightened reader, Collins, like many others, thinks that Christians are unenlightened. It is uncontroversial that Hobbes intended Charles II to be one of his readers and that Hobbes knew that Charles was a Christian. So how could Hobbes have intended Charles to get his secret message? In fact, the thesis that Hobbes expected the wise to get the secret message and the stupid, that is, the Christians, not to get it, is undermined by the fact that it was bigoted, and, I dare say, sometimes stupid, Christians in the seventeenth century who typically thought that Hobbes was intent on undermining Christianity.

Being overly suspicious sometimes results in seeing something that is not there (see Figure 12.1).[45] Collins correctly maintains that the page is evidence of Hobbes's Erastianism, that the sovereign "holds in one hand a sword, symbolizing temporal power, and in the other a large crozier, emblem of spiritual power" and that the two vertical panels "elaborate on the theme."[46] However, when he observes that the "royal fortress stands against an episcopal palace, a sovereign's crown against a bishop's mitre," he is seeing an opposition that is not there. The sovereign is holding both sword and crozier, a distinctive sign of a bishop, and they are angled to converge at a point above his head. For Hobbes, "the sword of justice and the shield of faith" are both held by the same person, "for a Church and a commonwealth of Christian people are the same thing."[47] In saying this, he was merely expressing seventeenth-century English law, according to which every Englishman was a Christian.

---

[45] Sometimes evidence seems to have a duck-rabbit kind of ambiguity such as Hobbes's illustrated title page, which various scholars have used to prove various theses. Some see the image of the sovereign's face as that of Cromwell and others see the visage of Charles I. Collins's interpretation of the title page does not turn on who, if anyone, is being pictured.

[46] Collins, 121.

[47] *Leviathan*, 39.5 and 42.80.

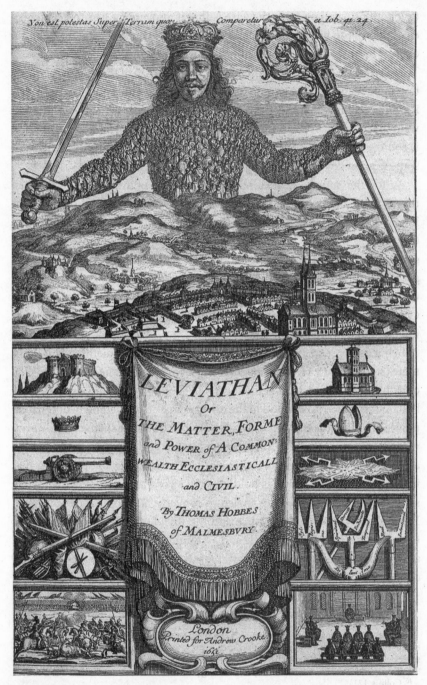

Figure 12.1 *Leviathan, or, the matter, form, and power of a commonwealth, ecclesiasticall and civil.* Harry Ransom Humanities Research Center, The University of Texas at Austin.

Hobbes wanted a state church so that there would be no possibility of divided loyalties.

If Hobbes had intended to indicate a negative attitude towards episcopacy, he should have had the sovereign hold a broken cozier, preferably one obviously severed by the sword, or had the crozier pointed downwards. Moreover, the represented sovereign is a king since he wears a crown. Neither the rule of the Rump Parliament nor that of Cromwell is being endorsed. For Hobbes, Constantine was the model of a Christian emperor (as for Protestants) and also a bishop.[48] So the crown and mitre rather than standing against each other are coordinate and represent king and bishop, as do the castle and what seems to be a cathedral, the seat of a bishop. Religious temporal authority is the two arms of the state.[49] Collins's remark that the symbolism in the other panels is "more ominous" is off the mark: "A charged cloud . . . is paired with a cannon. Demonic forked shafts labeled 'syllogism' and 'spiritual/temporal' also face an arsenal of weaponry."[50] In fact, Hobbes is merely extending the analogy between the secular and spiritual powers. Secular power is represented by a cannon and weaponry; the exercise of secular power is war. Correspondingly, spiritual power is represented by lightning and logic and its exercise is academic disputation. The lightning or "thunderbolts of Zeus" are a traditional sign of spiritual power; and disputation occurs within the walls of a college or university.[51] As long as the sovereign controls both secular and spiritual power, the instruments and exercise of spiritual power, paradigmatically episcopal, is not problematic. Moreover, Collins's description of the panel containing a pitchfork with the word "syllogism" and another with the words "spiritual" and "temporal" is incomplete. Another fork is labeled "directe" and "indirecte," as in direct and indirect syllogisms, another "real" and "intentionale," as in the distinction between real and intentional beings in philosophy. Finally, a pair of horns, cupping the forks, is labeled, "dilemmas." Hobbes has merely pictured the weapons of the university. Nothing in the illustrated title page endorses Independency.

[48] Ibid., 42.86.
[49] Ibid., 42.80.
[50] Collins, 121–2.
[51] See *The Two Gods of Leviathan*, 365–6.

4. Logical and Plausible Theories

One reason Collins is suspicious of Hobbes is that, according to him, "elemental features of Christian metaphysics were irreconcilable with his [Hobbes's] own political philosophy."[52] At best, this would show that Hobbes's theory was inconsistent, not that he was irreligious. Elemental features of mathematics were irreconcilable with Hobbes's own geometrical views—he tried to square the circle—but this does not show that he was anti-mathematical.

Collins writes,

> Hobbes's civil science depended on fear of death as the chief psychological force motivating humans to accept social constraint. If the fear of death was not the most basic of all fears, then it would not motivate naturally anti-social individuals into ordered society. Christianity, by promising eternal salvation and threatening eternal damnation, trumped the mere fear of death.[53]

What Collins does not mention is that Christianity promises eternal salvation to those who believe Jesus is the Messiah, and Jesus said, "Render unto Caesar the things that are Caesar's." Christianity is compatible with civil obedience. Even if fear is not the most basic fear of all, combined with the hope that reason can find a way out of the state of nature, it is motivation enough. Though God has greater power than men, the fear of the power of men is greater than the fear of the power of God.[54] Most Christians would agree.

Collins is also suspicious because he thinks that Hobbes guts Christian theology. He says that the "theology of *Leviathan* was intended to be both sufficiently Christian to attract the allegiance of the philosophically unsophisticated, and sufficiently detached from those aspects of Christianity that were irretrievably incompatible with sound civil science."[55] I find this judgment at odds with the text, the beliefs of seventeenth-century Englishmen, and human psychology. Hobbes's theology is philosophically quite sophisticated, and highly informed biblically. Philosophically unsophisticated people would not have been attracted by Hobbes's views. If Hobbes had wanted to

---

[52] Collins, 30.
[53] Ibid., 31.
[54] *Leviathan*, 14.31.
[55] Collins, 32.

attract them with some ruse, he would have espoused an utterly conventional and simplistic doctrine. Most unsophisticated people are comfortable with familiar doctrines, not novel ones.

One of the two main theses of my book, *The Two Gods of Leviathan*, is that Hobbes tried to prove that true Christianity was not politically destabilizing. Hobbes's theological positions that servants should obey their masters, that all should render unto Caesar the things that are Caesar's, and that Christ's kingdom is not of this world are politically engaged Christian doctrines. All of this is not just compatible with Erastianism but consonant with it.

Also suspicious according to Collins is Hobbes's view that the kingdom of heaven will be on earth, a view that he thinks is unbiblical and unchristian.[56] But Hobbes's interpretation is biblically based, as the references in chapter 38 of *Leviathan* show. Moreover, faced with the challenges of Copernican science—the earth is no longer the center of the universe; there is no "up" where heaven can be and no unearthly "down" where hell can be— Hobbes's view that heaven or the kingdom of God will be on earth is an ingenious way to save the doctrine of heaven, not to undermine it.

Concerning the Trinity, Collins objects that Hobbes defines "the Trinity in a remarkably earthly and political manner."[57] Collins presumably is thinking of Hobbes's definition of a person in terms of his idea that the sovereign is a person and a person is authorized to represent something. However, neither being earthly nor political is a sign of being non-Christian. Every legitimate religious concept has to be grounded ultimately in some "earthly" concept, because all ideas originate in sensation.[58] Augustine uses the earthly concepts of mind, intellect, and memory to explain the Trinity.

As for Hobbes's concepts being political ones, four comments should be made. The first is that his concept of a person is crucial to his political theory. If it failed to work as part of an explanation of the Trinity, then his concept of a person would become suspect, not the doctrine of the Trinity. It was not in his interest to use that concept in a failed application. Second, Collins gives no reason why a political concept should be any more suspect than a nonpolitical one. Indeed, using the concepts of substance[59] and relation, as Thomas Aquinas does, seems no more respectful than Hobbes's use of the concept of

---

[56] Ibid.
[57] Ibid.
[58] I ignore the possibility of innate ideas because Hobbes did not believe in them and neither do most contemporary philosophers.
[59] Following Boethius, Thomas defines a person as "an individual substance of a rational nature."

person because substances belong to species and God according to Thomas belongs to none, and relations are not things but are dependent upon things. The third comment is that Hobbes's concept of a person is not exclusively political. In the state of nature, one human being can authorize another to act on his behalf and thereby bear the person of the first. Although such a case may be rare and usually imprudent, it is possible. The fourth comment is that it's plausible that a political philosopher would use political concepts even outside of politics. In Renaissance Italy, Roman Catholic theologians explained the various kinds of grace in banking and commercial terms because that is what they and a large part of their audience knew.

Collins is probably bothered that Hobbes has Moses represent God the Father, Jesus God the Son, and the Apostles God the Holy Spirit.[60] Now this view is not political, since neither Jesus nor the early Church had political authority; but let's ignore that fact because it is more important that Hobbes's explanation of the Trinity will not work. Hobbes came to realize this and credited Bishop John Cosin with showing him that it will not work.[61] So Hobbes retracted that view in the Appendix to the Latin Leviathan.

When scholars criticize Hobbes's theory of the Trinity, one thing they virtually never do is to give a coherent and consistent theory of the Trinity.[62] If there is no such theory, Hobbes certainly could not have given one; and it is unjustified to think that simply by giving a theory, one is conveying a secret or esoteric message. Again, think of Hobbes's attempt to square the circle or Gottlob Frege's attempts to prove the consistency of his logical system. In Hobbes's particular case, the fact that he uses his fascinating concept of a person to explain the Trinity is evidence that he thought his theory was successful. For, if his concept of a person was not successfully used, then some doubt may attach to it.

5. The Interpretation of Evidence

As discussed earlier, Collins and I often disagree about the proper weight to assign to various pieces of evidence. I look at the illustrated title page of Leviathan and see a sovereign who wears a crown and holds a crozier, a

---

[60] Leviathan, 42.3.

[61] A. P. Martinich, Hobbes: A Biography (Cambridge: Cambridge University Press, 1999), 207–8.

[62] See A. P. Martinich, "Identity and Trinity," The Journal of Religion 58 (1978), 169–81, and "God, Emperor and Relative Identity," Franciscan Studies 39 (1979), 180–91.

sovereign who is a king and a bishop, and conclude that Hobbes prefers a monarch ruling an episcopal church, the very arrangement that Tudor and Stuart England had. Collins gives these features of the illustration little or no weight at all. He sees the title page as a pictorial representation of Hobbes's thesis that "disputes over 'precedence' between temporal and ecclesiastical authorities were the engines of civil war."[63] Whenever Hobbes makes a statement that can be construed as anti-Christian, Collins judges it to be sincere and to have great evidential weight. Whenever Hobbes makes a statement that is apparently favorable to Christianity, he judges it to be insincere and hence of doubtful evidential value. I hold something close to the opposite. My reason for discounting the statements that can be construed as anti-Christian is that they unnecessarily require more inferences or more complex inferences to arrive at that conclusion than a sincere rendering. That is, although an anti-Christian interpretation is possible, it is not necessary; and it requires more complexity than the alternative. Simplicity is as much a virtue in interpretation as it is in science. Moreover, as Hobbes pointed out in his debate with John Bramhall, once an interpreter is given free rein to hypothesize nonapparent meanings, he can arrive at almost any interpretation. Answering Bramhall's accusation of atheism, Hobbes wrote, "this atheism by consequence is a very easy thing to be fallen into" and then proceeded to show that Bramhall could be shown to be an atheist by consequence.[64]

Also, since there are many more apparent statements that affirm or presuppose Christian belief and since there are so many instances where Hobbes apparently is trying hard to reconcile Christian doctrine with either modern science or peace, it is more plausible to take Hobbes at his word than to be suspicious of him. Why should Hobbes labor so hard to give a coherent explanation of the Trinity, redemption, and the nature of the Church if he was insincere? I think it is psychologically more plausible that Hobbes would have affirmed the most conventional Christian views if he simply wanted to exploit Christian doctrine for secular political purposes. That would have made his views more palatable to his contemporaries. Also, the statements that Collins and others think suggest animosity or skepticism about Christianity do not have to be interpreted that way. They can just as easily—I think more sensibly—be interpreted in the way Hobbes indicates that they should be interpreted, namely, as directed against the abuses of biblical Christianity

[63] Collins, 122.
[64] Hobbes, *English Works*, ed. William Molesworth 4: 384.

by Roman Catholics, Presbyterians, and those members of the Church of England who resemble Roman Catholics in some respects.

6. Conclusion

Near the end of his book, Collins says that he "has argued that Hobbes's religious thought has two fundamental aims: to undermine religious belief among the wise, and to preserve Christianity's utility as a civil religion."[65] I agree that Hobbes had the second aim. He was inspired by the use of religion by King David and the Emperor Constantine. But the first alleged aim is not supported by the evidence that Collins presents. It is ironic that almost everyone who thought that Hobbes wanted to "undermine religious belief" was an enemy. Are these the enlightened readers that Collins refers to?

Collins also says, "It has been a fundamental premise of this book that Thomas Hobbes's Erastianism simultaneously drew on the variant theoretical traditions of Protestant ecclesiology and humanist civil religion. . . . Cromwell [believed] . . . the religious regime of the Interregnum was an enormous step on the road to the Godly state and the final achievement of the English Reformation."[66] I agree that Hobbes was Erastian and that he was influenced by both Protestantism and humanism, as many Protestant thinkers were. These facts suggest that Hobbes, like Cromwell, was trying to improve on the "achievement of the English Reformation."

[65] Collins, 252.
[66] Ibid., 205; see also 206.

13

Sovereign-Making and Biblical Covenants in *On the Citizen**

In *On the Citizen*, Thomas Hobbes describes two kinds of covenants. The first are covenants among human beings, most importantly sovereign-making covenants, which create human sovereigns. The second kind are the major biblical covenants, which have God as a party. Although Hobbes could have given a unified account of both kinds, his account of biblical accounts is truer to the biblical conception of covenants than to his account of non-religious ones. I will suggest that in *On the Citizen*, Hobbes wanted to make his theory of sovereign-making covenants as palatable to his readers as possible. The biblical associations of the idea of a covenant served his purposes. However, in sovereign-making covenants, the prospective sovereign is not a party to the covenant,[1] while God is a party to the prominent biblical covenants. My guess is that Hobbes wanted his own description of the biblical covenants to be as true to them as possible for fear of generating controversy when

* I want to thank Jo Ann Carson, Kody Cooper, Robin Douglass, Leslie Martinich, and Johan Olsthoorn for comments on earlier drafts.

Abbreviations used in this chapter are as follows:

DCo = *De corpore* (References are to chapter and section number.)
DCv = *De cive* (References are to chapter and section number.)
DH = *De homine* (References are to chapter and section number.)
EL = *Elements of Law, Natural and Politic* (References are to chapter and paragraph number.)
L = *Leviathan* s(References are to chapter and paragraph, followed by page numbers in Hobbes 2012.)
LL = *Latin Leviathan* (References are to chapter, followed by page numbers in Hobbes 2012.)

[1] According to the standard interpretation, a conquering sovereign is a party to the covenant with the vanquished. There is evidence for this view. However, I think a simple and better interpretation is that a conquering sovereign represents its subjects in a covenant with the defeated persons. The sovereign itself is an actor on behalf of its subjects (cf. DCv 7.17, 8.1, 8.14; and L 20.1/306).

Hobbes's Political Philosophy. A. P. Martinich, Oxford University Press. © Oxford University Press 2021.
DOI: 10.1093/oso/9780197531716.003.0014

England already had more than enough of it. So he was content to give a relatively straightforward description of the biblical stories and to restrict novelty to the secular covenants. A major unifying element of both kinds of covenants is faith.

Sovereign-Making Covenants

Covenants are indispensable to Hobbes's political philosophy. Without a covenant, there is no sovereign; without a sovereign there is no common-wealth; without a commonwealth, people are in a state of nature; and in the state of nature, human life is miserable. The fact that keeping one's covenants is among the first three laws of nature in each of his major political works sig-nals their importance. Covenants would be dispensable if people could get out of the state of nature in a different way, say, by having everyone making peace. That is the instruction of the first law: "*seek peace where it can be found*" (DCv 2.2, "*quaerendam esse pacem ubi haberi potest*").[2] This law is as helpful as the stock advisor's recommendation: Buy low, and sell high. How does one do this? The next law, derived from the first,[3] is only slightly more helpful. It instructs a person not to retain their right to all things but to transfer or lay down some of them (DCv 2.3; cf. L 14.5/200). This law leaves open whether rights should be renounced or transferred; and if the latter, to whom. Hobbes argues later that simple renunciation will not produce peace; and only one kind of transfer, each person transferring to the same one person, brings it (DCv 5.6; cf. DCv 2.4). Even if the second law were more specific, it would not suffice for the purposes of people in the state of nature. Laying down one's rights does not guarantee that a person would receive any rights or protec-tion to compensate for the loss. In other words, the second law of nature is compatible with making a gift of one's rights without any assurance that one would receive something of sufficient value in return (DCv 2.8). Suppose each person transferred his rights to the same one person. There would still

---

[2] Translations from the Latin text are my own.

[3] Hobbes's numbering of the initial several laws in *On the Citizen* may be confusing. After the "first and fundamental law," he discusses a derived law. But it is not given a number. The second law of nature, keep your covenants, is also the second derived law. The third derived law occurring in the chapter—"do not let someone who treated you well, regret doing so"—is the third law; and so on. See the Contents to DCv chapter 3.

be no guarantee that the person who accumulates these rights would have the job of protecting each person (cf. the third or fourth law of nature in DCv 3.8 and L 15.16/230).[4] What is lacking is "some right reciprocally transferred to himself," as Hobbes says, according to which each person is acting on the condition that all the others are acting to establish someone to protect them (L 14.8/202). It is what S. A. Lloyd (2009) has called "reciprocity."

Reciprocity is an essential element of covenants (L 14.9–11/204). As important as laying down rights is to covenants, it does not specify the content that is crucial to getting out of the state of nature. Simply requiring that everyone aim at the same goal is not sufficient. What is needed is a deduction from one or more of the first several laws to the conclusion that everyone subjects "his own *will*, to that of another *one*" for the purpose of protecting the covenanters (DCv 5.6; see also L 17.13/260).[5] The "therefore" ("igitur") that appears early in section six may be disconcerting. What were the premises? The answer is that Hobbes had shown that each "will" of social animals is attuned to acting cooperatively. In contrast, unification of all human wills into one will requires a special act to create a unity. The unification occurs when each person subjects his will to that of either one person or one council (DCv 5.6). In *Leviathan*, Hobbes will say that reason "suggest[s] Articles of Peace." But a suggestion is not a demonstration; and I do not see a demonstration of the articles of peace there. Earlier he had written that the wherewithal to get out of the state of nature is "Feare of Death; Desire of such things as are necessary to commodious living; and a Hope by their Industry to obtain" them, and "Reason" (L 13.14/196; cf. Lloyd 2009: 185–6). Fear, desire, hope, and reason are plausible conditions for using one's imagination creatively to arrive at plausible terms of peace.

The next matter to consider is whether the person to whom rights are transferred is a covenanting party or not. Hobbes's negative answer is to some extent a reaction to a view held by many of Charles I's enemies. According to them, the sovereign was a party to a "contract" with the people of England.

---

[4] I think that Hobbes did not consider an odd consequence of his view. Either the person who receives the rights is a natural or an artificial person. In either case (a) he lays down his right or (b) he does not. If (a), his ability to function as the protector of rights is diminished. If (b), then he seems to violate the second law of nature. Therefore, whether the person receiving the rights is natural or artificial, either his ability to distribute rights is diminished or he violates the second law.

[5] In the language of *Leviathan*, each party transfers their right to govern themselves to someone "to the end he may use the strength and means of them all, as he shall think expedient, for their Peace and Common Defence" (L 17.13/262).

Even some of Charles's supporters during the Civil War thought that he had a contract with the people (Hyde 1676: 49). The Royalists of absolutism, Hobbes among them, denied that the monarch could be a party to the covenant because English law held that the king could do no wrong; and if the king could be a party to the covenant, then he could do wrong.[6] Subjects, being human, would judge his actions and possibly conclude that he had done something wrong; and that would destabilize the civil state. Hobbes supplied other arguments. One is that a sovereign cannot make a covenant with "the whole multitude, as one party to the Covenant," because the multitude does not exist as a unity before they covenant (L 18.4/266). He does not argue conversely that the sovereign cannot be a covenanting party in the sovereign-making covenant, because during the process of covenanting, the sovereign does not yet exist (Hyde 1676: 49–51). Perhaps, he omits this argument because he does not want to highlight the fact that the sovereign is a creature of the people covenanting.

The unity of the sovereign raises a question. Are the natural persons who hold the office of the monarch and the artificial person of the monarch identical? They cannot be. The human being who is the "matter" of the sovereign exists before the sovereign is created and may die while the monarch lives on. Part of English law was that the king never dies. Hobbes does not always make clear whether he is talking about the natural person who is the sovereign or the artificial person of the sovereign (e.g., DCv 5.6; cf. L 28.25/496). When he says that each covenanter gives up the right to govern himself, he gives up the right "to this man or assembly of men," one may wonder about the precise reference of "this man." If "this man" is a natural person, the wrong person is getting the rights; they should be going to the artificial person. Similarly, if the "assembly" is a non-unified cluster of natural human beings, the wrong persons are receiving the rights. However, if "this man" refers to the relevant artificial person, then the correct person is receiving the rights; similarly for the phrase "assembly of men" mutatis mutandis.[7]

---

[6] Laurens van Apeldoorn (2019) presents strong evidence that Hobbes conflated the natural person with the artificial person that the sovereign is in order to criticize the view Parliament had taken to justify killing Charles Stuart. (I restrict discussion here to a monarch.) I think Hobbes need not have done this. He could have argued that to kill the natural person who is sovereign is in effect to destroy the sovereign by killing the person by which the sovereign acts.

[7] This understanding of his text may make one wonder how an artificial person is created before the covenanting has concluded (L 18.1/264; see for example, DCv 5.6–7 and L 17.13/262). The wonderment should be general for the apparent difficulty in creating artificial or institutional entities. For example, the Olympic Games open when the chair of the Olympic Committee says, "I declare the Olympic Games open." But how could he refer to the Olympic Games when they do

Pactum Vetus *and* Pactum Novum

Knowing that Hobbes has an extensive discussion of covenants in the Bible, one might wonder, and even expect, the theoretical account of those covenants to be very close if not the same as his treatment of covenants in Chapters 16 and 17. In addition to the unity suggested by the word "covenant" being applied to each, since nothing is universal but a word according to Hobbes, he would have a more general theory if he treated them similarly. To express this virtue from a different perspective, his theory would have been in better standing with metaphysics, which urges, "Do not multiply entities without necessity."

There was a practical advantage to be gained by a unitary account. Both the Presbyterians and the Independents challenged the king's claim to be supreme in religious matters even though the Act of Supremacy of 1534, renewed in 1559, said that he was. That he was the head of the secular government was too obvious to be said. Church and state intertwined in several ways. Bishops were members of the House of Lords because they were literally lords, owners of extensive wealth-producing land. Bishops also had often held secular posts, such as Chancellor. The monarch was crowned in Church, with the Archbishop of Canterbury typically presiding. Major events of ordinary human life, such as birth, entrance to adulthood, and marriage, occurred within a church. If Hobbes had shown that the covenant underlying the structure of English government was just like the covenant underlying covenants in the Old Testament, he would have undercut a major claim of the king's religious opponents, namely, that the ecclesial structure and liturgy of the Church were not dimensions of the English monarch's authority. In fact, like the monarch of England, Abraham, Moses (as God's representative), King David, and King Solomon were the head of both the religious and non-religious dimension of life. Cracks in that scheme were visible in the late sixteenth century; and Hobbes tried to repair that damage with his theory. Although absolute sovereignty would continue to flourish in some countries

not exist until the chair finishes saying "open"? Berengar of Tours (c. 999–1088) denied that the words of consecration, "This is my body," create the body of Christ. When the priest says "This," he must be referring to the bread; and when he says "my body," he must be referring to the bread again in order to be saying something true. The words "my body" cannot literally refer to the body of Christ because even on the account of those who believe in transubstantiation, his body is not present until after the priest finishes the words of consecration. He was condemned for this nifty reasoning. Divines of the Church of England sometimes used it against the Roman Catholic doctrine (Adams 1619: 65).

in Europe for more than a century, the future of English rule was already away from Hobbes's commitment to it. His theory was designed to preserve the past, not to create the future.

Neither the common law nor the civil law dictated the use of "covenant," to my knowledge, to express the authority of the monarch over the people (cf. Cowell 1607: sig. T3ʳ). The primary inspiration for it must have been the Bible. Hobbes explains that the two main parts of the Bible should be rendered in Latin as "Pactum Vetus" ("Old Covenant") and "Pactum Novum" ("New Covenant"), respectively, rather than the Vulgate's "testamentum." Notwithstanding the advantages for Hobbes to give a unitary account of sovereign-making and biblical covenants, we shall see in this section that he does not.

Hobbes says that from "the beginning of the world God reigned indeed... *by way of covenant* ["per *pactum*"],[8] over Adam and Eve" (DCv 16.2). The story of the first human beings in Genesis does not say anything about a covenant involving them and God. My guess is that Hobbes says this because of the influence of covenant theology, according to which God made two covenants with human beings, a covenant of works with Adam and a covenant of faith with all humankind.

Hobbes does not elaborate on the covenant of works because human beings are "all guilty of disobedience to Gods Law." Consequently, "now, not onely *Obedience* for the rest of our time, but also a *Remission* of sins for the time past [is required]; which Remission is the reward of our Faith in Christ" (L 43.3/930). As it applies to postlapsarian human beings, "The Obedience required at our hands by God, that accepteth in all our actions the Will for the Deed, is a serious Endeavour to Obey him" (L 43.4/930). One might think that Hobbes's use of "the Will for the Deed" is evidence that he was not an English Calvinist on the ground that an act of will or endeavor is a deed; and a deed is a work (Cromartie 2018: 96). The problem with this interpretation is

---

[8] Charles Cotton translated "pactum" as "contract" in the chapter on sovereignty by institution (DCv 7.5–7). In Chapters 16 and 17, he changed his practice and often translated "pactum" as "covenant'; for example, he translated, "*Pactum... inter Deum & Abrahamum*") as "*Covenant... between God and the Israelites.*" Occasionally Cotton translates "foedum" as covenant, even when it occurs close to "pactum." And Cotton can hardly be faulted, because Hobbes sometimes uses "foedum," not to mention "testamentum," to mean covenant (DCv 16.3; cf. DCv 16.1 and 16.4). Tuck and Silverthorne regularly translates both "pactum" and "foedum" as "agreement," including the titles of chapters 16 and 17, "The Kingdom of God by the Old Agreement [*pactum*] and "The Kingdom of God by the New Agreement [*pactum*]." Malcolm sometimes translates "pactum" as "pact." See his editorial note 34 to L 14.11/204. Hobbes sometimes uses "pact" in *Leviathan*, where he could have used "covenant."

that English Calvinist divines of the early and mid-seventeenth century often used the phrase "the will for the deed," sometimes citing 2 Corinthians 8:12 to support their view. They could use the phrase in good faith because the phrase means deeming a will to be a work, where deeming presupposes that the will is not a work. Although Hobbes uses "endeavor" as a technical term, his meaning is close to one of its ordinary meanings, and various Calvinist theologians said that God requires only an "endeavor" to obey God (e.g., Attersoll 1618: 736: "*God accepteth the will for the deed, and the endeavour to obey for perfect obedience*").

Although covenant theologians held that God was a party to the covenant made with Adam and Eve, Hobbes does not assert that. Rather, he says that "In the beginning of the world God reigned . . . *by way of covenant,* over Adam and Eve" (DCv 16.2). The interpretation that God was a party to this covenant comes by implication. Hobbes went on to say that God "wished no obedience to be given to him, beyond that which natural reason dictated, except *through a covenant* [*per pactum*]" (DCv 16.2). He is alluding to the command that Adam and Eve are not to eat of the tree of the knowledge of good and evil. God's authority to issue this command was a consequence of the covenant and not presumably from his omnipotence. Hobbes does not raise the issue of whether the covenant was a sovereign-making one.

Rather than demand good works of fallen human beings, as was demanded of Adam and Eve, God demanded only faith from their descendants. The penalty for disobeying God's commands would be remitted if they had faith because faith counts as repentance (DCv 17.7). What kind of faith? "[F]aith in Christ" (L 43.3/930).

In any case, the supposed covenant of works was soon voided "and never after renewed," as suggested above (DCv 16.2: "neque unquam post renovatum"). Hobbes then considers the first covenant that was significant for the character of the "old covenant," the one that involved Abraham.[9] It was not a sovereign-making covenant because Abraham was already a sovereign, under the rubric of tribal chief (DCv 16.6). As sovereign, Abraham had authority over "sacred as [much as] secular" matters. Hobbes goes on to say that the same covenant with Abraham was "renewed" with Isaac and Jacob. In other words, "by the form of the covenant itself," Abraham promised that his descendants would worship God, as much as he would (DCv 16.6). They

---

[9] God's covenant with Noah is not significant to the main theme of the old covenant, namely, the status of Israel as God's special people. An easy way to understand why is to consider that Noah was not a Hebrew or Israelite (cf. Bullinger 1624: 28–9).

would know how to worship God because Abraham was "the *interpreter* of all the *laws* and *words* of *God*" (DCv 16.7). Since God was a sovereign by nature over Abraham and all other people, Abraham's covenant did not acknowledge God simply as a god, "but *that God appearing to him [Abraham]*; just as the ritual worship, which Abraham owed to God" was the ritual worship "of *religion* and *faith*, . . . [that] God had *supernaturally* revealed" (DCv 16.4).[10]

Hobbes's description of the covenant with Moses is similar to the one with Abraham. He says that Moses had the right of interpretation entirely in himself. He supports his view by considering the absurdity of the alternatives:

> For if he [Moses] had not been the *interpreter of the laws and word*, that office must have belonged either to *each private person*, or to a congregation or *synagogue* of many, or to the *high Priest* or to other *Prophets*. First, that that office belonged not to private men, or any assembly composed of them, stands from this, [namely] that they were not admitted, indeed, they were prohibited with most heavy threats, *to hear God speak*, otherwise than through Moses. For it is written, *Let not the priests and the people cross the lines, to go up unto the Lord, lest he [God] kill them. So Moses went down to the people, and told them everything.* (Exod. 19:24–5; DCv 16.13)

The quotation from Exodus is rather bloodless compared to other stories that Hobbes alludes to or briefly describes in order to illustrate his view that Moses is the sole legitimate interpreter of Israelite religion. The story of the rebellion of Corah, Dathan, and Abiram, who led two hundred and fifty other Israelites to rebel against Moses, is more vivid. While Hobbes quotes two verses from the story of their deaths (DCv 16.13), a longer quotation is appropriate for contemporary readers:

> And it came to pass, as he had made an end of speaking all these words, that the ground clave asunder that was under them: And the earth opened her mouth, and swallowed them up, and their houses, and all the men that appertained unto Korah, and all their goods. They, and all that appertained to them, went down alive into the pit, and the earth closed upon them: and they perished from among the congregation. And all Israel that were round about them fled at the cry of them: for they said, "Lest the earth swallow us

---

[10] The Latin reads: "sed *Deum illi apparentem*, quemadmodum cultus quem *Abrahamus* debebat Deo, . . . quem Deum *supernaturaliter* revelaverat."

up also." And there came out a fire from the LORD, and consumed the two hundred and fifty men that offered incense. (Authorized Version, Numbers 16:30–5)

Given the religious challenges by puritans and Presbyterians to Charles's authority to dictate the proper form of worship in the late 1630s and early 40s, Hobbes must have had that controversy in mind when he wrote the words above. However, he also meant quite generally that no one should presume to interpret religion unless he is the sovereign. After the story of Corah and the others, Hobbes describes the subsequent official interpreters of the Israelite religion, such as Eleazar, the sovereign and high-priest (DCv 16.14–5). His summary statement is "Therefore, supreme civil power was owed *by right*, from the institution of God, to the High priest" (DCv 16.15: "Potestas itaque civilis summa debebatur *iure*, ex institutione Dei, Sarcedoti summa").

To return to Abraham, the covenant between God and Abraham was one between two sovereigns.[11] The biblical account of the Mosaic covenant is a different and more difficult case. The Hebrew slaves who fled Egypt and were wandering were approaching death's door. Although they were following Moses, they had not covenanted to make him their sovereign. They were a "stateless" group. Afraid and desperate, they implored Moses to ascend Mt. Sinai as their representative.[12] They needed a representative because they thought they would die if they were in the presence of God, and because the only way to make a covenant with God is through the mediation of a person in whom people have faith, Moses was needed (see also McQueen 2020). When Moses came down from Mt. Sinai, the sovereignty-making covenant had been completed. Hobbes does not say here whether God was a covenanting party. Whatever happened, God became the sovereign of the Israelites in extraordinary circumstances and Moses His representative.

That God became the special sovereign of the Israelites under Moses should have been an attractive feature for Hobbes's purpose. He could have explained the central covenant in the Old Covenant as consonant with his view about secular sovereign-making covenants. He could have

---

[11] One may wonder how God could lay down any rights as required in a Hobbesian covenant in light of his natural sovereignty. He could have concocted a mainstream answer: "Since God is infinite, laying down a right does not diminish his infinite power."

[12] Luca Ribarević suggested at a conference in Amsterdam that the Israelite covenant is one by acquisition, not by institution; and God is undoubtedly an object of fear. However, the Israelites were in immediate fear of starvation and dehydration. Hobbes does not indicate which kind of covenant it was.

written that God became the sovereign by accepting as gifts the rights to govern themselves offered by the covenanting former slaves (cf. DCv 2.5, 2.12; EL 15.11). As the special sovereign of the Israelites, God commanded the Israelites to obey the Ten Commandments (cf. Mendenhall 1954: 62), or more broadly, the dietary, purity, and ritual laws in Deuteronomy and elsewhere.[13] The divine and secular sovereign-making covenants each involved saving people from death. God in the Old Covenant saved the Israelites from death in the desert from thirst and hunger. In the New Covenant, he saved all human beings or gave them the means to be saved from the punishment of sin through the work of Jesus. Similarly, the civil sovereign, the lord of his subjects, saves them from the dangers of the state of nature. However, Hobbes does not interpret the covenant mediated by Moses in that way. He follows the standard view that God was a party to the covenant, despite denying a contractual part to the civil sovereign. It is not clear why he did not try to give a unified account of sovereign-making covenants. Although Hobbes had not yet expressed his theory of persons and authorization in On the Citizen, the ordinary concepts of authorization and representation would have been sufficient for this explanation to be acceptable. Perhaps he did not want to introduce a new interpretation of an important element of Judeo-Christian religion in the already revolutionary years of the early1640s. Perhaps he thought that the language of the Bible committed him to the standard position that God was a covenanting party (e.g., Ainsworth 1620: 93). Perhaps, he simply did not think about it.

In addition to the salience of covenants in books of the Old Covenant and the New Covenant and the popularity of covenant theology, Hobbes may have chosen the word "covenant" because of its use in the National Covenant (1638) by Presbyterian Scots as a pretext for resisting the religious policies of Charles I. The covenant purports to be between Scots, God, and the king. Hobbes had even more reason to be outraged by purported covenants with God without the king's approval or participation because the English parliamentarians had created the Solemn League and Covenant (1643), in order to win the assistance of Scottish Protestants to fight the King:

---

[13] Abraham, David, and Solomon were absolute sovereigns too; but not in virtue of a covenant involving God.

this pretence of Covenant with God, is so evident a lye, even in the pretenders own consciences, that it is not onely an act of an unjust, but also of a vile, and unmanly disposition. (L 18.3/266)

Hobbes was arguably right to condemn those who entered into new covenants. Those covenants were illicit because they were "repugnant" to a "former Covenant" by which they were obliged to the King (L 18.3/264).

Edwin Curley is not so sure: "Clarendon is right to complain" that Hobbes's statement about the possibility of humans having covenants with God is "destructive of our religion and against the express sense of Scripture" (Curley 2004: 200; cf. 201 and 206; the quotation is from Hyde 1676: 50). But Clarendon was wrong or seriously misleading when he wrote that Hobbes held that "no covenant can be made with God" (Hyde 1676: 50). What Hobbes said was that "there is no Covenant with God, but by mediation of some body that representeth Gods Person," and that the only one who can do this is "Gods Lieutenant, who hath Soveraignty under God" (L 18.3/266).[14] Curley says that Hobbes's claim in *Leviathan* that mediators are necessary in order for people to "know" whether a covenant should be accepted or not "is rather puzzling" (Curley 2004: 203, about L 14.23/210). Certainly, Hobbes should not have used the word "know" because of his strong conditions on knowledge. He should have used "appropriately believe" or something similar. However, my guess is that even if Hobbes's comment had been weaker, Curley's puzzlement would persist. He would still hold that Hobbes's statement that divine-human covenants need a mediator "doesn't square with those biblical texts which support the need for a mediator; they suggest that (ordinary) humans cannot be in the presence of God and survive the experience" (Curley 2004: 203).

Two related points may be made in reply. One is that Curley's word "ordinary" in parentheses points to the solution. Moses was not ordinary; and he was not ordinary because God chose him, just as the Israelites were not ordinary after God had chosen them. The other point is that Curley does not cite all of the relevant texts. While ordinary people would die in the presence of God, as Exodus 20:19 indicates (cf. Deut. 5:22), the Bible allows for an exception, Moses. The exception is necessary because a covenant with God requires the presence of a witness to God's acceptance. So God immunized

---

[14] The Latin *Leviathan* has: "Pactum enim cum Deo iniri non potest, nisi mediante aliquot, qui Deum representat; id quod solus facit is, qui Summum sub Deo habet Potestatem" (LL 18.3/267).

Moses against the death that otherwise would have struck him down. Hobbes sensibly says that human beings do not understand how God could have spoken to Moses. But Christians, Jews, and Muslims believe it.

The problem of the biblical mediator is analogous to the problem of interaction between mind and matter in Cartesian philosophy. They are too unlike in nature and causal power to interact. Descartes' pineal gland is the Moses of interaction. Since a gland is a body, it cannot reduce the gap between mind and body. More pertinently, Descartes chooses a body part to mediate between mind and body rather than something mental, because humans could never be sure of the existence of another person's mental thing. No one believes that the pineal gland solves the problem, except Cartesians. One has to have faith in Descartes. Similarly, Moses could be the mediator of the covenant with the Hebrews because they had faith in him.

Curley makes an additional point about Hobbes's treatment of the Old Covenant that requires a separate answer. In *Leviathan*, Hobbes says that "it is impossible for any man to make a covenant with God Almighty, farther than it hath pleased him to declare who shall receive and accept of the same covenant in his name" (Curley 2004: 204, quoting EL 15.11). Hobbes's text suggests that the aspiring covenanter with God would *know* whom God received and accepted. In his more reflective moments, Hobbes knew that no one could know that God had revealed himself. He sees it as a matter of belief and faith that "people should not believe *God's word*, before they believe his prophet. The people of Israel believed Moses because of two things; his *miracles* and his *faith* . . . Similarly . . . there is *faith in the God of Abraham* . . . If faith is absent, he is rejected . . ." (DCv 16.11)[15] In *On the Citizen*, Hobbes says that Abraham's acceptance of God's revelation was a "*matter of faith*" (DCv 16.4). About Abraham's subjects, neither faith nor knowledge was relevant. His subjects owed him obedience because he was their sovereign: "*the word of God* was to be fetched from his lips only, as being the interpreter of all the *laws* and *words* of God" (DCv 16.7; also 16.9; and McQueen 2020). He would say the same thing about Moses and the Israelites after they made a covenant with God: "But it is manifest that this power [of interpreting the word of God] had been completely in Moses when he was alive" (DCv 11.13). Hobbes considers the alternatives to his interpretation that Moses had that power or authority. It could not be a private person because such a person was "prohibited with most heavy threats from claiming to have heard God

---

[15] The Latin text is: "*Mosi* a populo *Israelitco* creditum est propter duas res, *miracula, & fidem.*"

speak otherwise than through the testimony of Moses (DCv 16.13; see Exod. 19:24–5).

Now Curley and other philosophers could still maintain that Hobbes's treatment of mediators is philosophically unacceptable: "If *we* cannot know, without a mediator, whether our covenant has been accepted, how can *the mediator* know?" And that may be true.[16] My point is that the root of the problem lies in the Bible. Hobbes is doing his best to defend a difficult position. Why would he do that? One answer is a rhetorical question. Why do theistic philosophers in the analytic tradition continue to defend what appears to most contemporary philosophers as an indefensible position? Another answer, namely, that Hobbes, the philosopher of paradox (Parkin 2016) intended the intelligent, careful reader to see that he was undermining the Christian position, is unpersuasive to me because of the absence of strong signs of duplicity in his defense. And his defense is more formidable than any other seventeenth-century defense I know of. To evaluate Hobbes's performance, one needs to compare it with other performances of the time. An athlete who pole-vaulted four meters in 1920 was a champion; one who did this in 2000 was mediocre.

The New Covenant

Hobbes treats the new covenant in chapter 17. According to standard Christian theology, the new covenant involves God, Jesus Christ, and all human beings. While the word "new" in "new covenant" would seem to commit Hobbes to describing a covenant that is, well, new, and thus a covenant distinct from the covenant or covenants with Abraham, Moses, and others, Hobbes tries to avoid making such a claim. Early in Chapter 17, he writes that Jesus had been sent "to renew a new covenant between them and God (DCv 17.3).[17] It is odd that he does not explain how one renews a new covenant. (Had he been a used car salesman, he might have sold a customer a new used car.) It is not obvious that the idea of a renewed, new covenant has any pay-off for him. Perhaps he thought that if the new covenant were simply a renewal, then he would not have to explain the role of God in a new way.

[16] Curley has pointed out several problems with Hobbes's treatment of biblical covenants. But I think Hobbes was in an impossible situation because the text of the Bible is false, contradictory, or unintelligible. See Curley's comments about Robert Filmer (Curley 2004: 212n21 and 213–4).

[17] The Latin text is: "ad renovandum inter ipsos & Deum *Pactum novum*."

Not odd, but problematic is figuring out the referents of "them" ("ipsos"). In its context, the plausible candidates are the people mentioned earlier. But this includes apostles, disciples, Pharisees, and unspecified people who hated Jesus. The role of Jesus was to renew the covenant with *them*. A group that is not mentioned at all is all human beings. The problem of finding a suitable reference for "them" continues at the beginning of the next section. Hobbes says the covenant [*foedus*] was between Christ and "the people" ("populum"). The people are the *them*, who are still unidentified. Hobbes ends this section with an unconvincing clause: "all Christians agree" (DCv 17.3).

Hobbes devotes a large part of chapter 17 to explaining the way that Christ's role on earth was similar to that of Moses. Jesus was a vice-roy [*Pro-regium*], just as Moses was (DCv 17.4). Hobbes explains that the kingdom of God the Father was not the kingdom of Jesus by interpreting several New Testament texts. He emphasizes the difference in roles between Jesus and God the Father. While God the Father was king, Jesus insofar as he was the son of God was not.[18] The Father commanded; Jesus counseled. Hobbes's main interest is to locate the second kingdom of God in the indefinite future, probably in order to make it irrelevant to current events.

In addition to the problem of identifying the referent of "populum" and the antecedent of "ipsos," there is a problem of identifying the antecedent of "ipsum" in the following section. Hobbes says, "Christ was sent from God his Father to make a *covenant* between him [ipsum] and the people" (DCv 17.4). Because of the Latin use of "ipse," its antecedent above is Christ, not God the Father. But that conflicts with what he said in section three and what he will say later: Christ had been sent to "*strike a Covenant* between God and men" (DCv 16.6: "ad *Pactum* inter Deum & homines *percutiendum*"); and "For the new, that is, the *Christian covenant*, it is covenanted . . . on the part of God, to *pardon their sins, and to lead them into his celestial kingdom*" (DCv 17.7: "*Pacto*, enim, novo, hoc est *Christiano*, Conventum est . . . ex parte Dei, ut *remitteret illis peccata, & in Regnum Coeleste ipsos introduceret*").

What might Hobbes have said instead of making either God or Jesus the covenanting party? About Jesus, he could have asserted his traditional role as mediator. Someone in whom the covenanters have faith has to attest to God's acceptance of sovereignty. As for the parties to the new covenant, these could be the first followers of Jesus, the apostles and disciples, who

---

[18] Cf. DCv 17.4: "manifestum est, . . . *Christus* Patri suo aequalis sit quoad naturam."

covenanted to take the God represented by Jesus as their special sovereign god. Although the first followers do not represent all human beings, the new covenant was open to all people. The apostles, in response to the instruction of Jesus, went to all nations (Matt. 28:19). When a sufficient number of people in a location could have their own assembly, they became a Christian church. When entire nations became Christian, national churches arose, similar to the way in which colonies became nations independent of their mother country. However, in separating from a nation, they did not necessarily take on a different sovereign. The former British Commonwealth was analogous. Queen Elizabeth II was the queen of the British Empire, and she remained the sovereign, as separate nations calved. Like Canada, Australia, and others, Great Britain retained Elizabeth. The dual sovereignty of King James VI of Scotland and I of England is nowhere near as good an example; but at least Hobbes could have pointed out how the same man could bear two sovereign persons (cf. DH 15.3), just as the same God could bear two (or more) artificial persons. (There are irrelevant differences between God's sovereignty over Christian churches and James's sovereignty over Scotland and England, so objections could be made to the analogy. But it is an analogy.)

Many interpreters of Hobbes believe that he often conveyed a secret message about the incoherence of Christianity. My simple reply is that philosophy is difficult. Human fallibility is generally a better explanation for a falsehood than communicative tergiversation. It is not surprising that Hobbes did not produce a perfect system in his lifetime, long as it was. He could have done a better job with just the conceptual materials he had at hand, as I think Bernard Gert did (Gert 2010; cf. Martinich 2012b). Hobbes certainly could have done more with the idea of gifts in the state of nature. For example, if a person gives his right to something to another person and then acts as if he still had the right to that thing, he acts "without right" and therefore unjustly. A covenant is unnecessary. Hobbes compounds his mistake in *Leviathan* when he says, "where there is no coercive *Power* erected, that is, where there is no Common-wealth, there is no Propriety [Property]" (L 15.3/220; cf. 14.10/204). Property can exist in the state of nature. If all the people in a particular region unilaterally transfer their right to something to a person *P*, then that thing should count as the property of *P* since *P* is the only person who has a right to that thing. *P* can call the thing "meum" by right (cf. DCv 6.1, and Green 2020).

Faith

Although faith has been mentioned extensively already in this chapter, it has not been a theme. But it needs to be one now because it is a salient element of *both* human sovereign-making covenants and the biblical ones. Faith is often thought of as primarily a religious phenomenon. The faith of Abraham, Moses, or some other revered figure from the Old Covenant are paradigmatic examples. But the phenomenon is much broader. People have faith in their friends, their spouses, and their Japanese or German automobiles. Faith sometimes has literally a cash value. Government issued bonds are backed by the "full faith and credit" of the issuer (see also the US Constitution, Article 4, section 1).

The belief that covenants are exclusively or primarily religious often elides with the idea that faith is inherently irrational. It is not. Whether faith in something is rational or not depends on whether the evidence available sufficiently supports it or not. Having faith in friends who have helped a person in difficult times and have always kept their word is rational. This is not to say that rational faith stays within the bounds of its evidence. Faith is projected into unknown areas, usually the future, but sometimes the past as in having faith that a reliable and considerate friend would have called if she had been able to.

The proper contrast to rational faith is non-rational faith; and it divides into the irrational and the non-irrational. Irrational faith goes against what the evidence indicates. Although many theists have an irrational faith, they are not the only ones. If Mr. Naïve has faith in his "friend" Ms. Con even though Con has repeatedly disappointed Naïve by breaking her promises and undermining Naïve's projects, then Naïve's faith in Con is irrational. That leaves non-irrational faith for discussion. People often have faith in someone for some project when the evidence available is insufficient to be rational and not so adverse as to be irrational. Here is an example: Walker is lost in a large city. Walker goes up to Bystander and asks, "Can you tell me how to get to Beacon Street?" Bystander says, "Go one block past the traffic signal and turn left. It's about three blocks down from there." If Walker follows Bystander's directions, faith has been placed in Bystander, even though Walker has no particular knowledge of Bystander or evidence of his trustworthiness.

Although the scenario with Walker and Bystander does not include a covenant, people in the state of nature have to have faith that their co-covenanters will not act without faith. This faith is not rational and not irrational faith, but non-irrational faith. Although Hobbes does not make a theme of non-religious faith, he does say that a contract involves mutual faith ["fides mutua"] (DCv 2.11). Shortly after, in the same chapter, he writes, "he who is held by a covenant is believed [he will keep it], for the chain [strength] of covenants is faith alone" (DCv 2.18: "ei qui pacto tenetur, creditur: pactorum enim vinculum sola fides est"). Hobbes continued to hold that covenants depend on faith. In *Leviathan*, he wrote, "he that is to perform [an action] in time to come, being trusted,[19] his performance is called *keeping of promise*, or *faith*; and the failure of performance, *violation of faith*" (L 14.11/204; LL 14.11/205: "ad Contractum exequendum altero prior esse potest; tunc posteriori *Credi* sive *Fides haberi* dicitur; & Promissio ejus *Pactum* dicitur; & non praestitisse, *Violatio Fide*").[20] Faith and covenants go together because, as Hobbes said, as regards a covenant, a person "is to perform in time to come." And Hobbes wrote that civil societies required faith and compacts in order to create civil societies (DCv 1.2 "born fit": "*sed Foedera, quibus faciendis fides & pacta necessaria sunt*").[21] Why Hobbes does not say more about faith is a matter of conjecture. Perhaps he thought it might look like a weakness in his political philosophy.

Relatively few people today think that any faith is knowledge. David Hume argued that people have a natural inclination to believe that the sun will rise tomorrow even though no one strictly knows that it will. But betting against the sun is a fool's bet; and lacking faith in the ten-year past performance of a mutual fund is no formula for success.

It should not be surprising that faith is not a distinctively religious concept. In order to be intelligible, concepts have to be traceable back to experiences or propositions about ordinary experience. It is fair to say that Hobbes realized this, given his discussions of the ordinary uses of words used in the Bible, such as "prophet" and "spirit." If a word does not make sense in a non-religious context, it cannot make sense in a religious one. The concepts of omnipotence, omniscience, and omnibenevolence intelligibly apply to the Judeo-Christian-Islamic God because those concepts result from combining

---

[19] As this quotation and the corresponding Latin text indicate, having faith in something is either the same as or very close to being the same as trusting. Faith and trust are discussed further below in the main text.

[20] The corresponding Latin is not an exact translation of the English. The Latin says in effect that if one party executes the contract before the other, then the second party is said to be believed or to have faith; and the promise is called a covenant; and not to satisfy it is a violation of faith. Noel Malcolm's translation in my opinion unnecessarily departs from English cognates of the Latin.

[21] Tuck and Silverthorne (in Hobbes 1998: 24) translate "foedera" as "alliances" and "pacta" as "agreements."

every with *power, science* or *knowledge*, and *benevolence*, respectively. That these terms are not distinctively religious language is evident from the true statement: "No animal is omnipotent."

Religious language absorbs sense from the non-religious language. Words that originated in ordinary experience may take on new semantic features that they did not have in their original usage. And those transformed words can be re-absorbed by non-religious language. As regards covenants, the Bible took that concept from ancient Near Eastern, non-Israelite cultures and applied it to relations with God (Mendenhall 1954). While Hobbes probably did not know of its origin, the situations in which covenants occur in the Bible was sufficient for him to understand what they were. Given the commonality of covenants and their prominence in Hobbes's discussions of politics and religion, a commentator cannot justifiably ignore the religious connotation of covenants. This is especially true of *On the Citizen*.

It is appropriate to comment here on Hobbes's uses of "fides" and "fiducia." Unlike English, the Latin words for faith (fides) and for trust (fiducia) are etymologically related. A sensible decision about translating these two words, especially when they occur closely in a passage would be to uniformly translate them as *faith* and *trust*, respectively, with a note about their etymological relation. Charles Cotton, who is probably the first translator of *On the Citizen* (Malcolm 2002: 234–58), obscures Hobbes's view by translating "fides" sometimes as *faith* and sometimes as *trust*. It appears that a desire to avoid using the same English word when "fides" occurs twice in close proximity motivates his practice. For example, at *On the Citizen* 2.20, shortly after Hobbes wrote that people who do not keep their oaths violate their faith, he wrote that those who violate their faith are accustomed to break their faith (DCv 2.23). However, Cotton translates the first occurrence of "fides" as *faith* and the second one as *trust*. Later in the same chapter, Hobbes says that a person "who is held by a covenant is *believed* (for the chain that a covenant has is faith alone)" (DCv 2.18). Since translating "creditur" as "he is believed" does not result in idiomatic English, Cotton understandably translated "creditur" as *he is trusted* (DCv 2.18). Without the Latin text, a reader would be misled. Cotton's practice can be excused to some extent because Hobbes himself sometimes translates "trust" as "fides" (L 7.6/102) and, in the same paragraph, "faith and trust" simply as "fides"; and in the paragraph following it "Beleefe, Faith, and Trust" simply as "fides" (L 7.7/102). The semantic proximity of faith, trust, and belief are indicated in this passage of *Leviathan*: "BeleefE, and FAITH: *Faith, in* the man; *Beleefe*, both *of* the man, and *of* the truth of what he says . . . To *have faith in*, or *trust to*, or *beleeve a man*, signifie the same thing; namely, an opinion of the veracity of the man" (L 7.5/100).[22]

Conclusion

In *On the Citizen*, Hobbes is primarily interested in explaining the logic of covenants that create sovereigns constituted by human beings. A central point is that the sovereign cannot be a party to the covenant. The biblical conceptions of covenant probably inspired him to some extent because of its prominence. However, the biblical authors did not construct their narratives about covenants involving God with any political theory in mind. For them, taking the idea of covenant from the culture of the Eastern Mediterranean, God was a party to the covenants that established his special sovereignty over particular people. Hobbes's words commit him to that position. He did not explain the discrepancy between ordinary and divine sovereign-making covenants. He had nothing to gain by doing so. If he had argued that God was not a covenanting party, his opponents would have criticized him for introducing a new interpretation of the Bible. Nonetheless, I think he had the resources to assimilate the structure of the divine covenants to secular ones. About the covenants with Abraham, he could have said simply that they were not sovereign-making. About the sovereign-making covenants with Moses and Jesus, he could have said that Moses and Jesus were the mediators or representatives necessary for completing a covenant among the people and in which God was only a third-party beneficiary. However, if he had said this, his opponents probably would have accused him of introducing a novelty into Christian theology. In the 1640s, he was not inclined to do that.

---

[22] In the parallel passage of the *Elements of Law*, Hobbes leaves out faith and explicates belief as "the admitting of Propositions upon *Trust*" (EL 6.9).

Bibliography

This bibliography contains publication information for those chapters which had their own bibliography in their first publication or had it in a bibliography for all the chapters in a book. It also contains some additional works by Martinich that are not referred to in any of the chapters but are relevant to his interpretation of Hobbes.

Abbot, Robert. 1594. *A Mirrour of Popish Subtilties Discovering Sundry Wretched and Miserable Evasions and Shifts.*

Abbot, Robert. 1617. *A Hand of Fellowship, to Helpe Keepe out Sinne and Antichrist.*

Abizadeh, Arash. 2013. "The Representation of Hobbesian Sovereignty," in *Hobbes Today*, ed. S. A. Lloyd. Cambridge: Cambridge University Press, pp. 113–52.

Abizadeh, Arash. 2017. "Hobbes's Conventionalist Theology, The Trinity, and God as an Artificial Person by Fiction," *The Historical Journal* 60/4: 915–41.

Achtemeier, Paul, ed. 1985. *Harper's Bible Dictionary.* San Francisco, CA: Harper & Row.

A. D. 1624. *The Food of the Soule.* London.

Adams, Thomas. 1619. *The Happiness of the Church.* London.

Adams, Thomas. 1633. *A Commentary or, Exposition Upon the Divine Second Epistle general, Written by the Blessed Apostle St. Peter.* London.

Ailesbury, Thomas. 1622. *A Sermon Preached at Paules-Crosse the Second Day of June, being the Last Sunday in Easter Term.* London.

Ainsworth, Henry. 1620. *Reply to a Pretended Christian Plea for the Anti-Christian Church of Rome.* London.

Ambrose. 1637. *Christian Offices Crystal Glass.* London.

Ames, William. 1630. *De Conscientia et ejus Jure.* Amsterdam.

Ames, William. 1639. *Conscience with the Power and Cases thereof Divided into V Books.* Leiden and London.

Ames, William. 1643. *Marrow of Sacred Divinity.* London.

Ames, William. 1983. *The Marrow of Theology.* Durham, NC: Labyrinth Press.

Anonymous. 1611. *Jacobs Ladder.* London.

Anonymous. 1623. *Elizabethan Homilies*, ed. Ian Lancashire. http://onlinebooks.library. upenn.edu/webbin/book/lookupid?key=olbp21565, accessed August 1, 2020.

Anonymous. 1642. *Discourse Presented to Those Who Seek Reformation of the Church of England.* London.

Anscombe, Elizabeth. 1981. "Mr. Truman's Decree," in *Ethics, Religion, and Politics*, 3 vols. Minneapolis: University of Minnesota Press.

Anselm of Canterbury. 2008. *Major Works.* New York: Oxford University Press.

Apeldoorn, Laurens van. 2019. "On the Person and Office of the Sovereign in Hobbes' *Leviathan*," *British Journal for the History of Philosophy*, online first: https://www. tandfonline.com/doi/full/10.1080/09608788.2019.1613632.

Arrowsmith, John. 1659. *Armilla Catechetica. A Chain of Principles.* London.

Attersoll, William. 1612. *A Commentarie upon the Epistle of Sainte Paul to Philemon.* London.

Attersoll, William. 1618. *Commentarie on the Fourth Booke of Moses, Called Numbers*. London.

Aubrey, John. 1898. "Thomas Hobbes," in *Brief Lives*, ed. Andrew Clark. Oxford: Clarendon Press, pp. 321–403.

Aubrey, John. 2020. *Enchiridion, or on Faith, Hope and Love*, tr. J. F. Shaw. http://www.leaderu.com/cyber/books/augenchiridion/enchiridiontoc.html, accessed August 15, 2020.

Austin, J. L. 1975. *How to Do Things with Words*, 2nd ed., ed. J. O. Urmson and Marina Sbisà. Cambridge, MA: Harvard University Press.

Bäch, Allan. 1982. "Aquinas on the Incarnation," *New Scholasticism* 56/1: 127–45.

Bäch, Allan. 1998. "Scotus on the Consistency of the Incarnation and the Trinity," *Vivarium* 36/1: 83–107.

Bacon, Francis. 1597. *Essayes: Religious Meditations*. London.

Bacon, Francis. 1642. An *Essay of a King*. London.

Bacon, Francis. 1648. *XVI Propositions concerning the Reign and Government of a King*. London.

Ball, George. 1617. *Short Treatise*. London.

Barlee, William. 1656. *Praedestination . . . In a Correptorie Correction*. London.

Barlee, William. 1658. *A necessary vindication of the doctrine of predestination*. London.

Barnes, [Robert]. 1573. *The Whole workes of W. Tyndall, Iohn Frith, and Doct. Barnes, Three Worthy Martyrs, and Principall Teachers of this Churche of England Collected and Compiled*.

Baskerville, Stephen. 1993. *Not Peace but a Sword*. London: Routledge.

Baumgold, Deborah. 2013. "'Trust' in Hobbes's Political Thought," *Political Theory* 20: 1–18.

Beard, Thomas. 1616. *A retractive from the Romish religion*. London.

Bennefield, Sebastian. 1615. *Sinne against the Holy Ghost Discovered and Other Christian Doctrines Delivered*. London.

Berman, David. 1988. *A History of Atheism in Britain: From Hobbes to Russell*. London: Croom Helm.

Bernard, Richard. 1626. *Rhemes against Rome: or, The removing of the Gagg of the New Gospell, and rightly placing it in the Mouthes of the Romists*. London.

Bevir, Mark. 1999. *The Logic of the History of Ideas*. Cambridge: Cambridge University Press.

Bevir, Mark, et al. 2000. *The Logic of the History of Ideas*, in *Rethinking History* 4/3: 295–373.

Bible, The HarperCollins Study, ed. Harold Attridge. 2000. New York: Harper One.

Bible, The New Oxford Annotated, 3rd ed. 2001. New York: Oxford University Press.

Bible, The King James Version, with the Apocrypha. 2006. London: Penguin Classics.

Blau, Adrian. 2012. "Anti-Strauss," *Journal of Politics* 74/1: 142–55.

Bloom, Alan. 1974 "Leo Strauss: September 20, 1899–October 18, 1973," *Political Theory* 2/4: 372–392.

Bolton, Robert. 1626. *Some General Directions for a Comfortable Walking with God*. London.

Bouwsma, William. 1988. *John Calvin*. New York: Oxford University Press.

Bramhall, John. 1655. *A Defence of True Liberty from Ante-cedent and Extrinsicall Necessity*. London.

Bramhall, John. 1656. *Replication to the Bishop of Chalcedon*. London.

Bramhall, John. 1657. *Castigations of Mr. Hobbes his Last Animadversions in the Case concerning Liberty and Universal Necessity wherein all his Exceptions about that Controversie are Fully Satisfied*. London.

Bramhall, John. 1658a. *The Catching of Leviathan, of the Great Whale*. London.

Bramhall, John. 1658b. *Schism Guarded and Beaten Back upon the Right Owners*. London.

Brown, Keith C., ed. 1965. *Hobbes Studies*. Oxford: Basil Blackwell.

Browne, Thomas. 1691. *An Answer to Dr. Sherlock's Case of Allegiance to Sovereign Powers*. London.

Bullinger, Heinrich. 1624. *Looke from Adam, and Behold the Protestants Faith and Religion*. London.

Byfield, Nicholas. 1615. *An Exposition Upon the Epistle to the Colossians*. London.

Byfield, Nicholas. 1626. *The Rule of Faith, or, An exposition of the Apostles Creed*. London.

Calvin, John. 1559: *Institutio Christianae Religionis*. Geneva.

Calvin, John. 1634. *Institution of Christian Religion*, tr. Thomas Norton. London.

Calvin, John. 1960. *Institutes of the Christian Religion*, ed. John T. McNeill, tr. Ford Lewis Battles. Philadelphia: Westminster Press.

Camden, William. 1626. *The Abridgment of Camden's Britania*. London.

Cartwright, Christopher. 1658. *A Practical and Polemical Commentary or Exposition on the Whole Fifteenth Psalm*. London.

Church, Henry. 1637. *Miscellanea Philo-theologica. Or, God, & Man*. London.

Clarendon. See "Hyde, Edward, earl of Clarendon."

Collins, Jeffrey. 2005. *The Allegiance of Thomas Hobbes*. Oxford: Oxford University Press.

Collins, John. 2004. *Introduction to the Hebrew Bible*. Minneapolis: Fortress Press.

Cooke, Paul. 1996. *Hobbes and Christianity*. Lanham, MD: Rowman & Littlefield.

Cooper, Kody. 2013. "Reason and Desire after the Fall of Man: A Rereading of Hobbes's Two Postulates of Human Nature," *Hobbes Studies* 26/2: 107–29.

Cowell, John. 1607. *The Interpreter: Or Booke Containing the Signification of Words*. London.

Cromartie, Alan. 2018. "Hobbes, Calvinism, and Determinism," in *Hobbes on Politics and Religion*, ed. Laurens von Apeldoorn and Robin Douglass. Oxford: Oxford University Press, pp. 95–115.

Curley, Edwin. 1992. "'I Durst Not Write So Boldly' or How to Read Hobbes' Theological-Political Treatise," in *Hobbes e Spinoza*, ed. Daniela Bostrenghi. Napoli: Bibliopolis, pp. 497–593.

Curley, Edwin. 1996a. "Calvin or Hobbes?" *Journal of the History of Philosophy* 34: 257–71.

Curley, Edwin. 1996b. "Reply to Martinich," *Journal of the History of Philosophy* 34: 285–87.

Curley, Edwin. 2004. "The Covenant with God in Hobbes's *Leviathan*," in Sorell and Foisneau 2004, pp. 199–215.

Darrel, John. 1602. *The Reply of John Darrell, to the Answer of John Deacon*.

Davidson, Donald. 1984. *Inquiries into Truth and Interpretation*. New York: Oxford University Press.

Davidson, Donald. 2005. *Truth, Language, and History*. New York: Oxford University Press.

Day, John. 1615. *Day's Festivals or, Twelve of his Sermons*. Oxford.

Dear, Peter. 1988. *Mersenne and the Learning of the Schools*. Ithaca, NY: Cornell University Press.

Deigh, John. 2016a. "Political Obligation," in Martinich and Hoekstra 2016, pp. 293–314.

Deigh, John. 2016b. "Reply to Martinich." European Hobbes Society, http://www. europeanhobbessociety.org/newpublications/debate-martinich-deigh-on-law-2-deigh/, accessed August 18, 2020.

Devigne, Robert. 1994 *Recasting Conservatism: Oakeshott, Strauss, and the Response to Postmodernism*. New Haven: Yale University Press.

Douglass, Robin, and Johan Olsthoorn, edd. 2020. Hobbes's *On the Citizen*. Cambridge: Cambridge University Press.

Drury, Shadia. 1988. *The Political Ideas of Leo Strauss*. New York: St. Martin's Press.

Eachard, John. 1672. *The Grounds and Occasions of the Contempt of the Clergy and Religion Enquired Into . . . With Mr Hobbs's State of Nature Considered in a Dialogue*. London.

Eliot, T. S. 1934. *Selected Essays: 1917–1932*. New York: Harcourt Brace.

Elton, G. R. ed. 1982. *The Tudor Constitution*, 2nd ed. Cambridge: Cambridge University Press.

Eusebius. 1968. *A New Eusebius*, ed. J. Stevenson. London: S. P. C. K.

Eutactus Philodemius. 1650. *An Answer to the Vindication of Doctor Hammond, Against the Exceptions of Eutacus Philodemius. Wherein is Endeavored to be Cleared What Power Man Hath*. London.

Evelyn, John. 1697. *Numismata, a Discourse of Medals, Ancient and Modern . . . : to Which Is Added a Digression Concerning Physiognomy*. London.

Evrigenis, Ioannis. 2020. "Hobbes: Prophet of the Enlightenment or Justice of the Peace," *Political Studies* 82/1: 129–33.

Filmer, Robert. 1652. *Observations Concerning the Original of Government, Upon Mr Hobbes's "Leviathan," Mr Milton against Salmasius, H. Grotius "De Jure Belli."* London.

Filmer, Robert. 1991. *Patriarcha and Other Writings*, ed. Johann Sommerville. Cambridge: Cambridge University Press.

Fitzherbert, Thomas. 1610. *The Second Part of a Treatise Concerning Policy and Religion*. Douai, n.p.

Foisneau, Luc. 2000. *Hobbes et la Toute-Puissance de Dieu*. Paris: Presses Universitaires de France.

Fotherby, Martin. 1622. *Atheomastix Clearing Foure Truthes, against Atheists and Infidels*. London.

Fotion, N. 1971. "Master Speech Acts," *Philosophical Quarterly* 21: 234–43.

Foxe, John. 1583. *Actes and Monuments of Matters most Speciall and Memorable, Happenyng in the Church with an Universall History of the Same, Wherein is Set Forth at large the Whole Race and Course of the Church, from the Primitive Age to these Latter Tymes of Ours*. London.

Franco, Paul. 2020. "Hobbes's Secularism: Pragmatic Civil-Theologian or Utopian Atheist," *Political Studies* 82/1: 126–9.

Gadamer, H.-G. 1989. *Truth and Method*, 2nd revised ed., tr. J. Weinsheimer and D. Marshall. New York: Crossroad.

Galileo. 1615. "Letter to the Grand Duchess Christina," in *Discoveries and Opinions of Galileo*, tr. Stillman Drake. New York: Random House, 1957.

Garfinkle, Steven. 2013. "Ancient Near Eastern City-States," in *The Oxford Handbook of the State in the Ancient Near East and Mediterranean*, ed. P. Fibiger Bang and W. Scheidel. New York: Oxford University Press, pp. 94–120.

Gaskin, J. C. A., ed. 1994. *Thomas Hobbes: Human Nature, and De Corpore Politico*. Oxford: Oxford World Classics.

Gassendi, Pierre. 1658. *Syntagma philosophicum*, in *Opera omnia*, vol. 2. Lyon: Laurentius Anisson and Joan Devenet.

Gaukroger, Steven. 2006. *The Emergence of a Scientific Culture*. Oxford: Oxford University Press.

Gauthier, David. 1969. *The Logic of Leviathan*. Oxford: Clarendon Press.

Gert, Bernard. 2001. "Hobbes on Reason," *Pacific Philosophical Quarterly* 82: 243–57.

Gert, Bernard. 2010. *Hobbes: Prince of Peace*. Boston: Polity.

Gibson, John. 1981. *Genesis*, vol. 1. Edinburgh: The St. Andrew Press.

Glover, Willis. 1965. "God and Thomas Hobbes," in Brown 1965, pp. 141–68.

Greaves, Richard. 1993. Review of "The Two Gods of *Leviathan*," *Church History* 62/4: 562–64.

Green, Michael. 2020. "Corporate Persons without Authorization," in *Hobbes's On the Citizen*, ed. Robin Douglass and Johan Olsthoorn. Cambridge: Cambridge University Press, pp. 145–160.

Grice, H. P. 1957. "Meaning," *Philosophical Review* 66: 377–88.

Grice, H. P. 1969. "Utterer's Meaning and Intentions," *Philosophical Review* 78: 147–77.

Grice, H. P. 1975. "Logic and Conversation," in Martinich, ed. 2001, pp. 165–75.

Grice, H. P. 1989. *Studies in the Way of Words*. Cambridge, MA: Harvard University Press.

Hakewill, George. 1616. *An Answere to a Treatise Written by Dr. Carier, by Way of a Letter to His Maiestie*. London.

Hall, Edmund. 1650. *Lazarus's Sores Licked*. London.

Hamou, Philippe. 2018. "Marin Mersenne," in *Stanford Encyclopedia of Philosophy*, https://plato.stanford.edu/entries/mersenne, accessed June 1, 2020.

Hampton, Jean. 1986. *Hobbes and the Social Contract Tradition*. Cambridge: Cambridge University Press.

Hawke, Michael. 1657. *Killing Is Murder, and No Murder*. London.

Hemmingsen, Niels. 1579. *The Way of Lyfe*. London.

Hildersam, Arthur. 1635. *CLII Lectures upon Psalme LI Preached at Ashby-Delazouch in Leicester-shire*. London.

Hill, Christopher. 1986. *Collected Essays*, 3 vols. Amherst: University of Massachusetts Press.

Hirschmann, Nancy. 2016. "Hobbes on the Family," in Martinich and Hoekstra 2016, pp. 242–63.

Hobbes, Thomas. 1647. *De cive*. Amsterdam.

Hobbes, Thomas. 1650. *Humane Nature*. London. (Referred to by chapter and section number, followed by a page number.)

Hobbes, Thomas. 1651a. *Leviathan*. London.

Hobbes, Thomas. 1651b. *Philosophical Rudiments Concerning Society and Government*. London.

Hobbes, Thomas. 1652. *De corpore politico, or, The Elements of Law, Moral and Politick with Discourses upon Severall Heads*. London.

Hobbes, Thomas. 1655. *Elementorum philosophae section prima De corpore*. London.

Hobbes, Thomas. 1656a. *The questions concerning liberty, necessity, and chance clearly stated and debated between Dr. Bramhall . . . and Thomas Hobbes of Malmesbury*. London.

Hobbes, Thomas. 1656b. *Six Lessons to the Professors of Mathematiques, One of Geometry, the Other of Astronomy* London.

Hobbes, Thomas. 1658. *De homine*. London.

Hobbes, Thomas. 1679. *Behemoth*. London.

Hobbes, Thomas. 1680. *Considerations upon the Reputation, Loyalty, and Religion of Thomas Hobbes*. London.

Hobbes, Thomas. 1681. *Vita Carmine Expressa*, in *Thomae Hobbes Angli Malmesburiensis philosophi vita*. London.

Hobbes, Thomas. 1682a. *An Answer to a Book Published by Dr. Bramhall . . . The Catching of the Leviathan*. London.

Hobbes, Thomas. 1682b. *Seven Philosophical Problems and Two Propositions of Geometry*. London.

Hobbes, Thomas . 1839a. *The English Works*, ed. William Molesworth. London. Cited by volume and page number.

Hobbes, Thomas. 1839b. *Opera Latina*, ed. William Molesworth. London. Cited by volume and page number.

Hobbes, Thomas. 1972. *Philosophical Rudiments Concerning Government and Society*. In *Man and Citizen*, ed. Bernard Gert. Garden City, NY: Anchor Books.

Hobbes, Thomas. 1994a. *The Elements of Law, Natural and Politic*, ed. J. C. A. Gaskin. Oxford: Oxford University Press.

Hobbes, Thomas. 1994b. *Leviathan*, ed. Edwin Curley. Indianapolis: Hackett Publishing Company.

Hobbes, Thomas. 1998. *On the Citizen*, ed. and tr. Richard Tuck and Michael Silverthorne. Cambridge: Cambridge University Press. Cited by chapter and paragraph.

Hobbes, Thomas. 2002. *Leviathan*, ed. A. P. Martinich. Peterborough, ON: Broadview Press. Cited by chapter and paragraph.

Hobbes, Thomas. 2011. *Leviathan*, rev. ed., ed. A. P. Martinich and Brian Battiste. Peterborough, ON: Broadview Press, 2011.

Hobbes, Thomas. 2012. *Leviathan: The English and Latin Texts*, 3 vols., ed. Noel Malcolm. Oxford: Clarendon Press.

Hoekstra, Kinch. 2004. "The *de facto* Turn in Hobbes's Political Philosophy," in Sorell and Foisneau 2004, pp. 34–73.

Hoekstra, Kinch. 2006. "The End of Philosophy (The Case of Hobbes)," *Proceedings of the Aristotelian Society* 106: 25–62.

Holden, Thomas. 2015. "Hobbes's First Cause," *Journal of the History of Philosophy* 53/ 4: 647–67.

Hollis, Martin. 1968. "Reason and Ritual," *Philosophy* 43: 231–47.

Hutton, Sarah. 1978. "Thomas Jackson, Oxford Platonist, and William Twisse, Aristotelian," *Journal of the History of Ideas* 39: 635–52.

Hyde, Edward, earl of Clarendon. 1645. *Transcendent and Multiplied Rebellion and Treason Discovered*. Oxford.

Hyde, Edward, earl of Clarendon. 1676. *A Brief View and Survey of the Dangerous and Pernicious Errors to Church and State, in Mr. Hobbes's . . . Leviathan*. Oxford.

Hyde, Edward, earl of Clarendon. 1995. *Leviathan: Contemporary Responses to the Political Theory of Thomas Hobbes*, ed. G. A. J. Rogers. Bristol: Thoemmes Press.

Isham, Gyles, ed. n.d. *The Correspondence of Brian Duppa and Sir Justinian Isham, 1650– 1660*. Northamptonshire: The Northhamptonshire Record Society.

Jackson, Nicholas. 2007. *Hobbes, Bramhall, and the Politics of Liberty and Necessity*. Cambridge: Cambridge University Press.

Jackson, Thomas. 1628. *A Treatise of Divine Essence and Attributes*. London.

James I (king). 1918. *The Political Works of James I*, ed. Charles Howard McIlwain. Cambridge, MA: Harvard University Press.

Jesseph, Douglas. 1999. *Squaring the Circle*. Chicago: University of Chicago Press.

Jewel, John. 1571. *The Second Tome of Homilees of such Matters as were Promised*. London.

Johnson, Paul. 1974. "Hobbes's Anglican Doctrine of Salvation," in *Thomas Hobbes in His Time*, ed. R. Ross, H. W. Schneider, and T. Waldman. Minneapolis: University of Minnesota Press, pp. 102–25.

Johnston, David. 1986. *The Rhetoric of Leviathan*. Princeton: Princeton University Press.

Judgment and Decree of the University of Oxford Past in their Convocation. 1683. Oxford.

Jue, Jeffrey K. 2006. *Heaven upon Earth: Joseph Mede (1586–1638) and the Legacy of Millenarianism*. Dordrecht: Springer.

Kain, Philip J. 1987. "Hobbes, Revolution and the Philosophy of History," in *Hobbes's "Science of Natural Justice,"* ed. C. Walton and P. J. Johnson. Dordrecht: Martinus Nijhoff, pp. 203–18.

Kavka, Gregory. 1986. *Hobbesian Moral and Political Philosophy*. Princeton: Princeton University Press.

Kelly, J. N. D. 1978. *Early Christian Doctrines*, rev. ed. New York: Harper & Row.

Kennett, White. 1708. *Memoirs of the Family Cavendish*. London.

Kettlewell, John. 1691. *The Duty of Allegiance Settled upon its True Ground*. London.

Kiparsky, Paul, and Carol Kiparsky. 1970. "Fact," in *Progress in Linguistics*, ed. Manfred Bierswich and Karl Erich Heidolf. The Hague: Mouton, pp. 143–73.

Kraynak, Robert P. 1990. *History and Modernity in the Thought of Thomas Hobbes*. Ithaca, NY: Cornell University Press.

Lawson, George. 1657. *An Examination of the Political Part of Mr. Hobbs his Leviathan*. London.

Leibniz, Gottfried. 1988. "The Common Concept of Justice," in *Political Writings*, 2nd ed., ed. Patrick Riley. Cambridge: Cambridge University Press.

Leith, John. 1973. *Creeds of the Churches*, 3rd ed. Atlanta, GA: John Knox Press.

Lilburne, John. 1646. *The Free-man's Freedom Vindicated*. London.

Lloyd, S. A. 1992. *Ideals as Interests*. Cambridge: Cambridge University Press.

Lloyd, S. A. 1997. "Coercion, Ideology, and Education in Hobbes's *Leviathan*," in *Reclaiming the History of Ethics*, ed. Andrewes Reath, Barbara Herman, and Christine Korsgaard. Cambridge: Cambridge University Press, 36–65.

Lloyd, S. A. 2009. *Morality in the Philosophy of Hobbes*. Cambridge: Cambridge University Press.

Locke, John. 1967. *Two Treatises of Government*, ed. Peter Laslett. Cambridge: Cambridge University Press.

Locke, John. 1993. "Second Tract on Government," in *Political Writings of John Locke*, ed. David Wootton. New York: Mentor.

Lucy, William. 1663. *Observations, Censures and Confutations of Notorious Errours in Mr Hobbes his Leviathan*. London.

Lyons, John. 1977. *Semantics*. Cambridge: Cambridge University Press.

Malcolm, Noel. 1988. "Hobbes and the Royal Society," in Rogers 1988, pp. 43–66.

Malcolm, Noel. 1994. *The Correspondence of Thomas Hobbes*. Oxford: Clarendon Press.

Malcolm, Noel. 2002. *Aspects of Hobbes*. Oxford: Clarendon Press.

Martinich, A. P. 1978. "Identity and Trinity," *The Journal of Religion* 58/2: 169–81.

Martinich, A. P. 1984a. *Communication and Reference*. Berlin: Walter de Gruyter.

Martinich, A. P. 1984b. "A Theory for Metaphor," in Martinich, ed. 2001, pp. 447–58.

Martinich, A. P. 1992. *The Two Gods of Leviathan: Religion and Politics in Hobbes's Philosophy*. Cambridge: Cambridge University Press.

Martinich, A. P. 1996. "On the Proper Interpretation of Hobbes's Philosophy," *Journal of the History of Philosophy* 34: 273–83.

Martinich, A. P. 1997. *Thomas Hobbes*. London: Macmillan Press.

Martinich, A. P. 1999. *Hobbes: A Biography*. Cambridge: Cambridge University Press.

Martinich, A. P. 2001. "Interpretation and Hobbes's Political Philosophy," *Pacific Philosophical Quarterly* 82/3–4: 309–31.

Martinich, A. P. 2004a. "The Interpretation of Covenants in *Leviathan*," in Sorell and Foisneau 2004, pp. 217–40.

Martinich, A. P. 2004b. "Hobbes's Reply to Republicanism," in *New Critical Perspectives on Hobbes's Leviathan*, ed. Luc Foisneau and George Wright. Milano: FrancoAngeli, pp. 227–39.

Martinich, A. P. 2005: *Hobbes*. London: Routledge.

Martinich, A. P. 2007. "Thomas Hobbes's Interregnum Place of Worship," *Notes and Queries* 252: 433–36.

Martinich, A. P. 2012a. "On Thomas Hobbes's English Calvinism: Necessity, Omnipotence, and Goodness," *Philosophical Readings* 4/1: 18–30.

Martinich, A. P. 2012b. "Egoism, Reason, and the Social Contract," *Hobbes Studies* 25: 209–22.

Martinich, A. P. 2013. "L'Auteur de Péché et Les Démoniques: Deux Problèmes Calvinistes chez Hobbes et Certains de ses Contemporains," in *Jean Calvin et Thomas Hobbes*, ed. O. Abel et D. Weber. Geneve: Éditions Labor et Fides, pp. 43–71.

Martinich, A. P. 2013. "Law and Self-Preservation: On Misunderstanding Hobbes, 1650–1700," in *The Persistence of the Sacred in Modern Thought*, ed. Chris Firestone and Nathan Jacobs (South Bend, IN: University of Notre-Dame Press, 2013), pp. 38–65.

Martinich, A. P. 2016. "Authorization and Representation in Hobbes's *Leviathan*," in Martinich and Hoekstra 2016, pp. 315–38.

Martinich, A. P. 2019. "Thomas Hobbes and John Bramhall on Free Will," in *Routledge Companion to Free Will*, ed. Kevin Timpe, Meghan Griffith, and Neil Levy. New York: Routledge, pp. 303–12.

Martinich, A. P., ed. 2001. *The Philosophy of Language*, 4th ed. New York: Oxford University Press.

Martinich, A. P., and Kinch Hoekstra, edd. 2016. *The Oxford Handbook of Hobbes*. New York: Oxford University Press.

McGee, J. Sears. 1998. "On Misidentifying Puritans: The Case of Thomas Adams," *Albion* 30/3: 401–18.

McGee, J. Sears. "Thomas Adams," in *The Dictionary of National Biography*, online: http://www.oxforddnb.com.ezproxy.lib.utexas.edu/view/article/131?docPos=3, accessed July 15, 2016.

McNeill, John. 1954. *The History and Character of Calvinism*. London: Oxford University Press.

McQueen, Allison. 2020. "'A Rhapsody of Heresies': The Scriptural Politics of *On the Citizen*," in Douglas and Olsthoorn 2020, pp. 180–98.

Mede, Joseph. 1641. *Apostasy of the Latter Times . . . or The Gentiles Theology of Daemons*. London.

Mede, Joseph. 1642. *Diatribae. Discourses on Divers Texts of Scripture*. London.

Mede, Joseph. 1664. *Works of the Pious and Profoundly-Learned Joseph Mede*. London.

Mede, Joseph. 1677. *Works of the Pious and Profoundly-Learned Joseph Mede*, 4th ed. London.

Mendenhall, George. 1954. "Covenant Forms in Israelite Tradition," *The Biblical Archaeologist* 17: 49–76.

Mill, David van. 2001. *Liberty, Rationality, and Agency in Hobbes's Leviathan*. Albany: State University of New York Press.

Miller, Perry. 1984. *Errand into the Wilderness*. Cambridge, MA: Harvard University Press.

Moore, Stanley. 1971. "Hobbes on Obligation: Moral and Political: Part One: Moral Obligation," *Journal of the History of Philosophy* 9/1: 43–62.

Moore, Stanley. 1972. "Hobbes on Obligation: Moral and Political: Part Two: Political Obligation," *Journal of the History of Philosophy* 10/1: 29–42.

Muller, Richard. 2004. "John Calvin and Later Calvinism," in *The Cambridge Companion to Reformation Theology*, ed. David Bagchi and David C. Steinmetz. Cambridge: Cambridge University Press, pp. 130–49.

Nagel, Thomas. 1986. *The View from Nowhere*. New York: Oxford University Press.

Nauta, Lodi. 2009. *In Defense of Common Sense*. Cambridge, MA: Harvard University Press.

Nelson, Eric. 2010. *The Hebrew Republic*. Cambridge, MA: Harvard University Press.

New Oxford Annotated Bible. See *Bible, The New Oxford Annotated*.

Oakeshott, Michael. 1975. "Dr. Leo Strauss on Hobbes," in *Hobbes on Civil Association*. Berkeley: University of California Press, pp. 132–49.

Osler, Margaret. 1994. *Divine Will and Mechanical Philosophy: Gassendi and Descartes on Contingency and Necessity in the Created World*. Cambridge: Cambridge University Press.

Osler, Margaret. 2009. "Becoming an Outsider: Gassendi in the History of Philosophy," in *Insiders and Outsiders in the History of Philosophy*, ed. G. A. J. Rogers, Tom Sorell, and Jill Kraye. London: Routledge, pp. 23–42.

Overall, John. 1690. *Bishop Overall's Convocation-Book*. London.

Overhoff, Jürgen. 1997. "The Lutheranism of Thomas Hobbes," *History of Political Thought* 18/4: 604–23.

Overhoff, Jürgen. 2000. *Hobbes's Theory of the Will*. Lanham, MD: Rowman & Littlefield.

Paganini, Gianni. 2003. "Hobbes, Valla, and the Trinity," *British Journal for the History of Philosophy* 11/2: 183–218.

Pangle. Thomas. 2006. *Leo Strauss: An Introduction to his Thought and Intellectual Legacy*. Baltimore: The Johns Hopkins University Press.

Parker, Samuel. 1671. *Discourse of Ecclesiastical Politie*. London.

Parkin, John. 2007. *Taming the Leviathan*. Cambridge: Cambridge University Press.

Parkin, John. 2016. "Hobbes and Paradox," in Martinich and Hoekstra 2016, pp. 624–41.

Pearson, John. 1659. *Exposition of the Apostles Creed*. London.

Pelikan, Jaroslav. 1971. *The Christian Tradition: The Emergence of the Catholic Tradition (100–600)*. Chicago: University of Chicago Press.

Perkins, William. 1592. *A Case of Conscience*. London.

Perkins, William. 1609. *Arte of Prophesying*. London.

Peters, F. E. 1967. *Greek Philosophical Terms*. New York: New York University Press.

Peters, R. S. 1956. *Hobbes*. Harmondsworth: Penguin Books.

Pierce, Thomas. 1655. *A Correct Copy of Some Notes Concerning Gods Decrees, Especially Reprobation*. London.

Pierce, Thomas. 1657a. *Divine Philanthropie Defended*. London.

Pierce, Thomas. 1657b. *Divine Purity Defended*. London.

Pierce, Thomas. 1658a. *Self-Condemnation*. London.

Pierce, Thomas. 1658b. *Self-Revenger*. London.

Pierce, Thomas. 1658c. *Divine Philanthropie Defended*, 2nd ed. London.

Pierce, Thomas. 1659. *Divine Purity Defended*, 2nd ed. London.

Pope, Walter. 1697. *Life of the Right Reverend Father in God, Seth, Lord Bishop of Salisbury.* London.

Preston, John. 1631. *Life Eternall, or, A Treatise of the Knowledge of the Divine Essence and Attributes.* London.

Pufendorf, Samuel. 1717. *Of the Law of Nature and Nations, Eight Books*, 3rd ed., tr. Basil Kennett. London.

Purkiss, Diane. 2006. *The English Civil War.* New York: Basic Books.

Quine, W. V. 1960. *Word and Object.* Cambridge, MA: MIT Press.

Quine, W. V., and Joseph Ullian. 1978. *The Web of Belief*, 2nd ed. New York: Random House.

Raz, Joseph. 1995. "Interpretation without Retrieval," in *Law and Interpretation*, ed. Andrei Marmor. Oxford: Clarendon Press.

Reik, Miriam. 1977. *The Golden Lands of Thomas Hobbes.* Detroit: Wayne State University Press.

Rogers, G. A. J., ed. 1988. *Perspectives on Hobbes.* Oxford: Clarendon Press.

Rosenberg, Roy. 1966. "Yahweh becomes King," *Journal of Biblical Literature* 85/3: 297–307.

Ryan, Alan. 1996. "Hobbes's Political Philosophy," in *The Cambridge Companion to Hobbes*, ed. Tom Sorell. Cambridge: Cambridge University Press, pp. 208–45.

Scargill, Daniel. 1669. *The Recantation of Daniel Scargill.* Cambridge.

Searle, John. 1969. *Speech Acts.* Cambridge: Cambridge University Press.

Searle, John. 1983. *Intentionality.* Cambridge: Cambridge University Press.

Shafte, J. 1673. *The Great Law of Nature, or, Self-Preservation Examined, Asserted and Vindicated from Mr. Hobbes his Abuses.* London.

Shapin, Steven, and Simon Schaffer. 1985. *Leviathan and the Air-Pump.* Princeton: Princeton University Press.

Sherlock, William. 1671. *The Case of Allegiance Due to Soveraign Powers.* London.

Sherlock, William. 1684. *The Case of Resistance of the Supreme Powers Stated and Resolved.* London.

Sherlock, William. 1691. *Their Present Majesties Government Proved to be Thoroughly Settled.* London.

Skinner, Quentin. 1969. "Meaning and Understanding in the History of Ideas," *History and Theory* 8/1: 3–53.

Skinner, Quentin. 1974. " 'Social Meaning' and the Explanation of Social Action," in Tully 1988, pp. 79–96.

Skinner, Quentin. 1976. "Motives, Intentions, and the Interpretation of Texts," in Tully 1988, pp. 68–78.

Skinner, Quentin. 1988. "Reply to My Critics," in Tully 1988, pp. 231–88.

Skinner, Quentin. 1996. *Reason and Rhetoric in the Philosophy of Hobbes.* Cambridge: Cambridge University Press.

Skinner, Quentin. 1998. *Liberty before Liberalism.* Cambridge: Cambridge University Press.

Skinner, Quentin. 2002. *Visions of Politics*, 3 vols. Cambridge: Cambridge University Press.

Skinner, Quentin. 2004. "Hobbes and the Classical Theory of Laughter," in Sorell and Foisneau 2004, pp. 139–166.

Skinner, Quentin. 2008. *Hobbes and Republican Liberty.* Cambridge: Cambridge University Press.

Socrates Scholasticus. 1729. *Ecclesiastical History of Socrates Scholasticus in VII Books*, 3rd ed. London.

Sommerville, Johan. 1993. Review of "*The Two God of Leviathan*," *Albion* 25/3: 493–94.

Sorell, Tom. 1986. *Hobbes*. London: Routledge.

Sorell, Tom. 1988. "Science in Hobbes's Politics," in Rogers 1988, 67–80.

Sorell, Tom, and Luc Foisneau, edd. 2004. *Leviathan after 350 Years*. Oxford: Clarendon Press.

Sorenson, Roy. 2015. "Fictional Theism," *Analysis* 75/4: 539–550.

Southgate, Beverley. 1993. "*Covetous of Truth*": *The Life and Work of Thomas White, 1593–1676*. Dordrecht: Kluwer Academic.

Springborg, Patricia. 2008. "The *Historia Ecclesiastica* and Hobbes's Philosophical Project," in Thomas Hobbes, *Historia ecclesiastica*, Critical edition, ed. Patricia Springborg, Patricia Stablein, and Paul Wilson. Paris: Honoré Champion, 201–36.

Sreedhar, Suzanne. 2013. *Hobbes on Resistance*. Cambridge: Cambridge University Press.

Stauffer, Devin. 2007. "Reopening the Quarrel between the Ancients and the Moderns: Leo Strauss's Critique of Hobbes's 'New Political Science,'" *American Political Science Review* 101/2: 223–33.

Stauffer, Devin. 2018. *Hobbes's Kingdom of Light*. Chicago: University of Chicago Press.

Steinberger, Peter. 2009. "Analysis and the History of Political Thought," *American Political Science Review* 103/1: 135–46.

Strauss, Leo. 1936. *The Political Philosophy of Thomas Hobbes: Its Basis and Genesis*. Oxford: Clarendon Press; reprinted in 1952 by University of Chicago Press, with an additional Preface.

Strauss, Leo. 1952. *Natural Right and History*. Chicago: University of Chicago Press.

Strauss, Leo. 1959. *What Is Political Philosophy? And Other Studies*. New York: The Free Press.

Strauss, Leo. 1965a. *Hobbes' politische Wissenschaft in ihrer Genesis*. Neuwied am Rhein: Hermann Luchterhand.

Strauss, Leo. 1965b. *Spinoza's Critique of Religion*, tr. E. M. Sinclair. (Originally published 1930: *Die Religionskritik Spinozas als Grundlage seiner Bibelwissenschaft*.) New York: Schocken Books.

Strauss, Leo. 1989. "Progress or Return?," in *The Rebirth of Classical Political Rationalism*, ed. Thomas Pangle. Chicago: University of Chicago Press, pp. 227–270.

Strauss, Leo. 2011. *Hobbes's Critique of Religion*. Chicago: University of Chicago Press.

Strawson, P. F. 1971. *Logico-Linguistic Papers*. London. Methuen.

Talaska, Richard. 1988. "Analytic and Synthetic Method According to Hobbes," *Journal of the History of Philosophy* 26/2: 207–37.

Tarcov, Nathan, and Thomas L. Pangle. 1987. "Epilogue: Leo Strauss and the History of Political Philosophy," in *History of Political Philosophy*, 3rd ed., ed. Leo Strauss and Joseph Cropsey. Chicago: University of Chicago Press, pp. 907–38.

Tenison, Thomas. 1670. *The Creed of Mr. Hobbes Examined*. London.

Tracy, Thomas. 1994. "Divine Action, Created Causes, and Human Freedom," in *The God Who Acts*, ed. Thomas Tracy. University Park: Pennsylvania State University Press, pp. 77–102.

Trinkhaus, Charles. 1996. "Lorenzo Valla on the Problem of Speaking about the Trinity," *Journal of the History of Ideas* 57/1: 27–53.

Tuck, Richard. 1979. *Natural Rights Theories*. Cambridge: Cambridge University Press.

Tuck, Richard. 1990. "Hobbes and Locke on Toleration," in *Thomas Hobbes and Political Theory*, ed. Mary Dietz. Lawrence: The University of Kansas Press, pp. 153–71.

Tuck, Richard. 1992. "The Christian Atheism of Thomas Hobbes," in *Atheism from the Reformation to the Enlightenment*, ed. Michael Hunter and David Wootton. Oxford: Clarendon Press, pp. 111–30.

Tuck, Richard. 2004. "The Utopianism of *Leviathan*," in Sorell and Foisneau, pp. 125–38.

Tulloch, John. 1872. *Rational Theology and Christian Philosophy in England in the Seventeenth Century*. Cambridge: W. Blackwood.

Tully, James, ed. 1988. *Meaning & Context*. Princeton: Princeton University Press.

Twisse, William. 1631a. *Discovery of Dr Jacksons Vanitie*. London.

Twisse, William. 1631b. *The Doctrine of the Synod of Dort and Arles*. London.

Twisse, William. 1632. *A Briefe Catecheticall Exposition of Christian Doctrine*. London.

Twisse, William. 1641. *The Apostacy of the Latter Times, in which . . . the World should wonder after the Beast*. London.

Twisse, William. 1653. *The Riches of Gods Love*. Oxford.

Tyndale, William. 1573. *The Whole Workes of W. Tyndale, John Frith, and Doct. Barnes*. London.

Vendler, Zeno. 1972. *Res Cogitans*. Ithaca, NY: Cornell University Press.

Vicens, Leigh. 2018. "Free Will and Theological Determinism," in *The Routledge Companion to Free Will*, ed. Kevin Tiempe, Meghan Griffith, and Neil Levy. London: Routledge.

Virgilius Maro, 1632. *Opera P. Virgilii Maronis*. Cambridge.

Vlastos, Gregory, Paul Sunstein, and Robert Gordis. 1986. "Further Lessons of Leo Strauss: An Exchange." *New York Review of Books*, April 24, 1986, http://www.nybooks.com/articles/archives/1986/apr/24/further-lessons-of-leo-strauss-an-exchange, accessed on 15 July 2013.

Waldron, Jeremy. 2002. *God, Locke, and Equality*. Cambridge: Cambridge University Press.

Wallis, John. 1690. *The Doctrine of the Blessed Trinity Explained, In a Letter to a Friend*. London.

Ward, Seth. 1656. *In Thomae Hobbii Philosophiam*. Oxford.

Watkins, J. W. N. 1973. *Hobbes*, 2nd ed. London: Hutchinson University Library.

Whitaker, William. 1585. *An answere to a certeine booke, written by Maister William Rainolds*. London.

Whitfield, Thomas. 1653. *A Treatise Tending to Shew that the Just and Holy God, may have a Hand in the Unjust Actions of Sinfull Men: and that in such a Way as shall be without any Impeachment of his Justnesse and Holinesse, or Diminution of his Power and Providence*. London.

Wilson, Thomas. 1600. *Exposition of the Two First Verses of the Sixt Chapter to the Hebrews*. London.

Wilson, Thomas. 1615. *Theologicall Rules*. London.

Wolfson, H. A. 1954. *Christology of the Later Fathers*, ed. Edward Hardy. Philadelphia: Westminster Press.

Wolfson, H. A. 1970. *The Philosophy of the Church Fathers: Faith, Trinity, Incarnation*, 3rd ed. Cambridge, MA: Harvard University Press.

Wren, Matthew. 1660. *Monarchy Asserted*. London.

Wright, George. 1999. "Hobbes and the Economic Trinity," *British Journal for the History of Philosophy* 7: 397–428.

Zuckert, Catherine. 2009. "Strauss's Return to Premodern Thought," in *The Cambridge Companion to Leo Strauss*, ed, Steven Smith. Cambridge: Cambridge University Press, pp. 93–118.

Original Publication Information and Permissions in Chronological Order of Publication

Index

For the benefit of digital users, indexed terms that span two pages (e.g., 52–53) may, on occasion, appear on only one of those pages.